STATIONS OF THE CROSS

STATIONS OF THE CROSS

Adorno and Christian Right Radio

Paul Apostolidis

DUKE UNIVERSITY PRESS   Durham and London 2000

© 2000 Duke University Press   All rights reserved

Printed in the United States of America on acid-free paper ∞

Typeset in Trump Mediaeval by Keystone Typesetting, Inc.

Library of Congress Cataloging-in-Publication Data

appear on the last printed page of this book.

This book is dedicated to

Jeannie Morefield.

Contents

Acknowledgments

Many people have helped me bring this project to fruition, and to them I offer my heartfelt thanks. Most of all, I owe gratitude to Jeannie Morefield, whose intellectual insights, political concern, and personal companionship have vitally contributed to my work on this book since its inception. I have also benefited immeasurably over many years from Susan Buck-Morss's great dedication as a dissertation adviser and friend. Additional thanks go to Isaac Kramnick and Theodore J. Lowi, both valued members of my dissertation committee, and to Anna Marie Smith, whose detailed comments on my work have continually provoked me to complexify my thinking. Timothy Kaufman-Osborn, Lisa Disch, Jodi Dean, and Jeremy Varon all read drafts of various parts of this book and rendered extremely useful comments and criticisms. This book would not have been possible without the benefit of sustained conversations over the last several years with Richard Clayton, Elizabeth Nishiura, Libbie Rifkin, Juliet Williams, and Douglas Usher. I owe another debt of gratitude to Douglas Kellner and the other (still anonymous) reader of my manuscript for their precise and knowledgeable comments, along with Valerie Millholland, Miriam Angress, Kay Alexander, and Laura Sell at Duke University Press. Thanks also to my copy editor, Paula Dragosh. The Graduate School of Cornell University funded my research trip to Colorado Springs with a travel grant, and Susan Marine and Meagan Day helped make the trip both productive and enjoyable. Alan Crippen was a gracious and helpful host during my visit to Focus on the Family, and my thanks also go to the many people working at Focus along with several progressive activists in Colorado Springs who agreed to be interviewed and supplied me with vital information. My gratitude also goes to my colleagues in the Politics

Department at Whitman College and to a great many Whitman students with whom my critical thinking about the Christian right has developed in new and important ways. I am especially grateful for the support and encouragement of many family members and friends, above all my parents, my sister, all the Morefields, and my wonderful daughter Anna.

Portions of chapter 2 were originally published under the title "Culture Industry or Social Physiognomy? Adorno's Critique of Christian Right Radio" in *Philosophy & Social Criticism* 24, no. 5 (September 1998) by Sage Publications.

STATIONS OF THE CROSS

Introduction

"Will He or Won't He?"

On September 21, 1995, the ABC news magazine program *Day One* featured a story on radio personality James Dobson. Dobson was then and remains one of the most enduring and powerful leaders of the Christian right in the United States. A psychologist and popular author, Dobson has been the head of Focus on the Family (Focus), a leading media organization of the Christian right, since its founding in 1977. Focus saturates the airwaves of evangelical radio with Dobson's interview and news programs and publishes a vast array of books, magazines, and videotapes covering issues from child discipline to welfare reform. Nevertheless, the mainstream media have paid little attention to Dobson over the years, in contrast to its coverage of leaders who have more directly attempted to heighten the Christian right's influence in the spheres of electoral politics and legislation, especially Pat Robertson and Ralph Reed.

On this particular day in 1995, the mainstream media had been drawn to Dobson because of his rhetorical interventions in the blossoming campaign for the Republican presidential nomination. *Day One* offered a general profile of Dobson's efforts at Focus on the Family, although the main angle was clearly the possibility of Dobson's entering the fray as either a kingmaker or a candidate. Dobson had spoken out publicly against the inclusive, "big tent" strategy advocated by Republican National Committee chairman Haley Barbour. Opposing compromise on "moral issues," especially abortion, Dobson had dedicated two days on his nationally broadcast and extremely popular radio program *Focus on the Family* to publicizing a speech by hard-right candidate Alan Keyes. But would Dobson attempt to channel his towering popularity and authority among evangelicals into a presidential bid of his own? So mused the ABC program.[1]

Eventually, of course, it became clear that Dobson was not interested in running. A less sensationalist and more measured article on Focus in the *New York Times*, which had appeared a few months earlier, had been closer to the mark in assessing the politics of Dobson and his organization. The article noted that Dobson's "voice is clearly heard these days in Washington," then continued: "Despite [Dobson's] political talk, Focus is a largely nonpolitical organization, and it has attracted many people who admire Dr. Dobson's views on marriage, bringing up children, and a host of other family issues."[2] Focus, the *Times* seemed to conclude, in concert with the organization's own self-presentation, was primarily concerned with matters pertaining to faith and family, and only occasionally with affairs of politics. Neither the *Times* story nor the *Day One* segment was succeeded by a follow-up report. To the ordinary consumer of the mass media in 1995 who happened to see either of these pieces, Focus on the Family would likely have sparked interest only by offering a moment of controversy in an otherwise dull election. As the *Times* intoned and ABC implied, Focus had little truck with things political.

Three years later, in 1998, Dobson's name surfaced once again in the mainstream media. As in 1995, Focus's leader drew the attention of major news organizations by striking out against GOP leaders whom he considered too quick to abandon moral imperatives on crucial matters of policy. This time, Dobson's target was the Republican Congress. Dobson warned that if federal lawmakers did not speedily pass measures requiring parental consent for abortion, defunding Planned Parenthood, and abolishing the National Endowment for the Arts, he would use every means at his disposal to urge evangelical conservatives to boycott the 1998 elections or to support third-party candidates. To *U.S. News and World Report*, which ran a cover story on Dobson in May of that year, Dobson's challenge heralded a "major shift in the attitudes of the Christian right toward politics" and the "crumbling" of the Republican coalition.[3]

Dobson's threats to "go nuclear" against GOP leaders in the fall of 1998 never materialized. Indeed, just a few days after the publication of the *U.S. News* story major newspapers reported that Dobson had "sounded conciliatory" following meetings with House leaders. " 'I believe the leadership of the Republican Party was listening,' Dobson said," in reference to his proposals for action on "bills to repeal the 'marriage penalty' tax, abolish the National Endowment for the Arts, and ban certain late-term abortions."[4] Perhaps Dobson had thrown down the gauntlet to influence the location of the political middle ground as the 1998 (and 2000) elections approached, by staking out a "purist" space on the far right. Perhaps, too, his remarks and their predictable casting in the media as examples of a confrontational, no-quarter Christian conservatism were intended to camouflage the extent to which Dobson and other Christian right leaders were actually operating very much within the boundaries of the political mainstream. After all, Dobson's policy demands tracked closely the items listed in the Christian Coalition's 1995 Contract with the American Family, a document that relied on focus groups and polls to fashion an agenda with broad public appeal. Following the 1996 elections, moreover, and notwithstanding the mixed successes of Christian right–supported candidates at the ballot box, the movement emerged with a stronger institutional base than ever within Republican party committees from the precinct to the national levels and with a new crop of political action committees (PACS) giving it unprecedented leverage in campaign finance.[5] Whatever the purpose of Dobson's 1998 actions, however, by the late 1990s major news organizations were beginning to take notice of Dobson more frequently. And this seemed to be happening because, in the words of the *New York Times*, Dobson had begun articulating an "overtly political message" with increasing intensity, intentionality, and publicity.[6]

Culture, Power, Ideology, and the New Right

This book analyzes the politics of Christian right culture by studying Dobson's radio program *Focus on the Family*. Ironically, despite the episodic flurries of excitement about Dobson's preelection defiance of Republican leaders during the 1990s, the media have probably overlooked the points of greatest political impact by Dobson and Focus on the Family. Focus is a major producer of Christian right culture—of organized, commercialized, mediatized evangelical conservatism. To understand Focus's contribution to the reshaping of the American political landscape at the close of the twentieth century, it is important to assess Focus's "overt" participation in legislative processes, voter mobilization, and party organizations. But it is also necessary to confront thornier questions concerning the politics of Focus's cultural offerings as such. Such questions, however, seem inarticulable within the constraints of the ordinary public discourse deployed by news agencies like the *Times*, ABC, and *U.S. News*. For the mainstream media, as their interrogations of Dobson illustrate, culture appears to have political significance only when its agents publicly involve themselves in the institutional and discursive channels of governmental action and partisan competition.

This journalistic "common sense" presupposes a specific conception of power along with a particular understanding of ideology. Both of these concepts require critical scrutiny. Here, power is a result of observable contests between individuals or groups of individuals, in which it is always at least technically (though sometimes not practically) possible to identify winners and losers. The former are held to enjoy power to the extent that they impose their will on the actions of the latter.[7] From this perspective, "ideology" refers to dimensions of both the ends and means of such struggles for power. In terms of ends, ("an") ideology is usually understood simply as a policy agenda: the goal of political power contests is considered to be the installment of one faction's policy concerns as the agenda of the whole. The Christian right's ideology would thus consist of a familiar list of policy prescriptions, including a legal ban on abortion, the reinstitution of vocal prayer in public schools, tax reductions, and the denial of civil rights protection for gays and lesbians. The power of the movement, in turn, could be measured by assessing the extent to which these policy stands had been incorporated into the platforms of major party candidates and into public law.

Similar though substantially more sophisticated assumptions regarding power and ideology infuse most social-scientific accounts of the Christian right and other social movements. Since the Christian right's inception as a national force in the late 1970s, a continually growing body of empirical research has analyzed the factors leading to the movement's initial mobilization and subsequent rejuvenations, the nature of its successes and failures, and the reasons behind its victories and defeats. Explaining the movement's coalescence and activation has provoked interesting controversies. Scholars have described the movement's early mobilization as rooted variously in a reaction to left-liberal social movements, especially the student, anti–Vietnam War, women's, and gay liberation movements; class resentment directed at the "New Class" of knowledge professionals; federal policy changes and court decisions that unsettled previous norms regarding church-state relations, in particular altering the tax rules for religious schools and prohibiting prayer and Bible reading in public schools; the long-term growth of evangelicals' affluence in the postwar era, making possible the vast spread of evangelical churches and "parachurch" organizations such as radio and television broadcasting systems; and deliberate efforts by secular neoconservative political leaders to forge "fusionist" coalitions among "moral traditionalists" and anti–welfare state free marketeers, centering rhetorically on anticommunism and emerging in full bloom with the Reagan-Bush '80 coalition.[8] Thus in the vocabulary of empirical social movement theory, some analysts have emphasized the Christian right's cultivation of political resources while others have focused on its advantageous responses to structures of political opportunities; still others have charted the movement's engagement in a "political process" incorporating these other activities while also involving changes in participants' sense of political efficacy.[9]

There has been a more limited divergence of views concerning the Christian right's achievements over the past quarter century. By and large, social scientists have taken a dim view of the hype over the movement in the left and mainstream media. They have emphasized that the movement has not gained any major victories in national policy (comparable, say, to the Nineteenth Amendment or the Civil Rights Act of 1964).[10] Furthermore, the Christian right's record at the state and local levels has been uneven and liable to setbacks, notwithstanding the prodigious reenergizing of the movement that occurred with the late-'80s/early-'90s reorientation to the grassroots—witness the judicial overturning of Colorado's Amendment 2, the only state ballot initiative precluding civil rights protection for gays and lesbians to have passed during the high tide of these campaigns in the early to mid-1990s.[11] Virtually all agree, finally, that the movement continues to face the problem of facilitating cooperation between confrontation- and compromise-oriented factions, with the direct action, antiabortion group Operation Rescue and Christian Coalition epitomizing the former and latter, respectively. This difficulty has intensified with the end of the cold war, the corresponding decline in utility of anticommunism as a unifying concern, and the endurance of legislative impasses on most components of even the supposedly accommodationist Contract with the American Family.[12]

These scholars' chastening of alarmists who lament the approaching takeover of the government by religious "extremists" is salutary, to a degree. However, their nearly ubiquitous emphasis on the debilitating effects of the movement's internal tensions and repetitious predictions of the movement's imminent centripetal breakup are somewhat misleading. We should question the assumption of social scientists and journalists alike that a major policy triumph for the Christian right can by definition only involve those "moral" issues, like abortion, school prayer, and homosexuality, that are the movement's most distinctive and widely publicized concerns. Simply because an issue bridges the demands of secular and religious conservatives does not automatically disqualify it as an indicator of Christian right strength. The Christian right contributed vital support at mass and elite levels alike to the Reaganites' "counterinsurgency" efforts in Latin America, the Bush administration's war on Iraq, and the bipartisan elimination of aid to the poor that culminated (at least temporarily) in Bill Clinton's signing of the Republican bill to abolish the federal entitlement to financial assistance for poor women and children.[13] More generally, tension within a movement may not always be a source of weakness. Instead, as Sara Diamond argues, internal diversity—even contentious or acrimonious diversity—can be a sign of maturity, strength, and flexibility: "A political movement is successful to the extent that it can accommodate many different types of organizations, so that activists of different dispositions can find useful outlets for their talents."[14]

In addition, social movement analysis need not limit itself to assessing the Christian right's political power solely in terms of its capacities to influence public policy and elections. Diamond suggests a broader conception of movement power when she calls attention to the new right's role in forging "consent" to established class relations through "educational and cultural institutions, such as churches, schools and the mass media." She points out, moreover, that the class valences of new right culture can be complex and perhaps contradictory. For although these institutions "are strongly influenced by society's dominant economic elites . . . they also partially reflect and serve the interests of other classes."[15] Such a view contrasts markedly with the more common approach that (1) measures the Christian right's power in terms of the numbers of activists it has mobilized, dollars it has raised, bills it has helped pass, and candidates it has assisted in electing; and (2) understands the movement's ideology in terms of a one-dimensional continuum running from "confrontational" to "compromise-oriented," and as a uniform, self-consistent "thing" that adherents somehow possess, just as they might own an anti-abortion bumper sticker expressing "their" ideology.

Understanding the politics of Christian right culture in nonreductive, more nuanced terms comprises the central task of this book. This project begins by assuming that culture can be politically consequential even when it does not directly address public policy issues or align itself with specific party leaders. The notion that culture's intrinsic qualities—the narrative forms employed by a religious tradition, the internal logic of a philosophical system, or the formal-aesthetic qualities of an artistic movement—can encode and emanate dynamics of social power was classically formulated in Marx's critique of religion. To be sure, Marx drew attention to religion's strategic cooperation with capital to attain "political" goals in the conventional sense. For example, he denounced the "conspiracy of the Church with monopoly capital" to facilitate the passage of laws hostile to the working class, such as those that closed down public-houses on Sundays.[16] But for Marx, the political significance of religion in general was much more far-reaching: "This state and this society produce religion, which is an inverted consciousness of the world, because they are an inverted world. . . . Religious suffering is at one and the same time the expression of real suffering and a protest against real suffering. Religion is the sigh of the oppressed creature, the heart of a heartless world and the soul of soulless conditions. It is the opium of the people."[17] Religion has power, for Marx, inasmuch as it epitomizes the worker's misrecognition of her objective misery. Religion reflects this situation—though in an "inverted" fashion—in its very essence, for instance in the yearning for an afterlife of peace and fulfillment. And religion reproduces oppression, by tranquilizing any stirrings of critical consciousness. Culture thus appears as a realm of power—and, more specifically, a domain where the political rule of the bourgeoisie is legitimated—without there needing to be an "overt" or direct connection to party or policy. Here, ideology operates in religion's cultivation of the inchoate sense that it would be futile to challenge structural power relations and that capitalist relations and bourgeois law are natural and God-given, rather than functioning (only) in the conscious and deliberate formulation of programs for reform or reaction. Nevertheless, in this passage from Marx, culture is clearly neither simply ideological nor exclusively a field of domination. For even religion, which for Marx was idealism in its quintessential form, is not merely a way to mask the true sources of misery but also "a protest against real suffering." This implies that a radical approach to religion does not merely dismiss it as a pack of capitalist lies, but tries to convert its protestative strength into different modes of historically concrete expression. In sum, using the example of religion, Marx shows that culture has political significance in three distinctive ways, at once reflecting, reproducing, and contesting power.

Marx's provocation to consider the politics of culture as a complex array of disparate and potentially contradictory effects provides a general orientation for this study of Focus on the Family. The organized, mediatized culture of the Christian right is most emphatically political, as this book demonstrates. It is political, not just because it provides a regular soapbox for the leaders of the movement's electoral and legislative projects. Nor is it political simply because it prepares the psychological ground for new right activists by inculcating horror at abortion, disgust at homosexuality, fear of adolescent sex, and a range of other issue-related *dis*positions (as well as, often, specific positions). Certainly, there is an instrumental relationship between Focus on the Family and the Christian Coalition or the Family Research Council (FRC), the leading arms of the Christian right in electoral, party, and legislative affairs. Focus generates networks of secondary associations (extending both family and church ties), patterns of everyday living (involving above all a receptivity to particular media styles and sources), and general social attitudes (such as those mentioned above), which facilitate attempts by the Coalition and the FRC to organize their constituencies on behalf of very conservative Republican candidates and proposals. In point of fact, the consumers of Focus's products have been regimented into mailing lists for lobbying and fundraising by the FRC for the benefit of Republican causes.[18] Yet Focus's cultural products are also political *in themselves*, and they are political in ways that are more complex and ambiguous than one might imagine from most accounts of the movement in the major media and the annals of social science. In short, the political significance of Christian right organized culture lies not only in its strategic relationship to new right political activism but also in its expression, reinforcement, and contestation of contemporary, social-structural relations of power.

The New Conservatism and Cultural Theory

If the mainstream media and social science literature on the Christian right have mostly declined to address the politics of conservative culture in other than instrumentalizing and subordinating terms, the same cannot be said of all academic writing on the new right. The political purchase of conservative culture has received central attention in some notable recent accounts of the rise of the new right in the United States and abroad. As one might expect, given the dominant intellectual currents of the past few decades, these studies have drawn more heavily on Foucault (or "post-Marxist" writings influenced by Foucault along with Lacan and Derrida) than on Marx in mapping the circulation of power through cultural passages, although they have also adapted Gramsci's concern with cultural politics. Stuart Hall, for example, has analyzed the new right in Great Britain as a hegemonic project to enable certain ways of making political sense of "everyday experience" in an era of social, economic, and national crisis:

> . . . Thatcherism discovered a powerful means of translating economic doctrine into the language of experience, moral imperative and common sense, thus providing a 'philosophy' in the broader sense— an alternative *ethic* to that of the 'caring society'. . . . The essence of the British people was identified with self-reliance and personal responsibility, as against the image of the over-taxed individual, enervated by welfare-state 'coddling', his or her moral fibre irrevocably sapped by 'state handouts'. . . . [Thatcherism] began to be spoken in the mid-1970s—and, in its turn, to 'speak'—to define—the crisis: what it was and how to get out of it. The crisis has begun to be 'lived' in its terms. This is a new kind of taken-for-grantedness; a reactionary common sense, harnessed to the practices and solutions of the radical right and the class forces it now aspires to represent.[19]

Hall shows how the British new right anchored its political power in a reconstructed sense of national identity. This identity was forged not simply through official political discourse, such as public statements by Margaret Thatcher, but more specifically through the conjuncture of such rhetoric with more local and informal levels of experience and knowledge. In particular, Hall contends, ordinary frustrations like passing time "in the waiting-rooms of an overburdened National Health Service" or changing daily routines in response to growing crime rates furnished the experiential, cultural context that lent validity to Thatcherite discourse.[20] The basic point here is that the cultural realm of everyday life is a terrain where political struggle is inevitably waged, rather than being merely auxiliary to politics.

Lauren Berlant has taken a complementary approach to charting the generation of a new notion of citizenship by the new right, among other cultural-political forces, in the United States. The antiabortion movement, in particular, has been effective not just in gaining legal reforms and influencing elections but also—perhaps more profoundly—in reconstituting the "conditions of American citizenship," the "aggregate meaning of nature, identity, and the body in the construction of American nationality."[21] From a critical study of representations of pregnancy, the fetus, and abortion in magazines and films, Berlant educes the emergence of an image/concept of the citizen whose chief characteristic is its "fetality." Like the fetus, whose stereotypical image is endlessly reproduced in popular culture as it floats innocently within the womb, unaware that at any moment it might be destroyed, the "fetal" citizen is defined by her ever-present vulnerability to victimization. The logic of "fetal" citizenship has particularly unfortunate consequences for women, according to Berlant, because it facilitates their treatment as perpetually endangered objects of protection (rather than autonomous agents) in a host of policy and legal areas, most vividly in efforts to regulate pornography.[22] Like Hall, Berlant thus demonstrates that the political efficacy of the new right can be understood only in a very constricted sense if it brackets out the movement's cultural energies—for her, the labor of shaping and "embodying" identities, particularly those of gendered and sexual subjects.

Scholarly attention to the politics of Christian right culture specifically is limited but growing. Linda Kintz has traced the relocation of emotional investment "directly and intensively into the sacred site of the family" by and in evangelical conservative books, videos, and public events. For Kintz, evangelical sex manuals and Promise Keepers rallies do not just furnish cultural preconditions or stimuli for (supposedly more distinctively) political phenomena like the Christian Coalition's lobbying efforts and recruitment by the U.S. Taxpayers Party. Rather, electoral activism and the enjoyment of cultural commodities and spectacles are interwoven in a contiguity of practices that collectively generate the "affective" commitment or "passion" that, for Kintz, is the basic substance of politics.[23] More recently, Kintz has coedited a volume (with Julia Lesage) attempting to link her postmodernist take on the Christian right, along with several other pieces similarly attuned to cultural theory, to empirical, social-scientific analyses of the movement.[24]

These engagements with new right social movements, interventions that highlight the significance of culture for conceptualizing the movement's political power, model several analytical precepts incorporated in this book. Above all, like the works mentioned above, this account of Christian right culture presupposes that a cultural phenomenon's political meaning is never wholly determined by its intrinsic features, although a close and thorough examination of these characteristics is indispensable to a successful critique. Rather, the high political stakes of cultural production—and cultural criticism—come to the fore when we analyze the place of cultural objects within structures of social power and fields of struggle. The politics of Promise Keepers become evident in some respects, for example, when its representations of masculinity are shown to carry antifeminist assumptions and traces of the Protestant-capitalist ethic. But a more complete picture of Promise Keepers' politics emerges, with significant implications for any plan of opposition to the organization, when we consider Promise Keepers' relationship to the historical moment of its emergence. This moment may be fruitfully characterized in terms of multiple and varying conceptions of power—perhaps as an era of crisis in gender identities, or as a period of intensifying class conflict. The key point in general, however, is that the political consequences of culture can be drawn especially vigorously when the theorist forges connections between a given cultural object and a historically elaborated domain that transcends the boundaries of the object itself.

In addition, this book draws lessons from these other studies by examining new right culture microscopically and, in a sense, sympathetically. If the goal here is to identify Christian right culture's entanglement with the operations of social power, then it is vital to assume an interpretative position near enough to specific cultural phenomena to sense their complex interactions with historical conditions. And it is equally crucial not to prejudge the ethical and cognitive sensibilities at work in these phenomena, as many critics of the Christian right do. Those who are not adherents or supporters of the movement can come to understand the reasons for its power all the more vividly the more they allow themselves a spontaneous response to the movement's appeals to widely shared hopes, fears, and experiences. This is precisely what Hall is getting at when he stresses that the embrace of Thatcherism constituted a "rational" and "ethical" response by British workers and other citizens, because Thatcherism translated into discourse the everyday annoyances and profound hardships of life under a self-contradictory social-democratic program. Similarly, Kintz urges her readers to try to hear Christian right rhetoric, or imagine listening to it, from the positions of a great many women today who "are destroyed by anxiety, as they question whether they are good enough and as they try to find their identity in accomplishments, paychecks, and titles," all the while feeling "deep, profound, inarticulable worries about children" and therefore responding to a discourse that "addresses them as mothers."[25] As both Hall and Kintz argue, an approach that listens closely and with some measure of earnest sympathy to Christian right culture gains the ability to identify the experiential elements within these cultural phenomena that do not necessarily or exclusively have to be articulated to the new conservatism, but can be affirmed and addressed in more radical venues.

This study is particularly concerned with the relationship between Christian right culture and certain broadly shared experiences of the post-Fordist political economy: the increasing exclusivity and declining quality of health care and other social services, the undermining of democratic accountability in elections and the public sphere, and the long backlash against movements to empower women, minorities, and children. The analysis of the radio program *Focus on the Family* here shows not only that certain elements of conservative culture *can* be turned to alternative purposes, but moreover that Christian right culture, at least in one of its most influential forms, already *is* in conflict with the social conditions it legitimates. *Focus on the Family* at once expresses, reproduces, and protests against these post-Fordist experiences, according to its very constitution.

The Dialectics of Culture: Reconsidering Adorno

Despite the affinities of this study with the projects in cultural and political theory discussed above, the perspective here also differs from them. Above all, it stands apart in laying greater stress on the abiding *autonomy* of cultural phenomena from social power relations. This notion might at first seem to conflict with my criticism of approaches assigning a supplemental, subordinate, or auxiliary role to culture in relation to the political, and my insistence on the political significance and efficacy of cultural phenomena. It also goes against the grain of much contemporary work in cultural studies and political theory for which Foucault and Gramsci provide intellectual beacons, as they do for Berlant and Hall. Yet the idea that cultural phenomena can be in some sense autonomous of social power relations is central to the *dialectical* sensibility that guides this book, a sensibility that this study in turn attempts to refine into a productive method for the critical analysis of the present-day Christian right and contemporary popular culture in general.

Dialectics is conceptualized in this study as a methodological framework for interpreting the politics of culture in a way that keeps cultural criticism open to the following nearly paradoxical possibility. On the one hand, social power relations inundate any given cultural object, shaping its significance through and through. They wholly undermine culture's usual claim to provide a critical perspective lying "outside" society, just as they belie the assumption that the politics of the Christian right or any other social movement can be adequately understood through approaches that relegate the movement's cultural aspects to a subaltern role. On the other hand, the cultural object may momentarily transcend its entanglement in social power relations and raise a genuine protest against power. It is the insistence on the latter point that distinguishes this study from Foucauldian and Gramscian approaches to the critical analysis of culture.

Without a doubt, the politics of culture come to life when we view culture in a way influenced by Foucault: as a plurality of modes in which power circulates, of networks that always already involve discourses and institutions of law and capital in combination with those organizing pleasure, faith, and morality, in which the latter are radically indistinguishable from the former—since all, quite simply, are paths in which power is produced, moves, and operates. In turn, cultural studies has yielded profound insight into the new right in the United States and Britain by interpreting popular culture with the aid of Gramsci's theory of how "hegemonic" struggles function to elicit broad consent to historically specific conceptions of nationality.[26] Critical analysis gains something additionally important, however, when it considers cultural experiences and objects not only as thoroughly enmeshed in "disciplinary" mechanisms and "hegemonic" contestations but also as *different and apart* from these power dynamics, if only in the most transient and embattled moments. The critical theory of Theodor W. Adorno can aid us in elucidating this distinctively dialectical relationship of culture to social power.

The first two chapters explore Adorno's theories of cultural criticism, mass culture, and right-wing politics in some detail in order to clarify the important contribution that Adorno makes to my critique of a core element of Christian right culture today. Adorno is famous—to some, infamous—for having classically articulated the theory that "mass culture" in late-capitalist society is definitively shaped by processes of commodification and marketing and is therefore entirely ideological, in the sense of fostering a conformist subjectivity and an authoritarian social and political order. Such was the gist of the essay on the "culture industry" that Adorno wrote with Max Horkheimer as part of *Dialectic of Enlightenment*

(1944). Portions of chapters 1 and 2 provide a critique of this essay, and my own approach to *Focus on the Family* depends more centrally on other aspects of Adorno's theory. Still, Adorno's extreme pessimism regarding mass culture's potentialities was partly justified insofar as the theory of "state capitalism" on which it was based provided an accurate account of capitalist society in the mid–twentieth century. This theory, developed by Adorno and his colleagues at the Frankfurt Institut für Sozialforschung (Institute for Social Research), emphasized the centralization of planning authority with respect to production and consumption in large corporations and swelling states and the accompanying constriction of the domains for autonomous, individual action. Adorno and Horkheimer's theory of the culture industry, in turn, demonstrated the increasing envelopment of cultural experiences within these processes.

The advancing ensnarement of culture in the service of corporate profits was of world-historical consequence for Adorno because of the revolutionary potential he attributed to aesthetic experience, and also because of his distinctive conception of cultural radicalism. In sharp contrast to Gramsci, who viewed the synthesis of an "intellectual and moral unity" as a vital element of the "party spirit" on which the success of any hegemonic or counterhegemonic struggle relied, Adorno argued that the emancipatory energy of culture could only be released in cultural experiences that offered critical distance from all forms of instrumentalist thought and action—including party-building on the left.[27] For Adorno, "instrumental reason" comprised the "spirit of capitalism" in its advanced-industrial epoch. Under late capitalism, that is, the subject was on the verge of completely forfeiting the ability to reflect critically on socioethical ends, as consciousness and behavior tended to become oriented exclusively toward the solution of technical problems, or questions of means. For cultural experience to afford the subject any sort of break with these historically specific conditions of domination, the cultural object had to retain at least a residue of "nonidentity" with all instrumentalist processes, even though it was inevitably composed according to sociohistorical necessity. From an Adornian perspective, then, the progressive or liberatory aspect of the cultural object lies not in its positive contribution to a reconciliation of social contradictions assumed to be already existent, at least in a germinal sense (for instance, in the "state spirit" of the counterhegemonic party of the working class), but rather in its assertion of the *hope* for reconciliation in the face of actual, persistent domination. This critical capacity of culture is resolutely *utopian*, in the sense that it envisions a radical restructuring of society as a whole. But it is also determinedly *negative*, in that it does not explicitly define the nature of utopia but rather is content to let a dim sense of the utopian emanate from the aporias generated by culture's

manifestation of social contradictions. Discerning culture's utopian negativity, in turn, hinges on an interpretive approach to culture that at least
initially grants the cultural object's claim to be something that transcends
or is autonomous of political and economic instrumentalisms. It was precisely this autonomous character of culture that Adorno considered to be
absent from the products of the culture industry.

The culture industry theory is still of some use in interpreting the politics of Christian right media culture today, since the techniques of cultural
mass production characteristic of the Fordist era, which formed the historical context for this theory's formulation, have hardly disappeared. However, there were problems with this theory even in the period of its origina-
tion, when it seems to have most aptly described the political economy of
Hollywood, radio, and other elements of the culture industry. These difficulties stemmed above all, as the first chapter argues, from the fact that
Adorno carried out very few protracted and detailed examinations of individual artifacts of mass culture. Ironically, this made Adorno's theory of
the culture industry vulnerable to his own critique of vulgar Marxism: that
social theory uninformed by the sympathetic, microscopic, dialectical
critique of culture in its specific manifestations loses its capacity to be
critically self-reflective and begins to take its truths for granted as abso-
lutes, because it lacks exposure to culture's negative-utopian resources.
Nevertheless, Adorno took a significant (if hesitant) step toward this kind
of dialectical critique when he analyzed Depression-era Christian right
radio in the United States in "The Psychological Technique of Martin
Luther Thomas' Radio Addresses" (1943). A critical retrospective of this
traditionally overlooked text within Adorno's oeuvre thus occupies the
second chapter of this book, setting the stage for the subsequent analysis of
Focus on the Family.

The central argument of the first part of this book is that Adorno's theory
of dialectical cultural criticism offers a potentially more lasting legacy for
analyzing the politics of culture under late capitalism than does the theory
of the culture industry. The method that Adorno named *social physiognomy* sought to discern the presence of society's contradictions in the
self-contradictory composition of the cultural object. For Adorno, as long
as society remained riven by antagonisms rooted in political-economic
domination, no cultural object could ever be created in a way that was
genuinely harmonious—for culture always reflected and reproduced social
conditions. It was primarily in the analysis of "high"-cultural phenomena
such as Arnold Schoenberg's atonal string quartets, Samuel Beckett's enigmatic drama *Endgame*, and Søren Kierkegaard's paradoxical contortions
in *Either/Or* that Adorno deployed and honed his critical method, not in
his more perfunctory and less individualized reflections on movies, re-

corded popular music, and television. Nonetheless, no inherent features of social physiognomy preclude its application to cultural objects that Adorno would have called "mass-cultural"—as long as one recognizes, as Adorno did not, that mass-cultural phenomena can have an internal coherence, that they can strive to attain an aesthetic wholeness and a continuity with a distinctive historical tradition. These pivotal qualities make it possible to interpret the ruptures preventing this coherence from fully being realized as *contradictions within a whole*, as opposed to mere breaks within an object that itself is no more than a conglomerate of instrumental effects. Viewing elements of highly commercialized and widely distributed culture in this way can shed light on their ideological tendencies, beyond those stemming from the employment of standardized production, stereotypical construction, and scientifically managed distribution and promotion. In addition, by following Adorno's lead in taking seriously—though by no means accepting at face value—the claims even of mass-cultural objects to constitute an autonomous realm apart from politics and economics, theory can bring attention to the unexpectedly radical political sensibilities that such objects sometimes carry with them—even the products circulated by the Christian right's culture industries.

Christian Right Narratives and Post-Fordism

Rather than moving directly to an explanation of how Adorno's theory informs my specific interpretation of *Focus on the Family*, I want to clarify this relationship by describing briefly the path I took in developing my reading of Dobson's program. My hope here is to give the reader a sense of how certain concepts I adapted from Adorno—above all, aesthetic structure, contradiction, and dialectics—came by degrees to seem capable of offering analytical leverage with respect to the phenomenon. I do this to underscore an important point: my method of examining *Focus on the Family* has not been lifted in mature form from Adorno's texts, but instead has evolved through my sustained engagement with Dobson's broadcasts. (In corollary fashion, this encounter with Christian right radio has been essential to the formulation and refinement of my critique of Adorno.) Proceeding in this way requires a temporary shift out of the dense, theoretical discourse pursued in the previous sections. Although this modulation might be slightly jarring to some readers, it allows me to convey how my critical approach has been elaborated more authentically than if I were to omit mention of this developmental process.

The material analyzed in this study is taken from roughly eighty half-hour broadcasts of *Focus on the Family* aired in the mid-1990s. These broadcasts cover a broad range of subjects: "family" concerns, most prominently child discipline and marital vitality; public policy issues, in both the domestic and international arenas; health problems, both mental and physical; financial matters, personal and societal alike; and questions of religious faith.[28] In monitoring Dobson's program, I gradually came to the conclusion that what binds many of the individual shows together, more than topical similarities, are shared patterns in the ways the featured issues are addressed It became clear to me, first, that narrative or story-telling constitutes a central mode of communication in these broadcasts. For example, a broadcast series on homosexuality examined in more detail below does not simply offer an objectivistic argument that gay men are "deviant" or that gay and lesbian politics are undermining the nation. Instead, *Focus on the Family* makes these points by having a "formerly gay" man and his therapist tell Dobson their stories of working together and bringing the client into a new, heterosexual "lifestyle."

Second, I began to see that often a unified narrative is conveyed by multiple and varied stories told in different shows. In each of these more pervasive narrative "undertows," various radio personalities on the shows who fit a particular mold fill in the features of a distinctive main figure, a unique character-type. Thus the individual stories of the therapist in this episode on homosexuality, the psychiatrists who discuss "false memories" of child abuse in another broadcast, and Dobson himself perform the con-tinuous retelling of a single, broader narrative. This more general narra-tive, a narrative centering on the experiences of a compassionate, profes-sional caregiver, along with the other two narratives examined in the chapters to follow, largely constitute the foundational aesthetic structures of the program. Moreover, these are distinctively evangelical-Christian narratives: narratives of salvation through compassion, humility, and for-giveness. Retold in ways that attempt to reconcile them to very contempo-rary experiences, they nonetheless establish a new phase in a historically continuous, religious tradition.

Finally, every one of these narrative figures is deeply rent by internal inconsistencies. To be sure, the casual, intimate, reflective conversations between Dobson and his guests unfailingly convey the impression of nar-rative coherence. Listening carefully to these broadcasts, however, I was repeatedly struck by the manifest contradictions between the basic as-pects of each character-type. For instance, the figure of the evangelical professional represented by Dobson and others at first seems a model of universal compassion, ethical self-determination, and scientific-practical expertise. Ultimately, however, the "compassionate professional" reneges on each of these promises, refusing to extend compassion to certain kinds of people, abandoning autonomous ethical decision making for heterono-mous obedience to a system of cosmic order, and offering the solace of a new identity (membership within the pure community) in place of concrete, healing aid. Similar, constitutional contradictions characterize each of the other two narrative figures discussed in the chapters ahead, the "humble leader" and the "forgiving victim."

Of course, the narrative form as such lends coherence to each character-type, as personal stories of trial and triumph commence, unfold, and attain closure. At least an appearance of aesthetic harmony thus emanates from Focus's narratives—the appearance, that is, of a reconciliation of the two conflicting halves of the narrative figure's persona. Yet this narrative coherence remains, at bottom, both forced and false. Deep tensions between the two faces of each character-type boil just below the surface of each figure's harmonious countenance.

Foucauldian/postmodernist and Gramscian forms of critique join hands, unexpectedly, with empirical social science in interpreting the meaning of the ruptures in Christian right culture with reference to political *strategy*. For many social scientists, the discontinuities I discern within the narrative structures of *Focus on the Family* would be taken as evidence of the movement's constant battle to keep the peace among those who yearn for confrontation and others who favor compromise with the less "ideologically" pure of the right and center. Gramscian analysis, in turn, would respond to these discursive breaches by searching out the class-structural or intranational tensions of which Christian right culture is the "lived experience," an experience that results from intentional hegemonic practices of intellectuals and popular elements from specific social groups. Thus the contradictions within Focus's figure of the "compassionate professional" might be seen as resulting from the class-heterogeneity of a major faction of the Christian right, represented vividly though not exclusively by Focus and its constituents, in which segments of the professional strata exert intellectual leadership for a mass base whose membership, although predominantly middle and upper middle class, also includes working-class constituents.

Meanwhile, some postmodernist theorists would stress that Christian right culture's incoherencies may counterintuitively help "discipline" Americans in a Foucauldian sense by causing power to circulate ever more productively and intensively through new right institutions and discourses. Meryem Ersoz, for example, notes that the radio stations transmitting *Focus on the Family* typically use "a pastiche of programming devices borrowed from a variety of adult contemporary stations and reinscribed within [a] conservative Christian political and religious context."[29] The incorporation of secular styles, such as signature themes that copy "rock-music format stations" and objectivistic news reporting that mimics the major networks, might seem to undercut religious-traditional messages that demonize the "liberal" media and rock's celebration of sexual pleasure—just as the invocation of expert-scientific knowledge by Focus's "compassionate professional" appears to contradict fundamentalist denunciations of humanism and scientific skepticism. Yet precisely these jagged edges can be seen as constituting new pathways of power that enable the desires and knowledge-modes conventionally associated with secular media and entertainment forms to find expression in evangelical-conservative contexts, thereby strengthening the "effects of truth" of the latter.

Foucauldian/postmodernist, Gramscian, and positivist perspectives thus suggest distinct interpretations of the narrative contradictions within *Focus on the Family*. Nonetheless, they maintain an important commonality by approaching these inconsistencies as manifestations of the strategic dynamics of the Christian right. A similar emphasis on strategy would most likely guide Foucauldian and Gramscian analyses of the disparities between the twenty-one broadcasts chosen for detailed analysis below and the remaining shows among the seventy-eight total broadcasts selected for the study that only partially exhibit the characteristics of one of the three major narratives discussed in chapters 3–5.[30] Foucauldian critics would likely interpret these variations on the narrative structures of *Focus on the Family* as evidence that Focus's discourse has emerged through "genealogical" processes characterized by discontinuities and capricious deployments of power-knowledge rather than a more unified, developmental unfolding.[31] From a Gramscian perspective, these disjunctures between (as well as within) the various editions of *Focus on the Family* might well appear as signs of the clashes or uneasy alliances between distinct hegemonic forces, such as the Christian right, the libertarian movement, and the corporate interests involved in the new right coalition.

In contrast to such efforts to unveil *Focus on the Family*'s claim to be religious culture as political strategy, I propose that we take the reformulation of religious narratives in *Focus on the Family* seriously as a coherent, tradition-bound religious phenomenon, at least initially. We might engage the possibility, that is, that Dobson's program is in fact saturated not only with strategy but also with theology; and that this theological sensibility does not exhaust its political vitality inasmuch as it is "theocratic," cloaking authoritarian power in holy vestments, but also endows *Focus on the Family* with a dialectical claim to autonomy from political and economic instrumentalisms. By virtue of this autonomous moment, *Focus on the Family* can be seen as retaining a weak but abiding negative-utopian ferment. I do not mean that simply because *Focus on the Family* calls on Christian traditions, it keeps alive a set of positive, theologically rooted values on the basis of which to criticize social injustice. Rather, Focus's necessarily unsuccessful attempt to rearticulate a coherent narrative of religious salvation, in a society rent by antagonisms but still sporting the pretense of harmony, negatively illuminates those antagonisms and thereby preserves the hope of their radical, historical transcendence.

More specifically, the contradictions in Focus's narrative figures express, reinforce, and negatively protest against an assortment of contradictions of post-Fordism. As chapter 3 demonstrates, Focus's figure of the compassionate professional reflects the dissonance of an increasingly exclusive and ethically barren "system" of health care and social services with the legitimating rhetoric of communitarianism propounded by the Clinton administration along with many corporations. This rhetoric mounts as older, Fordist structures that ensured a more universal provision of human services become increasingly wobbly, necessitating a search for an ideological mooring for the post-Fordist state and economy that moves beyond Reaganite liberal productivism. The narrative of the "humble leader," analyzed in the fourth chapter, reproduces the conflict between post-Fordist electoral institutions, in which politicians' democratic accountability has been compromised to an unprecedented extent by the capitalization of campaigns and the media, and the aura of revitalized populism that leaders like Bill Clinton and Newt Gingrich have cultivated through their use of innovative media styles and techniques. Chapter 5 deciphers Focus's figure of the "forgiving victim" as expressing the declining power of women, minorities, and children in post-Fordist society, while efforts to roll back the gains of feminism and the civil rights movement advertise themselves as fulfilling rather than subverting the social justice claims raised by the radical movements of the 1950s–1970s.

In these ways, narrative structures of *Focus on the Family* reflect and reproduce the political-economic conditions of post-Fordism. By virtue of their ultimate failures as coherent stories of salvation, however, these narratives furthermore contain a negative-utopian wish that these social contradictions might one day be overcome. Perceiving this *dialectical* relationship of a major component of Christian right culture to the post-Fordist social totality furnishes social theory with vital, self-critical energies. Attentiveness to the dialectics of culture can help prevent the reification of "the right" and evangelicalism as monolithic forces, as the pure enemy that must be conquered, rather than as sources (albeit counterintuitive and spare ones) of radical energies. At the same time, this approach also preserves a perspective that hopes for broad social transformation, not just the microscopic, capillary instantiations of resistance that Foucault invites us to desire. And it finds grounds for this hope in the observation that it is sheltered and maintained not only among weary veterans of "the Movement" but, startlingly, also in the most unlikely corners of American culture.

Critique alone, of course, can no more transform the negative-utopian moments of *Focus on the Family* into institutional changes than can these radio broadcasts themselves. Thus the practical implications of this study demand reflection in their own right, and this is undertaken in the concluding chapter. The contemporary United States presents an ideological and institutional environment in which the public philosophy of liberalism holds sway. Not surprisingly, given this context, critical responses to evangelical conservatism from influential interest groups, religious institutions, and academia have generally grounded their claims on liberal premises. They have thus emphasized the movement's subversion of the principles of free speech, religious disestablishment, toleration, and "instrumentalist" governance dissociated from substantive moral considerations.[32]

My analysis of *Focus on the Family*, it turns out, does indeed speak to one of the central concerns of liberalism: the value of protecting and encouraging autonomous individuality. That is, each of the three narrative figures analyzed expresses a wish for the actualization of a certain kind of individual autonomy—the cultivation of an empowered subject capable of "governing" itself in matters of ethical judgment and political citizenship. The dominant liberal discourse, however, lacks sufficient conceptual space to comprehend the clear message of this study of *Focus on the Family*: that the Christian right cannot be successfully resisted on the basis of concern for rights and liberties alone. Rather, the liberal project must be joined to an explicit challenge to the structural transformations in the political economy described here, because these changes are undermining the autonomous individuality that lies at the core of the liberal vision. It must furthermore enjoin a commitment to nurturing ethical sensibilities, looking beyond the Christian right's illiberal desire to inject private morality into public policy, in the awareness that despite all its talk of "values" the Christian right ultimately proffers a politics of disillusioned anti-ethics insofar as it cynically rejects the notion of the individual's moral autonomy. Again, liberalism is predicated on this very notion and cannot survive its historical hollowing-out.

Finally, however, political practice must avoid treating culture in exclusively instrumental terms. Activists need to take stock of the dessicated condition of liberal-left popular culture and respond to Christian right pop culture by creating new narratives of social transformation. A major conclusion of this study, explored in the final chapter, is that Christian idioms themselves can provide fruitful grounds for generating such narratives, enabling the articulation of critical theory's claims within the political struggles of specific, historically situated communities. Those who attempt to forge these links of solidarity by generating new and politically consequential narratives, however, must bear in mind Adorno's insight that it is precisely the cultural object's autonomy from the instrumental purposes of specific social or political groups that safeguards the protestative dimension of its political power. At the same time, acknowledging this autonomous character of the object enables the creator and critic of culture alike to perceive moments in the object's construction that can properly be termed *utopian*. The utopia of which these moments allow a passing glimpse is neither the positive articulation of a state of total redemption nor the negative gesture toward such a condition that was a constant motif in Adorno's writings. Instead, as the analysis ahead shows, the utopian moment within Christian right popular culture presents itself as an *anticipation* of a radical unsettling of given social and political relations—a sense of the simultaneous presence, absence, and imminence of a condition in which alienated groups would at least begin to recognize their common experiences and concerns. In more concrete terms, listening carefully to *Focus on the Family* yields the unlikely experience that shared ground exists among Dobson's listeners and, for example, welfare rights advocates, or campaign finance reform activists, or nonviolent resisters of racism. Were such flashes of the utopian in Christian right popular culture to be given more acute, consistent, and self-conscious expression in alternative cultural forms, entrenched dichotomies between "left" and "right" might not so strongly inhibit attempts to build a broad, democratic-populist resistance to the new market-based, political-economic fundamentalism.

"Turning Hearts toward Home": A Brief History of Focus on the Family

Entertaining thoughts like these can only be done in good conscience, however, with eyes open to the everyday struggles faced by progressive activists who confront the new right in all of its organizational, financial, and technological might. Focus on the Family has received far less attention from scholars and journalists than the other major institutions of the Christian right, especially the Moral Majority, the Christian Coalition, and Pat Robertson's television empire. Nevertheless, as researchers are beginning to discover, Focus exercises enormous influence both within and beyond the evangelical conservative subculture.

As anyone who even occasionally pushes the search button on her or his car radio knows well—whether listening to AM or FM, and whether traveling in cities, suburbs, or rural areas—evangelical conservative radio is hardly a thing of the past, despite the more spectacular and better-documented expansion of televangelism from the 1950s through today. In 1994, the leading evangelical magazine *Christianity Today* reported that "Christian radio" had "mushroomed to the extent that it is now the third most common format on the dial, behind country and adult contemporary."[33] As of 1997, there were between twelve hundred and sixteen hundred stations with a "Christian" format in the United States, accounting for roughly one-tenth of all radio stations in the nation, with over two-thirds of these stations being for-profit enterprises.[34] In the world of evangelical radio broadcasting, no organization has made a larger impact than Focus on the Family. *Christianity Today* has dubbed Focus's president and founder, James Dobson, "the undisputed king of Christian radio."[35] In 1995, *Focus on the Family* was the third most listened-to radio show in the country, after the Rush Limbaugh and Paul Harvey programs.[36] An estimated 20.6 million people listen to evangelical radio programming at least once a week—and 4 million listeners heed cohost Mike Trout's call to "turn our hearts toward home" with *Focus on the Family* every day.[37] In the United States, the thirty-minute show is transmitted almost fourteen thousand times per week on about fifteen hundred stations, or nearly all of the stations with "Christian" formats.[38]

Focus on the Family was founded in 1977, when James Dobson opened a small office in Arcadia, California, to support his weekly radio broadcasts on family-related issues such as disciplining children and maintaining a healthy marriage.[39] The son of a preacher in the Protestant fundamentalist Church of the Nazarene, Dobson claims to have been able to pray before he could talk and to have felt God's calling from as early as age three, when he toddled up to the altar in response to his father's Sunday morning exhortation that the unsaved offer their lives to Jesus.[40] Dobson chose not to enter the ministry, however, feeling beckoned instead to pursue a career in psychology. During the 1960s, Dobson received his Ph.D. in Educational Psychology from the University of Southern California and earned credentials in school psychology, school psychometrics, and junior high school and elementary school teaching, as well as state licenses in psychology and marriage, family, and child counseling. Dobson worked as a teacher, counselor, and psychometrist in public schools while attending graduate school. He also coauthored six articles that were published in professional journals, including two in the *New England Journal of Medicine.*[41]

Dobson became a public figure in 1970 when his first popular book, *Dare to Discipline*, was put out by Tyndale House Publishers, an evangelical press located in the evangelical heartland of Wheaton, Illinois. *Dare to Discipline* faulted "permissive" child-rearing practices for the "cataclysmic social upheaval" of the late sixties in which "the young" had declared war on "authority in all its forms" and generated worldwide "chaos, violence, and insecurity."[42] An obvious though not explicit rebuttal to popular parenting expert Benjamin Spock, who had become not only a leading critic of some traditional child-rearing practices but also a vocal opponent of the Vietnam War, Dobson stressed the need to apply physical punishment to children whose conduct reflected "willful, haughty disobedience" and directly challenged the parent's (usually the mother's) authority.[43] Although Dobson has been unfairly caricatured as an advocate of child abuse by some opponents, his language in *Dare to Discipline* tended to dehumanize disobedient children, seemed sometimes disconcertingly enthusiastic about the application of pain to such children, and in general undermined its initial contextualization of discipline within a "framework" of parental love by ultimately figuring discipline and respect for parental authority as the foundation of love.[44] *Dare to Discipline* thus embodied significant tensions between moments of hopeful idealism and stronger currents of repressive authoritarianism—tensions that, as we shall see, have continued to pervade Dobson's communications projects with Focus on the Family. Moreover, in drawing parallels between disobedient children and radical students, endorsing parents' use of incentives to stimulate acquisitive behavior by children, and construing parental, political, and divine authority as a unified structure of order, Dobson forged a template in 1970 for the fusion of "traditional family values," economic neoliberalism, and political authoritarianism that would shortly thereafter catalyze the new right's conquest of national power. Finally, *Dare to Discipline*'s reception foreshadowed the congenial relationship that would soon develop between the new Christian right and the Republican party: besides becoming a popular best-seller (selling three million copies), the book was "specially bound and placed in the White House library" in 1972.[45]

After concluding his graduate study, Dobson worked on the Attending Staff of Children's Hospital in Los Angeles and then began teaching at the USC School of Medicine as an associate clinical professor of pediatrics. However, the popularity of *Dare to Discipline* and two subsequent popular books on child-rearing and marital relations launched Dobson on a parallel career as a public speaker and writer. In the mid-1970s, Dobson resigned from Children's Hospital to pursue more vigorously such enterprises as conducting seminars on family issues, producing a video series based on these seminars, and carrying out his new radio broadcasting project. Formatted as a talk show spotlighting professional voices, *Focus on the Family* provided a break from most of the other fare on evangelical radio, which was dominated at that time by preachers ("pulpit thumpers," in the words of an advertising consultant quoted in Dobson's biography). The program was soon expanded from a weekly to a daily broadcast and in 1981 was lengthened from a fifteen-minute program to its current half-hour duration.[46] Meanwhile, Dobson's video series, also titled *Focus on the Family*, opened up uncharted territory in Christian right visual culture. This series inaugurated the production of an innovative type of Christian right product: the "talking-head"-style recording of "the professional lecturer specializing in Christian lifestyle issues." Dobson's videos were wildly successful. They generated a new industry trend, as "Dobson clones" soon rushed into the market, and enabled unprecedented modes of penetration into everyday life by Christian right media.[47]

Since 1980, Focus's staff has grown from twelve to over thirteen hundred employees. Its headquarters expanded from a small group of offices in Arcadia, California, to a thirteen-acre site in Pomona, California, in 1987. Just four years later, Focus moved to its current facilities: a forty-seven-acre corporate campus with three buildings and a zip code of its own in Colorado Springs, Colorado, home to the largest concentration of Christian right organizations in the country.[48] Focus's fifty-two "ministries" today go far beyond radio broadcasting, ranging from book publishing to professional counseling, from direct mail to video production, from magazine publication to an academic program for college undergraduates, and from a "corporate library" outreach project to conferences for physicians and attorneys.[49] Focus has established affiliates in Canada, Europe, Russia, Australia, and South Africa, and international versions of *Focus on the Family* reach as many as 550 million listeners throughout the world— in several languages besides English—with a particularly high density of broadcasting in Central and South America. The program is carried abroad not only by the U.S. Armed Forces Radio Network but also by a number of "foreign state radio networks," including "the two major radio networks in Russia." Focus's broadcasts are among the five most popular radio programs in Zimbabwe, and it was reported in 1998 that "500 state-owned radio stations in China [were] about to begin the Focus broadcast."[50] Accumulated primarily through individual contributions, Focus's annual operating budget topped $100 million in 1994 and continues to increase. The budget more than doubled between 1990 and 1994 and by the mid-1990s was over five times the size of the Christian Coalition's budget and more than half as large as that of Robertson's for-profit media corporation International Family Entertainment (IFE), which owns the Family Channel (formerly the Christian Broadcasting Network, or CBN).[51] Nonetheless, Focus remains strictly a not-for-profit institution. Focus's employees respond to ten thousand letters from constituents every day, mail copies of Dobson's monthly letter to 2.1 million people, and receive two hundred thousand visitors per year at Focus's Colorado Springs "Welcome Center."[52]

Notwithstanding this massive financial growth and operational diversification, the radio personality of James Dobson still stands at the heart of Focus on the Family as the primary symbol of the organization's unity and purpose. The fortunate visitor who arrives on a day in which Dobson is in the studio, as I did when I journeyed to Colorado Springs in early 1996, is usually welcomed to watch and listen to the recording of *Focus on the Family* from a special gallery separated from the taping area by large glass windows.[53] The decor of the broadcast studio makes a visual statement that accords with the stylistic tenor of the conversation between Dobson and his guests. Flanked by dark, wood-toned shelves of books and lush green plants, the discussants generate the air of a relaxed and informal—yet serious, learned, and occasionally impassioned—exchange of thoughts among respected professionals. Dobson clearly possesses a charisma that enables him to inspire devotion and admiration in his constituents, as fully 75 percent of Focus's constituents report having listened regularly to *Focus on the Family* for five years or more.[54] An imposing physical presence because of his unusual height, Dobson, at sixty years of age, has the aura of an earnest, kind, and wise elder who retains much youthful vigor and possesses confidence in his own moral authority. Moreover, judging from his popularity among the millions of evangelicals who think well of him but have never seen him in the flesh, Dobson seems to have a gift for projecting these qualities over the radio.

In the wake of the cynicism spawned by the televangelists' scandals and Pat Robertson's having sullied himself with the dirt of political ambition, Dobson has come to represent a voice of integrity to most conservative evangelicals. He also seems to speak for (and to) a socioeconomically comfortable or even privileged constituency (and many who at least aspire to such status), despite his homespun anecdotes and periodic references to the lean years he and his wife Shirley experienced as a young couple. This is borne out by the available demographic information about Focus's supporters, whom the *New York Times* described as "suburban," "middle- and upper-middle-class people": about half have four-year college or graduate degrees and 80 percent have some college education; the "vast majority" are married with two or more children.[55] Ultimately, however, Dobson's traditional and almost complete avoidance of the medium of television has been instrumental to his image as the one conservative evangelical leader with class and a clear conscience. By shaping his media identity almost solely through the use of radio in a television age, Dobson appears at once both less manipulative and more authentically conservative than other prominent figures of evangelical conservatism.[56]

Thus, though Dobson does not hesitate to use stereotyped images of socioeconomic and cultural humility to his advantage, he and his constituency undermine, at least to a degree, the common perception of evangelicals as poorly educated, low to lower middle class, mainly rural folk. Focus represents a major arm of the Christian right whose cooperation with antitax groups and other conservative organizations prioritizing economic issues has been facilitated by the fact that, sociologically, Dobson and many of his constituents are among those who have benefited from the types of economic growth characteristic of the transition to post-Fordism. These evangelicals are hardly the working-class dupes of manipulative elites, engaged in a cultural politics running counter to their (immediate and narrowly construed) economic interests. Instead, they tend to be beneficiaries rather than victims of the "growing social subsidization of the new middle strata through ongoing degradation of job creation and erosion of mass Fordist consumer norms."[57]

Accordingly, Focus has been adept at harnessing the political technologies developed and perfected by the countermobilization of the middle and upper classes against the poor, minorities, and women in the conservative resurgence of the 1970s–1990s.[58] Focus's metamorphosis into a powerful force within electoral and public policy–making institutions has paralleled that of the Christian right more broadly. Initially, during the 1980 presidential campaign and then during the Reagan years, the focus was on the national level and depended heavily on the publicly visible interventions of prominent individuals—in the movement as a whole, Jerry Falwell; for Focus, Dobson himself. Dobson served on an advisory committee to the Carter administration's ill-fated White House Conference on Families, at which Christian right participants made national headlines by staging a walk-out in response to what they viewed as the scuttling of their concerns by the conference leaders. Of no little significance in securing this role for Dobson was the fact that "he announced on his radio show that he would like to be [included in the committee] and thousands of listeners called the White House."[59] This incident typified the style of the early Christian right (although it has by no means been abandoned by the current movement): a rapid response by mass audiences to the exhortations of a national media spokesperson, bringing pressure to bear inside the Washington, D.C., beltway. And it previewed the growing significance of talk radio as a tool of new-right political mobilization, which would reach new heights in the 1990s.

Dobson subsequently served on several advisory committees under the Reagan administration: the National Advisory Commission to the office of Juvenile Justice and Delinquency Prevention (1982–84); the Citizens Advisory Panel for Tax Reform, which he cochaired (1984–87); the Attorney General's Commission on Pornography (1985–86); the United States Army's Family Initiative, which he eventually chaired (1986–88); the Attorney General's Advisory Board on Missing and Exploited Children (1987); and the Secretary of Health and Human Services' Panel on Teen Pregnancy Prevention. The Bush administration did not offer Dobson any similar appointments, but Focus's official biography of Dobson states that Dobson "consulted with President George Bush on family related matters." Senator Bob Dole named Dobson to the Commission on Child and Family Welfare convened by Senate Republicans in December 1994.[60]

In the late 1980s, as Dobson was becoming increasingly known in the nation's capital, Focus's organizational commitment to public-policy intervention intensified. Although Focus remained officially nonpartisan and uninvolved in fundraising or other election-oriented activities, in 1988 Dobson's group purchased the Family Research Council and soon remodeled it into one of the country's foremost evangelical conservative lobbying organizations. Gary Bauer, for eight years a high-level official in the Reagan administration, directed the FRC from its founding until 1999. Over the past several years, spokespersons from the FRC have been increasingly heard in the mainstream media offering conservative soundbites on current issues. However, reporters rarely note the organization's link to Focus, upon which the FRC is no longer dependent financially but with which the FRC continues to coordinate activities extensively. Dobson himself has described the FRC as "the lobbying/research arm of Focus on the Family."[61]

In addition, Focus devotes approximately 5 percent of its own annual budget to public policy–related activities. This amounts to several million dollars that support a surprisingly extensive range of functions, since sophisticated communications technologies allow a relatively small staff to maintain a wide array of contacts. In 1996, Focus's computerized fax system had been programmed to transmit op-ed pieces written in Colorado Springs to about 130 editors of major newspapers around the country, as part of a recent effort to cultivate relationships with media professionals. Sitting in front of cubicle walls adorned with signed personal photographs taken with President Ronald Reagan and Lieutenant Colonel Oliver North, Public Policy Information Manager Caia Mockaitis told me that she furnished material to the mainstream media without waiting to be asked first, knowing that effective political maneuvering means supplying the terms according to which issues are debated.[62] Other staff members working in or with the policy department compiled and sent out information packets on fifty-eight different issues, as well as nineteen academic studies called "social research briefs" and "youth culture reports."[63] Focus's news reporting and commentary program, *Family News in Focus*, was being aired over nineteen thousand times per week in the United States and Canada on more than sixteen hundred radio facilities.[64] And though the circulation of Focus's policy magazine *Citizen* had recently fallen to 108,000 from its 1992 peak of about 300,000, Focus had expanded its cybernetic communication with constituents through the World Wide Web.[65]

Focus also has promoted the formation of semi-autonomous organizations to conduct lobbying and public information activities at the state level. This project was initiated in 1989, the same year that Pat Robertson and Ralph Reed founded the Christian Coalition in the wake of Robertson's movement-reenergizing 1988 campaign for the presidency. Thus, once again, Focus steered a course typical of the Christian right's development as a whole, in this case by shifting the locus of recruitment and activism closer to the grassroots. "Family policy councils" (FPCs), as Focus calls them, existed by 1996 in at least thirty-two states (Focus does not provide the exact figure), with especially active FPCs located in California, Colorado, Texas, Michigan, Pennsylvania, North Carolina, South Carolina, and Virginia, and with New York and New Jersey being the only large states in which no FPCs had been founded.[66] Like Bauer and other FRC representatives, spokespersons for the FPCs who are quoted in media reports are rarely if ever linked to Focus. Officially, Focus simply "stands willing to assist and serve the FPCs" in the areas of "board development," "strategic planning," "fund development," and "issue strategy support," and only provides consultation on these activities if invited to do so by a self-starting group in a given state.[67] In practice, Focus's coordination of the founding and operations of FPCs may well be quite a bit more proactive, as a series of community-based events sponsored by Focus in the early 1990s suggested.[68]

Focus helped generate mass constituencies for the FPCs by running a program of "Community Impact Seminars" (CISs) throughout the nation from 1992 to 1995. Usually hosted by an FPC, these daylong events featured two Focus representatives who provided mostly monologic presentations on an assortment of general themes ranging from the philosophical to the practical, from the decline of Western culture through the influence of secular humanism to "a model for church action."[69] Seminar participants received a packet of materials with a complete conference curriculum, along with complementary copies of several additional information sources, including *Citizen* magazine, a programming schedule for *Family News in Focus*, several FRC "Community Impact Bulletins," and the FRC's newsletter "Washington Watch." The packet also referred attendees to a variety of other media and information outlets, offering promotional materials for the sponsoring FPC and subscription forms for "Washington Watch" and Focus's fax service, "Family Issues Alert." The CISs thus vividly illustrated the Christian right's signature adroitness at using its media and public events to promote additional media, thereby energizing a vast network of communications with a panoply of interface sites.[70]

At the same time, the two CISs I observed evinced a strikingly peculiar disregard for the exigencies of current combat in the spheres of elections and public policy. The presentations and curricula for the CISS changed negligibly in style and substance over the several years and multiple locations in which Focus conducted the program. A sprinkling of locally resonant humor was virtually the only difference between the two 1994 CISS that I attended. This was remarkable, since the first took place in Kennewick, Washington, the day after a statewide initiative to prevent the statutory guarantee of civil rights for gays and lesbians had failed to gain the requisite number of signatures for inclusion on the 1994 general election ballot. The second, in turn, was held in a suburb of Rochester, New York, barely a month after the Republican party had gained control of Congress for the first time in generations. Neither the Kennewick nor the Rochester CISS remotely resembled a serious debriefing among committed activists to evalute political victories or defeats and plan future actions accordingly, in contrast to the organizing conferences sponsored by the Christian Coalition (one of which I observed in Syracuse, New York, in the fall of 1995).[71] Although the seminar urged attendees to engage in community activism through church-based "community impact committees," there was no coordinated effort to establish such agencies or to link them into a highly efficient vehicle for lobbying and getting out the vote.[72] Instead, these committees seemed conceived more along the lines of a high-school athletics booster club or volunteer-based meals-on-wheels program.

How can these apparent lapses of strategic acumen be explained? It is certainly reasonable to consider Focus's silence regarding current events that were doubtless of extreme interest to most seminar participants as part of a more grand movement strategy, according to which, to paraphrase Diamond, different actors and organizations take responsibility for separate tasks in line with their distinct strengths and interests. For Diamond, the CISS contributed an intellectual, reflective dimension to the movement that the Christian Coalition's tactical seminars naturally precluded. According to the movement's "division of labor," that is, Focus has taken charge of blending "activist training with more subtle cultural programming aimed at a potentially broader audience" than the Coalition's membership.[73] The media and information links generated through the conference packet, in turn, facilitate the mutual nourishment of the different wings of the movement.

Yet the puzzling reticence of Focus's seminar leaders concerning the headline developments in the movement's conquest of electoral and policy-making influence can, I believe, be interpreted in another way. For it is emblematic of the fact that neither Focus's nor the Christian right's political power and significance is entirely a function of deliberate strategy and instrumentalist action—notwithstanding the financially well-heeled, geographically extensive, and technically sophisticated apparatus for such action that Focus and other movement organizations have gradually built since the 1970s. The politics of Focus on the Family are also very much a matter of silences, of aporias, of spaces between contradictory narrative strands that gesture mutely toward the chasms that mark the growing divisions between the secure and the exploited in America today. This book investigates these disjunctures in which the politics of Christian right culture in the post-Fordist era are produced, search for their valences with—and their defiances of—the forces that are propelling this country toward an increasingly antagonistic future.

1

Adorno on Mass Culture and Cultural Criticism

Baby with the bath water.—Among the motifs of cultural criticism one of the most long-established and central is that of the lie: that culture creates the illusion of a society worthy of human beings which does not exist; that it conceals the material conditions upon which everything human arises, and that, comforting and sooth-ing, it serves to nourish the bad economic determinacy of existence. . . . This is the notion of culture as ideology. . . . But precisely this notion, like all expostula-tion about lies, has a suspicious tendency to become itself ideology.—Theodor W. Adorno, *Minima Moralia*, 1944

Marx famously concluded his *Theses on Feuerbach* by declaring: "The philosophers have only *interpreted* the world, in various ways; the point is to *change* it."[1] Many Marxian theorists over the past century have received this injunction as a warning against theory becoming so preoccu-pied with the analysis of culture that it loses touch with concrete efforts to revolutionize society. This suspicious predisposition toward cultural critique has been further bolstered by the example Marx himself seems to have set, as he moved from the critique of Hegelian philosophy to the critical analysis of political economy.

Adorno's distinctive position among twentieth-century Marxist theo-rists stems largely from his steadfast repudiation of this predisposition and his ardent defense of cultural criticism as a valid and necessary task for Marxist theory. To be sure, various forms of cultural critique have fea-tured prominently in the writings of Adorno's Frankfurt School colleagues (notably Max Horkheimer, Herbert Marcuse, and Jürgen Habermas) and other thinkers from outside this tradition (especially Antonio Gramsci and Raymond Williams). But Adorno's texts are unusual in the intensity and centrality that the exhortation toward cultural criticism assumes within them. For Adorno, it was both intellectually axiomatic and historically imperative to recognize that theory which dismissed intellectual and artistic phenomena as "mere ideology"—that is, as essentially just instruments for perpetuating class domination—was itself ideological. Aspiring to critical insight into society meant resisting the delusion that abstract, social-theoretical categories provided all the knowledge of their objects that was needed to penetrate ideology. Instead, Adorno argued, under late capitalism critical thinking hinged on subjectivity preserving a critical, yet also empathetic and spontaneous, experience of the cultural object. For Adorno, engaging cultural phenomena in this way could generate both self-critical theory and transformative praxis, in an era when the petrifying instrumentalization of thought not only permeated bourgeois social relations but moreover threatened socialist politics from within.

The major portion of this book is devoted to locating the position of *Focus on the Family* within the contemporary structure of U.S. society and to extracting lessons from this endeavor for critical social theory today. Adorno's method of cultural criticism systematically informs this account of Christian right radio. Before delving into the details of James Dobson's program, therefore, it is first necessary to explain the method of dialectical criticism (or "social physiognomy"), as Adorno conceived of it. We shall also explore the specific historical experiences, along with the distinctive social-theoretical conceptualizations of these experiences (above all, the theories of state capitalism and the culture industry), in relation to which this method was initially formulated. Why did Adorno consider cultural criticism so crucial for Marxian theory? What was this intellectual practice supposed to reveal about the cultural object? In what sense, for Adorno, were the object's relations to the social totality and to social theory "dialectical," and how were these "dialectical" relationships associated with transformative politics? Why was "mass culture" almost entirely hostile to revolutionary theory and practice, in Adorno's view, and what aspects or possibilities of "mass culture" did this view exclude? These questions furnish the guiding concerns of this chapter. In the next chapter, I glean important lessons for a critique of the contemporary Christian right from Adorno's own study of fundamentalist radio in the Depression era. Chapter 2 then confronts the issue of how changing historical conditions, specifically the transition to post-Fordism, should influence the development of a method of cultural analysis that preserves vital insights from Adorno but is also appropriate to the current social situation.

Social Physiognomy and Culture's Utopian Negativity

Adorno did not characteristically engage in straightforward and systematic reflection on theoretical and philosophical methods in his writings.

Instead, the greater part of his written work focuses directly on cultural phenomena—above all, modern music and philosophy—making an implicit argument for dialectical criticism by demonstrating its interpretive power rather than describing a method step-by-step and building a logical case for it. *Negative Dialectics* (1966), the last major work that Adorno completed, did indeed concentrate on issues of philosophical method and presents the closest approximation to a formal program of dialectical thought that can be found among Adorno's writings. Yet the method of negative dialectics had taken shape over many years and in many different documents, some of which openly addressed matters of critical methodology. Crucial elements of this approach were already foremost in Adorno's mind in his 1931 inaugural lecture, "The Actuality of Philosophy."[2] The essay "Cultural Criticism and Society" (1955) offers a particularly vivid and concise argument for Adorno's distinctive mode of dialectical reflection on culture. This short piece provides a suitable point of departure for several reasons: the essay's reflections are rigorously and explicitly methodological yet unencumbered by the creeping formalism that at times besets *Negative Dialectics*; it manifests one of Adorno's boldest attempts to set himself apart from other Marxists; and it articulates Adorno's method of dialectical criticism in the context of historico-critical reflections on mass culture.

In "Culture Criticism and Society," Adorno argues that the very concept of "culture" as an intellectual realm distinct from and ideally untarnished by the realm of material necessity is ideological. Rather, he writes, "all culture takes part in society's guilty coherence; it ekes out its existence only by virtue of injustice already perpetrated in the sphere of production, much as does commerce." For Adorno, this injustice is specifically "the radical division of mental and physical labor," from which culture itself originates. Thus the "traditional" cultural criticism that responds to the rise of "consumer culture" by denouncing "the entanglement of culture in commerce," though it claims to be "criticism of ideology," is itself "ideology." Such cultural criticism, Adorno contends, implicitly sanctions the division of mental and physical labor by asserting culture's essential difference from the sphere of physical necessity.[3]

However, Adorno contends further that although cultural criticism perpetuates a deception by overlooking the fundamental complicity of culture with domination, a more demystifying critique must still insist on the autonomy of culture rather than unequivocally opposing this notion. For culture "draws its strength" (*Kräfte*) from its independence from that which is necessary at a given historical moment for socioeconomic production and reproduction, even if this independence is not absolute. Adorno defines this "strength" as "the preservation of an image of existence pointing beyond the compulsion which stands behind all labor."[4] In other words, culture has the potential to contribute to the radical transformation of society, insofar as it maintains an aspect that is both *negative* and *utopian* in relation to sociohistorical conditions.

Adorno asserts that Marxist social theory cannot do without this negative-utopian "ferment," for this is the "very truth" of culture. And he directly attacks "dialectical theory which shows itself to be uninterested in culture as a mere epiphenomenon" of the economic "base" and which treats cultural objects simply as tools either to bolster or to subvert class rule.[5] Such "economism" not only fails to recognize the autonomous protest that culture may lodge against power, but moreover signals that its epistemological basis for criticism is suspect. According to Adorno, critical subjectivity can only emerge on the basis of a "spontaneous relation to the object"—an "experience of the object" prior to theoretical understanding and therefore providing mind with the capacity to call its own concepts into question.[6] This notion of spontaneous experience stands at the very core of Adorno's theory of critical thought. It suggests an empirical sensibility, in the sense that it connotes a direct encounter with the object that is not mediated by theoretical lenses—that is, a prior conception of the object's meaning in relation to other objects or to society. This experience, however, is decidedly *not* "empirical" in the (positivist) sense that it examines the object in order to formulate generalizations about abstract categories of which the object will ultimately be seen as an exemplar. Nor does Adorno here join hands with existentialism and fundamental ontology, which he detested because of their presupposition that full knowledge of the object was attainable without the mediating rigors of dialectical thought.[7] Rather, Adorno's idea of the spontaneous "experience of the object" reflects the Hegelian underpinnings of his thought, inasmuch as it presupposes that critical subjectivity can neither generate itself from within the architecture of its own conceptual labyrinths nor spring up fully formed on the basis of unmediated contact with "being" (like Athena emerging from the head of Zeus), but becomes actual only when a subject enters into an immediate relation with an object outside itself and then raises this "true" experience to self-consciousness, thereby exposing the poverty of its concept of the object. Adorno crucially differs from Hegel as well, however, because he denies that the subject ever actually "finds itself" in its object and contends that the subject's sense of identity with the object is not the ground of freedom but rather the seed of domination. In *Negative Dialectics*, Adorno argues that thought can only extricate itself from its propensity toward a form of thinking that is in league with domination by granting "precedence to the object."[8] That is, thought must ground its self-reflection in an experience of the object that recognizes that the object is distinct from the subject (and thus from the subject's concept of the object, which Hegel's idealism, social-scientific positivism, and existentialism's "jargon of authenticity" all alike forget) and "loves" the object without forgetting that distinctness.[9]

Adorno contends in "Cultural Criticism and Society" that much cultural analysis performed in the name of dialectical materialism shuns precisely this kind of experience and thereby develops "an affinity to barbarism."[10] He allows that the characteristically "ambivalent attitude of social theory toward cultural criticism" is justified, acknowledging that "the hypostasis of culture" makes culture both a distraction from and a "complement to horror."[11] In other words, Adorno insists that cultural criticism must not become an end in itself, for such "enthrallment in the cultural object" is simply a reversion to "idealism"—that is, to the installation of mind as the ultimate reality and the consequent mystification of material oppression.[12] Adorno thus by no means advocates dispensing with the project of analyzing culture from a standpoint that transcends culture so as to determine "the role of ideology in social conflicts."[13] But to abandon cultural criticism altogether on the grounds that all culture is "superstructure," Adorno argues, amounts to "idealism" in a different guise, since theory here subsumes cultural objects under an abstract category of theory's own devising and absolutizes thought by erroneously identifying the object with that abstraction. To Adorno, this theoretical move betrays a contempt for precisely that experience of the object that alone would enable thought to achieve critical self-reflection. Adorno hesitates to say that social theory that considers cultural criticism irrelevant must necessarily become the slave of domination. He insists, however, that "no theory, not even that which is true, is safe from perversion into delusion once it has renounced a spontaneous relation to the object," and he repeatedly draws attention to the coexistence of an economistic attitude toward culture with totalitarian rule in the Soviet Union.[14]

As an alternative to both traditional cultural criticism and vulgar Marxist economism, Adorno proposes a method of dialectical criticism that he names "social physiognomy." Although refusing to formalize this method, Adorno etches out its contours in his distinctive, deliberately antisystematic mode of writing in "Cultural Criticism and Society." This critical procedure grounds itself in a spontaneous "experience of the object" by taking "immanent criticism" as its starting point. "Immanent criticism" involves the reflection on the theorist's spontaneous perception of the object's immediate appearance in light of an analysis of the object's structural composition.

Through immanent criticism, the theorist analyzes the object's structural form in terms of the relationship between the *general idea*, which the object is meant to express, and the *particular elements* (or "moments," or materials), which have been combined so as to give that idea concrete expression. For traditional cultural criticism, the knowledge of the object gained through such an analysis (that is, its success or failure in fulfilling historically developed principles of aesthetic form) would constitute an end in itself. "The threshold of dialectical over cultural criticism, however," writes Adorno, "is crossed when the former intensifies the latter until the concept of culture itself is at once fulfilled, negated, and transcended" (bis zur Aufhebung des Begriffs der Kultur selber).[15] Social physiognomy accomplishes this Aufhebung or transcendence of cultural criticism, which both completes and cancels the latter, by interpreting the results of immanent criticism in relation to social theory. Adorno argues that the character of the relationship between the general and the particular within the object's structure unintentionally but inevitably bears the traces of social power relations. It follows that no complete reconciliation of the general and the particular within the object's form is possible as long as social contradictions remain unresolved. Counterintuitively, then, the object's "truth-content" does not lie in its positive achievement of the formal task that the artist sets for herself, but instead in its inability to complete this endeavor: "The moment in the work of art which enables it to transcend reality . . . does not consist in the harmony achieved, of the dubious unity of form and content, the internal and the external, the individual and society, but rather in those features in which discrepancy appears, in the necessary failure of the passionate striving toward identity."[16] Inasmuch as the object's "failure" is "necessary," then, the theorist can decipher the object's formal deficiencies as the gaps subsisting between the general idea of society as a reconciled community of human beings and society's actual existence as a historical totality fraught with antagonism. Social physiognomy thus means "naming what the consistency and inconsistency of the work in itself expresses of the constitution of the existent. . . . Where it comes across inadequacy it . . . seeks to derive it from the irreconcilability of the object's moments. It pursues the logic of the object's aporias, the insolubility located in the task itself. In such antinomies it perceives those of society."[17]

Adorno's procedure of immanent criticism thus presupposes a carefully formulated hermeneutical approach to the cultural object. It moreover appears to assume a particular kind of object, a work of art constructed in conscious relation to a historically situated style or formal tradition that defines the prerequisites for attaining a certain sort of "harmony." In short, by virtue of its very conceptualization social physiognomy seems predisposed toward the analysis of those cultural phenomena furthest removed from the domain of commodities and mass consumption. Yet, for Adorno, commodification as such does not preclude the object's capacity to internalize and express social contradictions, or even to preserve a small stock of negative-utopian "strength." Indeed, Adorno argues that at least under the conditions of classic, liberal capitalism, commodification positively endows the object with a critical truth-content.

As a commodity, the cultural object emanates the appearance of particularity and uniqueness, and seems capable of satisfying the idiosyncratic desire of the consumer. At the same time, it appears as the fruit of a naturalized social order that transcends the subject, harmonizing and ensuring the fulfillment of all subjects' desires. In fact, however, the commodity's purchase confirms its universal fungibility with all other objects within the exchange process, realizing the object's constitution for the sake of exchange value rather than use value while both legitimating and obscuring the exploitative social relations according to which the object was actually produced. Nevertheless, Adorno argues, the commodity's reified appearance is not simply an illusion but moreover the promise of fulfilled life—that is, life in which the social and the individual are utterly reconciled. Adorno thus writes the following in an essay on Thorstein Veblen published contemporaneously with "Cultural Criticism and Society": "Commodity fetishes are not merely the projection of opaque human relations onto the world of things. They are also the chimerical deities which represent something not entirely absorbed in the exchange process, even while they themselves arise from the primacy of this process."[18] Hence, precisely as commodities, cultural objects are endowed with utopian "strength," whether or not they enter into society as elements of an esoteric cultural realm that claims autonomy from the processes of production and social class relations.

Nevertheless, for Adorno, it is not solely by virtue of the object's commodity-character that it possesses the capacity to express the contradictions of society as well as the hope that they might be overcome. Adorno argues that works of art can make their inherent protest against social contradictions explicit by bringing to the surface their own essentially conflicted character and thereby the contradictory constitution of society: "Immanent criticism calls successful not so much the work which reconciles objective contradictions in the illusion of harmony, but much more so that which expresses the idea of harmony negatively by engraving the contradictions, pure and uncompromised, in its innermost structure."[19] Thus in Adorno's view, cultural objects can express their promise of fulfilled life to a greater or lesser extent through their formal constitution. The object can subvert the ideological character of its own claim to autonomy and freedom, vis-à-vis the heteronomous imperatives of socioeconomic necessity, if its structural composition thematizes contradictions rather than glossing over them.

Adorno's exhortation that cultural criticism practice the dialectical *askesis* of social physiognomy is not grounded merely in an abstract logic of philosophical aesthetics, however. Rather, Adorno's method and his critical judgments alike have their foundation in a theory of late capitalism, even as his cultural criticism seeks to raise this theory to a higher level of self-reflectivity. It is to Adorno's theory of society that we must therefore now turn.

State Capitalism and the Culture Industry

In historical and critical accounts of the Frankfurt School, Adorno tends to acquire the reputation for having been a lousy intellectual collaborator with more empirically oriented scholars. Martin Jay describes the bumpy relations that characterized Adorno's associations with Robert Lazarsfeld and others involved in the Princeton Radio Research Project around 1940, whose empiricist perspective Adorno could never quite bring himself to respect (at least, not until much later in his life).[20] Similarly, Rolf Wiggershaus emphasizes Adorno's role in allowing the Institute for Social Research's commitment to the interdisciplinary mingling of philosophy, cultural criticism, and empirical research to dwindle during the period of emigration.[21] Axel Honneth's distress at "the peculiar irrelevance of empirical sociological questions for [Adorno's] late work" complements these judgments.[22] Yet Adorno was an active member of the Institute during its most fertile years as an experiment in interdisciplinary social research (from about 1932 until roughly 1942). As a consequence, his cultural criticism bears the unmistakable imprint of his exposure to the political economy of his colleagues, especially Horkheimer and Friedrich Pollock. Indeed, without the element of social theory borrowed from others, Adorno's social physiognomy could not have achieved its dialectical interpretation of culture.

Pollock's 1941 essay, "State Capitalism: Its Possibilities and Limitations," decisively influenced both Adorno and Horkheimer. Pollock argues that a new "model" of capitalist society has taken shape in the mid–twentieth century, a political-economic structure that is most fully realized in the "totalitarian" countries but also clearly ascendant in "democratic" nations such as the United States. For Pollock, "state capitalism" supersedes the arrangements of turn-of-the-century monopoly capitalism, even though the latter has prepared the ground for the former. The central characteristic of state capitalism is the fact that the market has been "deposed from its controlling function" and replaced by the planning apparatus of the state. Even though some market or "pseudo-market" institutions remain in operation, they serve as instruments for correcting administrative errors (e.g., an overestimate of the demand for a certain commodity) rather than as the "last guarantee for the reproduction of economic life." According to Pollock, this tectonic shift of institutional power has in turn transformed social relations. Whereas under private capitalism "all social relations are mediated by the market," with the advent of state capitalism "men meet each other as commander or commanded," and the "profit motive is superseded by the power motive." Pollock contends that both the "concentration of economic activity in giant enterprises" and the "principle of command and obedience" have been achieved to a great extent in the context of monopoly capitalism. Nonetheless, for Pollock, the elevation of the state to its new role as the directing agency of the economy "changes the character of the whole historic period."[23]

Let us postpone for the moment the question of this theory's empirical validity as an account of mid-twentieth-century late capitalism. Instead, we shall first focus on the foreboding consequences that Adorno draws from this analysis for his own cultural interventions. In the increasing subordination of the market economy to centralized political administration in Europe and North America, Adorno recognizes the structural source of culture's neutralization as a revolutionary force. Stripped of its ability to *mediate* the relationship between society and the individual, and transmuted instead into a mere conduit of direct domination, the cultural commodity loses precisely that aspect which enabled it (under liberal capitalism) to gesture toward reconciled life: its paradoxically both deceptive and truthful surface-appearance, its claim to be something other than the symbol and concrete result of exploitation. For Adorno, these social circumstances make extremely urgent the struggle to rescue culture's utopian "strength" by identifying elements of culture that still make this claim. The conditions of state capitalism thus certify the demand for social physiognomy as a critical-interpretative practice, since this method prises the object's appearance of reconciliation from its constitutional self-contradictoriness. Historical conditions furthermore predispose Adorno's critique toward seeking radical cultural residues in the fine arts rather than in consumer culture, since it is precisely the extinguishing of culture's ideological claim to be autonomous from socioeconomic necessity that Adorno discerns in the coordinated planning of culture as the "leisure" economy by the culture industry.

Although Pollock had noted the growth of the leisure industry as a prominent feature of state capitalism in general, it remained for Adorno and Horkheimer to develop a full-fledged theory of the culture industry, a task famously carried out in *Dialectic of Enlightenment*.[24] The main empirical reference point for this theory is the United States, where the new state-capitalist form had attained only an immature realization in comparison to the other industrialized countries. Nonetheless, Adorno and Horkheimer argue that the American culture industry is state-capitalist in its tendencies, if not in its actual administration. They note, first, that the aesthetics of mass politics are already largely derived from the patterns established by the entertainment industry: "Films, radio and magazines make up a system which is uniform as a whole and in every part. Even the aesthetic manifestations of political opposites resemble one another in singing the praises of the system's steely rhythm."[25] In addition, the culture industry has spawned the technologies that have proven vital to Nazism (that is, full-blown, totalitarian state capitalism), above all radio broadcasting. Radio enables the Führer's voice to "penetrate everywhere," and "the immanent tendency of radio is to make the human word . . . absolute."[26] The public opinion management techniques developed by the great entertainment corporations, moreover, furnish the propaganda machinery of the fascist state and accustom the population to its mundane employment.

Above all, however, the culture industry anticipates fully formed state capitalism because it supplants market institutions with the structures of a command economy. Thus the indispensability of advertising leads to the concentration of economic power, first in an oligopoly of giant private firms and ultimately in the state:

> Only those who can continuously pay the exorbitant rates charged by the advertising agencies, foremost of which are the radio networks themselves; that is, only those who are already owned by financial and industrial capital, or are coopted by capital's decisions, can enter the pseudo-market as sellers. The costs of advertising, which eventually flow back into the pockets of the combines, spare these entities the trouble of competition with disagreeable, subordinate outsiders. They guarantee that decisive power will remain with these interests, not unlike those decisions of economic councils by which the establishment and conduct of business operations are controlled in the totalitarian state.[27]

The reign of advertising over culture furthermore installs what Pollock refers to as the "principle of command and obedience" as the main mode of social relations, for it deprives the masses of any meaningful choice over the culture they consume even while fostering the illusion that the industry is the humble servant of democratic tastes:

> The constitution of the public, which ostensibly and actually favors the system of the culture industry, is a part of the system and not an

excuse for it. . . . The consumers are the workers and employees, the farmers and petite bourgeois. Capitalist production so confines them, body and soul, that they fall victim without resistance to what is offered them. . . . [The public] demands Mickey Rooney over the tragic Garbo and Donald Duck over Betty Boop. The industry obeys the vote which it has itself evoked.[28]

On the other hand, the culture industry markets its products as emblems of particularized lifestyles, and not simply as the demands of the majority—for instance, by generating pseudocompetition between "the Chrysler and General Motors series" or between "A and B films."[29] Nevertheless, this pseudodifferentiation of products only serves to incorporate all individuals more effectively into the system of cultural consumption, since the competition is fictional, itself the product of advertising. In turn, the role adopted in the consumption of culture binds the consumer ever more forcefully to her role in the production process, because the rituals of leisure merely rehearse those of work:

Under late capitalism, amusement is the prolongation of labor. It is sought after by anyone who wants to evade the mechanized labor process, in order to be able to cope with it again. At the same time, however, mechanization has such power over the one who seeks leisure and the happiness therein—it so fundamentally determines the manufacture of amusement commodities—that the individual can experience nothing more than the after-images of the labor process itself. The ostensible content is merely a faded foreground; what sinks in is the automated sequence of standardized operations. The labor process in the factory and office can be evaded only through the approximation to it in leisure time.[30]

Thus the culture industry complements the transformation of the production process, such that the "principle of command and obedience" comes to overlay the whole spectrum of social relations. For Adorno and Horkheimer, in sum, the culture industry represents the partial completion of a teleological process of political-economic development culminating in totalitarian state capitalism: "The ruthless unity of the culture industry testifies to what draws nigh in politics."[31]

But if this process is teleological, is it also inevitable? Such a conception would be starkly incompatible with the authors' lifelong rejection of a mechanistic theory of history. Yet in *Dialectic of Enlightenment*, it is hard to avoid the sense that Adorno and Horkheimer have given up hope that the forces driving industrialized societies toward totalitarian state capitalism can be vanquished. For here, the essential, cultural impetus to revolutionary praxis seems to be thoroughly precluded by the culture industry. In a situation where "the free market is coming to an end," the cultural object becomes "a paradoxical commodity. It is so completely subject to the law of exchange that it is no longer exchanged; it is so blindly enthralled in use that it can no longer be used."[32] In other words: (1) the termination of competitive market relations tends to eliminate the *exchange-value moment* of the cultural commodity, even as it extends the rule of commodity fetishism over greater psychic and social territories than ever before. Thus Adorno frequently refers to the totalization of the "exchange society," where absolute "interchangeability" becomes the guiding characteristic of subject-object and human social relations alike. At the same time, however, the exchange process itself loses its previously spontaneous quality and thereby ceases to exercise the decisive, socially mediating function that it had possessed prior to late capitalism. (2) The culture industry furthermore obliterates the *moment of use value* that the cultural commodity had preserved under liberal capitalism, in terms of both the object's capacity to manifest a wish for the reconciliation of the social and the individual and its ability to satisfy the consumer's material desires. Regarding the latter, Adorno and Horkheimer argue that the culture industry's products never even begin to provide the fulfillment they pledge. Instead, they stimulate desires and then order the individual to make herself satisfied with the desires themselves:

> The culture industry perpetually cheats its consumers of what it perpetually promises. The promissory note which it draws on pleasure, with its plots and layouts, is endlessly prolonged; the spectacle actually consists in only the promise itself, which spitefully intimates that the real point will never be reached, that the guest should find satisfaction in reading the menu. . . . [Culture] merges with advertising . . . as its product incessantly reduces to a mere promise the enjoyment which it promises as a commodity, it ultimately collapses into advertising, which it needs because it cannot be enjoyed.[33]

The public all the more voraciously and anxiously consumes the products of the culture industry, in other words, precisely because the latter offer no real satisfaction, and precisely to the degree that these products shrilly insist on the enjoyment they will provide. When the mass-cultural object guarantees fulfillment, however, it identifies satisfaction not only with its own consumption but moreover with the smooth functioning of the apparatus that makes the pledge in the first place. Thus Adorno and Horkheimer write: "Under monopoly, all mass culture is identical, and its skeleton, its artificial and abstract framework, begins to show through. . . . Movies and radio need no longer pretend to be art. They use the truth that they are just business as ideology, which is supposed to justify the rubbish they deliberately produce."[34] According to Adorno and Horkheimer, that is, the mass-cultural object no longer claims any autonomy from the demands of socioeconomic necessity. Quite to the contrary, it triumphantly invokes the latter—its economic success, as measured by ratings and ticket sales—as the fountain of its legitimacy. Thus with the advent of the culture industry, culture's ideological function becomes just as paradoxical as does its commodity-form: the object's appearance refers to no utopian condition to which the status quo aspires, but instead simply announces the facticity of the existing social totality and the imperative of conformity to its norms. Ideology in the classic (Marxist) sense thereby ironically ceases to exist at the very moment when culture's ideological function becomes all-consuming. Or as Adorno puts it in "Cultural Criticism and Society": "Today, ideology means society as appearance. . . . If ideology is defined as socially necessary appearance, then the ideology today is real society itself in so far as its integral power and inescapability, its overwhelming existence-in-itself, surrogates the meaning which that existence has exterminated."[35] In short, then, the end of the mediation of culture by market mechanisms deprives the cultural commodity of its element of use value, in both the sense of the anticipation of the utopian condition and the gratification of actual desires. Cultural commodities thereby relinquish the liberatory potential that previously accrued to them precisely as commodities.

Adorno and Horkheimer clinch their case against the culture industry, finally, by arguing that the mass-cultural object's formal composition (that is, its internal constitution as well as its surface-appearance) makes it structurally incapable of negativity. For just as business considerations alone determine the object's surface-appearance, its claim concerning its own identity, so likewise the imperatives of the bottom line exercise total sway over the object's inner composition. For Adorno and Horkheimer, the mass-cultural object acquires its constitution exclusively through stereotypical design, standardized production, mechanical reproduction, and planned distribution. The engineers of the culture industry thus dispense altogether with the problematic of formally constructing a "work," which has been the traditional task of artistic creation, and which involves striving for the reconciliation of the object's general idea with its particular elements:

The development of the culture industry has led to the predominance of the effect, the obvious touch, and the technical detail over the work itself. . . . [But] [t]hough concerned exclusively with effects, [the culture industry] crushes their insubordination and subjugates them to the formula, which replaces the work. The same fate is inflicted on whole and parts alike. The whole stands inexorably opposed to the details, bearing no relation to them. . . . The whole and the particular carry the same features; there is no antithesis and no connection. Their prearranged harmony is a mockery of what had to be striven after in the great bourgeois works of art.[36]

Since the typical object produced by the culture industry contains no genuine, *aesthetic* tension between whole and parts to begin with, the possibility of the object negating a facile resolution of such a contradiction is precluded—and thus, so is the possibility of *socially* revolutionary culture.

Cultural Radicalism and Modern Music

Where, then, does Adorno locate the seedbed of cultural radicalism? Given the dissolution of aesthetic form in the culture industry, radical culture can only be found among those objects that uncompromisingly resist their appropriation and redeployment by the culture industry. Moreover, dialectical criticism alone is capable of demonstrating the object's reflection of historical conditions in a way that neither hypostatizes social theory as scientific truth nor overlooks the negative-utopian capacities of the object. Despite the bleakness of *Dialectic of Enlightenment*, Adorno thus does not surrender the hope for revolutionary culture entirely. Nevertheless, he sees this hope as beleaguered and forced into a deeply defensive position by the cultural dynamics of late capitalism.

The music of Arnold Schoenberg and Adorno's critique of Schoenberg in *Philosophy of Modern Music* (1948) offer paradigmatic instances of radical culture and dialectical cultural criticism, respectively, from Adorno's point of view. For Adorno, Schoenberg represents the quintessence of aesthetic radicalism, which is perforce a radical posture in relation to society. Whereas the culture industry dispenses with aesthetic form altogether, Schoenberg recognizes that music's "truth" is inseparable from its capacity to handle self-consciously its place within a historical tradition of artistic creation. The rules of Schoenberg's twelve-tone compositional technique are thus "configurations of the historical force in the material" inasmuch as they respond to the evolution of musical form during the modern era, from the "classicism" of Mozart through Beethoven, Romanticism, and finally Wagner.[37] Since the formal problems of musical composition express social antagonisms, in turn, Schoenberg's solution attains political status as a cultural response to the stages of modern, capitalist society.

Adorno sees in Beethoven the historically unprecedented emergence of "autonomous aesthetic subjectivity, which strives to organize the work freely from within itself." Whereas previous composers had allowed conventions of form to determine the work's composition, with Beethoven "the development (*Durchführung*)—subjective reflection upon the theme which decides the fate of the theme—becomes the focal point of the entire form."[38] Social physiognomy reveals that this moment in musical history reflects the heroic, revolutionary stage of bourgeois individualism in Western society, beyond inaugurating a new era in musical composition as such.[39] Late Romanticism and Expressionism, by contrast, reflect the decay of autonomous subjectivity in society at large through their hypostatization of "the dream of subjectivity," the foregrounding of "outbursts" that are liberated from stylistic conventions but also cut off from any developmental relation to the thematic material. As Adorno puts it succinctly, "society becomes manifest" in the "isolation" of Expressionism's "absolute subject."[40] In Wagner, finally, this irresponsible subjectivism degenerates into a "nominalism of musical language," an arbitrary deployment of "leitmotiv and programmatic content" that stands in for a genuine, critical engagement with the historical tendencies of musical "language."[41] The social physiognomy of Wagnerian opera is thus fascist, not simply because Wagner famously supplied Hitler with mythological content for the National Socialist imaginary but rather because of the structure of the music itself, wherein subjectivity assumes a stance of blind domination of the musical material.[42]

By contrast, Adorno argues that Schoenberg self-consciously and critically draws the consequences of music's historical trajectory. Schoenberg sees that the dialectical counterpart of musical "nominalism," of the pretended omnipotence of subjectivity vis-à-vis historical objectivity as crystallized in aesthetic form, is the aesthetic subject's virtual liquidation. With the advent of the twelve-tone system, "the subject dominates music through the rationality of the system, only in order to succumb to the rational system itself."[43] In twelve-tone composition, ". . . every single tone is transparently determined by the construction of the whole work, [and thus] the difference between the essential and the coincidental disappears. . . . There is no longer any unessential transition between the essential moments, between the 'themes'; consequently, there are no longer themes at all and, in the strictest sense, not even a 'development' " (*Entwicklung*).[44] Sociohistorically, in turn, this banishing of autonomous subjectivity from the musical composition expresses the dialectic of enlightenment in society as a whole, in which the advance of instrumental reason leads to the subject's (self-)enslavement to the forces of late-capitalist domination. Schoenberg's position is authentically radical, for Adorno, because it refuses to perpetuate the myth that autonomous subjectivity any longer exists. Schoenberg's music thereby rejects collaboration in the cultural legitimation of the social order as a peaceful community of free individuals—in contrast, Adorno contends, to Stravinsky's ideological attempt to engineer a "restoration" of the autonomous aesthetic subject (and, of course, contrary to the culture industry as well).[45]

The irony in Adorno's stance is patent and deliberate. Fidelity to the promise of a reconciled society of critical subjects can only be guaranteed by renouncing the "development" of the work, the labor by which the subject mediates the relation between whole and parts such that the whole is freely developed into something different than its inherent tendencies would "fatalistically" yield of themselves. Thus, Schoenberg's string quartets and Paramount Pictures' blockbusters alike manifest *in their structures* the virtual extinction of critical reason under late capitalism. But Schoenberg does this in an historically attuned, self-conscious and evidently negative manner, and thereby preserves a genuinely utopian hope. This hope, moreover, looks forward (negatively) not only to a reconciliation among human beings but also to a transformed relationship between subject and object, between humanity and nature. For in yet a further irony, Adorno contends that only music which most stubbornly refuses any easy enjoyment by the individual confronted with its enigmatic sound-textures has the power to denounce the antiseptic cleansing of culture in general of all but the last traces of use value.

Qualifying the Theory of the Culture Industry

The central argument of this book is that the organized culture of the Christian right today can be interpreted, through a variation of social physiognomy, as expressing negative-utopian truths about the contemporary social order. Obviously, the theoretical perspective that informs this project has traveled some distance from Adorno. It presupposes that Adorno's culture industry theory leads us to miss crucial, potentially radical aspects of mass-cultural phenomena—even those associated with the political right wing. Such an opinion is common enough today, given the enthusiasm with which cultural studies theorists have embraced the critical analysis of "popular culture" in search of its emancipatory moments. It often escapes notice, however, that Adorno's own theory provides compelling terms according to which the intellectual deficits of the culture industry theory should have been anticipated by Adorno himself. Specifically, the central problem with the theory of the culture industry lies in the fact that this theory was not made self-reflective through the dialectical criticism of specific, mass-cultural objects. Instead, Adorno let his approach to mass culture be guided by an a priori understanding of the operations of state capitalism and the function therein of industrialized cultural production.

Before elaborating this criticism, it is important to point out that Adorno's hostility to mass culture is often exaggerated by his critics, especially within cultural studies.[46] The chapter on the culture industry in *Dialectic of Enlightenment* represents mass-cultural phenomena in the bleakest light. It is also Adorno's most widely read intervention concerning mass culture and is usually taken as definitive of his position on the issue of mass culture's critical capacities.[47] Yet in other texts, especially certain essays that were not written (as was *Dialectic of Enlightenment*) in the situation of extreme anxiety and despair provoked by World War II and the horrors of fascism, Adorno leaves open the possibility that some mass-cultural phenomena might preserve moments of utopian negativity. The essays "Die Form der Schallplatte" (The form of the phonograph record) (1934), "Prolog zum Fernsehen" (Prologue to television) (1953), "Culture Industry Reconsidered" (1963), "Free Time" (1969), and "Transparencies on Film" (1967) all in various ways take up in earnest the problematic of how mass-cultural phenomena might have an immanent construction that would grant them negative-utopian capabilities.[48]

It has been argued, furthermore, that Adorno did on occasion employ social physiognomy to analyze mass culture. Susan Buck-Morss contends that Adorno's 1936 article on jazz "used a dialectical method of immanent criticism to interpret the sociohistorical truth of the phenomenon which Adorno later called 'social physiognomics.' "[49] Buck-Morss describes how Adorno here discerned the modern schema of the individual's relationship to society "within the musical material itself":

> In the improvisational "breaks" of jazz music which pretend to be individualistic, hence progressive, Adorno saw the image of archaic ritual. The musical alteration of verse and refrain, the solo breaks followed by thematic repetition, paralleled the primitive dancer performing for the collective, and this in turn was an image of the relationship between the individual and society in which the former, powerless, made a "sacrifice to the collective."[50]

To Adorno, Buck-Morss writes, the "images of the archaic" evoked by jazz showed "not that jazz music was authentically primitive" but rather that "precisely as commodity, precisely in those elements which determined it as a phenomenon of mass culture, it possessed qualities which bore the name of the primitive."[51] The pseudo-individualistic features of the music making it appear to be new and eccentric so as to enhance its attractiveness to consumers, in other words, constituted the music as an image of the archaic. Dialectical analysis of the phenomenon, in turn, interpreted this recapitulation of the archaic within the phenomenon's structure as an image of the growing powerlessness of the modern individual. For Buck-Morss, "Über Jazz" thus shows plainly that "far from belittling mass culture, Adorno took it extremely seriously, applying to its phenomena the same sophisticated analytical method, the same intellectual spleen, which he used in interpreting Husserl, Kierkegaard, and Stravinsky."[52] Buck-Morss demonstrates that Adorno approaches jazz in the 1936 essay with a dialectical sensibility, and thus forces a reevaluation of earlier accounts that Adorno had "emphatically reject[ed] any kind of purely aesthetic analysis of jazz in favor of psychosocial critique."[53] She also soundly refutes those who accuse Adorno of dismissing mass culture as "low-brow" or holding it in contempt out of personal snobbery against persons with less education or a lower class standing than his own, emphasizing that Adorno consistently leveled his critique at the form of the object rather than the sociological characteristics of the audience.[54]

Nonetheless, Buck-Morss's defense of Adorno is too generous. To the extent that Adorno does not deem it necessary to study individual jazz performances or performers in the 1936 essay, but rather applies his criticisms to the "genre" (*Gattung*) as a whole, he cannot be said to approach jazz with an equal seriousness to that which animates his analyses of modern music and philosophy.[55] In this sense (though not in the sense which she intends), Buck-Morss is correct to say that the first "analysis of jazz provided a model for all Adorno's later critiques of mass culture," inasmuch as Adorno's subsequent studies of radio, film, and television almost never devote concentrated attention to particular broadcasts or movies but instead analyze each mass-cultural mode as a whole.[56] In other words, in these later studies, as in the 1936 essay on jazz, Adorno consistently holds his criticism aloof from a genuinely spontaneous experience of the mass-cultural object, and in doing so he short-circuits the entire process of dialectical analysis.

Consequently, Adorno's interpretation of jazz in the 1936 essay (as well as in its 1955 successor, "Perennial Fashion—Jazz") remains driven unreflectively by his (then embryonic) theory of mass culture, and both the theory and the analysis itself thereby suffer. Adorno's judgments that jazz is "a commodity in the strict sense," that "the genre is dominated by function and not by an autonomous law of form," and that the individualistic features of jazz are "exclusively determined in accordance with stereotype" are in later writings generalized to apply to mass culture in toto.[57] Just as Adorno finds nothing reminiscent of the artistic "work" in the musical structure of jazz—no thoughtful and purposive relationship of general idea and particular elements that might have been different from that which the music possessed by virtue of its standardized production— so does he subsequently deny that the products of the culture industry possess any trace of utopian negativity. Thus, "Über Jazz" does not so much testify to Adorno's willingness to see fruitful ground for immanent criticism in mass-cultural phenomena as provide an initial indication of the narrow scope of Adorno's approach to mass culture.

If the theory of the culture industry was deprived of self-reflectivity by Adorno's abstention from the dialectical criticism of mass-cultural objects, then in turn the same problem redounded to the more general theory of state capitalism. Almost certainly, this theory erred by elevating the structure of war-mobilized fascism to the status of a general model that all industrialized nations were bound sooner or later to approximate. Even in the early 1940s, Pollock's theory was criticized by others associated with the Institute who argued that the private-monopolistic branch of the industrialized economy still possessed structurally decisive power.[58] More recent writings by James O'Connor and Claus Offe have advanced more nuanced accounts of the distribution of power among the monopoly, competitive, and state sectors of the economy under late capitalism.[59] In addition, the theory of state capitalism underestimated the degree of state intervention in the liberal-capitalist economy.[60]

Beyond these challenges to Pollock's political economy, however, legitimate questions have been raised concerning Adorno's assumption that cultural mediation of the relationship between the social totality and the individual under liberal capitalism was exclusively carried out by the market, and thus was definitively bound up with the fate of the cultural commodity. For Axel Honneth, the single-minded focus on "the end of mediation" by the market blinded Adorno to

> the places of social communication that lie outside [the market]—the institutions of the bourgeois public sphere, the proletarian cooperative enterprise, or the plebian subculture, all of which delay the path of capitalist industrialization—as well as the interest organizations directed toward it, in which social groups attempt to realize their economic interests. . . . Adorno is driven to the disquieting conclusion of a totally administered society, since his analysis of the structural changes in capitalism is guided from the outset by an extremely reductionistic conception of the internal social relations of capitalism. . . . This view of capitalist society, hardened into a one-dimensional picture, lets fade out of view the deeper dimensions of those pre-state domains of action in which normative convictions and cultural self-interpretations, as well as the purposive-rational deliberations of individuals, become socially effective.[61]

According to Honneth, that is, the conclusion that culture no longer mediates between the individual and society under late capitalism, but rather is merely a tool of the collective's direct domination of the individual, only makes sense if one ignores the existence of diverse realms of cultural interaction under liberal capitalism that were primarily organized neither by markets nor by states. Honneth proposes that the remedy for this blindness on Adorno's part would have been more energetic cooperation with colleagues engaged in empirical social research, and he has a point, although the proposition that any cultural realm lies definitively "outside" an area where it is vulnerable to the shaping influences of economic life surely needs to be questioned just as strenuously as Adorno's vision of the complete and undifferentiated saturation of all culture with the logic of exchange value (or, in the "administered society," with the logic of "command and obedience"). Adorno's own writings, however, suggest an additional means for rescuing his theory of the culture industry, as well as the theory of state capitalism, from intellectual petrification: a more focused and dialectical analysis of specific, mass-cultural phenomena.

But must the near total absence of such analyses from Adorno's writings—precluded, it would seem, by the totalizing bleakness of the culture industry theory—be judged merely as a failure, whether by this we mean a failure to realize the Institute's promise of interdisciplinary social research or to follow through the logic of Adorno's own injunction that cultural criticism never waver from its "intransigence toward all reification"? A critical account of Adorno's theory of the culture industry would not be complete without a discussion of the premeditated aim that informs (without entirely excusing) Adorno's evocation of the specter of the totalized world in general and "absolute reification" in the realm of culture specifically: the sense that this rhetorical motif harbored a kernel of inspiration toward transformative social praxis.

Catastrophe, Moral Recognition, and Praxis

In exploring the reason why Adorno did not treat mass culture with more analytical seriousness, we must first recall that his repeated invocation of the "administrated world" served to provide a historical imperative for the critical-methodological turn to social physiognomy. Still, it might then seem especially questionable that Adorno would paint the historical situation in such unsubtle tones, since presumably the firmer the historical grounds for his theoretical innovation were, the more compelling his argument on behalf of the latter would have been. Had Adorno attempted to render historical conditions in an exact and precisely qualified manner, however, he would have risked subverting the logic of his own critique of positivism. This critique denied the possibility that thought could render exact representations of social conditions by recognizing that thought inevitably subsumes certain "nonidentical" features of its object under its own abstract concepts.[62] In "Cultural Criticism and Society," Adorno appears to have dealt with this problem by deliberately providing conflicting images of the sociohistorical situation. The juxtaposition of these discordant images motions toward the "true" representation of historical conditions while indicating that this truth cannot be stated outright. For example, Adorno seems to give up entirely on the possibility of critical thought and autonomous culture when he writes: "The sinister, integrated society of today no longer tolerates even those relatively independent, distinct moments which the theory of the causal dependence of superstructure on base once supposed."[63] No sooner does Adorno write these totalizing and doom-filled words, however, than he equivocates on them: "In the open-air prison which the world is becoming, it is no longer important to know what depends on what, such is the extent to which everything is one."[64] Adorno thus generates an ambiguity: is the world "becoming" an "open-air prison," or has it already become totally "integrated" such that the fusion of society and ideology have left thought no potentially critical breathing space? Adorno simply lets the contradiction persist, shunning any conclusive resolution. By provoking this ambivalence concerning the very possibility of autonomous culture and dialectical criticism, Adorno escapes the concept-reifying consequences that would have followed from any claim to possess definitive knowledge of the historical situation.

More importantly, this ambivalence allows Adorno to elude the fetishization of dialectical criticism as either an end in itself or the sole key to social transformation. In this sense, Adorno's exaggerated depictions of the late-modern peril of critical subjectivity and autonomous culture ought not to be read as literal, constative assertions, but rather as rhetorical devices gesturing toward something beyond critical thought as such, which he sensed was necessary for radical change. Adorno hints at the necessity of political praxis in the 1955 essay:

> Immanent criticism holds in evidence the fact that all mind (*Geist*) has always been under a spell. On its own it is incapable of the resolution (*Aufhebung*) of contradictions toward which it labors. Even the most radical reflection of the mind on its own failures is limited by the fact that it remains only reflection, without altering the existence to which its failure bears witness. Hence immanent criticism cannot take comfort in its own idea.[65]

The concluding lines of the same essay echo these thoughts: "The more total society becomes, the greater the reification of the mind and the more paradoxical its effort to escape reification on its own. . . . Absolute reification . . . is now preparing to renounce mind entirely. Critical thought [Geist] cannot be equal to this challenge as long as it confines itself to self-satisfied contemplation."[66] Indirectly—negatively—Adorno invokes a sense of precisely that which his extreme version of thought's late-modern predicament prohibits him from stating directly: the indispensability of transformative social practice.

At the same time, however, Adorno's apocalyptic ruminations play an important and justifiable role in the polemical aspect of his theory not only because they gesture toward something which they are not, but also in themselves. With his references to the "sinister, integrated society" for which there are "no more ideologies" but "only advertisements," Adorno invites the reader to gaze momentarily into the abyss. But this gaze need not remain transfixed on despair, and Adorno himself does not leave it so. Instead, such temporary confrontation with disaster can evoke the shocking recognition of just how deplorable circumstances are and may yet become, along with the irresistible desire to denounce those circumstances, without which no radical praxis can even commence. Adorno's handling of the symbol and event of "Auschwitz" functions in precisely this manner. In "Cultural Criticism and Society," Adorno renders the famous lines: "To write poetry after Auschwitz is barbaric. And this corrodes even the knowledge of why it has become impossible to write poetry today."[67] For Adorno, "Auschwitz" is the apotheosis of the antidivine. Much as, for the Christian, the incarnation of God in Jesus simultaneously realizes the kingdom of God and expresses the expectation of a transcendent reality not yet realized—so, for Adorno, the historical experience of the concentration camps at once actualizes "absolute negativity" and signals that the engulfment of the world in seamless negativity is approaching.[68] In "Cultural Criticism and Society," as well as eventually in *Negative Dialectics*, Adorno installs "Auschwitz" as both the primary symbol and the concrete reality of the late-modern historical situation, where thought is at the same time both increasingly and actually incapable of wriggling free from social domination (and thus of producing poetry that could do anything other than ideologically justify suffering). Adorno's vision of the world as a concentration camp, simultaneously in anticipation and in actuality, need not be understood as merely a lament over critical thought's dire incapacitation. Instead, Adorno's glances at the worst imaginable—or the unimaginably horrific—state of things generate moments of moral recognition, in which the most profound sadness kindles the greatest determination to engage in transformative action.

To return to the question of Adorno's one-dimensional characterization of mass culture, then, Adorno mobilizes the monolithic image of the culture industry as part of a rhetorical strategy to ignite ethical commitment and to invite political practice. This explains to some degree his abstention from a more careful and individualized treatment of mass-cultural phenomena. Nevertheless, this strategy exacts a significant cost in the consequent hypostatization of the notion of "mass culture" and the failure to bring the theory of the culture industry to a higher level of self-reflectivity. This interruption of dialectics in cultural criticism, in turn, makes Adorno's vision of praxis at best inchoate, at worst confused. On the one hand, the argument above counsels that Adorno not be taken too literally when he writes that "the unideological thought is that which does not permit itself to be reduced to 'operational terms.'"[69] Carried to its logical extreme, this injunction would of course preclude any praxis at all, and this does not seem to be what Adorno intends. On the other hand, since Adorno strenuously insists on the integrality of culture to revolu-tionary praxis, and given his judgment that negative-utopian cultural resi-dues survive only in the arcane and ascetic rigors of high-modernist music and art, it is extremely difficult to see how any coherent, mass-based movement of praxis could be possible. For such a movement obviously would have to depend to some degree on the critical energies within a more collectively accessible culture.

Thus although Adorno does not give up on praxis entirely, contrary to the claims of many of his critics, his theory gravitates toward the ques-tionable conclusion that collective, transformative action has become historically impossible, at least at the particular juncture of late-capitalist development reached in the mid–twentieth century.[70] This tendency is implicit in Adorno's treatment of mass culture, however much this aspect of his theory also preserves the hope of radical praxis. It becomes explicit, moreover, when Adorno endorses a politics of nonconformism, a highly individualist refusal to cooperate with society's expectations. In *Minima Moralia*, for example, Adorno speculates:

> In the face of the totalitarian unison which directly proclaims the eradication of difference as its purpose, even part of the liberating social force may have temporarily withdrawn into the sphere of the individual. If critical theory lingers there, it is not only with a bad conscience. . . . For the intellectual, inviolable isolation is now the only way of showing some measure of solidarity. All collaboration, all the human worth of social mixing and participation, merely masks the tacit acceptance of inhumanity. . . . [Nevertheless,] [t]he detached observer remains as entangled [in domination] as the active partici-pant; the only advantage of the former is the insight into this en-tanglement and the happiness at the infinitesimal freedom that lies in knowledge as such.[71]

To be sure, the embrace of isolation and nonconformity as a way to vouch-safe fidelity to the value of solidarity resonated deeply with basic conditions of late capitalist society in the 1940s and 1950s. Even if the ultimate specter of fascism had not been realized in the United States, the midcentury compromise among capital, labor, and the state did seem to block most major routes to radical transformation. In certain other respects, however, Adorno's "melancholy" vision of praxis was out of touch with historical circumstances. It ignored the extent to which the causes of groups excluded from the wartime and postwar social compact, particularly African Americans, women, and people in "Third World" countries, cried out for affirmative solidarity. It furthermore evinced no sense of the possibility that this sociohistorical formation might eventually fall prey to its own contradictions, creating new prospects for critical culture and transformative political practice alike.[72] Perhaps, had Adorno devoted more attention to the structural contradictions—rather than just the instrumentalities—within specific mass-cultural phenomena, he might have found a more prominent place for social contradictions within his social theory and for collective action within his theory of praxis.

We must not lose sight here, however, of Adorno's signature insight that in the formulation of praxis no complete harmony between theory and political practice can or indeed should be desired. For theory, to Adorno, is charged with the task of actualizing and preserving within human experience the notion of a life where objects and subjects are recognized and valued as things "in and for themselves" (an und für sich), without being attached to any purpose outside themselves—the notion, that is, of the utopian condition. A completely coherent resolution of the conflicting demands for practical change, on the one hand, and for the experiential sustaining of this utopian idea, on the other hand, is not to be anticipated under any historical circumstances short of utopia's realization. The attempt to theorize as though such a resolution *were* possible thus should be resisted today with as much vigor as Adorno showed. Nevertheless, the fact that theory's efficacy in bringing about this sort of experience gives it a share in praxis that transcends critical reflection does not justify the further conclusion that theory as such, even so conceptualized, can ever wholly suffice as praxis.

Cultural Criticism and the Right

Although Adorno tended to be frustratingly elliptical and sparse in his remarks concerning radical politics and culture, he took a much more active interest in the political culture of the right. This was thoroughly in character, of course, given the fundamentally negative orientation of Adorno's theory. Adorno thus did not "gaze into the abyss" in a poetic sense alone. To the contrary, the critical analysis of fascism became a major area of substantive research for Adorno, especially during the 1940s. Naturally, Adorno left the examination of fascist political and economic organization per se to others, concentrating instead on the elements of fascist culture, above all the style and techniques of fascist oratory and the indirect manifestations of fascism in the individual personality.[73] Moreover, because Adorno completed the bulk of his work on fascism while living in the United States and on the basis of research directed at American phenomena, his writings inevitably emphasized implicit rather than explicit expressions of fascism. In short, Adorno's critique of fascism was intertwined to a great extent with his cultural criticism and, in particular, with his work on the culture industry.

Exploring fascism as a cultural presence in the United States meant that sooner or later Adorno was bound to confront a distinctively American feature of right-wing political culture: its interweaving with Protestant fundamentalism. More specifically, this project brought Adorno face-to-face with a right-wing fundamentalism that had risen from the tomb of public ridicule (where it had been cast by the Scopes "monkey" trial in the 1920s) to become a powerful new force in the mass medium of radio. As the next chapter shows, just as Adorno discerned anticipations of fascism when he examined the culture industry, so likewise did he see the iron hand of the culture industry at work when he contemplated political phenomena of the right such as the radio broadcasts of the fundamentalist preacher Martin Luther Thomas.

Before drawing conclusive lessons from Adorno for the analysis of the contemporary Christian right, then, it makes sense to take a closer look at Adorno's own critique of the Christian right in his day. Adorno points us in a direction that has been too little pursued by contemporary theorists and social scientists: the analysis of Christian conservatism as mass culture. Nevertheless, as the discussion in the preceding pages indicates, the serious limitations of Adorno's analysis of mass culture must be recognized if his theory is to inform productively our interpretation of Christian right mass culture today. Above all, we must consider the possibility that the products of the Christian right's culture industry are more than simply the instruments of power, regardless of these facts: (1) that they are subject to many of the same market-subordinating processes utilized by the mainstream culture industry; and (2) that their own character as commodities is thus as ambiguous as that of the mainstream culture industry's products. Instead, the former just might display that "necessary failure of the passionate striving toward identity" that, when analyzed dialectically, yields at least traces of utopian negativity. Adorno himself moves a step along this path in his critique of Martin Luther Thomas's radio addresses, inasmuch as he uncharacteristically devotes sustained attention to a singular mass-cultural object, doing precisely what he avoids in his criticism of jazz as a genre. In turn, the analysis of Focus on the Family's radio shows occupying the latter portion of this book follows this path all the way through to its unlikely intellectual and political conclusions.

2

Adorno's Critique of Christian Right Radio

in the New Deal Era

I believe that the day of denominations is practically a thing of the past. I mean there will be no further advancement along the lines of the denominations. I refer to Baptists, Congregationalists, Presbyterians, but listen, there is a great advancement today of a vital Christianity, and it is coming primarily as a result of the radio.—Martin Luther Thomas, 1935

It may well be the secret of fascist propaganda that it simply takes men for what they are: the true children of today's standardized mass culture.—Theodor W. Adorno, "Freudian Theory and the Pattern of Fascist Propaganda," 1951

Specters of Hegel: Radio and the Right

Adorno's writings on mass culture were fundamentally shaped by his experiences in the United States, where he lived from 1938 to 1948. The essay on the culture industry in *Dialectic of Enlightenment* was written while Adorno and Horkheimer lived in Los Angeles, near the geographic and institutional heart of the American entertainment business—Hollywood. Yet the theory of the culture industry was not intended as an exercise in cultural anthropology, but rather as a study of one manifestation of a historical spirit that Adorno considered to be worldwide in breadth. For Adorno and Horkheimer, this spirit of "instrumental reason" defined not only mass culture in the United States but also the administrated cultures of the Third Reich and Stalin's Soviet Union. This world spirit was actualized, they maintained, in the technological and administrative rationalities mobilized by Paramount Pictures, Nazism, and Stalinism alike.

In particular, for Adorno and Horkheimer, the medium of radio constitutes a concrete point of affinity between Hitler's totalitarian state capitalism and the anticipatory version of state capitalism in the American culture industry:

> Chesterfield is merely the nation's cigarette, but the radio is the megaphone of the nation. In dragging cultural products wholly into the sphere of commodities, radio utterly renounces bringing its own cultural products to people as commodities. In America it collects no fees from the public. Radio thereby acquires the deceptive form of disinterested, impartial authority which suits Fascism admirably. The radio becomes the universal mouthpiece of the Führer: his voice rises from the street loudspeakers, blending with the howling of sirens announcing panic—from which modern propaganda can scarcely be distinguished anyway. The National Socialists themselves knew that the wireless gave concrete form to their cause, just as the printing press did to the Reformation. The metaphysical charisma of the Führer invented by the sociology of religion has finally turned out to be no more than the omnipresence of his radio speeches, which demoniacally parodies the omnipresence of the divine spirit. The gigantic fact that the speech penetrates everywhere replaces its content, just as the benefaction of the Toscanini broadcast takes the place of its content, the symphony. No listener can grasp their true connection, while the Führer's speech is lies anyway. The immanent tendency of radio is to make the human word, the false commandment, absolute. . . . One day the edict of production, the specific advertisement (whose actuality is presently concealed by the pretense of choice) can turn into the open command of the Führer.[1]

Fascistic impulses, Adorno and Horkheimer thus argue, are inherent in the very technological structure of radio broadcasting, which can invade even the most private spaces, never ceases its activity, and permits no reply by the audience.[2] Moreover, radio fundamentally alters the aesthetic structure of cultural forms transmitted over the airwaves, a point to which the authors merely allude here but which Adorno develops more fully in several contemporaneous essays on the radio broadcasting of classical music. For Adorno, radio transforms the delicate "interrelationship of unity and manifoldness" at the musical core of the symphony into the monotonous repetition of well-known themes and plugs for famous conductors. (This aesthetic transmutation, in turn, stems from technological factors, such as radio's flattening of "coloristic differentiation" in symphonic sound and the ability of the listener to avoid being caught up in the music's totality by turning the radio on or off at will.)[3] By thus "merging with advertising," the radio symphony is deprived of its aesthetic integrity, its mission of achieving a compositional reconciliation of the general and the particular. And, as Adorno's theory of social physiognomy suggests, it is thereby divested of its power to inspire the public to "criticiz[e] social realities," a power contingent on the symphony's demonstration of its inevitable failure to fulfill this mission.[4]

For Adorno and Horkheimer, finally, radio's relative independence from the market makes it an even more potent agent of thought's reification than other mass-cultural forms such as movies. "Radio, the progressive latecomer of mass culture," they write, "draws all the consequences at present denied the film by its pseudo-market."[5] As the previous chapter has explained, these "consequences" are the elimination of the competitive market through the expansion of a monopolistically and, eventually, state-planned economy; and, as a result, the paradoxically simultaneous omnipresence and negation of the commodity-form, along with its socially mediating moments of exchange value and use value. To Adorno and Horkheimer, radio broadcasting thus epitomizes the culture industry's parodic realization of the world spirit of freedom theorized by Hegel: it actualizes a unity of thought and social practice in which pure domination is established, and it reveals more than any other cultural phenomenon that even the relatively immature state capitalism of the United States is barely a step away from the totalitarianism of Nazi Germany.

Adorno, however, did not limit his exploration of the growth of fascism in the United States to these speculative extrapolations from the theory of the culture industry. He also analyzed the deployment of radio broadcasting to cultivate a substantively fascist political movement in his 1943 study, "The Psychological Technique of Martin Luther Thomas' Radio Addresses," as well as in several related essays.[6] As we shall see, Adorno's critique of right-wing radio in the United States drew productively on his cultural theory, providing an instructive example of how political rightism might be critically analyzed as a *cultural* phenomenon characteristic of late capitalism. More precisely, his critique retains its provocative edge today chiefly on account of its suggestive failures, although to an extent also by virtue of its genuine accomplishments.

In the Thomas study, Adorno devoted sustained and detailed attention to the immanent particularities of Thomas's radio addresses that was highly uncharacteristic of his predominant approach to mass culture. In doing so, he took an unmistakable step in the direction of social physiognomy. Here Adorno did not merely speculate in general terms that certain practices of production (such as montage) might favor the emergence of negative potentialities within mass culture, as he did in the essay "Transparencies on Film," for example. Nor did he simply confront right-wing radio as a genre, as he did with jazz. Instead, he engaged a specific object of mass culture with unusual regard for its singularity and complexity, and derived insights into socioeconomic conditions from the object's distinctive contours. Let us recall from chapter 1 that although dialectical criticism for Adorno presupposed both immanent (or aesthetic) and transcendent (or social-theoretic) moments, theory had to *begin* by granting "precedence to the object," for thought could only resist its own reification by drawing "strength" from the negative potentiality harbored within the object.[7] This is exactly what Adorno did in the Thomas study, at least initially. He would thus seem to have affirmed here in practice rather than in the abstract that mass-cultural phenomena could be aesthetically constituted with an integrity beyond the contrived unity forced on them by the culture industry, and thus with the capacity to express and inspire social transformation. The Thomas study ultimately did not follow through on this promise, as I demonstrate below. Nevertheless, the study offers evidence of a different order than scholars have heretofore presented that Adorno did on notable occasions stretch the intellectual horizons of his theory of mass culture.[8]

At the same time, the study provides an expanded basis for reaffirming the continuing productiveness of the theory of the culture industry for the contemporary analysis of mass culture, in particular Christian right mass culture. As I show below, Adorno appears to have accomplished a significant amount of groundwork for the theory of the culture industry through his critique of Thomas's radio broadcasts. This makes the study interesting for intellectual-historical reasons.[9] However, there are also political considerations that make the specific function of the culture industry theory within the Thomas study worth reexamining today. In the study, Adorno drew attention to the marriage of American Christian conservatism and mass culture in its earliest years and analyzed the Christian right *as* mass culture. By using elements of the culture industry theory to analyze Christian right radio, the Thomas study thus raises the possibility that mobilizing a similar intellectual framework today could shed new, critical light on phenomena that, by fusing the avid exploitation of the industrial techniques catalogued by Horkheimer and Adorno with the outright declaration of a "cultural war" on modern values, have taken the dialectic of enlightenment to a newly explicit extreme (in America, at any rate). The following discussion thus provides a prelude to those portions of subsequent chapters that analyze contemporary Christian right radio as "culture industry" in Adorno's specific sense.

Nonetheless, critical analysis of the Christian right today must navigate beyond the instrumentalist assumption that the broadcasts and publications of Christian conservatives are simply the product-lines of an expanding subsidiary of the corporate cultural machinery. To steer criticism of Christian conservative mass culture solely according to the compass supplied by the theory of the culture industry is to exclude from the outset the possibility that these phenomena may not seamlessly breed cynicism and disillusionment, but sometimes (if only negatively) nourish their audiences' most utopian hopes. Failing to consider these instances, in turn, obviates any possibility that progressives and Christian conservatives might ever find common ground and form populist coalitions that could unsettle entrenched structures of political and economic power. This brings us back to the necessity of the mode of critique toward which the Thomas study beckons us: immanent criticism of the mass-cultural object, dialecticized through social physiognomy, which both deciphers the "secret code" according to which the object expresses and reproduces social domination *and* recognizes the object's "enigmatic" and utopian denunciations of injustice.[10] In the penultimate section of this chapter I speculatively construe a social physiognomy of Thomas's rhetoric that might have emerged had Adorno engaged in a full-fledged immanent criticism of this phenomenon. I then summarize the principles, admonitions, and sensibilities that my own critique of Christian right mass culture excavates from Adorno's texts.

Before moving into a detailed discussion of the Thomas study, however, we should note the study's thematic and institutional proximity to two other works: *The Authoritarian Personality* (1950), by Theodor W. Adorno, Else Frenkel-Brunswik, Daniel J. Levinson, and R. Nevitt Sanford; and *Prophets of Deceit: A Study of the Techniques of the American Agitator* (1949), by Leo Lowenthal and Norbert Guterman. All three writings were originally conceived as contributions to the American Jewish Committee's (AJC) project on anti-Semitism, which was both a mainstay of financial support and the primary locus of collaborative research for Adorno and other members of the Institute for Social Research during the 1940s. *The Authoritarian Personality* is today the best-known product of this massive research undertaking. According to the original plan of the project, however, the empirical study of protofascist personality traits, the analysis of which became the content of *The Authoritarian Personality*, was to represent only a fractional component of a much broader endeavor. In particular, to complement the analysis of subjective attitudes, Adorno, Lowenthal, and Paul Massing carried out separate studies of the radio broadcasts of three right-wing preachers—of protofascist ideology, in other words, as an objective social phenomenon.[11] The Thomas study was one of these exercises. The AJC had planned for these studies to lead to "the publication of a popular handbook, with sketches, which would help to expose the tricks used by fascist agitators and so disarm them and immunize the public against them."[12] Like many other components of the overall project, however, this handbook never emerged in print. Instead, *Prophets of Deceit* was published in 1949 as "a scholarly version of the planned popular handbook."[13]

Adorno never prepared the Thomas study for publication, and the piece therefore escaped the severe discipline of editing by which Adorno usually constrained himself. Although some parts of the Thomas study present a relatively coherent argument, the sprawling, 130-page text as a whole is plagued by incomplete thoughts and methodological inconsistencies. In light of the effort required merely to plod through this unruly document; considering, in addition, the difficulty of disentangling and evaluating the divergent strands of argument wound together throughout the text; and in view of the inconsequentiality of its object in conventional political terms (major historical accounts of the American right wing and anti-Semitism in the United States do not even mention Thomas or his movement), it is understandable that the Thomas study has hitherto received little attention from scholars. That is unfortunate, however, because in certain respects this study is both politically more radical and theoretically more sophisticated than either of the two published texts that the AJC's project finally yielded.

Prophets of Deceit *and the Snare of Idealism*

Prophets of Deceit follows a conventional mode of Marxist ideology-critique. Lowenthal and Guterman assume that cultural phenomena can be analyzed as vehicles for the inculcation of class-based ideology and thus as functional assets to the maintenance of capitalist domination. In pursuing this form of ideology-critique, the theorists continue in the analytical mode characteristic of Lowenthal's earlier writings for the Institute. For example, in an article for the *Zeitschrift für Sozialforschung* Lowenthal analyzes the reception of Dostoyevsky among the German petite bourgeoisie in the years preceding World War I. He argues that Dostoyevsky's popularity with members of this social class was due to the author's offer of a spiritualist and nationalist "consolation" that absolved the individual from confronting social problems on the levels of politics and economics.[14]

The core thesis of *Prophets of Deceit*, in turn, is that Christian right-wing "agitation" prevents audience members from responding to their "social dissatisfaction" rationally—that is, by attempting to "trace" their feelings to "a clearly definable cause."[15] According to Lowenthal and Guterman, a "social malaise" has readied the psychological turf for the Christian right's incursions among large portions of the population. This malaise involves the suspicion that mysterious social powers are perpetrating a "hoax" on the majority of the people and depriving them of society's fruits; a "sense of helplessness and passivity"; a "general premonition of disasters to come"; and a deep "disillusionment" and cynicism regarding society's "values and ideals."[16] The important point, however, is that this psychological malady has "objective causes" in "social reality":

> This malaise reflects the stresses imposed on the individual by the profound transformations taking place in our economic and social structure—the replacement of the class of small independent producers by gigantic industrial bureaucracies, the decay of the patriarchal family, the breakdown of primary personal ties between individuals in an increasingly mechanized world, the compartmentalization and atomization of group life, and the substitution of mass culture for traditional patterns.[17]

Lowenthal and Guterman contend that while the malaise is initially only "a psychological symptom of an oppressive situation," it can ultimately prevent the transformation of that situation if the agitator manipulates it so that it "veils and distorts" objective reality:

> The agitator does not try to diagnose the relationship of this symptom to the underlying social situation. Instead he tricks his audience into accepting the very situation that produced its malaise. Under the guise of a protest against the oppressive situation, the agitator binds his audience to it. Since this pseudo-protest never produces a genuine solution, it merely leads the audience to seek permanent relief from a permanent predicament by means of irrational outbursts. The agitator does not create the malaise, but he aggravates and fixates it because he bars the path to overcoming it.[18]

To Lowenthal and Guterman, then, Christian right agitation is a form of sophisticated trickery leading the public away from rational insight into historically rooted oppression and toward a state of emotionally overwrought and despairing obsession with its own suffering.

Prophets of Deceit precisely catalogues the techniques used by the agitator to promote irrationalism in his audience. For each technique or "theme," the authors detail both the relationship to the malaise and the psychopolitical effects of the agitator's words. For example, they analyze the agitator's habit of "simultaneously damning and praising the accepted ideologies" of the social and political mainstream. This technique, they argue, aggravates listeners' "disillusionment with ideals, values and institutions" yet inhibits serious opposition to the mainstream by offering no concrete alternatives.[19] Likewise, the agitator's constant suggestions that catastrophe is imminent enervate the audience's diffuse sense of anxiety. At the same time, they "relieve the individual of responsibility for struggling with his problems" by never actually identifying the agents of the impending "doom," and encourage the listener to yield to the authority of "the available spiritual *elite*" out of fear.[20] Perhaps the most potent device in the agitator's arsenal is the construction of enemy-figures. According to Lowenthal and Guterman, these foes facilitate the agitator's delicate balance of provoking and suppressing the bile of his audience. For instance, the agitator rails against bureaucrats for usurping the people's power and despoiling public resources for personal gain. He thereby suggests that "representative government in this country is a sham." Nevertheless, he stops short of explicitly condemning the "basic structure" of political life, and the counterweight of his "eulogy of established institutions" ensures that his listeners maintain a posture of "respect for authority" and political passivity.[21] For Lowenthal and Guterman, the Jew emerges as the enemy-figure into which all variations (including bureaucrats, communists, bankers, and immigrants) are condensed, and as the "resting place" for the audience's "accumulated resentment."[22]

Lowenthal and Guterman stress that for the agitator, the audience's "aroused fury is to be kept in a kind of indefinite suspension, a perpetual and never fulfilled threat."

> The verbal fury of the agitator is only a rehearsal for real fury. . . . it would be erroneous to infer that he preaches free and wild joy in aggression. For with every gesture that urges his audience to indulge in violence, he reminds his followers, no matter how indirectly, that their aggression involves the forbidden, that they are still weak and can free themselves from the enemy's tyranny only by submitting unconditionally to his leadership. In the anticipated hunt, the followers can expect no spoils: they must be satisfied with the mere hunt itself. . . . The agitator's gift to his audience—his permission to indulge in violence—is a Trojan horse. . . . All that remains is the immediate condition of constantly renewed excitement and terror.[23]

In the end, the theorists conclude, the only satisfaction the agitator allows the audience is that of indulging in its own feelings of anger at being the "dupes" of shadowy powers. The agitator kindles fury and resentment as ends in themselves, rather than as catalysts to rational reform or revolution. Moreover, he "condition[s] the audience to authoritarian discipline" by ironically positioning it as merely the "inverted reflection" of the furious enemy forces. In the absence of a powerful fascist political movement, this means submission to the political and economic status quo that has caused the audience's malaise.[24] However, Lowenthal and Guterman also view Christian right agitation in the 1940s as a nascent form of fascism that could one day envelop American society—as Max Horkheimer puts it in the introduction, as a "latent" but very real "threat against democracy."[25] Given certain "historical circumstances," above all "social and economic" crises that might intensify and broaden the malaise and open up new points of influence for agitation, fascism on a mass scale could develop in the United States. In the meantime, however, the agitator's manipulation of his audience's discontent still exercises a significant social effect, inasmuch as it "functions objectively to perpetuate the conditions which give rise to that discontent."[26]

Prophets of Deceit provides a painstakingly careful and precise exposition of the substantive characteristics of Christian right ideology in this era. As the subsequent discussion of Focus on the Family shows, moreover, Lowenthal and Guterman's astute explication of the predominant themes of midcentury Christian right oratory remains salient today. The present-day Christian right, too, directs its wrath toward enemy-figures simultaneously ridiculed as impotent and feared as omnipotent (above all, as chapter 3 discusses, gays and feminists). And contemporary Christian right media reiterate historic patterns by blending reverence for traditional American institutions (especially the Constitution and the imperative of national security, as we shall see in chapter 4) with wildly alarmist talk of total societal collapse.

Nevertheless, methodological problems at the core of *Prophets of Deceit* sharply constrain its usefulness for a contemporary analysis of the Christian right. As rich and elaborate as the authors' presentation of the ideological material is, the linkages between this material and the social theory that is supposed to unlock its meaning are frustratingly shaky. The theorists do not even systematically relate most of the agitational "themes" to the concept of the malaise, which we must remember is not itself the decisive aspect of the historical situation for the ideology-critique but only "reflects" the determining socioeconomic forces. To be sure, the interpretations of these "themes" often recall elements of the malaise. For instance, the theorists argue that the figure of the plutocrat plays on the audience's sense of its "exclusion" from the enjoyment of "forbidden fruit."[27] But here the theorists do not explain how the plutocrat's particular characteristics—as a financier rather than an industrialist, as an enemy from a bygone era rather than a present-day threat, as somehow both a communist and a banker, and as a Jew—resonate with this aspect of the malaise, much less with specific socioeconomic circumstances. Finely differentiated though the authors' "microscopic" observations of the exact details of the figure of the plutocrat and the Jew in Christian right ideology are, they remain largely imprisoned under the magnifying lens.[28]

The disconnect between social theory and the object of cultural-ideological analysis in *Prophets of Deceit* can be traced to the authors' unrefined and economistic Marxism. Since the authors' descriptions of the agitational themes are not well integrated with their social theory, the connections between theoretical speculation and ideological material ultimately depend by default on the authors' general classification of the methods of agitation as strategic "irrationalism." The Christian right agitator's "irrationalism" is in turn defined largely through its contrast with an ideal type that Lowenthal and Guterman label "the reformer/revolutionary." Whereas the former appeals to his audience's irrational urges, the theorists claim, the latter attempts "to define the nature of discontent by means of rational concepts" and leads individuals to an undistorted awareness of objective circumstances with the clinical comportment of the "competent doctor." This blunt dichotomy between "irrational" fascism and "rational" radicalism obviously presupposes a rigid distinction between ideology and scientific truth, in which the former proceeds from the stifling or perversion of rational faculties while the latter results from unfettered reason. This begs the question of how the critical standpoint of *Prophets of Deceit* is grounded epistemologically, a question to which Lowenthal and Guterman provide no answer. Since they do not problematize the foundations of their knowledge of society, the theorists display precisely that "hybris of the mind" which Adorno insightfully criticizes as contrary to a philosophically rigorous historical materialism. From an Adornian perspective, that is, the Marxism of *Prophets of Deceit* abandons dialectics, reverts to idealism, and thereby betrays itself by ascribing an a priori truth to theoretical assumptions and renouncing the need for theory to become self-reflective through thought's "spontaneous relation to the object."

The irony here is that *Prophets of Deceit* overflows with remarkable, spontaneous insights into the minute twists and turns of Christian right ideology in this period. But these insights remain within the realm of what Adorno would have called "immanent" criticism, because the theorists do not show specifically how these ideological minutiae reproduce the social totality or how social theory might be reinvigorated by virtue of their labors. Above all (and this heightens the irony), even though the authors thoroughly document the incessant contradictions within the agitational material, there is no sense here that cultural contradictions reflect social contradictions, and thus that even protofascist culture might harbor a negative-utopian potency. Instead, the substantive relationship between culture and society is construed in wholly instrumental terms. And this is of a piece with the authors' methodological instrumentalism, their mechanical application of Marxist social theory and Freudian psychology to the ideological material.

Adorno's contributions to the AJC's project on anti-Semitism predictably exhibited more acutely dialectical sensitivities than did those of his colleagues. In the case of *The Authoritarian Personality*, a collaborative endeavor between Adorno and several less dialectically minded scholars, this made for some interesting inconsistencies in the final product. Nevertheless, as we shall see, neither in this work nor in the Thomas study did Adorno himself entirely escape the dialectical paralysis that besets *Prophets of Deceit*.

Traces of Dialectics in The Authoritarian Personality

The Authoritarian Personality analyzes fascism by focusing on the "consumer" rather than the "production of propaganda," unlike *Prophets of Deceit* and the Thomas study.[29] Nevertheless, particularly in those aspects of the study where Adorno exercised the greatest influence, *The Authoritarian Personality* exhibits more than superficial similarities to these other two writings in its theoretical sensibilities. Above all, the parts written by Adorno emphasize the imperative to interpret individual-level psychological phenomena with reference to the social totality, just as "Cultural Criticism and Society" lays this same burden on the critique of culture by calling for social physiognomy. However, this move ultimately does not make *The Authoritarian Personality* sufficiently dialectical in Adorno's strong sense—that is, such that the analysis of the particular phenomenon enables social theory to become self-reflective.

The Authoritarian Personality seeks to generate a highly specific account of the relationship between fascist ideology and individual personality structures. The authors begin with the axiom that "anti-Semitism is based more largely upon factors in the subject and in his total situation than upon actual characteristics of Jews."[30] They also presuppose that the scientific study of personality structures offers a vital "safeguard against the inclination to attribute persistent trends in the individual to something 'innate' or 'basic' or 'racial' within him," a tendency highly characteristic of Nazi propaganda.[31] The cornerstone of the study is its development of a list of variables that the authors dub the "F-scale" and that comprises a finely-tuned set of personality traits indicating a psychological "susceptibility" to fascist propaganda. The study uses this scale in surveys of a large number of respondents, but also probes beneath the plane of quantitative data by conducting more detailed "qualitative" or "clinical" interpretations of some of the interview material.

At the outset of the book, the four authors of *The Authoritarian Personality* make it clear that they do not mean to ascribe to personality structure the exclusive or decisive capacity to determine whether or not an individual adheres to fascist ideology. Instead, they claim more cautiously that "one place to look for determinants of anti-Semitic opinions and attitudes is within the persons who express them." In turn, the authors collectively disavow making any effort "to account for the existence of anti-Semitic ideas in our society," even while acknowledging that the domains of psychology, sociology, and history "can be separated only artificially."[32] Thus the jointly written introduction creates the sense that the analysts are deliberately restricting their focus for the sake of depth and clarity, although they are aware that any complete explanation of the origins of fascism must include the examination of nonpsychological data, such as an individual's "membership in social groups": "The soundest approach, it would seem, is to consider that in the determination of ideology, as in the determination of any behavior, there is a situational factor and a personality factor, and that a careful weighing of the role of each will yield the most accurate prediction."[33]

No little tension subsists between the chapters written individually by Adorno and the positivistic assumptions of this introductory material, including above all the latter's mechanical notion of causation and predictive aspirations. Nor, indeed, does Adorno seem to feel bound by the authors' collective refusal to speak directly of the social forces that spawn anti-Semitism. To the contrary, Adorno initially echoes the parsimonious piety of the introduction, only to negate it in the very next line:

> The data discussed so far permit at least the assumption that personality could be regarded as *one* determinant of ideology.
>
> Yet it is just the area with which we are now concerned [political and economic ideas] that most strongly forbids any simple reduction to terms of personality. . . . on a deeper level, probably for *all* ideological issues, there appears to be at work another determinant which, in numerous issues, blurs the distinction between high and low scorers and refuses to be stated unequivocally in terms of personality. This determinant may be called our general cultural climate, and particularly the ideological influence upon people of most media for moulding public opinion. If our cultural climate has been standardized under the impact of social control and technological concentration to an extent never known before, we may expect that the thinking habits of individuals reflect this standardization as well as the dynamics of their own personalities.[34]

Whereas the authors collectively only claim to interpret an individual's "political, economic, and social convictions" as "an expression of deeplying trends in his personality," Adorno breaks ranks and reads the interview transcriptions as expressions of social forces, in particular the spread of the culture industry's reifying effects. Together, the authors concede that whether or not anti-Semitic propaganda actually proliferate depends "primarily upon the situation of the most powerful economic interests, upon whether they, by conscious design or not, make use of this device for maintaining their dominant status."[35] On his own, by contrast, Adorno discerns within the study's psychological data the imprint of a social totality determined by monopolistic forces of production and tending toward totalitarian state capitalism. Moreover, Adorno gives the clear impression that the study expresses social truths not only in its positive conclusions but also by virtue of its ultimate failure, or negativity: for precisely the inevitable breakdown of the basic "distinction between high and low scorers" evokes the truth about society's brokenness.

Adorno thus repeatedly deciphers specific characteristics of respondents' statements regarding prejudice, politics, economics, and religion as manifestations of various aspects of the social totality. For example, he interprets certain respondents' anti-Semitism as a reaction to economic "monopolization," in the context of which the Jew comes to represent the "misfit bourgeois" who refuses to embrace the conformity and dependence mandated by the new corporate order. For others, anti-Semitism functions as a form of displaced resentment against subjugation to the "technological rationality" that is the guiding principle of monopoly business and the administrative state alike, and in the context of which the Jew's purported "clannishness" seems to retain vestiges of the intimate familialism destroyed by modern capitalism.[36] Likewise, the phenomenon of "pseudoconservatism," or maintaining fidelity to traditional economic values while embracing an ethnocentrist authoritarianism that undermines the American tradition of political and economic liberalism, is for Adorno the product of "objective social conditions" rather than simply an underdeveloped ego. Pseudoconservatism reflects "those developmental tendencies of our society which point into [sic] the direction of some more or less fascist, state capitalist organization."[37] Additionally, the respondents' "disposition to view religion as a means instead of an end," as a "cultural good" to be chosen from a selection of worldviews "after the pattern of choosing a particularly well advertised commodity" and then "consumed," witnesses to the "neutralization" of religion that accompanies its redefinition in the course of modernity as a "leisure" activity and its consequent recomposition as an "agency of social conformity"—its reconstitution, that is, in the image of the culture industry.[38]

Adorno's approach to the psychological data gathered for the study of the authoritarian personality is thus fundamentally more dialectical than that of his colleagues inasmuch as it locates the meanings of particularities in the data in their relations to the social whole. And in precisely this way, Adorno's handling of the data here surpasses Lowenthal and Guterman's interpretations of the agitational material in *Prophets of Deceit*. Nevertheless, this alone does not make Adorno's comments in *The Authoritarian Personality* dialectical in the strong sense set forth in other writings of his such as "Cultural Criticism and Society." For Adorno's dialectical mediations of the interview material do not go so far as to yield any self-reflectivity of the social theory he employs. Instead, the ideological investments of the respondents are simply interpreted as reflections of broad social forces—period. This short-circuiting of dialectics thus hypostatizes the theory of state capitalism and the culture industry.

One key symptom of the dialectical shortfall in even those sections of *The Authoritarian Personality* penned by Adorno is the mechanism with which Adorno often incorporates psychoanalytical theory within his interpretation of the data. For instance, Adorno contends that anti-Semitism operates as a regressive wish-fulfillment for the individual who longs to understand society's "laws" but finds them to be impenetrable and is therefore overwhelmed by "alienation":

> The opaqueness of the present political and economic situation for the average person provides an ideal opportunity for retrogression to the infantile level of stereotypy and personalization. The political rationalizations used by the uninformed and confused are compulsive revivals of irrational mechanisms never overcome during the individual's growth. This seems to be one of the main links between opinions and psychological determinants.[39]

Here, psychoanalytic categories enable Adorno to conceptualize the concrete mechanisms through which social tendencies become translated into individual attitudes. The resulting interpretation is certainly plausible, but it is too pat; and it seems likely that in his more rigorously dialectical moments Adorno himself would have tried to complicate the picture, perhaps by drawing attention to the contradictions within personality structures rather than simply mapping their smooth operation according to the requisites of power. This alternative approach would have perhaps allowed fissures in the social totality to emerge by shedding light on the inconsistencies within personality structures, thereby sketching a "social physiognomy" of the authoritarian personality that could have unleashed the latter's negative-utopian potential. Instead, Adorno makes the complicity of high scorers on the F-scale with totalitarian state-capitalist tendencies monolithic, positing their "desire for an unjust state of affairs in which the exchange of equivalents has been replaced by distribution according to unmediated and irrational power relationships." With this, moreover, Adorno wades into intellectually hazardous waters (behind Lowenthal and Guterman) by seeming to embrace a reductionist dichotomy between fascist "irrationalism" and rational radicalism. For Adorno, in short, the authoritarian personality is the "microcosmic image of the totalitarian state at which he aims." But this image apparently possesses no negative-dialectical fortitude that might allow the analysis of it to render original insight into the structure of society.[40]

Frankfurt School historian Martin Jay contends that the radical-political deficit of *The Authoritarian Personality* stems from the fact that this study of individual psychology was sundered from the more evidently Marxist, social-theoretical account of anti-Semitism in *Dialectic of Enlightenment*.[41] There is more social theory in Adorno's sections of *The Authoritarian Personality* than Jay allows, however. A deeper root of the study's insufficient radicalism than its severance from Adorno's more seminal work is its unwillingness to carry through the theorist's most stringent program of dialectics. Precisely this problem also surfaces in Adorno's own examination of anti-Semitism from the perspective of its "production" (as opposed to its "consumption") in the Thomas study.

Dialectics Defused: Adorno's Study of Martin Luther Thomas

One need look no further than the opening passages of the Thomas study and *Prophets of Deceit* to recognize in the former the distinctive impact of Adorno's concern that cultural criticism proceed dialectically, by energizing a "force-field" between social theory and a spontaneous "experience of the object." Lowenthal and Guterman start with a three-page "quotation" from their agitational material—actually, a composite made up of excerpts from the speeches of several different agitators. This curious prologue has the effect of mystifying the relationship of theory to the material. On the one hand, the material is not mediated by theory, since it is presented in a lengthy manner and is followed not by interpretation but by general, contextualizing statements about the "steady audiences" the agitators attract even though they have failed to win mass followings.[42] On the other hand, the agitational material is thoroughly mediated by virtue of its artificial construction. Since the authors do not make their theoretical perspective explicit and self-reflective, however, the overall impact of this introductory quotation is merely impressionistic: its bombastic content is little more than an attention-getter. Lowenthal and Guterman then abruptly shift into the classical style of empirical, social-scientific writing: after constructing a preliminary typology of political activists and forms of political rhetoric, they state their hypothesis and then launch into a detailed examination of the agitators' tactics, offering evidence to validate their argument.

Adorno, by contrast, begins from an analytical position that avoids both the suppression of theory and the complete immersion in the object that is implicit in his colleagues' composite citation. Yet Adorno also remains nearer to the object, when mediating his perception of the object through theory, than do Lowenthal and Guterman. The opening sentence of the Thomas study identifies, apparently at random, a particular feature of Thomas's radio addresses: "The fascist leader characteristically indulges in loquacious statements about himself." Adorno goes on to speculate on the historical, social-psychological circumstances that the agitator's "personalism" reflects:

> The detachment from personal relationships involved in any objective discussion presupposes an intellectual freedom and strength which hardly exists within the masses today. Moreover, the "coldness" inherent in objective argumentation intensifies the feeling of despair, isolation, and loneliness under which virtually each individual today suffers—a feeling from which he longs to escape when listening to any kind of public oratory. This situation has been grasped by the fascists. Their talk is personal. Not only does it refer to the most immediate interests of his listeners, but also it encompasses the sphere of privacy of the speaker himself who seems to take his listeners into his confidence and to bridge the gap between person and person.[43]

Adorno then proposes additional reasons for the agitator's personalistic "attitude," thereby linking his diagnosis of individuals' emotional experiences of "despair, isolation and loneliness" to a broader conception of social conditions: "The more impersonal our order becomes, the more important personality becomes as an ideology. The more the individual is reduced to a mere cog, the more the idea of the uniqueness of the individual, his autonomy and importance, has to be stressed as a compensation for his actual weakness."[44] Finally, Adorno speculates on the precise psychological dynamics by which the agitator influences his listeners: "Since this [compensatory activity] cannot be done with each of the listeners individually or only in a rather general and abstract manner, it is done vicariously by the leader. It can even be said that part of the secret of totalitarian leadership is that the leader presents the image of an autonomous personality actually denied his followers."[45]

Two crucial distinctions differentiate Adorno's procedure from that of Lowenthal and Guterman. First, as his immediate and critical engagement with the agitational material suggests, Adorno does not structure his study as the linear unfolding of a unified, deductively construed, causal scheme, as do Lowenthal and Guterman. Rather than constructing his analysis as the confirmation of an abstract hypothesis through the appraisal of concrete phenomena as exemplary evidence, Adorno composes his study as a series of discrete interventions that analyze distinct features of Thomas's speeches one by one, according to each one's unique structure. (Precisely this deliberate detotalization of the causal framework and monadological contemplation of individual interviews, in turn, characterizes Adorno's contribution to *The Authoritarian Personality*.) Second, within each intervention, Adorno does not begin on the level of theory and then move on to contemplate the object's characteristics, but instead proceeds in the inverse fashion (again, just as he does in *The Authoritarian Personality*). In both the general form and specific procedure of the Thomas study, then, Adorno prioritizes his own "spontaneous relation to the object," a position that his colleagues' ideology-critique declines by prioritizing a theory of society.

A few additional examples illustrate the operation and provocative consequences of Adorno's method in the Thomas study.[46] Each of Adorno's critical interventions in the study follows a series of steps similar to that which characterizes his interpretation of Thomas's "personalistic" rhetoric. In each case, Adorno articulates (1) the description of the speech-phenomenon he identifies; (2) the social-psychological conditions that this phenomenon indicates exist; (3) the socioeconomic circumstances from which these conditions spring; and (4) the personality-based psychological mechanism by which Thomas's speech-device exerts certain effects on the individual. In short, Adorno's critique decodes the surface-appearance of the material, deriving from it a speculative formulation of the relationship between the individual subject and the social totality.

Like Lowenthal and Guterman, Adorno pinpoints the agitator's "emotionalism" as a key object of analysis. Adorno names Thomas's derision of stoic "self-control" and encouragement of tears and wild rage the "'emotional release' device." This speech-device suggests to Adorno that "people want to 'give in,' to cease to be individuals in the traditional sense of a self-sustaining and self-controlled unity." Adorno theorizes that people desire to relinquish their psychological coherence as individuals simply "because they must," because of changes in the socioeconomic structure. The postbourgeois, monopolistic structure of the economy, Adorno argues, no longer rewards the "emotional self-control" that was the necessary "attitude of the independent individual of the liberal era of free competition." Instead, this new, advanced-capitalist structure demands that people yield to its overwhelming, economically proletarianizing and psychologically disintegrating forces. According to Adorno, Thomas's proddings toward "emotional release" convey to the audience that the safety of conformity sanctions their rebellion against traditional social taboos, thereby inciting them to irresponsible and even violent behavior in their ego-impoverished state.[47]

This sounds very much like the notion, set forth in *Prophets of Deceit*, that the agitator prescribes and models "irrational outbursts" for psychic "relief" from the traumas instigated by advanced capitalism's dysfunctions. The key differences here, however, are as follows: (1) Adorno does not elevate the motif of "emotionalism" to an abstract, categorial dimension of Thomas's rhetoric as a whole, but contemplates it in its concreteness as a singular feature of these broadcasts; and (2) Adorno's representation of social conditions springs monadologically from this "spontaneous relation to the object" in its specificity, rather than foregrounding the interpretation of the agitational material in toto. By dint of these critical gymnastics, Adorno's handling of Thomas's speeches accords with his insistence that theory can only participate in social liberation if it allows "precedence" to its object, heeding the object's claim to be approached empathetically as something existing both in and for itself rather than always already subsuming the object under thought's categories.

Another example of Adorno's procedure is his analysis of what he calls the " 'great little man' device." Adorno notes that Thomas portrays himself not only as a strong leader but also as a humble person who is on "equal footing with those whom he addresses," and incessantly "plays the beggar" by referring to his "financial worries." This rhetorical device unintentionally reveals "the universal feeling of insecurity of the masses in the present economic phase," in which the individual cannot see "himself as the master of his economic fate any longer" but instead feels "himself" to be "the object of huge blind economic forces working upon him."[48] These forces, Adorno argues, actually can reduce the individual to abject poverty at their whim. Adorno speculates that Thomas's begging provides relief from the fear of sudden impoverishment through a psychological mechanism of identification: "[Thomas] takes it upon himself psychologically to do the begging himself, to undergo psychologically the very same humiliation of which his follower is afraid, and thus to 'redeem' him symbolically of the shame of being a beggar by assuming this function vicariously and hallowing it, as it were."[49] Adorno thus contends that Thomas's " 'great little man' device" has the effect of encouraging listeners to accept with humility their actual position of social powerlessness.

For Adorno, however, the psychological mechanism of identification cuts two ways. Adorno notes that Thomas frequently employs the " *'fait accompli'* technique," which "consists of presenting an issue as one that previously has been decided." Moving to the level of social psychology, Adorno speculates that this rhetorical device betrays the longing among members of Thomas's audience, who feel themselves to be socially impotent, to identify with something strong. Since individuals feel helpless to determine their lives by their own "free will," in an era marked by the "dwindling of economic free enterprise and initiative," this desire for identification with strength finds its object in society itself—that is, in the given state of affairs that the social totality irresistibly produces. Not only the structural tendencies of the economy but moreover the institutionalization and daily barrage of commodity advertising, in Adorno's view, promote a "bandwagon" mentality and a crudely majoritarian disposition. Satisfaction of the general urge "to accept and even to adore the existent," Adorno argues, results on an individual level in the "transformation of the feeling of one's impotence into a feeling of strength."[50]

The speculations about socioeconomic and social-psychological circumstances that Adorno derives from his analysis of Thomas's rhetorical techniques illuminate various aspects of a society where socioeconomic power has been concentrated in the hands of the few, leaving the many with profound feelings of helplessness and insecurity. With each intervention, Adorno moves his critique beyond the spontaneous relation to the object from which it begins, into a transcendent position vis-à-vis the object that comprehends both society and the object as the products of historical power relations. He thus generates dialectical representations of Thomas's remarks, insofar as he first exposes the formative influences of social conditions on specific features of the addresses, and then shifts attention to these features' nurture of psychological traits perpetuating those conditions. Adorno thereby demonstrates how Thomas's radio speeches reflect sociohistorical circumstances, as do the defining traits of the authoritarian personality. But he also shows that Thomas's radio addresses reproduce these circumstances through their effects on subjectivity—that is, by generating authoritarian dispositions on the psychological level.

Like *The Authoritarian Personality*, however, the Thomas study ultimately fails to carry dialectics through to a sufficient degree. Superficially, opposite difficulties appear to beset these two texts. If in the former Adorno represents the object of critique (the authoritarian personality) as having an exaggerated coherence, in the latter he exerts too little effort to conceptualize the structure of Thomas's rhetoric as a whole. The implication is the same in both cases, however: neither text furnishes an immanent criticism of the cultural object that might serve as the basis for unveiling that object's social physiognomy. In the Thomas study, Adorno's strategy of examining each component of Thomas's rhetoric as a self-contained "device" or "trick" simply does not amount to immanent criticism of the material. Such analysis would have conceptualized the elements of Thomas's radio commentary in terms of their relations to one another within a complex whole and teased out any moments of incongruity, disjuncture, or antagonism that might have spoiled the harmony of those relations. Then, these immanent, binding and unbinding dynamics

could have been interpreted as expressing the dynamics of social domination, leading social theory toward self-reflectivity by unleashing the object's negative-utopian force. Without being anchored in immanent criticism, however, Adorno's speculations regarding the historical conditions
expressed in the object's features seem arbitrary, even as they receive
thereby the aura of absolute, scientific truth.

In other words, in the Thomas study dialectical criticism makes a
false start. Without any effort to articulate the internal constitution of
Thomas's rhetoric—that is, without immanent criticism in its full sense—
the spontaneous experience of the object yields no critical reflection on
the theory of the social order. In turn, the study's blindness to the moments of disorder within the object's composition precludes any original
insight into the contradictions of the social totality. Instead of generating
a dialectical force field between object and concept, Adorno produces a
unidirectional flow of critical energy from concept to object, thereby laps-
ing into the same idealist tendency that hampers *The Authoritarian Personality* and *Prophets of Deceit*.

The Thomas Study and the Theory of
the Culture Industry

Despite this structural fault in the Thomas study, it does have something
of importance to contribute to the critical analysis of the contemporary
Christian right. The study's value in this regard lies both in its gesture,
however incomplete, toward immanent criticism of the mass-cultural
object and in its use of the culture industry theory to analyze right-wing
political culture. Unfortunately, these two achievements seem to have
worked at cross-purposes to one another.

It is worthwhile to ask why Adorno dispensed with the immanent criticism of Thomas's broadcasts, when he had so carefully defined their constitutive elements and so imaginatively reflected on them. A plausible
answer emerges if we consider two distinct but related undercurrents of
the text. These are, first, the similarities that Adorno repeatedly draws
between aspects of Thomas's speeches and features of mass-cultural phenomena in general; and second, Adorno's consideration of the political
and religious ideas expressed in Thomas's rhetoric only in terms of their
value as "devices" of manipulation.

Apart from the pulpit, Thomas's main medium of communication was
radio. As we have seen, *Dialectic of Enlightenment* declared radio to be
the incarnation par excellence of the pallid world spirit of instrumental
reason defining administrated mass culture in the United States and Nazi
Germany alike. In the Thomas study, in turn, Adorno mobilizes and re-
fines the concepts developed to analyze the culture industry, which he

understood as implicitly fascist, in order to interpret fascism in a more explicit though still germinal form. The fact that Thomas relied on radio broadcasting to disseminate his message made it all the more natural that Adorno would do this. For Adorno, however, casting Thomas's radio commentary as a creature of the culture industry meant dismissing from the outset the possibility of submitting it to a thoroughgoing immanent criticism, much less sketching its social physiognomy with any substantial degree of coherence.

The debt owed by the Thomas study to the developing theory of the culture industry is readily apparent when one reads the study with *Dialectic of Enlightenment* in mind. To the extent that the analysis possesses a unifying thread at all, that thread is constituted by Adorno's analysis of Thomas as a purveyor of mass culture. "Thomas is an advertising expert in a highly specialized field, that of the transformation of religious bigotry into political and racial hatred."[51] To Adorno, Thomas's radio addresses "are largely to be interpreted as advertising for the nonpublic, esoteric activities" of "the nucleus of his followers" who attend Thomas's church and belong to his political organization.[52]

Sometimes Adorno explicitly compares Thomas's speech-devices to the tactics of commercial advertising. Thus, for Adorno, the "fait accompli device" not only expresses the growing prevalence of the "bandwagon" mentality as a social-psychological disposition (which the culture industry has helped create), but moreover is directly "borrowed from commercial advertising" as a promotional technique.[53] Likewise, Adorno views Thomas's frequent assertions "that the situation is desperate and has reached a peak of crisis, that some change must be made immediately" as incorporating a "common pattern of advertising: 'This offer holds good only for a few days.'"[54] True, Adorno immediately adds that this interpretation "scratches only the surface of the phenomenon," and ultimately locates the reason for Thomas's employment of the "last hour" device in the "objective situation" of Thomas's listeners, who are probably "deeply discontented and also even destitute."[55] Nonetheless, it remains the case that Adorno analyzes Thomas's action itself as a form of advertising that manipulates the attitudes stemming from consumers' "objective situation."

Many of Adorno's interpretations of Thomas's techniques introduce ideas that would eventually become core themes of the chapter on the culture industry in *Dialectic of Enlightenment*. Of Thomas's propensity to make emotional "confessions" regarding his personal weaknesses, for example, Adorno writes:

This is a universal feature in present-day mass culture. It is catered to by the gossip columns of certain newspapers, the inside stories told to innumerable listeners over the radio, or the magazines that promise 'true stories.' . . . it is a function of the attitude of snooping, deep-rooted in the unconscious psychological process which longs for the gratification of catching a glimpse of one's neighbor's private life—an attitude closely akin to fascism.[56]

A year later, in *Dialectic of Enlightenment*, Adorno and Horkheimer would articulate a similar point in more social theoretical, more philosophical, and less psychoanalytic terms:

> Inwardness, the subjectively restricted form of truth, was always more at the mercy of the outwardly powerful than they imagined. The culture industry turns it into an open lie. It is now experienced as the mere twaddle which is acceptable in religious bestsellers, psychological films, and women's serials as an embarrassingly agreeable garnish, so that genuine human emotion in real life can be all the more reliably controlled.[57]

Similarly, Adorno argues that Thomas's "emotional release device" stimulates "no real pleasure or joy, but only the release of the feeling of one's own unhappiness and the achievement of a retrogressive gratification out of the submergence of the self into the community. In short, the emotional release presented by fascism is a mere substitute for the fulfillment of desires."[58] This insight reappears later, woven into the more intricate argument that the culture industry extinguishes not only critical reflection on cultural objects but moreover the spontaneous enjoyment of them:

> The culture industry perpetually cheats its consumers of what it perpetually promises. . . . The culture industry does not sublimate, but rather represses. . . . In the culture industry, jovial denial takes the place of the pain present in ecstasy, as in asceticism. The supreme law is that they shall not satisfy their desires at any price, and in precisely this must they find laughing satisfaction. In every product of the culture industry, the permanent denial imposed by civilization is once again unmistakably demonstrated and inflicted on its victims.[59]

Adorno furthermore notes that Thomas bestows a "fetish character" on the term *leader* by constantly referring to leadership as though it were a good in itself. In doing so, Adorno contends, Thomas adapts to his own purposes the modus operandi of the advertising industry: "Incessant and omnipresent repetition which is planned rationally but blunts the conscious discrimination of the prospective consumers."[60] These remarks prefigure Adorno and Horkheimer's later reflections on the culture industry's mobilization of "the power of monotony" to convince people that they must accept the entertainment which the industry provides for them.[61] Finally,

Adorno observes that Thomas exhorts his public to give up on its foolish "utopian" hopes, to "be practical," and to take advantage of the "deal" he offers: inclusion in the movement to save America from ruin by the New Dealers, at the price of just a small donation.[62] The notion that Thomas's practical and thrifty affect is ideological contains in embryo the subsequent argument that the culture industry uses the diffident claim of being "just business" ideologically, to justify the utter subservience of its products to the status quo and their consequent lack of a utopian element.[63]

Inasmuch as religion is a part of Thomas's rhetoric, in turn, for Adorno it is present merely as an emotional and "associational background" that Thomas shrewdly calls up to heighten the effectiveness of his "advertising" scheme. Adorno describes a number of Thomas's speech-devices as dependent on "secularizations of religious stimuli which he still expects to operate within his listeners."[64] Adorno elaborates: "The '*fait accompli*' technique is reminiscent of the Protestant doctrine of predestination; the 'last hour' device, of the apocalyptic mood of certain sects; the dogmatic dichotomy between 'those evil forces' and 'the forces of God,' of Christian dualism; the exaltation of the humble folk, of the Sermon on the Mount."[65] Adorno devotes one of the four sections of the study to examining Thomas's use of "the religious medium."[66] This section identifies a number of additional techniques whereby Thomas turns attitudes, beliefs, and theological motifs associated with Protestant fundamentalism to his advantage. Aside from those mentioned above, these predispositions include the audience's receptiveness to theatrical sermonizing and belief that "hysterical" speech and behavior, such as "speaking with [sic] tongues," may be a sign of spiritual inspiration. Thomas knowingly plays on these religious associations, Adorno argues, to legitimize his bombastic emotionalism.[67] Likewise, Adorno contends, Thomas makes his anti-Semitism acceptable by denouncing "the Pharisees" (for Adorno, a code for Jewish intellectuals) and interpreting the crucifixion as a sign that the nation's salvation demands the literal "shedding of blood" (to Adorno, "the pogrom").[68] Thomas also invokes the notion of fidelity to the "faith of our fathers" to evoke enthusiasm for an "aggressive nativism" and his own "paternalistic authority" as a leader.[69] Thus, for Adorno, Thomas's "principal appeal" and "trademark" as an agitator is the "use of religion for fascist purposes and the perversion of religion into an instrument of hate-propaganda."[70]

Adorno's cataloguing of Thomas's tactics for twisting religious ideas and feelings toward fascist ends is highly specific and generally plausible. Yet the claim that religion only assumes a role within Thomas's radio addresses by virtue of its disintegration, or as an amorphous jumble of isolated impulses, is an assumption that Adorno does not critically evaluate. Undoubtedly, this notion originates in the sociological thesis of religion's "neutralization" that Adorno outlines in *The Authoritarian Personality*. But it agrees all too comfortably with Adorno's general approach to Thomas's broadcasting as a phenomenon of the culture industry—a cultural form, that is, lacking any compositional structure that could be analyzed in terms of its formal contradictions and negative-utopian powers.[71] For if any element of Thomas's rhetoric were to serve as a source of contradiction to the fascist dynamics that Adorno discerns, it would likely be the religious element. By insisting that religion functions within the speeches merely as a hodge-podge of inchoate affects that Thomas manipulates at will, like a "shrewd mass-psychologist" or "advertising" technician, Adorno conveniently evades the need to probe the structure of the addresses further to see whether their religious substance participates in structural tensions that in turn could illuminate further these addresses' dialectical relationship to social-structural contradictions.

In fact, by dwelling here on Thomas's personal ingenuity, ambition, and agency, the Thomas study misses one of the central insights of the culture industry theory: that the dominating apparatus operates as a system rather than being determined by the subjective motives and machinations of individual managers. Moreover, in the Thomas study Adorno seems content with the simplistic claim that the audience listens to Thomas and subscribes to his newspaper because it is deceived, or because its judgment is clouded by emotion. He offers no hint of the more subtle insight in *Dialectic of Enlightenment* that consumers paradoxically consent to be deceived (or seduced) by the culture industry, buying up its goods and imitating its stars "even though they see through them."[72] The Thomas study is at its weakest at points where Adorno's retreat toward an apparently naive rationalism is most baldly exposed, particularly in his occasional calls for "counterpropaganda" to combat Thomas's influences. For example, Adorno flatly asserts: "Counterpropaganda should point out as concretely as possible in every case the distortions of democratic ideas which take place in the name of democracy. The proof of such distortions would be one of the most effective weapons for defending democracy."[73] Such unnuanced appeals to a rationalistic common sense are so out of character for Adorno that they can only be plausibly interpreted as testimonies to the work's unfinished nature and/or halfhearted concessions to the liberal political goals of the larger project on anti-Semitism to which the Thomas study originally belonged—as did *The Authoritarian Personality*, which displays a similar dichotomy between the rational and the irrational.

Regardless of these inauspicious moments, however, the coupling of reliance on (and development of) the critique of the culture industry with a clear gesture toward social physiognomy stands as the central tension of the Thomas study. Adorno turned to the theory of the culture industry as a primary source of analytic concepts for the Thomas study, and perhaps also used Thomas's broadcasts as experimental material with which to continue refining that theory. Even as he did so, however, he ventured beyond the theory's boundaries. In the context of Adorno's oeuvre as a whole the Thomas study comprises a rare moment in which Adorno assumed an uncharacteristically "spontaneous relation" to an object of mass culture, thereby raising the prospect of analyzing that object's dialectical relationship to sociohistorical conditions. It is the intimation of an ambivalence regarding the potentially negative-utopian character of mass-cultural phenomena within the actual practice of criticism vis-à-vis a particular object that distinguishes the Thomas study from other writings of Adorno that register this ambivalence in a more abstract or hypothetical fashion. And it is this glint of possibility that makes the Thomas study instructive for a critique of Christian right radio today.

Thomas Reconsidered: Narrative Contradictions and the New Deal

But is the assumption that Thomas's radio addresses can, in fact, be analyzed through social physiognomy justified? What if Thomas's broadcasts really were nothing other than instruments of power—built with techniques borrowed here from Hitler, there from Madison Avenue—to manipulate the minds of resentful fundamentalists? What would an immanent criticism of these speeches look like, and in what sense can they be shown to have had a dialectical relationship—in the strongest, negative-utopian sense—to the social totality in which they were transmitted?

Adorno's many lengthy quotations of Thomas offer a sizeable amount of material to work with in forming hypothetical and very provisional answers to these questions. Rereading these fragments indicates that Adorno may well have missed a dimension of aesthetic wholeness and integrality in Thomas's rhetoric, as well as a way in which Thomas addresses himself to a historically distinctive cultural tradition. These aspects of Thomas's broadcasts stem from their narrative qualities. These narrative features do not give rise to a constitutional tension between a "general idea" and "particular elements," as, for example, Adorno locates in Beethoven's symphonies.[74] Nevertheless, Thomas's speeches are indeed structured in a fundamentally self-contradictory manner, inasmuch as they are organized according to two major and antagonistic narrative frames.

One of these narratives is utopian and triumphant: it is a version of the narrative of the Christian "crusade" to win souls for God and to establish

God's reign through earthly intermediaries. Thomas describes his "crusade" as a great movement of ordinary people to aid Christ in inaugurating the kingdom of God on earth. This movement ostensibly unites its participants in a harmonious and nondiscriminatory celebration of their common purpose, regardless of the participant's gender, "class," or "race."[75] According to Thomas, ultimate fulfillment both spiritually and materially awaits all who generously contribute their resources and efforts to the cause.[76] Nonetheless, this corporate endeavor preserves and vitally depends on the individual integrity of every member and affirms that the personal experience of truth is essential to collective "revival."[77] Thomas exhorts his listeners to have the courage to speak their minds and to believe in themselves.[78] In short, he preaches a rejuvenation of individual sinew and communal spirit alike for those who commit themselves to his cause.

Thomas undermines this narrative of hope and inclusion, however, with a different account of his "crusade" that emphasizes impending catastrophe and urges listeners to defend themselves against the enemies of the Lord. In part, this counterposed narrative looks forward apprehensively to the onset of another "great world war" that will likely be even more destructive than the previous war.[79] In addition, Thomas warns, Americans face the "imminent peril" of a communist putsch that is already all but accomplished because of the machinations of traitors in the government and banking system.[80] Indeed, the end of the world itself approaches, with the reign of "the Antichrist" in the Soviet Union, the militarization of Europe and Asia, and the portentously increasing frequency of natural disasters such as earthquakes.[81] At this "tremendous hour," when "storms" of every kind threaten the very foundations of creation, Thomas counsels genuine patriots to reinvigorate the lifeline connecting them to their origins as a people.[82] Citizens must "guard the freedom that our forefathers have given to us," reestablishing America as a "Christian nation" by undergoing a national repentance.[83] Such repentance means restoring fidelity to "God and his righteous law" and resisting all idolatrous faith in "legislative enactments to regulate man's conduct"—especially laws providing for "the dole," which deprive individuals of "the joy of working," "pauperize millions of people in this country of ours," and give "free money" to the "millions of people in this country who don't want to work and who would not accept a position if they had that opportunity."[84] It also means purging from the national body those "devilish" and "evil forces" that threaten "Western," "Anglo Saxon," and "Christian civilization."[85] Finally, it means taking up arms in "the firing line" and being willing to die (and kill) to "defend . . . this great institution."[86]

How might the friction between the divergent strands within Thomas's narrative of the Christian crusade, so incompatible in both tone and substance, be dialectically deciphered as a figuration of social conflict? The Great Depression and the New Deal suggest themselves as obvious empirical reference points for a social physiognomy of these radio broadcasts. And indeed, the tension between utopian-triumphant and catastrophic-defensive narrative moments in Thomas's rhetoric expresses a fundamental tension within American society during the early New Deal. At the time of these broadcasts, the economically stabilizing effects of the Social Security Act of 1935 had not yet begun to be felt. Meanwhile, "the early work programs such as the Civilian Conservation Corps and the Works Progress Administration were interim measures designed to occupy workers until a viable labor market was restored."[87] The New Dealers had billed their agenda as a crusade to provide unprecedented guarantees that all citizens would be included in the distribution of society's economic fruits, and thus had redefined the American social contract by incorporating into it a new and utopian notion of the welfare state. But despite the vigor and optimism of Roosevelt's first hundred days, the first major components of the New Deal instituted a "patchwork welfare state" that "did not emerge from a coherent social vision," did not succeed in stimulating sufficient growth to allay fears that the economy would never recover, left millions out of work and destitute, and initiated a long-standing pattern of program administration that stigmatized the needy rather than responding to their need as a societally generated condition.[88]

In sum, the mid-1930s witnessed the ambiguous coexistence of an official ideology of utopian mission with a concrete set of elite responses to economic and political crisis that were defensive, discriminatory, and incrementalist. Thomas's radio addresses, in turn, expressed this social tension within their narrative structure through the undermining of the hopeful and forward-looking element by the catastrophic and backward-gazing element. Moreover, the speeches arguably fostered acquiescence to the culmination of the New Deal's utopian aspirations in defensive measures by virtue of that same narrative structure, in which the call to realize a transcendent sense of community was represented as congruent with the call to arms defending the tradition of authentic patriots against stigmatized outsider figures. Thomas's radio addresses certainly did nothing to make explicit their own constitutive contradictions, and thereby those of society. That is, they offered no sense that there might be social, structural impediments to the realization of a genuinely coherent vision of a "crusade for Christ." They thus remained fundamentally reactionary phenomena—but for different reasons than Adorno's own interpretation of them would lead us to suspect.

What is more, by taking seriously the claim of the agitator's speeches to be something other than they are—that is, to be an invocation of the good society rather than merely an ad campaign stressing the necessity and inevitability of authoritarian policies—we can at last feel the fleeting jolt of this cultural phenomenon's radical potentiality. The latter accrued to it in the same measure that its structural self-negation belied America's claim in the early New Deal period to be a harmonious society. This negative-utopian moment, in turn, might conceivably have helped ener- gize a critical rethinking of social theory and practice among a Depression- era American left that failed to appreciate the signs of an emerging and unprecedented solidarity in the U.S. working class. While Thomas ranted over the airwaves, America witnessed an era of general strikes in major cities and "massive violent confrontations between labor and capital." The period of the mid-1930s has been referred to as "the highwater mark of the class struggle in modern American history." Instead of disintegrat- ing into a morass of factional feuding, disorganization in the face of re- pression by capital and the state, and gravitation toward the Democratic party—and far from retreating into the hermitage of lonely nonconform- ism erected by Adorno—the left might have responded to historical cir- cumstances with a utopian crusade of its own.[89]

From the New Deal to Post-Fordism

This book seeks to define the relationship of the contemporary Christian right to the post-Fordist political economy. It formulates the significance of the new Christian right with respect to those social conditions that have supplanted the Fordist regime of accumulation, regulation, and labor organization that defused and postponed the class struggle of the early twentieth century. The writings discussed in this chapter supply three clear and different models for carrying out this task. The Thomas study throws light on the outlines of yet a fourth approach.

Following Lowenthal and Guterman, we might consider analyzing the new Christian right as a vehicle for disseminating ruling-class ideology, a mechanism that works by provoking "irrationalism" and resentment among evangelical conservatives. Although the dubious distinction be- tween "rational" and "irrational" politics would be an unfortunate inheri- tance from *Prophets of Deceit*, there is still an element of truth in the claims of those who, like Frances Fox Piven, see the new Christian right's ascendancy since the mid-1970s as "the rise of irrational politics":

When people are blocked from dealing with the problems of liveli- hood, community, respect, and security through politics, they be- come more susceptible to fundamentalist appeals. When institutional reforms seem impossible, frustrated publics are more likely to respond to calls for a politics of individual moral rejuvenation, typically coupled with calls to mobilize against some vulnerable group.[90]

Piven argues that the scapegoating of welfare recipients signals "the failure of political leaders, Democrats and Republicans alike, to articulate rational solutions to the economic hardships and insecurities that dominate the popular mood."[91] Blaming the mythical "welfare queen" substitutes for policies that would redress the actual causes of widely experienced economic decline in the United States: the recent and successful onslaught against labor and restructuring of the state by organized capital. To an extent, Piven is right. But must we assume that either Christian right culture or evangelical conservatives themselves are uniformly "irrational" in their responses to social conditions? Might not their relationship to the social totality be a good deal more complicated than Piven allows?

Alternatively, we could follow the lead of Adorno et al. in *The Authoritarian Personality* and approach evangelical conservatism as a psychological malady that bears the mark of historical conditions. Randall Balmer moves toward such a view when he characterizes the "reliance on rigid, legalistic morality" and other key aspects of contemporary evangelicalism as a form of "sustained adolescence":

> No stage of life is more prone to hero worship than adolescence. An adolescent is strongly influenced by group conformity and the expectations of other people; it's a stage in which self-consciousness is at its height. "I see the evangelicals' penchant for gazing inward to assess their own spirituality as a heightened form of self-consciousness," [one unusually reflective evangelical preacher] said. "They're constantly comparing themselves to the standards of spiritual behavior they've established and asking 'How am I doing?' and 'Am I good enough?' and 'How do I appear to others?'" Spiritual appearances are very important to evangelicals, just as an adolescent spends a lot of time in front of the mirror.
>
> Adolescence is also a period of rebellion, a search for individuality, identifying yourself in opposition to authority—feeling on the one hand that you have to submit to authority and on the other hand chafing under it and wishing you could be your own boss. "My instinct is that evangelicals don't love God very much, that they relate to God the way a child or an adolescent relates to an authority figure."[92]

The vocabulary here is not Freudian, but the methodological implication of this argument closely parallels that of Adorno and his colleagues: that evangelical conservatives tend to display a distinctive personality type, and a distinctly regressive one at that. Of course, the Adornian moment missing from Balmer's musings is the relation of the individual personality structure to the structure of society, such that the prolonged adolescence of evangelical conservatives would become a figure for retrogressive social tendencies. Still, Balmer's account provides a step in this direction. But Balmer's own record of his experiences with widely varying elements of the American evangelical subculture testifies to the reality that these believers cannot be easily pigeonholed with regard to their creeds, moral values, politics, or personalities. And even if a specific personality structure were characteristic of most adherents of the Christian right, might it not exhibit contradictions problematizing the assumption that its political disposition would always favor right-wing authoritarianism?

The Thomas study poses the possibility of charting the Christian right's relationship to post-Fordism along the lines demarcated by the theory of the culture industry. At the same time, the Thomas study hints at the prospect of interpreting Christian right media culture with the assistance of social physiognomy, seeking contradictions within the cultural object that express the contradictions of the social totality and perhaps contest the latter as well. Alone among the various approaches summarized here, such a critique offers the hope of enabling social theory to become self-reflective or, to put it in Adorno's terms, of igniting negative-dialectical thinking.

Changing sociohistorical conditions since the World War II and postwar eras, however, may have altered the terms on which Adorno's theory can be appropriated for the criticism of Christian right culture today. The theory of the culture industry was intended to describe the fate of culture within a historically specific political-economic system. Under Fordist conditions (1) open class conflict was prevented by state planning and administration, labor's disavowal of radicalism, and capital's guarantee of high wages and stable employment; (2) the labor process was organized in ways oriented toward the mass production of standardized commodities, including especially the linking of wages to precisely defined tasks and seniority, the application of Taylorist principles by management, and the strict segregation of mental (or skilled) and physical (or semiskilled) labor; (3) economic growth was predicated on high demand for consumer durables among the general population in the most industrialized countries, organized as stable and predictable markets for mass quantities of standardized commodities; (4) capital underwent a phase of material expansion (or an epoch of "continuous change" requiring extensive investment in fixed capital goods), as opposed to a finance-led expansion (or a period of "discontinuous change" when investment is concentrated in money capital); (5) the U.S. political, economic, and military hegemony in the West, and eventually the cold war balance of power globally, minimized international economic competition and ensured relative political stability worldwide.[93] Adorno and Horkheimer's thesis was that these rigidities of mass production, mass consumption, "administrated" class struggle, capital investment, and international order were to a great extent secured by the planning, regimentation, and standardization of culture. In turn, social physiognomy as a method of cultural criticism received its commission from these same social conditions, inasmuch as they replaced the competitive market's mediation of culture with administrated culture and thereby divested cultural objects of their claims to autonomy.

Given the dramatic changes in political-economic life since the early 1970s, can a historical basis still be identified on which a redeployment and rethinking of social physiognomy and the culture industry theory today make sense? Let us briefly review these changes. (1) The fiscal and legitimation crises of states, capital's decreasing profitability and organizational restructuring, the steadily diminishing power of unions, and declining wages and job security have yielded newly antagonistic and polarized class relations. (2) Taylorist production methods and specifically defined job roles have given way to "flexible specialization" among more privileged workers and more brutal forms of exploitation among the less well situated. (3) Policies for stimulating broad demand for consumer durables have been succeeded by corporate "niche marketing" of specialized commodities and the intensified targeting of state subsidies to middle- and upper-class constituencies. (4) The world economy has entered into a new phase of financial expansion, nullifying many commitments to economic stability and security associated with the prior material expansion. (5) All of the above trends have been magnified by a more competitive international economy and the new obscurity of global political relations.[94] What, then, are the implications of these political-economic shifts for cultural criticism that hopes to retrieve something of present value from Adorno?

The answer hinges on whether the transition to post-Fordism mitigates or aggravates the danger that culture is losing its claim to autonomy from political and economic necessity. And on this issue, no conclusive or unequivocal judgment is possible at the moment. On the one hand, we might reasonably have some confidence that the freedom of culture from "administration" will increase, given (1) the state's steps toward the deregulation of industry, the reduction of welfare state services, and, in the United States, the defunding of the arts and public broadcasting; (2) the resurgence of "free market" ideology among major party leaders and in public opinion; (3) the evident lack of fit between an old model of cultural tastes oriented toward a limited number of stereotyped images and goods and a post-Fordist economy that depends on greater eclecticism and multi-culturalism in consumption habits; (4) the failure thus far of efforts to bring into being modes of international regulation functionally comparable to those exercised by individual nation-states and the United States during the Fordist era. On the other hand, the following considerations lead to the opposite conclusion: that the autonomy of culture is at least as precarious under post-Fordism as under previous Fordist conditions. (1) Although the state's form of cooperation with capital is being renegotiated, the state is not necessarily being disempowered in absolute terms, as the continued exorbitant levels of military expenditure and the expansion of police and prison institutions illustrate. (2) Ideological neoliberalism and neoconservatism have been accompanied not by a return to nineteenth-century conditions of capitalist competition but rather by an unprecedented concentration of capital through mergers and acquisitions, notably in the cultural industries. (3) Planning for more specialized and volatile markets is still planning, and with the tremendous growth of the advertising industry it is arguable that scientific marketing has become more influential than ever before. (4) The high premium that "flexible accumulation" strategies place on information has led to a situation in which "capitalism is becoming ever more tightly organized *through* dispersal, geographical mobility, and flexible responses in labour markets, labour processes, and consumer markets." In particular, the acceleration of international financial trading to ever more breathless paces has gone hand in hand with "the emergence of greatly enhanced powers of financial co-ordination," even if such coordination depends less now than previously on state power.[95]

Thus there is as much or more reason to fear that culture's instrumentalization marches on under post-Fordism just as it did in the Fordist era, even if its step is timed to a more eccentric drumbeat. This means that elements of the theory of the culture industry might still illuminate domination-reinforcing aspects of Christian right culture today, just as it aided Adorno in his interpretation of Martin Luther Thomas's radio addresses, even though the broad thesis that the culture industry's mass production of consciousness ensures compliance with mass production in the labor process no longer has as much currency as it did a half century ago. In addition, the culture industry theory maintains its interest and applicability to the degree that Fordist structures of production, consumption, regulation, and accumulation remain in effect despite the far-reaching changes described above. And there is indeed much agreement among political economists that Fordist practices continue to shape life in certain key domains of the domestic and international economy, such as the military industries.[96]

More importantly, the current political economy provides plenty of impetus for the mission to rescue culture's negative-utopianism from the confines of instrumentalist control, in the spirit of Adorno's social physiognomy. Now, as before, only culture that preserves a claim to autonomy from political and economic necessity has the potential to lend a self-critical capacity to social theory. And now, perhaps even more than before, structural developments in the social totality threaten the cultural object's disingenuous yet emancipatory protestation of its worth in and for itself.

As the above sketch of a dialectical criticism of Martin Luther Thomas's radio addresses suggests, however, how social physiognomy conceptualizes the contradictions in the cultural object and in society may need to change in light of the peculiarities of its object. The main issue here is the precise nature of the hermeneutic guiding immanent criticism. Where does one look to find the formal structure of a Christian right radio program, a structure not reducible to a mélange of techniques adapted from the culture industry at large? If formal composition implies confrontation with a process by which culture undergoes historical development (as Schoenberg, for example, grappled with the evolution of modern music), then where does Christian right radio face history and what specific historical trajectory does it encounter?

Answers to these questions cannot be found through any a priori logic. They require the sustained study of specific phenomena within Christian right organized culture. Still, the experimental social physiognomy of Thomas's rhetoric above suggests that the solution might have something important to do with religious narrative. Perhaps Adorno greatly exaggerated when he dismissed religion as mere garnish on the "administrated world," a trick of the light deployed by manipulative admen. Maybe, today as in Thomas's era, religious narrative instead furnishes the core themes, rhythms, and character types that give Christian right media phenomena qualities of aesthetic wholeness, integrality, and historical groundedness. And perhaps religious narrative secures these objects' claims to autonomy and thereby enables their reflection and reproduction—and negative-utopian contestation—of the contradictions of post-Fordism.

3

Christian Professionals and the Fraying
Fabric of Health and Human Services

No one is forgotten; everywhere there are neighbors and welfare workers, Dr. Gillespies and parlor philosophers whose hearts are in the right place and who, by their kind, person-to-person intervention, make curable individual cases out of socially-perpetuated miseries—so long as there is no obstacle in the personal depravity of the unfortunate. . . . By emphasizing the "heart of gold," society confesses to the suffering it has created.—Max Horkheimer and Theodor W. Adorno, *Dialectic of Enlightenment*, 1944

The collapse of the Fordist compact among capital, labor, and the state has rendered the future of the American welfare state highly indeterminate. The return of the Democrats to executive power in the 1990s did not bring a reversal of the cutbacks and reorganizations initiated in the Reagan-Bush years. To the contrary, in a policy move that symbolized the structural changes underway, the Clinton administration ended the federal entitlement to financial assistance for poor families with dependent children that had been in place since 1935. And despite widespread discontent with a wasteful, costly, and inequitable health care system, the state's attempts to achieve reforms in this area have yielded only the most marginal adjustments. The call to replace statist solutions to poverty and other social problems with citizens' voluntary efforts, a leading theme under the Reagan, Bush, and Clinton administrations alike, further indicates that the imperatives imposed by post-Fordism have shaped recent public policy in ways that transcend partisan differences.

Although the state's commitment to social welfare programs has grown increasingly tenuous, a new sort of welfarism has emerged in a place where we might not expect to see it: in certain quarters of the Christian right.

Evangelical churches have traditionally been less oriented toward social mission than Catholic and mainline Protestant churches, in part because of their more individualist theologies and norms.[1] Yet with the help of publicity provided by leading Christian right media institutions like Focus on the Family, a new crop of programs and services aimed at meeting human needs has sprung up within the evangelical subculture. Scholars and the media have devoted much attention to the Christian right's mobilization of electoral and lobbying groups, including most prominently the Moral Majority and the Christian Coalition. But they have largely missed the simultaneous proliferation of Christian right agencies "ministering" to people in various unfortunate circumstances.

Focus on the Family has advanced many of these efforts through the nationwide distribution of its radio broadcasts, publications, and videotapes as well as a call-in counseling and referral service. From the topological height of its headquarters near Pikes Peak, Colorado, Focus acts as a national (indeed, global) force of steering and coordination for an increasingly dense network of local agencies spread over much of the country. Focus's founder and president James Dobson emblematizes this quasi-welfarist face of the Christian right. Dobson conveys the public persona of a compassionate, evangelical professional: he appears to be motivated by Christ's example of universal love; to draw on specialized training, thus providing effective aid in a modern society; and to exercise leadership within a vast and growing community of people of goodwill dedicated to helping those in need. The daily radio talk show by which Dobson is best known to millions of ordinary people, *Focus on the Family*, features a steady stream of guests who present themselves in similar ways.

The above quotation from *Dialectic of Enlightenment* points toward the possibility that testimonies and exhibitions of compassionate professionalism on *Focus on the Family* may not be simply, or at all, benign demonstrations of Christian good-neighborism. Adorno and Horkheimer's point is that the culture industry reifies historically rooted (and therefore avoidable) suffering, making it seem to be simultaneously a natural and inevitable feature of human existence and a condition that is thoroughly regulated and controlled by society. The stereotype of the "heart of gold" in the culture industry, they maintain, is cut from the same historical cloth as the burgeoning apparatus of scientific "human resource" management in corporate personnel departments, and of the welfare state. State capitalism itself thus comes to appear as an immutable order of things, and the ideology of person-to-person goodwill serves to justify the liquidation of authentic individuality and the perpetuation of suffering.

The welfare state is in decline today, but personnel management certainly is not—indeed, it is one occupation that has demonstrated continued expansion with the onset of post-Fordism, partly to facilitate the "adjustments" demanded by new systems of "flexible specialization" and diminished job security. Nor, in turn, has the stereotypical figure of the "heart of gold" vanished from U.S. media culture. If anything, television and radio abound as never before with this stereotype, with the explosion of talk shows in the 1990s. Recent trends in political advertising, too, have made this type more central than ever in the mainstream media. Ronald Reagan was highly popular even among many who disagreed with his policies because, the common refrain went, at least his "heart was in the right place." As Lawrence Grossberg argues, Reagan connected with voters more because he seemed to care deeply about certain things than because citizens shared his substantive commitments.[2] And Bill Clinton has fashioned the quivering lip and empathetic tear into a major motif of his image, a motif highlighted when that image was refunctioned in the best-seller and movie versions of *Primary Colors*.[3]

Given this wider context, it is arguable that *Focus on the Family*'s propagation of the "heart of gold" in the personae of Dobson and his guests ideologically supports post-Fordism in the manner suggested by the culture industry theory. If "neighbors and welfare workers" are energized as never before to help their fellows, then isn't it obvious that those who suffer are either bound to be taken care of or are so depraved as to be beyond hope of assistance? And if the evidence is all around that individuals' and local communities' efforts to reach out to people in need are bearing abundant fruit, then why not simply accept the neo-individualist and communitarian paeans to "flex-spec," along with the blunt pronouncements that welfare state programs "just don't work"? Such would be the intrepid logic of Christian right radio qua culture industry. As culture industry—through the manipulative dissemination of stereotyped figures geared toward the implantation of an acquiescent and critically dull conformism—*Focus on the Family* ensures the obedience of the people to their new masters. The latter are no longer the postwar "experts" of social planning, now discredited along with Aid to Families with Dependent Children and proposals for universal health care, but rather the wizards of global finance and the prophets of corporate downsizing.

This analysis contains a basic element of truth. For all its much-publicized outrage against the Disney corporation and other strongholds of mainstream commercial culture, the Christian right's media culture stylistically often resembles the latter quite closely. And as Adorno and Horkheimer point out, features of style can bear the most fundamentally decisive mechanisms of ideology. *Focus on the Family* clearly exercises an instrumental function within the Christian right as a social movement by explicitly promoting certain leaders, activities, and policy positions.

Adorno and Horkheimer help us see the program's instrumentality to the political economy more generally.

But what if we were to consider seriously the claim of *Focus on the Family* to stand apart from the necessities involved in the self-reproduction of the social totality (and, more narrowly, the mobilization of the Christian right)—to take it seriously, that is, not with the goal of evaluating the subjective intentions of Dobson and his fellows but rather in anticipation that this claim might in part define the program's historical significance? Dobson and his guests present themselves as agents of transformation, liberation, and renewal for society and individuals alike. They do this by invoking several versions of a traditional narrative living at the very core of American evangelical Protestantism: the narrative of personal salvation. Moreover, their communication in and through this narrative addresses two problems that the narrative has frequently attempted to solve: the status of the individual's spiritual and ethical autonomy with respect to her salvation, and the relationship between individual salvation and the redemption of society. In other words, by speaking with the terms furnished by the evangelical salvation narrative, Dobson and other spokespersons on *Focus on the Family* establish the program as part of a historical tradition. They thereby endow the broadcasts with a distinctive form that is both historically rooted and characterized by a structural wholeness and integrality. Precisely these features make it conceivable that a social physiognomy of the program could be developed, in a manner analogous to the procedure advanced by Adorno. By conceptualizing the narrative contradictions of *Focus on the Family* as structurally related "antinomies" of "the object's moments" rather than as discrete tools within a kit of "devices" for psychological and political control, dialectical criticism might show that the program expresses certain contradictions in the social totality. The constitutive tensions of *Focus on the Family* might even reserve a small stock of negative-utopian energy, enabling them not only to reflect but also (weakly) to contest social antagonisms. Radical cultural and political activists should not be indifferent to this ingredient, however minor, in Christian right culture. So suggests the reasoning of Adorno's theory of social physiognomy, and so counsels the closer examination of *Focus on the Family*'s figure of the compassionate professional.

Boosting the "Slow Learner"

Dobson first achieved a national reputation as a specialist in the psychology of child development. One standard format of *Focus on the Family* has Dobson simply expound on a particular topic in child psychology over the course of several broadcasts, uninterrupted except for the occasional interjections of cohost Mike Trout.[4] Dobson has produced series of this sort on marriage ("Love Must Be Tough"), child discipline ("Dare to Discipline"), and assorted issues faced by parents ("Parenting Isn't for Cowards"). Even though the most recently produced shows are more likely to experiment with diverse formats, Focus periodically reruns episodes from these and other series. Dobson's public persona as a compassionate, Christian professional—the very embodiment of the "heart of gold"—comes through with particular clarity in these shows. It is thus useful to begin with some examples from them in formulating a sense of the characteristic features and narrative elements at play in the composition of this figure, which ultimately proves to be far more complex than any mere stereotype.

Introducing a three-broadcast series on "human intelligence," Dobson announces that he and Trout will pay special attention to "the classic underachiever," "the intellectually disabled child," and "raising your child's IQ."[5] While Trout commences the discussion in an objectivistic vein, explaining that the program deals with "questions such as 'How do we think?' or 'What facilitates learning?'" Dobson immediately modulates the tone of the broadcast by adding what sounds like a moral commitment to helping the less fortunate. This initial interchange sets a pattern that is repeated throughout the broadcast series. Trout's comments periodically create opportunities for Dobson to contrast his own appreciation and compassion for "underachievers'" needs to society's devaluation and ridicule of them. For instance, Trout ashamedly admits that "as a parent, I suppose I could be accused of comparing my children to other children at various times" and adds that "one of the areas where all parents are guilty of comparison is intelligence and how well their children learn."[6] In effect, this statement and others like it function as cues for Dobson to reiterate his concern for children of average and below-average intelligence, as measured by conventional means like IQ tests, and to denounce the "elitism which holds that bright kids are worthy and valuable and slow learners or ordinary children are less valuable."[7]

The cumulative effect of such comments is to generate the sense that Dobson's love for the unfortunate knows no limits, that he holds dear those whom the world despises in a way that seems intentionally to follow the example of Christ as depicted in the Gospels. Dobson's patience and compassion seem especially vivid when he describes his internship at Pacific State Hospital for "mentally retarded" children. Dobson recalls being mobbed by a frenzy of love-starved children on entering the hospital each day:

> There would be 30 or 40 or 50 children who were 8 years of age, and I would step onto that ward and here they would come, just screaming

"Daddy! Daddy! Daddy!" and press me from all sides, until they would nearly knock me down. Because in many cases the parents who have handicapped children like this feel so guilty about it that they sometimes don't visit them as often as they ought to and those children are starved for emotional support. And as I say, I developed a real soft spot in my heart for youngsters who go through this difficulty.[8]

To the evangelical listener who is well schooled in the Bible, these remarks are bound to bring to mind the image of Jesus surrounded and "pressed from all sides" by the sick and lame who clamor for his healing touch. Trout responds by musing: "One of the greatest examples of unconditional love can be seen in the expressions of a mentally retarded child." But it is clearly Dobson himself whom the conversation most pointedly paints as the bearer of Christlike, "unconditional love," and whose compassion for the hospital's wards is not diminished in the least by their incessant and unfulfillable demands on him.

In contrast to Jesus, however, Dobson's fervor for helping others is complemented by scientific expertise and professional status. Dobson sprinkles his remarks with medical jargon, conveying his thorough knowledge of neurology. At Trout's behest, Dobson relates his involvement in a study by "15 major medical centers" of phenylketonuria, a metabolic disorder that can cause brain damage, and describes the physiological etiology of the disease in minute detail. Dobson and Trout also take up the topic of memory several times during the series, and this gives Dobson several occasions to demonstrate the breadth and complementarity of his studies in physical anatomy and psychology. For instance, he explains that memory is formed when "information" is "coded" onto the end of a neuron, telling that cell "when to fire and when not to fire." Memory "blocking" occurs when an individual lacks sufficient "confidence and emotional security": "emotional stress . . . changes the chemistry in that little gap called a synapse between the cells, and the spark is unable to jump the gap. In order for the brain to work properly, it's a matter of timing."[9] Dobson seems well versed in the professional literature of medicine and psychology. He explicitly bases his advice for the parents of "slow learners" on the results of the "Harvard pre-school study," a 1965–1975 research project that Dobson claims identified "the environmental factors that seem to correlate most with future intellectual ability" for children. Reviewing each of the six factors that the study regards as decisive influences on the development of children's intelligence, Dobson emphasizes Harvard scholars' confirmation of the vital importance of mothering. This leads him into a diatribe against feminists: by valorizing women's employment, he claims, feminists foolishly ignore children's scientifically demonstrated needs for constant maternal care. They also fail to see that traditional "mother love" is something that "God built into" the mother-child relationship: "You can . . . see the wisdom of Scripture in the findings" from the Harvard study, Dobson declares.[10] The key point here, though, is that Dobson does not rely only on a moral-religious argument about what is right or wrong to justify his support for traditional motherhood. Instead, he disputes the research employed by feminist scholars and insists that "the data are clear" regarding the impossibility of adequately substituting for constant maternal care—"those are the *facts*, Mike," he concludes.[11] Dobson thus embodies a figure of Christian compassion in which the elements of Christlike love and professional-scientific expertise are of equal significance.

What we see here are the basic outlines of a distinctive narrative regarding the demonstration of Christian compassion. Focus builds on the biblical narrative of Jesus' supreme selflessness and awe-inspiring concern for others, a narrative developed through parables like that of the Good Samaritan and stories of Jesus' work among the poor, ill, and outcast. And inasmuch as these biblical stories are meant to illustrate the path of salvation, Focus's narrative likewise takes on the character of a redemption narrative. But Focus's story modulates the traditional material by incorporating the sense that scientific expertise and professional position are, or can be, integral to Christian compassion and salvation. This narrative not only defines what Christian compassion is but does so in a way that discloses the proper relationship between personal salvation and the historical development of society. For it implies that the crucial sources of social power and knowledge in modernity harmonize perfectly with the Christian life. It moreover posits the coherence of socialization and achievement according to modern, scientific-professional norms with the ethical autonomy of the individual believer who perceives biblical examples of compassion and resolves to "go and do likewise."

But while Focus's narrative of the compassionate professional attempts to hold together these different pieces without any rupture or inconsistency, tensions among them eventually surface. Dobson's representation of personal salvation, societal redemption, and divine command as a flawlessly cohesive whole ultimately belies the insinuation that Dobson exemplifies a love from which none are excluded. For it becomes clear during the broadcast series that certain people are indeed situated beyond what appears to be the legitimate purview of compassion, and that the compassionate professional's extension of service has more to do with the maintenance of boundaries than the concrete ministry to human needs. Meanwhile, the ethical autonomy that seems fundamental to Dobson's self-presentation as a compassionate professional gradually dissolves.

When Dobson discusses memory, for example, anatomical traits, social conventions, and God's intentions combine to constitute a seamless totality that tolerates compassion only within its sharply defined limits. As we have seen, Dobson's explication of the physiology of memory leads him into a discussion that affirms "mother love" as a norm that is both validated by scientific research and mandated by divine law. Dobson concludes these remarks by insisting ominously that "you can't go messing with that without creating some major problems for that individual child and for the culture. . . . that is the way the system was designed, and guess who designed it!"[12] The sense here is that people fall into two binarily opposed groups: one either fits into or is rejected by the "system." And indeed, the rejection of those who do not meet the "system's" requirements is total. First of all, it is spiritual: Dobson implies that the child whose brain receives insufficient or improper "stimulation" (meaning inadequate mothering) may well be sentenced to eternal damnation. Recalling a research project showing that all experiences are "locked" into the brain's anatomy and can be fully remembered when proper stimuli are applied to the brain, Dobson concludes:

> When the Bible says that we're accountable for every idle word, every thought and deed and so on, that it's all written down—it's written in your *brain* as well as in *heaven*, and nothing is ever really lost. That's why it's so important that we do pay attention to experiences that a child has—not that you can eliminate every difficult moment, and he even profits from some of those, but he may *look* like he isn't aware that they're going on—believe me, he's not only aware of it but it's being *stored* there, and it will have some influence on him.[13]

When Dobson refers to the inscription of words and deeds "in heaven" and to individuals' "accountability" for those words and deeds, he suggests that children whose mothers do not properly care for them are more susceptible to immorality and thus condemnation by God. Dobson thus welds biology, society, and the unseen realm into a single chain of order: disruption of "normal" physiological processes through transgression against cultural tradition ultimately leads to spiritual evil and divine retribution.[14]

The seamlessness of this unified order, moreover, makes it logically necessary that the ostracism of those who contradict the principles of order not be delayed until the afterlife but manifest itself in this life as well. This logical necessity explains the significance of a number of key interludes in Dobson's narrative, in which Dobson characterizes individuals whose life experiences are at odds with those that are supposed to follow from the smooth functioning of the cosmic order. Each anecdote involves the representation of children whose intellectual capacities are physiologically damaged and whose mothers do not care for them sufficiently. In every case, the image of the child that the tale evokes has a repulsive quality that sharply undercuts the story's compassionate tone. Ultimately, these anecdotes do not so much provoke compassion for the victim as confirm that the individual is doomed to remain an "outsider" in relation to the "system" of physical, social, and spiritual order.

Notwithstanding Dobson's professed "soft spot" for developmentally disabled children, his description of the "screaming" mobs who repeatedly nearly knocked him to the floor of Pacific State Hospital depicts these children in an unsympathetic and threatening manner. The "unconditional love" that Trout attributes to them seems out of control and dangerous. Undertones of Trout's remark, furthermore, convey that these children are fundamentally not like other people. Dobson criticizes parents who do not visit their institutionalized children, but it seems nonetheless that these children's separation from their parents is inevitable—perhaps even necessary for the parents' own protection.

Along with the developmentally disabled, the poor are cast as "outsiders" and stranded beyond the boundaries of the compassionate professional's quasi-mechanical cosmic order. Noting that proper mental stimulation in early childhood activates "enzyme systems" that cannot be "turned on" beyond a certain age, Dobson continues:

> This is believed to be at least part of the reason that children raised in a very impoverished environment, perhaps a ghetto setting where children are not stimulated—they may not be talked to very much, and not held very much, and not exposed to a lot of adult conversation, and so their brains don't have that kind of stimulation—those youngsters, it is believed, will forevermore be *different*, will be less capable than they might have been for having gone through that flat time, that unstimulating time, during this critical period.[15]

The interchange that immediately follows identifies "ghetto" children as "different" from "normal" children by linking the former with "mentally retarded" children, whose "otherness" Dobson has already established:

> Trout: You wrote about this a number of years ago in your first published book, a graduate textbook that perhaps most of our listeners aren't aware of. Has much changed since then?
> Dobson: That book was called *The Mentally Retarded Child and His Family*.[16]

Like the developmentally disabled, moreover, "environmentally disabled" children are "different" in a menacing way that counteracts the implication that these children deserve compassion. Dobson's prior reference to a psychology experiment studying the effects of sensory deprivation on brain activity has already alerted the listener to the effects of insufficient mental stimulation:

> The brain starts to unravel under these circumstances. They begin to hallucinate, they see pink elephants and bananas with eyes and ears on it, they see weird things. They not only think weird things but they see them, you begin to actually hallucinate, you begin to see and hear things that do not exist. . . . the mind will generate input one way or the other. If it doesn't come from the outside, it'll resort to its own resources.[17]

Dobson's listeners know from other broadcasts that "ghetto" children have plenty of "outside resources" to help them "hallucinate" besides their spontaneous imaginings. Here, Dobson inspires fear of "ghetto" children by suggesting that they use drugs to fill the void left by irresponsible mothers, which means having criminal and antisocial tendencies (again, in the context of other editions of *Focus on the Family*).[18] For Dobson, "ghetto" children thus are prone to live in a world isolated from everything that really "exists," and the supposed fact that these individuals are both spatially and intellectually unreachable seriously compromises Dobson's message of sympathy.

The most distressing anecdote in this broadcast series concerns a girl whose parents "severely abused" and neglected her for the first thirteen years of her life. According to Dobson, the parents imprisoned their daughter in a "back room" of their house, often forcing her to sleep tied down and sitting on a toilet. Dobson describes his work with this girl after she was discovered and brought to Children's Hospital:

> Well, it was very hard for that child, even at 13 or 14 years of age, to make up for that lost time. She may have had a normal brain, a normal potential for intellectual functioning, at birth. But by the time we found her, she couldn't *accept* love, she couldn't *give* love—but there were also certain *concepts* that seemed to be totally beyond her. I haven't heard about the follow-up, I haven't heard what's happened to her since then—one of the staff members took her into his home and actually either adopted her or made her very much a part of his family—but he talked about the *gap* that was there intellectually, that you just couldn't get past.[19]

Dobson uses this anecdote to demonstrate the validity of the Harvard study's conclusion that healthy intellectual development requires that children be given "free access to the living areas of the home." The story fails to do this convincingly, however, because it presents a case of such extreme divergence from the imputed norm. Ultimately, the story functions less as a compelling confirmation of Dobson's scientific theory than as a means of evoking a sense of the radical alterity and horror of the world of "outsiders" in relation to the unified, cosmic system of order. Dobson's remarks gesture once more toward compassion when he praises his fellow staff member for treating the child warmly. Nevertheless, Dobson has already established that such compassion will have no effect on the girl, who is capable of neither offering nor receiving love. Dobson's comment on her debilitation in this emotional and spiritual sense seems out of place in the context of the cause-and-effect relation he posits between "free access" to living spaces and intellectual development. Yet this comment is perhaps the most important element of the story, because it completes the totalized contrast between the physical, social, and spiritual characteristics of the godly cosmic order and the features of this order's demonic counterworld where the abused child is condemned to remain even after her mistreatment ends.

Even those who are classified as insiders according to this cosmic schema, however, do not receive the benefits promised by the compassionate professional. Dobson simultaneously offers and withholds genuine assistance. Dobson and Trout periodically remind the listener that the series addresses "raising your child's IQ." In fact, however, Dobson never recommends how to improve children's intelligence but rather describes how to prevent children's failure to reach a genetically (and divinely) destined level of intelligence. Moreover, Dobson ultimately dismisses the Harvard study's conclusions as superfluous, saying that his advice really comes down to the simple mandate to "do what God intended," which means for women to fulfill the role of the traditional mother.[20] To be sure, Dobson's fetishlike invocation of Harvard, along with his pointed review of his own publication record and experience as a medical educator, serve to legitimate his own and other professionals' positions within the system of godly authority. Nevertheless, for insiders and outsiders alike, the intervention of the compassionate professional on *Focus on the Family* anchors the addressee's relationship to the monolithic structure of natural, social, and spiritual authority, rather than furnishing the promised, concrete aid.

Focus's narrative of the compassionate professional thus profoundly contradicts itself. On the one hand, Dobson offers an example of salvation through the extension of limitless, effective, and freely given compassion to all who need it, especially those who need it most. On the other hand, the related images of the screaming developmentally disabled child, the hallucinating ghetto kid, and the loveless abuse victim congeal into the appalling visage of a being that simply cannot fit into the natural-social-divine continuum. And this forsaken entity seems inevitably to be the offspring of women who abandon the responsibilities of traditional motherhood. The universal, wondrous compassion of Christ gives way to the segregation of outsiders from insiders according to a family's acceptance or rejection of this fundamentalist value. Indeed, as a whole, this alternative countenance of the compassionate professional might usefully be termed a "fundamentalist" aspect, for it displays not only the substantive patriarchalism of American Protestant fundamentalism but moreover the latter's binarizing tendencies in matters of identity and belief.[21] In conformity with these tendencies, in turn, the subject of salvation abandons ethical autonomy and takes up the task of policing the universal order, of continually reinforcing this order's boundaries and reestablishing insider and outsider identities.

The main point here is not to pass judgment on the genuineness of Focus on the Family's offer of compassionate aid to its listeners. Clearly, Dobson's self-presentation as the consummate Christian good neighbor is not to be taken merely at face value. Yet appreciating the features of this aspect of Focus's compassionate professional, and acknowledging its abiding contradiction with this figure's other, more foreboding, fundamentalist countenance, are vital to understanding the basic narrative form active in the broadcasts. In turn, grasping this narrative form yields the prospect of discerning the social physiognomy of the series, as Adorno's theory suggests: that is, of reading the narrative contradictions of Dobson's broadcasts as reflecting, reinforcing, and possibly contesting sociohistorical contradictions. (Again, note the difference between this way of interpreting the politics of Focus on the Family and the route suggested by the culture industry theory, which would direct attention primarily to the apparatus of production and distribution while treating the program's content simply as an assemblage of advertising gimmicks.) Before moving into this dialectical mode, however, let us fill out the immanent criticism of the phenomenon by examining several additional episodes of Focus on the Family. For here we are dealing with a narrative that provides the basic, formal structure for a great many of Focus's broadcasts, a refrain that makes each one intelligible in much the same way regardless of differences in subject matter, rather than a story that is told just once.

Fighting "False Memory Syndrome"

Regular listeners to Focus on the Family understand well that despite Dobson's unique status as a cultural leader, the show's host remains just one of many compassionate, Christian professionals in the evangelical subculture. Indeed, Focus on the Family actively cultivates the sense that Dobson and his guests belong to a broad-based, community-spirited movement of people spreading healing care throughout society. Participation in the beloved community thus frequently complements the elements of ethical autonomy and universal compassion in the most immediately apparent, the most spontaneously perceptible salvation narrative in episodes of *Focus on the Family* that feature the compassionate professional.

Each of these aspects of the compassionate professional's salvation narrative appears in the broadcast series on "false memory syndrome." For these editions of *Focus on the Family*, evangelical psychologists Paul Meier, Paul Simpson, and David Gatewood join Dobson in the studio. Dobson begins by defining "false memory syndrome":

> This is a kind of general category of problems that are related to a person, perhaps with the help of a therapist or a psychologist or psychiatrist, who may have been [*sic*] so-called "regressed" to an earlier time of life; and they remember abuse, they remember *murder*, they remember *terrible* things that happened in their early childhood that they feel they have forgotten, they have repressed. And then, with the help of this therapist, it all comes out—then, of course, what next? Well, you go accuse the people that you think *did* those terrible things and you can imagine the shock, you can imagine the pain and the sorrow and the grief and the embarrassment that goes with that circumstance, when those parents or those others *didn't really do it!*[22]

This discussion among Dobson and his guests takes the form of a muckraking exposure of psychologists who employ "regression therapy," an ostensibly fraudulent technique that leads patients to think they remember real, traumatic events when in fact these "memories" have only arisen because of the therapist's suggestive remarks. Although the speakers note that actual cases of child sexual abuse and satanic "ritual abuse" do occur, they express particular concern for families that have been traumatized by "false accusations" stemming from "false memories." Meier propounds the benefits of "insight-oriented therapy," or therapy that operates wholly "on a conscious level" and only deals with memories that are "specific" and "verifiable" as opposed to vague recollections for which no evidence can be marshaled. They discuss several examples of families in which daughters have wrongfully accused their parents of satanic "ritual abuse" or incest. And Dobson bemoans "the pain and the sorrow and the grief" these parents feel—experiences, he notes, that are generally ignored in a culture where it is assumed that "everybody is a victim." Dobson emphasizes that Focus has spent many months preparing this broadcast series to ensure that the "facts" were presented in an accurate, objective manner: "We waited six months or longer to do this program, because I didn't want to give an excuse to those who *have* abused their children. I didn't want to not *hear* those who had been abused and make them feel like we're saying, 'you're lying.' But there's another *side* to it, and that's that there's another *victim*, the adult who's been accused of horrible things they didn't do."[23] Dobson and his guests thus cast their remarks on "false memory syndrome" as an effort to provide balance, moderation, and solid information in a public discussion dominated, Simpson claims, by the self-serving political agendas of "a very radical feminist element," a broad "new age" contingent, and regrettably even some "conservative caring Christians" who are obsessed with satanic cults. Together, they contend, these strange bedfellows have allowed "regression therapists" to escape accountability for their manipulative and harmful practices.[24]

Like their host, Meier, Simpson, and Gatewood present themselves as compassionate Christians with professional, scientific credentials. Dobson and his guests premise their discussion on a moral commitment to exposing and redressing the plight of a group of "victims" whose hardships go unnoticed by society. These individuals above all include parents who have been unjustly accused of abusing their children, as well as children who have fallen under the sway of "regressionism" propagated by quack psychologists. Still, the speakers stress that their concern also extends to children who have actually been abused. As in Dobson's solo series on children's intelligence, moreover, Christian compassion is not just a commitment of the heart but also a matter of professional intervention. Dobson explicitly fuses these two elements of the narrative:

Mike, we researched this subject for *months* before we did this broadcast because we didn't want to make one of the two mistakes. We didn't want to make the mistake of telling people who *had* been abused that it never happened, because in many cases it *has*. But we also did not want to endorse the false memory syndrome when *that* has occurred. So that is a delicate balance. I think people will see that there is a motive of compassion here, as we deal with this subject.[25]

For Dobson, compassion and the search for an objective, comprehensive, and scientific account of the problem imply one another. As Meier puts it, the panelists approach "false memory syndrome" by "reporting it factually, the way it really is," and explicitly call on their professional knowledge and experience to authorize their judgments. Meier, for example, argues that when "regression therapists" use hypnosis to help clients recover supposed memories from early childhood, they merely reactivate the "fantasies" typical of infancy. These "fantasies" are a characteristic of personality development, he claims, that child psychology has firmly established.[26] Simpson cites research that "has *very* consistently shown" that people are more likely to remember than to repress traumatic events, and dismisses the notion of "traumatic amnesia" as "on the fringe of what we're doing, in terms of accepted knowledge of modeling of memory."[27] Simpson and Gatewood furthermore show that their professional expertise extends beyond psychology per se when the former cites the "litigation rate of former clients now suing their therapists for implanting false memories" while the latter notes the amount of damages assigned in a highly publicized case won by the plaintiffs.[28] In addition, Dobson advertises his guests' professional credentials in psychiatry, psychology, and social work.[29]

In this series as in the episodes on child intellectual development, then, Focus's narrative of the compassionate professional displays its characteristic combination of biblically evocative, Christlike love for the unfortunate with the professional status and knowledge needed to make caring intervention count in the modern world. Again, modern apparatuses of power and knowledge place no obstacles in the road to salvation, but instead accelerate the believer's race toward heaven. Personal salvation, the subject's ethical autonomy, and the science-driven trajectory of modern social history seem wholly compatible with one another. In addition, the series on "false memory syndrome" augments this redemption narrative with the notion that salvation through compassionate professionalism involves joining a community-based effort to bring healing to those who need it. Rooting out "false memory syndrome" and comforting those who have suffered its traumatic effects is not just the job of trained specialists. Rather, the panelists stress, it is a collective endeavor in which ordinary people can participate in many ways. The latter can do this through spreading awareness of the phenomenon in their church communities and families. They can also help publicize and attend the educational seminars offered around the country by Meier and Simpson's organization, Project Middle Ground, which seems to embody the spirit of local activism involving professionals and nonprofessionals alike generated by the panelists' enthusiastic remarks.[30]

Once again, however, the strain on the narrative structure produced by internal tensions ultimately becomes apparent. The universal scope of the panelists' compassion contracts as once more the narrative reorients compassion exclusively toward those allowed within the borders of a cosmic order of physiological, social, and spiritual health. Dobson and his guests give the impression that "false memories" of abuse are much more common than "true memories" of abuse, without even superficially discussing the known circumstances of actual abuse. What is more, they suggest that those who believe their recollections of abuse to be true suffer from deep-seated psychological and physiological abnormalities. According to Gatewood, the latest "research" shows that having a "fantasy-prone personality" accounts for most cases of "false memory syndrome."[31] This psychological condition, in turn, has a biological basis. For the panelists, proper functioning of the memory means the precise and accurate retrieval of information stored in the brain as a result of empirically verifiable experiences. Since it is simply natural, as well as ordained by social convention and divine decree, that parents love their children, logic forces the conclusion that real memories will prevent family discord by causing children to recollect the loving care their parents have given them and to honor their parents accordingly.[32] Those whose memories suggest otherwise thus come under suspicion of being not only physiologically unwell but moreover agents of social disintegration and spiritual strife. In a word, they become the "other" to the unified system of cosmic order, and this directly contradicts the element of universal compassion in the narrative.

Paralleling the discussion of child intelligence, in this series a set of anecdotes positions children who voice memories of abuse radically outside the cosmic system. The speakers persistently link memories of child abuse with putatively absurd visions like stumbling on neighbors performing satanic rituals, being abducted by aliens from outer space, and reliving experiences inside the womb.[33] Tales ranging from the unsettling to the horrifying punctuate the discussion. Simpson tells the following story about "a beautiful Christian couple in their mid-fifties":

> Their Christian daughter went into therapy and was able to remember her mother being a high satanic priestess; that as a family, for a couple decades, they sacrificed animals on the backyard barbecue; that a pizza boy came to the door and that he was murdered by that family, and that they barbecued him on the grill and *ate* him. And the police department investigated all of it; they were reported; this family is being devastated—four grandchildren that the mom, the grandmother in this case, hasn't been able to see—and the police department found there are no missing pizza boys during this year that this was alleged to have happened, and yet the daughter still believes her images, and this family is left devastated. And as I go across the country doing the seminars and working with families, you hear these stories *over and over and over again.*[34]

Dobson and his guests then briefly dispute the extent to which sensationalistic rumors exaggerate the actual number of satanic cult sacrifices; Meier counters Simpson with the story of an actual, cultic sacrifice of a baby. Skepticism prevails, by the force of Dobson's citations of FBI statistics showing that virtually no "satanic cult activity" exists, along with Simpson's reminder that the medieval witch burnings were eventually exposed as a plot of "the accuser of the brethren [Satan] . . . to hit us within the body" (that is, "the body of Christ," meaning the community of the saved).[35] But the point is that in dismissing "satanic cult activity" as the concoction of disturbed minds, Dobson and Simpson assign the same status to individuals' claims to have suffered child abuse. For the discussion of satanism leads directly back to a conversation about "false" memories of child abuse:

> Dobson: David, talk about the people who call and write Focus on the Family from the perspective of false memory syndrome.
> Gatewood: Maybe I could just read a letter that we got. This is from a constituent that says: "Five years ago, my daughter had marital difficulties. She sought counseling and underwent hypnosis—and then began the nightmare. The evening of the hypnosis, she telephoned me from another street to tell me she had been sexually abused by her father. She called her father with the same information. I was shocked and found it very hard to believe. Her father denied the abuse categorically. Throughout this period, she blamed me for not defending her, protecting her from his assaults. It was the heartbreak of my life. I found that unless I agreed with the therapist and kept my mouth shut, they were not willing to do any dialogue. It was very difficult for us."
> Dobson: Well, you can imagine the pain of being accused in that way, if you were absolutely innocent and you'd *raised* that child in love and had *given* yourself.[36]

By creating an analogy on the formal level of the narrative between fantasies of flaming delivery boys and accusations of incest, Dobson and his guests lump the victims' accusations together within the realm of the absurd. Suspicion dislodges compassion as one individual who recalls child abuse and another who remembers cannibalism are jointly defined as possessed by Satan, as instruments of the Enemy of the believer, the family, the Church, the nation, and God. Only the individual's unequivocal renunciation of such accusations as the fruit of evil dementia can bring about assimilation to the cosmic "system" and eligibility for healing compassion. Meanwhile, just as the FBI has established the truth of satanism's limited appeal, so does the compassionate professional assume the role of policing the boundaries of the truths regarding insider and outsider identities generated by the godly, fundamentalist order.

As the ethical autonomy and universal compassion of the Christian professional evaporate, so does the tangible quality of the assistance he offers. The speakers' advice simply reaffirms evangelical "fundamentals" regarding children's duty to obey and honor their parents. And the organized, community-based efforts of these psychologists and others like them to combat "false memory syndrome" are ultimately focused on this basic end. Despite Project Middle Ground's aura of professionalism, the group's intervention strategies seem to come down to a few ordinary reminders about living the Christian life. For parents, Meier says, this means finding comfort in remembering that Jesus "know[s] what it's like to be accused and to be not guilty." For the accusers, Simpson adds, it means "retracting" false claims and seeking "restoration" into parental favor. Simpson recommends that syndrome-afflicted daughters and their fathers undergo a ritual of "restoration" in which the father literally "speaks his blessing over to the daughter."[37] Thus substantive, professional care is denied even to those who "recognize" their errors. Instead, the therapies advocated reconfirm the identity of the cosmic order from the point of view of the insider, legitimate the authority of the credentialed professional within that order's social dimension, and instruct insiders on how to demonstrate ritually their loyalty to established norms—here, the norms of patriarchy. At the same time, Project Middle Ground, which at first seems like one sturdy shoot in a garden of civic efforts to create a more inclusive community, turns out to be an agent to keep weeds from sprouting up within the *pure* community.

Offering "Hope for the Homosexual"

Dobson's broadcast series on "curing" homosexuality furnishes another instructive example of the contradictions that rend Focus's narrative of the compassionate professional. "Compassion" is not the first word that springs to mind when one thinks of Christian right attitudes toward gays and lesbians. Yet as antigay politics escalated in the 1990s, so likewise did the rhetoric of compassion for gays and lesbians in the Christian right media become more widespread. It is certainly a prominent theme in Focus's series on therapeutic treatment for homosexual desire, broadcast on *Focus on the Family* in April 1994.

At the start of this three-part series, Dobson's featured guest, psychologist Joseph Nicolosi, announces his intention to provide "encouraging" advice for people whom Dobson claims "are struggling with this problem" but "are not being encouraged." Dobson elaborates: "Mike, can you imagine the tragedy of, say, a fourteen-year-old young man who has these inclinations and feelings, and his parents are concerned about it and they send him to a therapist, and the therapist says, 'you need to *give* to [*sic*] these inclinations, your problem is that you're *homophobic*, we need to help you get over your *attitude* toward homosexuality—not to deal with the root *cause* of it!"[38] Dobson and Nicolosi demonstrate their motivation to help those who feel "trapped" in their "homosexual lifestyle" by the way they relate to another guest in the studio: "Allen Smith," a client of

Nicolosi's who testifies pseudonymously to his personal battle against "unwanted homosexual feelings" and to the healing power of Nicolosi's therapy. Superficially, the broadcast series seems to focus on "Smith's" personal story of successfully overcoming "sin," a "witness" to redemption of the sort that has been characteristic of American evangelicalism since the revivals of the early nineteenth century.[39] It soon becomes clear, however, that in the main narrative at work here "Smith" plays a minor role in comparison to Dobson and Nicolosi. That is, the narration and renewed demonstration of Dobson's and Nicolosi's performance of Christian service occupies the major part of the series' airtime, displacing "Smith" from the central subject-position of the narrative that he at first appears to occupy. Thus, for instance, when "Smith" presents himself as having "turned to" homosexuality because of his emotional vulnerabilities, this gives Dobson (who has prompted this confession in the first place) the chance to display his sensitivity:

> Dobson: When you were younger, when you were five, six, seven, did you have any idea that you were kind of drifting in that direction?
> "Smith": No, but I was somewhat effeminate, and I remember that; and I remember being made fun of, and I remember other boys ostracizing me. So that was always a hurt—it still sometimes is a hurt.
> Dobson: Sure it is, it's always difficult to be ridiculed as a child.[40]

Dobson in turn lauds Nicolosi's abundant concern for the unfortunate: "What I appreciate about *you*, Joe," he remarks, "is that you do have a *great* deal of *compassion* for people who are *in* that situation."[41] As in the other series, then, the biblically based narrative wherein showing compassion to the needy leads to salvation clearly resounds here.

Moreover, the subject of this redemption narrative again displays the apparently complementary aspects of *caritas* and professional, scientific expertise. Dobson emphasizes "Dr." Nicolosi's "great deal of background and experience" in the psychology of same-sex desire, noting Nicolosi's position as "Clinical Director of the Thomas Aquinas Psychological Clinic in Encino, California," and promoting Nicolosi's two books.[42] In turn, Nicolosi portrays himself as a renegade truth-teller within the health professions, which he claims have fallen under the sway of gay activists' self-interested political machinations. Nicolosi and Dobson speak out against "the gay agenda" not just by declaring its "values" profane but also by branding its empirical claims as politically opportunistic pseudoscience:

> Nicolosi: It is a campaign, it's a political campaign, and I think a lot of people don't realize that in the last few years, the three major studies that have come out—so-called scientific studies that show homo-

sexuality to be biologically based, were done by three gay activists. So the scientists themselves are gay and politically active in their gay agenda. When you look closely at these studies, you see that there is nothing substantial there, there is nothing conclusive.

Dobson: One of 'em, as I understand, that was done on *cadavers* showing differences in brain structure, was done on patients who died of AIDS!

Nicolosi: Of course! There were many flaws with that, including the fact that Simon LeVay had to guess at some of the brains—he didn't know if some of them were gay or straight, so he took a guess. And one interviewer said to him, "well, what if you guessed wrong?" And he said, "but what if I guessed *right?*"

Dobson: (chuckling contemptuously) Ugh, that's *science?*

Nicolosi: (laughing) That's science!

Dobson: And yet it made the papers all over the country.

Nicolosi: Front pages, absolutely.

Dobson: You know, just from a genetic perspective, when genetic material is not passed on to the next generation because you don't reproduce, we all know what *happens* to it.

Nicolosi: It dies *out.*

Dobson: It's eliminated from the *gene* pool, so if you have a fewer number of homosexuals reproducing than the heterosexual community, which is a pretty fair hypothesis at least, you would gradually *eliminate* those genes from the gene pool.[43]

Debunking the arguments of "gay" scientists by exposing their ostensibly fraudulent methods and pointing out imputed gaps in their logic, Dobson and Nicolosi establish their own scientific-professional credibility. Nicolosi augments his own authority in this regard by displaying his confident grasp of the jargon of psychotherapy. He contends that homoerotic tendencies arise through childhood experiences of "the triadic relationship," defined as "the sensitive boy; the overinvolved, possessive, domineering, controlling mother; and the distant, detached, or hostile father." Under these family-systemic conditions, a boy becomes "alienated—unidentified, so to speak—from his own masculinity" because of his inability to experience "masculine bonding with his father." Homosexuality results, Nicolosi claims, when "those unmet needs become eroticized." But "homoerotic attractions" can subside when the individual "gets his other emotional needs met" through successful, masculine relationships. The "information" and "techniques" offered by Nicolosi and other therapists who view homosexuality as a "developmental disorder," in particular "identification" with the therapist as a "male role model" or "father figure," help put clients on the road to forming "healthy" relationships with other men and obtaining relief from their same-sex desires.[44]

The series on "curing" homosexuality thus fosters the clear impression that Nicolosi and Dobson not only are motivated by the best of intentions but are moreover equipped with the expertise to make good on their promises of healing. Of additional and vital importance, however, is the fact that the listener to this edition of *Focus on the Family* comes away with the optimistic sense that the leaders she has heard are part of a broad-based, organized, and communal response to pressing human needs. That is, the broadcast series does not simply extol the virtues of the compassionate professional as an individual. It also contextualizes this testimony within the celebration of a larger, cooperative mobilization of resources to provide assistance to those who urgently require it. The series thus culminates in an excited discussion of the fact that an increasing number of "support services" for "recovering homosexuals" exist on the local level. These services involve a nationwide "network" of psychiatrists and psychologists like Nicolosi, the National Association for the Research and Therapy of Homosexuality. In addition, Nicolosi describes an "ex-gay ministry network" of support groups run by and for individuals who have been through the kind of therapy these professionals offer. Professionals, therapy veterans, and ordinary people concerned about helping "homosexuals who want to change" all contribute, finally, to a multitude of evangelical "ex-gay ministries" such as Exodus International and Transformation Ministries.

Perhaps most importantly, the broadcast series does not merely advertise that these projects exist, but moreover suggests that the taping of the series has itself ignited this sort of community-based, helping resolve. For in the last part of the broadcast, Dobson and Nicolosi field questions from an enthusiastic fifty- to seventy-five-person studio audience, all of which revolve around the theme of what individuals and church communities can do to "reach out" in a "compassionate" way to "homosexuals."[45] In general, then, the proffer of healing aid to "homosexuals" acquires a halo of not only loving hospitality and medical legitimacy but also communitarian politics. Far from struggling alone against the societal powers that be, the compassionate professional labors alongside others who share a practical commitment to building the good community.

In short, then, in the series on "curing" homosexuality the compassionate professional again seems inspired by an autonomous and unqualified compassion for all, able to provide specialized and effective care, and devoted to a cooperative mission of cultivating civic concern. He represents the mobilization of resources by the caring community to aid its unfortunate members in a manner preserving both individual moral integrity and technical rationality. The way of redemption illuminated by this narrative thus precisely parallels that indicated in the other broadcast series.

Yet once again the most spontaneously apparent "face" of the compassionate professional tendentially gives way to a colder, harder countenance. First, the claim of Christlike, all-inclusive compassion is belied by the narrative figure's willingness—even duty—to stigmatize and ostracize outsiders whom he considers undeserving of succor. The latter propensity becomes evident when Dobson and Nicolosi sharply distinguish between the "homosexual" who deserves their support and the "gay" who does not:

> Nicolosi: To me, the difference between the nongay homosexual or [sic] the militant gay is a difference of values. . . . The gay person will say, "this is who I am, I like it, and if anybody has a problem with it it's their problem." *My* clients are heterosexually identified in their value system. They cannot identify with the gay culture—it's too *radical* for them—so their *feelings* are *homosexual*, but their *value* system is *heterosexual*, and so there's a clash between values and sexuality.
> Dobson: And the Church simply must understand that distinction, because in its revulsion for the *activists* who are out there trying to *change* society, and *have* to resist that [sic], but they *must* not lose their compassion for the individual, who is *caught* there—people like "Allen."

The psychologists then entrench a sense of "revulsion" for those who are gay and proud by positioning "the militant gay" beyond the pale of a cosmic unity of psychological and physiological wellness, social harmony, and moral-religious rectitude. "Smith" emphasizes the "stresses" and "anxiety" that accompany being gay. Dobson describes the "gay" person as someone who spends "*all* day long, every day, concentrating on sex." Nicolosi definitively classifies the "gay" "condition" as abnormal: "The high promiscuity and the number of sexual contacts that gay men engage in—*and* not only that but the *kinds* of sexual behaviors they get involved in, which would be rather repulsive to most of us—tells us that there's something pathological about the condition."[46] The imputed "pathology" of the "gay" is not simply emotional and behavioral but all-encompassing for that individual. It is *physiological*, most centrally because being "gay," for Dobson and Nicolosi, implies being infected with HIV as well as threatening others with infection. Dobson bemoans the "recruitment" of vulnerable teenagers by "gays" through "AIDS hotlines that try to capture these kids and have 'em call, and they get 'em into that [gay pornographic] material and just kind of *entice* them." The "gay" pathology is furthermore *social*, to Dobson and Nicolosi, in that "gays" emerge from severely troubled families (in particular, families with sexual abuse) and then act out their distress by waging subversive politics. They thus become "fully *identified* with" their pathology in a way that links the intimate self to public conduct. The touted compassion of Focus's narrative figure thus stops short of extending to those whom Focus itself portrays as especially wounded and unfortunate individuals. Instead, Dobson and Nicolosi incite feelings of "revulsion" at the outsider (whom they describe literally as "out there").[47] Finally, according to Nicolosi, the pathological status of "gays" is *spiritual.* Denouncing churches that "buy into the gay agenda and believe that there are gay Christians," Nicolosi declares:

> The *Christian* view is a heterosexual view. There's no such thing as a gay Christian, that is a contradiction in terms. We were born to be heterosexual, we were born to be drawn to the opposite sex, and that's the foundation; and our relationship to *Jesus* is a *masculine* relationship, it's one more male in our life. . . . I believe that "gay" and "Christian" is a contradiction in terms. It's a philosophy; it leads to a gay anthropology, which is to say that some of us are just born this way, and that is totally against the natural law and biblical teachings.[48]

Focus's compassionate professionals thus weave a seamless fabric in which nature, social convention, and scriptural truth blend together to form the basis for "identifying" and distinguishing outsiders and insiders.[49]

Does not the figure of the recuperable "homosexual," however, blur these lines of distinction between the godly interior and the satanic exterior? Ultimately not, since "Smith" claims that Nicolosi's therapy has "cured" him of all feelings of sexual attraction to men, rid him of fascination for "the gay lifestyle," enabled him to experience "the big zing" of desire for women (and to guffaw about it with Dobson), and given him hope that one day he will marry and start a "Christian" family.[50] In other words, for Dobson and Nicolosi, "homosexuals" can and should assume an imputedly normal identity. They can do this if, and only if, they place themselves under the authority and discipline of an appropriate therapist/father-figure and strive to erase all traces of being "homosexual" (not to mention "gay") from their identities, both internally and externally. For Dobson, the "homosexual" who consents to this "treatment" is then "in exactly the same situation . . . as the unmarried heterosexual" who feels tempted to abandon her or his commitment to abstinence, but who can overcome her or his lust through obedience to scriptural law.[51] In the meantime, the broadcast series implies, "homosexuals" within "the Church" should stay as invisible as possible. Colonizing and refunctioning queer rhetoric about coming out, Dobson declares: "This is a secret population. See, we hear about the gays all the time, but this other population of individuals, they just want to take care of their problem and blend into the woodwork and just get on with their life."[52] Even while he draws attention to this "secret population," however, Dobson clearly intends for it to *remain* closeted, as his metaphor about vanishing "into the woodwork" and his repeated, emphatic statements that it is best for "Smith" not to disclose his real name demonstrate.

For the insiders as well as the outsiders, then, the compassionate professional's invocation of the scientific, social, and spiritual order of the cosmos furnishes an identity made from whole cloth. Moreover, those toward whom the narrative figure's compassion is supposedly directed receive little else besides that identity. The caregiver's promise of scientifically substantive, professional aid goes unfulfilled (as it inevitably must, of course, given that their diagnoses and prescriptions comprise the real pseudoscience here). According to "Smith's" and Nicolosi's descriptions, the decisive component of the therapy seems to have been the latter's admonitions to stop "whining" and to meet the "challenges" of playing sports and dating women. Nicolosi does appear to have helped "Smith" acknowledge his genuine feelings of dissatisfaction in his relationship with his father. However, Nicolosi himself does not seem to see this process of becoming self-aware as integral to the main dynamic of "Smith's" "healing." Instead, the latter hinges on "Smith's" learning how to lose gracefully in athletic competition while developing his skills so that he can eventually become a winner and form "healthy" masculine friendships with his male teammates. Finally, "Smith" establishes his "cured" condition by conveying his newfound ability to exert power over women:

> "Smith": I myself had some female supervisors who were feminists, and who did not like any sort of assertion on my part, or just basically standing up for my own rights. And it was great in therapy because Dr. Nicolosi would say, "now, no, you don't back *down*, you're a *man*, you have the right to politely *assert* yourself, to protect your own rights."
> Dobson: He was *teaching* you how a man thinks and behaves.
> "Smith": Exactly.[53]

Ultimately, the main "therapy" Nicolosi offers is the dogmatic insistence that "Smith" conform to a traditional, fundamentalist masculinity defined by athletic prowess, willful assertiveness, and dominance over women.

In sum, the figure of the compassionate professional that takes shape within Focus's series on homosexuality ultimately offers little in the way of either compassion or professional care. The narrative foresees the liquidation rather than the fulfillment of autonomous ethical decision, as the figure's goodwill toward all is superseded by his embrace of the duty to police the boundaries of a cosmic system of physical, social, and spiritual truth. With this suspension of the Christian ethic, the revival of inclusive community spirit proclaimed by the narrative is revealed as the exclusionary attempt to maintain the body of the elect in its pure and sanitized state. Finally, the compassionate professional not only strands outsiders within a realm of radical alterity, beyond the reach of compassionate engagement, but even cheats insiders by substituting the stabilization of order-maintaining identities for the provision of the promised practical aid.

Interlude: On the Politics of Focus's Compassionate Professional

Considering these three broadcast series together, it is plain to see that *Focus on the Family*'s cultural mission is thoroughly instrumental to the Christian right's public policy goals. The episodes considered above both kindle and comprise politicocultural attitudes that are homophobic, anti-feminist, and disempowering of children. Focus thus generates favorable dispositions among target populations for organizations like the Christian Coalition, which attempt to direct patriarchal and antigay sentiments toward support for specific public policies, candidates, and party organizations. For example, Dobson's and Nicolosi's vitriol against gays belongs to a more general strategy pursued by the Christian right to demonize gays and lesbians, who have served as powerful negative symbols in the movement's drive to mobilize a traditionalist constituency behind neoconservative reforms. In this respect, Focus's broadcast series is simply one of a great many publications, products, and public statements by the movement that carry out politically opportunistic scapegoating, such as "The Gay Agenda" videos produced by the Lambda Report. The politics of *Focus on the Family* thus materialize in campaigns to pass state ballot initiatives depriving gays and lesbians of their civil rights, protests against the National Endowment for the Arts for funding homoerotic photography, and the passage of federal legislation defining marriage as exclusively an act between one man and one woman.

Adorno reminds us, however, that the politics of a cultural phenomenon need not be conceived of in purely instrumental terms. Indeed, by analyzing culture simply as a trove of devices to accomplish predetermined goals, cultural criticism apes the gestures of domination inasmuch as it "thus gives official approval to that tendency of the bourgeois consciousness to degrade all intellectual formulations to a simple function, an object which can be substituted for some other object, or—in the final analysis—an article of consumption." Above all, such an approach precludes from the outset any possibility of finding a negative-utopian moment in the cultural object, of seeing this object not as a "mere exponent of society" but rather as "a ferment for [social] change."[54]

At the beginning of this chapter, we saw how elements of Adorno's culture industry theory evoke a sense of *Focus on the Family*'s utility not only to the Christian right movement but moreover to the post-Fordist social totality. In turn, in the unfolding of Focus's narrative of salvation through compassionate professionalism—that is, with the "immanent criticism" of the narrative, which recognizes the program's claim to autonomy from political and economic necessity—we now have a basis for a more dialectical interpretation of the program. The contradictions within the narrative can now be juxtaposed to resonant contradictions in the social totality. This may fortify our sense of the ideological character of Dobson's broadcasts while also bringing to light any capacities they possess to protest social antagonisms and to make social theory more self-reflective, as the preceding two chapters suggest.

The centrality of the figure of the compassionate professional within the narrative structure of *Focus on the Family* indicates that the politics of the program have much to do with current historical conditions governing the provision of professional care for the needy in society at large. That is, not only the strategic realities of Christian right movement politics in the nineties define the political thrust of *Focus on the Family*. The constitutive contradictions within the program's narrative structure imply that the shows featuring the compassionate professional might ironically, if only negatively, harbor a utopian wish for the transformation of the very social circumstances that the new right has helped create, specifically in the areas of health care and social services.

Health Care in the Compassionless Society

The Continuing Crisis and Managed Care. When the Clinton administration took office in 1993, broad agreement existed in the United States that the country's health care system was in crisis. The rhetoric of the Clinton-Gore 1992 campaign had helped accelerate momentum for reform, and after several false starts on other issues the administration trained its sights on health care reform as a major policy initiative. Although the right did not support Clinton's call for greater government regulation of the health industry, even archconservatives like Senator Phil Gramm acknowledged that some public response to the health system's problems was needed and proposed their own grand renovations (in Gramm's case, a voucher program). By the end of the 1990s, however, most political and media leaders no longer spoke with such urgency and alarm about the failing health care apparatus. Following the election of Republican Congresses and the reorientation of the administration toward less divisive policy matters, fundamental health care reform dropped out of the national policy agenda, leaving only a few marginal reform efforts in its place.

Nevertheless, the health care crisis itself remains very much a reality. The dysfunctionality of health care in the United States is commonly understood with reference to two central, long-term problems: skyrocketing costs and diminishing access to insurance coverage and care. Private households' expenditures for health services and supplies increased from $23.7 billion to $247 billion (or by over 1,000 percent) between 1965 and 1991. Private businesses' expenditures of this nature rose from $6 billion to $205.4 billion (or by nearly 3,500 percent) during the same period; public expenditures for health services and supplies grew from $7.9 billion to $254.5 billion (or by over 3,000 percent).[55] Public spending on health care continued to expand by nearly 10 percent each year from 1989 to 1996.[56]

The rapidly rising health expenditures of employers and the increasing overcapacity among providers have driven the structural shift in the health industry from fee-for-service provision toward what is known as "managed care." In theory, managed care yields "more emphasis on prevention, less use of high-cost new technologies, and price reduction in the cost of health care services due to large group buyers of health care." Heightened competition for consumers among insurance companies and providers stimulates the reduction of costs and the implementation of administrative measures to make care provision more economically efficient. Moreover, managed care is intended to increase the quality of health services by eliminating incentives toward the prescription of unnecessary procedures. These adjustments presuppose the transfer of substantial power in the health industry from individual hospitals and physicians to the corporations that manage the provision of health care.[57]

Since 1990, enrollment in managed care plans has grown at a rapid pace for participants in public insurance programs and private employer-sponsored arrangements alike. In 1992 36 percent of the population was insured through managed care plans; by 1996 the proportion had risen to 60 percent of the population. Spending has continued to reach unprecedented heights, topping $1 trillion nationally for the first time ever in 1996. However, the rate of expenditure growth slowed markedly in the mid-1990s: in 1996, national spending on health care as a proportion of the national gross domestic product was unchanged for the fourth straight year. From 1991 to 1996 the annual growth rate of employer-sponsored insurance premiums decreased by over 50 percent.[58] Although the duration of this relief from cost pressures remains uncertain, it seems clear that managed care has at least temporarily slowed the tremendous expansion of health care spending.

These figures represent only part of the recent picture, however. Analysts generally agree that the deceleration of health care spending increases has largely been due to diminished consumption of health care services, which in turn results from financial incentives in both private and public plans that have made it more complicated for services to be ordered. Whether or not this reduction in consumption has been entirely a matter of "trimming the fat" from a wasteful system is a matter of no little contestation. In fact, abundant evidence exists that the expansion of managed care is making basic health care less accessible than ever to the working and unemployed poor.

As health costs exploded, the uninsured population mushroomed. From 1980 to 1992, the percentage of persons under the age of 65 who were uninsured rose from 12.5 percent to 17.2 percent. The uninsured population was estimated at 37 million for 1993 and had grown to 40.6 million just two years later.[59] The majority of the uninsured in 1991 belonged to "full-time, full-year working families"; only 15.3 percent of the uninsured population belonged to families with "nonworking heads." Still, access to health care divides unequally along class lines: low income, low educational attainment and unemployment all correlate with lack of access to regular health care and lack of insurance. Race plays a crucial role as well: in 1996, 17.2 percent of Hispanic children had no usual source of health care, while the figures were 12.6 percent for black children and 6 percent for white children; and 27.2 percent of Hispanic children were uninsured, as compared to 17.6 percent of black children and 12.2 percent of white children. These differences translate into worse health for minorities and the poor.[60] Perhaps nowhere is this ongoing crisis in the health care system more vivid than among Native Americans, who suffer mortality rates that vastly outdistance those of the population at large for alcoholism, tuberculosis, diabetes, pneumonia, influenza, and suicide.[61]

Managed care supposedly benefits the uninsured population by easing the budgetary pressures caused by skyrocketing costs and thereby expanding the political latitude for public health benefits. Such policy reforms have not materialized, however. Since the failure of the Clinton initiative in 1994, the federal government has made only slight progress in extending more health services. Congress mandated insurance "portability" for persons who lose their jobs, but did not guarantee anyone's ability to pay for continued insurance.[62] The federal government has also launched a program to insure an additional 2.8 million previously uninsured children, using matching contributions from states, but this initiative offers no help to the over 8 million other children and 30 million adults who lack insurance.[63]

Meanwhile, previously established systems for providing "uncompensated care" (that is, health services to people who are unable to pay for them) have been major casualties of the shift to managed care. Although no nationally coordinated plan for serving this population has ever existed, "urban public hospitals, community health centers, some inner-city teaching hospitals, and local health departments are generally considered to be the core safety-net institutions."[64] Managed care has greatly increased financial pressures on these institutions and threatened their capacity to serve their clients, sometimes even to survive. It has created an environment favoring "a system based on price competition in which both private and public purchasers want to pay only for the cost of the services their enrollees receive."[65] Meanwhile, uncompensated care has become more concentrated than ever in those hospitals that have previously provided services to this population at disproportionate levels.[66] At the same time, the sources of public funding that have enabled safety-net institutions to make ends meet in the past are drying up in a variety of ways. (1) The introduction of managed care for Medicaid recipients, along with the recent constraint on health care price increases, has intensified competition among providers for these patients; this means that safety-net providers are more likely to lose these clients and, along with them, public funding streams. (2) This problem is exacerbated by federal and state policies slowing increases in expenditures for Medicare and Medicaid. (3) "In response to the fragile situation of these hospitals, local governments are making decisions to sell tax-supported hospitals or further reduce their support";[67] such divestment in turn ratchets up competitive pressures, making the process of safety-net financial destabilization followed by privatization self-reinforcing. Finally, the increasingly shaky financial prospects of safety-net institutions have compelled them to cut back a wide range of additional services they have traditionally offered to poor communities, "ranging from poison control to Meals-on-Wheels programs," from housing referrals to counseling.[68]

In general, then, established norms and networks enabling the provision of some health and health-related services (although hardly adequate care) to those unable to pay for them have been superseded by the virtual consensus that valorizes budgetary efficiency above all other ends and competition among private business interests above all other means. This consensus is industrywide: it includes mental as well as physical health services. And the accumulating inequities in the area of mental health are even greater than those in the industry as a whole. In the past, "coverage for mental health care has been substantially more restricted than coverage for general medical care." This has been due in part to abiding suspicions that more extensive coverage will lead to unreasonable use of services, partly to the phenomenon of "adverse selection" where insurance companies recognize the mentally ill as "bad risks" because "many mental and addictive disorders are more persistent than other illnesses," and partly to a reliance on safety-net providers for mental health services.[69] Employer coverage of mental health services fell precipitously during the early 1990s cost explosion, with the percentage of large firms offering equal coverage for mental and other infirmities dropping from 27 percent in 1988 to 14 percent in 1993.[70] The new emphasis on ridding the health system of "unnecessary" services through competition and more efficient management thus impacts a mental health arena that already systematically restricts services to many who may desperately need them. Shifts to managed care in mental health have lowered costs dramatically, mainly by decreasing the consumption of services. Although some evidence suggests that managed care does not result in the denial of care to those who genuinely need it, these studies concentrate on health care plans offered by government and large business employers with unionized workforces.[71] It is more likely that adverse selection has intensified with managed care's multiplication of mechanisms for influencing enrollment and service use.[72] As in health care as a whole, finally, legislative reforms concerning mental health have only marginally modified existing arrangements and trends.[73]

Post-Fordism and the Health Care Revolution. Let us now relocate this brief survey of recent changes in health care within the context of the broader, historical political-economic shifts discussed at the end of the preceding chapter. The growth of managed care is one particularly important element of the more general transition to post-Fordism, one major area of society in which relations among capital, labor, and the state are being renegotiated and new forms of domination are emerging. The Fordist compact in the United States never produced national health insurance, as it did in virtually all other advanced-industrial countries. Yet through the state's regulation of labor-management relations, the codification of collective bargaining practices, and the general presumption that capital, labor, and the state all had interests in maintaining high levels of consumer demand, Fordism did institutionalize standard practices guaranteeing health security (along with income security) for the majority of the population, including large segments of the working class. Chief among these practices was the inclusion of employer-sponsored, private health insurance as a key constituent of the basic package of fringe benefits for many wage workers and members of the salariate alike. (Unemployment compensation, workers' compensation for job-related injuries and disabilities, and the Social Security old-age pension program, in turn, secured the incomes of these employees, as did the inclusion of a private employee pension program as a standard benefit.) In addition, during the postwar era "the federal government pumped public funds into the medical industry, subsidizing private health insurance, hospital construction, and medical education and research." This massive investment, along with the Medicare and Medicaid programs, helped engineer a steady expansion of access to and use of health services among the general population during the postwar era.[74] The growing availability of health care and other human services, in turn, was vital to the legitimacy of the state under Fordism.

Post-Fordism has witnessed a reversal of this trend. The shift to flexible accumulation means that businesses now rely less on stable, predictable mass markets for mass-produced, standardized commodities. A compelling rationale thus no longer exists for corporate and government policies that ensure mass demand by keeping the workforce financially, physically, and emotionally secure. The infamous "rigidities" of labor contracts ironed out among organized labor, big business, and the expanding state have been succeeded by more "flexible" commitments to workers' health, safety, and security. In terms of health care specifically, this has meant (1) reduced benefits or switches into managed care for workers in traditional, skilled, or semiskilled jobs; and (2) the concentration of job growth in low-skilled service occupations offering no benefits at all (an employment trend at the forefront of which, ironically, is the health industry itself). But the proliferation of unmet needs is not being answered by the welfare state, which continues to experience a secular decline characterized by fiscal crisis, budget cuts, program excisions, bureaucratic reorganizations, and foundering legitimacy. In the realm of health policy, these tendencies manifest themselves most directly in the long-term erosion of value of Medicaid benefits, periodic tightenings of restrictions on Medicare payments to providers, the shift to managed care for Medicaid patients, and the increasing support in Congress for proposals to terminate Medicaid and/or to reconfigure Medicare in ways that place greater financial responsibilities on users.[75]

The health industry furnishes the scene for several other adjustments central to post-Fordism. The preoccupation with cost-cutting in this industry directly responds to employers' drive to lower labor costs in the face of declining profits and increased international competition, by reining in expenditures on employee benefits. The tremendous expansion of for-profit health care provision and management transforms health services into an especially dynamic and profitable arena of growth, offering new opportunities for investment in the wake of the decline of industries geared toward the production of consumer durables and the uncertainties in military production associated with the end of the cold war. Managed care itself increases the demand for capital by health plans and hospitals by raising administrative and other overhead costs, and this both nourishes and is fed by the epochal transition from the previous era of material expansion to the current stage of finance-led expansion. Additionally, despite the prevalent rhetoric of efficiency through market-based competition, managed care represents no more of a return to the "free market" than does post-Fordism generally. What *is* happening is the redistribution of the capacity to organize markets, as hospital chains, health plans, and physician organizations struggle to increase their "market share" and "market power" through a variety of strategies, most obviously mergers but also product diversification and labor cost reduction through downsizing staff.[76] Finally, the health industry also reflects the indeterminacy of the post-Fordist transformation and its lack of a wholesale rupture with Fordism, inasmuch as the promotion of managed care exhibits a similar faith in technocratic solutions to social and individual problems to that which carried the day under Fordism.[77]

In short, the new bottom-line mentality and the intensifying exclusivity of care provision in the health industry, of which managed care is the primary agent, are post-Fordist phenomena. These tendencies attest to and accelerate the evaporation of the ethical commitment to ensuring the availability of health care to all citizens that was embodied, albeit profoundly imperfectly, in the institutions administrating the Fordist compromise. The emerging system defines only those who can pay as deserving of care, as the resources previously set aside for uncompensated care dwindle. The ranks of those excluded from basic care swell while the boundaries of the system become decreasingly porous. Now, more than before, when it comes to receiving health care one is either an insider or an outsider—period.

The increasing precedence of profits and efficiency over all other values in the political economy of health care also undercuts the ethical autonomy of individual providers of services. Throughout most of the twentieth century, physicians have worked with a high degree of professional independence. As the corporation became the dominant, organizational form of private enterprise in the early and middle years of this century, medical professionals were almost uniquely able to resist the absorption of their work, capital, and profits by large, bureaucratic companies. The economic, social, and cultural authority of the physician grew alongside the corporation rather than being eclipsed by it. The business-labor accord emerging from the New Deal and facilitated by the postwar expansion confirmed not only the private status of health care provision but also the autonomous stature of physicians, since health insurance benefits operated by means of reimbursement rather than the direct provision of services. Thus, while the early and mid–twentieth century witnessed the subsumption of much professional work under the auspices of bureaucracies in both government institutions and private corporations, medicine persisted as "the heroic exception that sustained the waning tradition of independent professionalism."[78]

The expansion of managed care, however, has greatly undermined physicians' autonomy. By the early 1980s, the U.S. health industry had decisively entered a phase of corporate consolidation of "a hitherto decentralized hospital system" and "a variety of other health care businesses."[79] Whether under for-profit or nonprofit auspices, institutions have had to conform to the new regime of "centralized planning, budgeting, and personnel decisions." Power within the industry has correspondingly shifted away from doctors and toward administrators, marketing managers, and investors.[80] Meanwhile, physicians face the increasing intrusion of administrative tasks into their day-to-day work along with routine pressures to minimize services—indeed, to minimize "compassion," as one industry analyst puts it—as the compatibility of their efforts with the goals of profit- and efficiency-optimization comes under greater scrutiny.[81] This is not to idealize the ethical integrity of the physician or the medical profession under the old fee-for-service system. The betrayal of professional ethics for the sake of power and profit certainly occurred under the previous regime, and indeed the ethical code of the physician was structurally instrumental to the profession's collective acquisition of financial and political sway.[82] To be sure, the private, entrepreneurial physician and the medical profession have not been sufficiently accountable to society's needs, despite the earnest efforts of many doctors of good will. But the point is that under managed care, an incomplete fit between ethical standards and actual conduct has been replaced by an abandonment of ethics as such by the steering forces in the industry, sharply circumscribing the ethical autonomy of the individual caregiver.[83]

Similar consequences from managed care have resulted for social workers in the field of mental health and other service areas. Mental health care, residential social services, and even welfare case management have taken "for-profit, proprietary forms" and emerged as attractive new ventures for private corporations.[84] This trend toward privatization and corporatization in social services has significantly altered the character of the provider-client relationship:

> The new services being offered by practitioners and developed by agencies are increasingly disconnected from the circumstances of clients. The greater emphases on volume (productivity) in the face of resource scarcity is redefining service encounters in ways that are more likely to meet the quantitative fiscal needs of the agency and less likely to meet the qualitative service needs of the client or the professional needs of the worker. The service agency is increasingly

emphasizing uniform, factory-like (industrial) practices in order to address the deepening dilemma of expanding service needs and intensifying cost-containment policies. These more uniform or industrial practices are restructuring the content, timing, and rhythm of encounters between worker and client, and contributing to a process of professional deskilling. Fundamentally, these new priorities are stimulating an ever-widening gulf between the service worker and the client.[85]

Ironically, as post-Fordism eclipses Fordism in the political economy as a whole, an antediluvian "super-Taylorism" seems to have emerged among the social workers called on to deal with the dysfunctional side effects of this transition. But the overall transformation of social work remains thoroughly consonant with post-Fordist tendencies: the abandonment of institutional arrangements making good on the social, ethical promises of the Fordist compact goes hand in hand with the diminution of caregivers' ethical autonomy.

This process implies, moreover, that even those fortunate enough to end up inside the system rather than stranded outside its gates are less likely to receive the care they require. To be sure, it is an empirical question, and a disputed one, whether patients under managed care and clients in privatized social work arrangements are getting better or worse care than they would have under previous systems. However, physicians' and social workers' warnings that the bureaucratic management of their practices interferes with their ability to care properly for their clients should not be dismissed as merely the opportunism of professional groups that feel their financial and political interests to be under attack. Nor should assessments of public opinion that find no consistent pattern of user satisfaction or dissatisfaction with managed care lead us to consider the system innocent until proven guilty.[86] For the public's sense of the options to which it is entitled has surely contracted with the numbing repetition by media, corporate, and political opinion-makers that private, competitive, managed care is a fait accompli. Given this constraint on "subjective" data, critical analysis of "objective" tendencies is vital. And such reasoning tells us that when sick patients have to go through "gatekeepers" before obtaining the medication or specialized care they need, when physicians and social workers are saddled with a new burden of administrative tasks, when the number of therapy visits per year is capped without regard to individual case needs, and when the costs to consumers continue to rise despite slowed rates of expenditure growth (while health care spending in other industrialized countries is decreasing), those who have access to health and human services are receiving decreasingly effective care—or at the very least getting less value for the money they spend.

Contradictions of Post-Fordism: Visions of "the Village." Nevertheless, public discourse is dominated by voices promising that managed care will both improve the quality of health services and deliver these services more efficiently. Such assurances come not only from health management companies themselves but also from a broad, bipartisan amalgam of political leaders, including the president and most leaders in Congress. They furthermore generate misleading images of physicians under managed care as autonomous caregivers concerned only with the clinical needs of their patients.[87] These voices echo, moreover, throughout the domain of human services as social work is privatized and corporatized. For instance, much of the rhetoric surrounding the elimination of Aid to Families with Dependent Children proposed that the new block grant program would make services to the poor substantially better than under the entitlement system.[88]

When we consider the discourses that are called on to legitimate the current structure of health and human services, it becomes clear that post-Fordist society not only promotes inequality, ethical irresponsibility, and practical incompetence but is moreover self-contradictory. Above all, political and corporate leaders have sought to justify their generation of and insufficient response to the crisis of human needs by ratcheting up the rhetoric of the ethical community. Initially, the transition to post-Fordism seemed tied up with an ideological shift from "Fordist productivism" to "liberal productivism," with the competitive individualism, moral traditionalism, and free market rhetoric of the Reagan and Thatcher governments emblematizing the latter paradigm.[89] Yet these leading exponents of liberal productivism sponsored policies that conflicted with their ideological commitments, in particular by eventually conceding the need for "negotiation, multilateralism and partnership in international relations, and the active responsibility of states in the regulation of demand."[90] Conversely, the succession of the Reagan and Bush administrations by the "new Democrats" has meant an intensification rather than a reversal of the welfare state cutbacks initiated by the Republicans. With regard to ideology, however, the electoral success of Clintonism indicates that liberal productivism needs some sort of communitarian supplement to function as an effective strategy of legitimation.

The new communitarianism of the political establishment shines through in Hillary Rodham Clinton's 1996 book *It Takes a Village, and Other Lessons Children Teach Us.* Rodham Clinton's best-seller begins with the declaration, "Children are not rugged individualists," and proceeds to extol the benefits of community-based and broadly social contributions to children's welfare. *It Takes a Village* works hard to demonstrate the Clintonites' commitment to the traditional family even as it criticizes those who openly "espouse family values" without supporting a nation that "values families and children."[91] The book weds this family-oriented discourse to rebukes of contemporary American society for its failings as a community, and abounds with anecdotes that exemplify the values of "the village" in action, helping families raise their young. "We don't join civic associations, churches, unions, political parties, or even bowling leagues the way we used to," notes Rodham Clinton (tacitly invoking Clinton adviser Robert Putnam's theory of the decline of "social capital" in the United States). Nevertheless, she insists in a more upbeat vein, "Americans everywhere are searching for—and often finding—new ways to support one another."[92]

For instance, Rodham Clinton writes: "There's probably no area of our lives that better illustrates the connection between the village and the individual and between mutual and personal responsibility than health care." She laments the inaccessibility and unaffordability of prenatal care for many citizens, the country's relatively high infant mortality rates, the rising number of uninsured Americans, and the growing "influence of profit-driven medicine." And with apocalyptic gravity she declares that "until we are willing to take a long, hard look at our health care system and commit ourselves to making affordable health care available to every American, the village will continue to burn, house by house."[93] This sounds vaguely like a call for another major reform effort, perhaps even a national public health system. Rodham Clinton's concrete illustrations of hale "village" life, however, suggest that the path to such fundamental change lies through the gradual accumulation of voluntary efforts and piecemeal public-private partnerships in the context of expanded managed care, of which Rodham Clinton clearly approves. Thus, for example, the first lady lauds efforts to expand the affordability and accessibility of health care through an Arkansas state program advertising a coupon book for pregnant women compiled by "local merchants," with discounts on milk, diapers, and other necessities; the Haggar Apparel Company's commitment "to pay 100 percent of employees' medical expenses during pregnancy if they seek prenatal care during the first trimester of pregnancy"; public service ads on infant care in "the electronic village"; and a South Carolina program in which "experienced mothers" volunteer to teach parenting skills to "pregnant teenagers."[94]

Ultimately, the "village" seems to spring to life whenever virtually any individual or organizational effort is made to provide some sort of service, from the action of a single volunteer to the passage of legislation in Congress. But what is crucial here is not so much the frustratingly nebulous nature of Rodham Clinton's "village." It is rather the pointed invocation of communitarian rhetoric in a text that defined the administration's image at a pivotal juncture—after the Republican takeover of Congress, before the 1996 election—and sought to legitimate the state largely by virtue of an appeal to civic sentiments. Broadly speaking, Rodham Clinton employs communitarianism to justify the general sense that post-Fordist conditions such as the need to mold a "globally competitive economy"— and the shift to managed care—are quasi-natural forces to which Americans simply must adjust.[95]

On a more specific level, heavily advertised federal policy initiatives have indeed been shaped in conjunction with this new ethos of community. The ideals articulated in *It Takes a Village* knitted together key themes of the administration's first term, burnished the frankly neoconservative policy record of the first Clinton administration with a compassionate sheen during the 1996 presidential campaign, and resounded in the first two State of the Union addresses of President Clinton's second term. An ideological commitment to "the village" yielded a much-touted drive to recruit thousands of volunteers to serve in public schools as a central component of its education policy. The administration's expansion of state surveillance powers and carceral capacities has marched ahead under the banner of a "self-consciously communitarian" set of crime-related programs, the most publicized piece of which was a plan to restore "community policing."[96] President Clinton has also appealed to a communitarian spirit in repeatedly urging business owners to bear their share of the social burden by hiring and training welfare recipients whose benefits have been terminated.[97] Even some leading Republicans, including 1996 vice-presidential candidate Jack Kemp and others within the new right (especially the Christian right), have echoed the communitarian ideas of the "new Democrats," in particular highlighting the theme of volunteerism that was in fact a significant element of Reaganism, although in a more stridently antistatist permutation.[98]

Finally, the rhetoric of community has permeated not only official government discourse but moreover the public relations of corporations— perhaps nowhere more thoroughly than in the health industry. Hospitals might in fact be moving toward ever more exclusive operations and dropping the extra services that enabled them to reach out to local communities and especially the poor in diverse ways. Nevertheless, that has not kept industry leaders like the Health Insurance Association of America and Lee Kaiser from celebrating managed care as though it were catalyzing the creation of a new multitude of "community networks."[99]

The Historical Face of Focus's Compassionate Professional

What happens when consumers and providers of managed health and social services, or those who are unable to obtain such services, listen to

Focus on the Family? If they happened to tune in on 22 July 1994, they would have heard Phyllis Schlafly excoriating the Clinton health reform plan (which favored "managed competition") as "socialized medicine," a recipe for aggravation, overtaxation, ill health, and government tyranny to boot. They would have heard that "everybody gets essential care—even the illegal aliens who come across the border to have their babies in the United States so they can be American citizens." They would have heard that "the problem with health care is not the quality—it's admitted by everybody, we have the best quality health care in the world." And they would have heard Schlafly urge that citizens and policymakers not forsake their trust in the professional ethics and expertise of private, individual physicians.[100]

If these listeners decided to "focus on the family" with Dobson and Trout on a more regular basis, moreover, then consciously or not they eventually would have found these explicit assertions to be implicitly confirmed by the most spontaneously perceptible elements of Focus's narrative of the compassionate professional. As we have seen, this strand within the narrative fosters the sense that humane and sensitive care is available to all, or at least could be universally accessible if physicians and mental health professionals were to act with the exemplary compassion of Dobson and his guests. It suggests, furthermore, that such care is (or could be) provided by ethically honorable and autonomous individuals and that the services rendered actually (or could actually) meet and remedy pressing needs. In any case, a large-scale reorganization of mental health services or health care in general would be strictly inadvisable, according to this branch of the narrative. It advises that the failings of the health system are not structural but rather reflect the moral shortcomings of individuals and communities.

Nonetheless, regular listeners to Dobson's program also encounter a narrative pattern that icily contradicts Focus's explicit policy talk and its foregrounded figure of compassionate professionalism alike. For a different constellation of elements within the narrative of the compassionate professional expresses the disturbing historical situation of health and human services, post-Fordist-style, which we have reviewed above. The compassionate professional's ethical self-subordination to a vast and obdurate cosmic order reflects the growing disjuncture between individual ethics and organizational necessity in health services and social work. Likewise, the Manichaean dualism of this universal order expresses the tendency of the health and social services system to treat the needs of certain groups as simply inaudible and invisible, for government and industrial policymaking purposes. The narrative figure's substitution of outsider and insider identities for practical assistance, finally, bears the imprimatur of the hardening indifference of health and human service institutions even to those individuals fortunate enough to have access to them—the declining quality of care as such.

Focus's narrative of the compassionate professional not only expresses this historical situation, however, but furthermore actively reproduces it by encouraging certain subjective attitudes on the part of listeners. The forced resolution of the contradiction between the narrative figure's autonomous and heteronomous ethical moments is bound to breed a cynical disbelief that autonomous moral commitment could ever actually be the foundation for addressing social needs. Dobson's listeners are therefore likely to be so much the less disposed to challenge political and economic changes that are making the instances of such ethical conduct increasingly scarce. They are likewise prompted to see communitarian intonations of society's responsibility toward all of its members as compatible with corporate and government policies that meet the needs of only some citizens, when the narrative attempts to reconcile the compassionate professional's inclusionary and exclusionary aspects. Finally, Focus cultivates listeners' disillusionment that social institutions can effectively respond to socially created but individually felt needs, and thereby their acquiescence to the provision of fewer and lower quality services, when the narrative figure gently reneges on his offer of practical aid.

Is there, then, no discontinuity between listening to *Focus on the Family* and compliant adjustment to the political-economic transformations that comprise its historical context? Have I perhaps just done exactly what Adorno cautioned against: degraded *Focus on the Family* to "a simple function [of the social totality], an object which can be substituted for some other object," in this case an empirical account of health and human services in the contemporary United States imbedded in a theory of post-Fordism? Is Dobson's program in no way, even conceivably or potentially, a "ferment for change" of a progressive sort?

There is certainly no logical necessity that Dobson's listeners absorb the ideological effects of the broadcasts described above in exactly the manner suggested by the formal features of the compassionate professional's fundamentalist aspect. Perhaps *Focus on the Family* has indeed inspired some listeners to think and act in ethically autonomous ways, to devote themselves to community projects without viewing these as substitutes for the imputed evils of "big government," and to provide services that genuinely meet the needs of others—even in the face of the parts of Focus's narrative bluntly discouraging such responses. Whether or not some listeners have thus selectively and/or critically reacted to these broadcasts is an empirical question that lies beyond the scope of this book.

The crucial point here is that in its formal composition *Focus on the*

Family at least creates an opening for critical receptions and responses. What is more, the very failure of the narrative of the compassionate professional to harmonize fully its contradictory internal elements endows the program with an indelible "truth-content," to borrow a phrase from Adorno, a truth that confirms the narrative's historical force in and for itself. The acute contradictions of legitimating ideology with the growing denial of care to the needy, the withering of caregivers' independence, and the declining quality of care even for those who get it are reproduced in the contradictions that rend Focus's narrative of the compassionate professional. *The social physiognomy of Focus's compassionate professional is the conflict-ridden countenance of post-Fordist society.* Within the narrative, the fundamentalist face of the compassionate professional does not entirely eclipse this figure's other visage. Rather, the former subsists in a tension with the latter, the resolution of which is exceedingly superficial and fragile. Everything hinges, however, on the fact that the program clings to this resolution with all its might, forcing together the irreconcilable elements of a contemporary narrative of salvation through compassion. The very fact that this narrative reflects social antagonisms as the self-betrayal of its own claim to offer a utopian vision, a glimpse of a society that has reconciled its contradictions, imbues the narrative with a negative potency vis-à-vis the historical conditions that put their mark on it. In a sense, the narrative thus counterposes itself to these sociohistorical conditions in a stance of accusatory judgment. To one who attends to the internal disruptions within the narrative of the compassionate professional, this negative-utopian moment cannot but declare itself.

Can this negative-utopian ferment within Focus's narrative, however, tangibly alter the chemistry of the social theory called on to make its presence manifest? Pursuing the negative dialectic between *Focus on the Family* and a theory of post-Fordism still lies ahead of us. It is a task best deferred, however, until after the exposure of the expressions, reproductions, and contestations of other major features of post-Fordism by additional narratives spun out over the airwaves by Dobson and his friends.

4

Christian Politicians and the Decline of
Democratic Accountability

The image that he presents of himself is that of the "great little man" with a touch
of incognito, of he who walks unrecognized in the same paths as other folks, but
who finally is to be revealed as the savior. He calls for both intimate identification
and adulating aloofness.—Theodor W. Adorno, "The Psychological Technique of
Martin Luther Thomas' Radio Addresses," 1943

Conspiracy Gone Public?

Conspiracy theory, right-wing politics, and Christian fundamentalism
have had a long history of mutual association in the United States. Cataloguing the techniques of Depression-era agitators such as Gerald B. Win-
rod and Gerald L. K. Smith, Leo Lowenthal and Norbert Guterman identified warnings of conspiracies as the weapon of choice for anti-Semitic
fundamentalists on the airwaves to stir up the resentments that fortified
their reactionary movements. According to Lowenthal and Guterman, for
example, Carl H. Mote, who edited the journal *America Preferred* and
openly sympathized with Hitler, told his followers they were "dupes"
who were "cheated systematically, consistently, and perpetually" by a
"comprehensive and carefully planned political conspiracy."[1] For Mote
and his ilk, the threat to America lay not so much in the manifest expan-
sionism and authoritarianism of the Nazis as in the covert machinations
of Communists and Jews. Not only the governments of modern Europe
and the United States, they proclaimed, but indeed ruling bodies stretch-
ing all the way back to Nebuchadnezzar's Babylon had been infiltrated by
a "secret society" that had finally blossomed into an "International Invisible Government."[2]

It is tempting to hear in these remarks the quaint echoes of a long-ago era, a time antiquated by the defeat of fascism, the disgrace of Senator Joseph McCarthy, and the end of the cold war. To find comfort in historical distance, however, would be to ignore the resonances of these agitators' words with the ideology of the insurgent right in recent years. The racism, militarism, and fundamentalism of Christian patriot rhetoric, especially that of the Christian Identity movement, are interwoven with multiple strands of conspiracy theory.[3] In addition, warnings of conspiracies are a regular feature of what would otherwise seem the most innocuous domain of Christian right political culture: televangelists' broadcasts such as Pat Robertson's *700 Club* and radio talk shows like James Dobson's *Focus on the Family*. With their passionate emphasis on the intimacies of personal salvation and family life and their unflagging, keyboard-enhanced cheeriness, these programs would seem to offer unlikely fora for conspiracy theories. Yet Robertson's news commentaries on *The 700 Club* constantly hint at the influence of covert cabals on the Clinton administration.[4] Meanwhile, although Dobson enjoys an untarnished reputation among evangelicals for integrity and professionalism, the broadcasts monitored for this study contained allusion to nefarious efforts to install "an abortion clinic on every corner," to "recruit" adolescent boys into "the homosexual lifestyle," and to wage smear campaigns in the media against Christian right organizations.[5] Conspiracy theory in the classic sense still flourishes within the Christian right today. Indeed, it arguably reaches far greater audiences than ever before.

Conspiratorialism, however, neither encompasses nor typifies the critique of political institutions that the Christian right media most commonly disseminate. For the contemporary Christian right, at least in its most broadly influential and appealing variants, the problem with U.S. political life today lies not so much in its manipulation by conspiracies as in its captivation by an overweaning and destructive "publicity." Besides making the familiar assertion that government has grown too large and that there are too many government programs, the Christian right voices an additional grievance: that the incessant publicizing of political events is encroaching unbearably on both the private lives of ordinary citizens and the proper discharge of public officials' duties. In a sense, the mainstream Christian right today paradoxically invests publicity as such with a conspiratorial character, inasmuch as it suggests that the forces of publicity plot their saturation of society with public affairs in secret, exert power of unfathomable dimensions, and are impervious to challenges to their authority. However, since the agents of a dilated publicity are known to all, as the news anchors, talking heads, and public officials that purvey public affairs in the media, it is more precise to argue that Christian right organized culture has shifted the rhetorical frame from bringing to light what is hidden to protesting the glare of that on which Americans are purportedly forced to gaze.

In the aftermath of the right's intrepid drive to impeach President Clinton and remove him from office, of course, it seems highly ironic that this theme has been so prominent on *Focus on the Family*. From the early stages of the scandal through the conclusion of the Senate trial, conservative politicians, pundits, and activists energetically directed the public's attention toward the most prurient and sordid details of the president's infidelities. Dobson himself contributed to the momentum toward impeachment by dedicating his September 1998 newsletter to a scathing denunciation of "the dalliances of the commander in chief." True to form, Dobson's "family-friendly" newsletter did not explicitly describe Clinton's notorious failings of "character," as did the report of Independent Counsel Kenneth Starr that was beamed through cyberspace at around the same time that Dobson's letter was being read by Focus's constituents. Still, Dobson had nothing but praise for Starr. The letter hailed the independent counsel as a "courageous public servant" and a "Christian man" who "has taken the heat to get at the truth."[6] Dobson's missive, moreover, very likely helped persuade Republican congressional candidates that fall to maintain their calls for impeachment and build pressure on Capitol Hill for bringing articles of impeachment against the president. In short, when it has seemed politically opportune to do so, the Christian right has aggravated the very conditions it protests—the saturation of private space with public discourses and images, and the amplification of public talk about matters previously normativized as unspeakably intimate.

The Christian right's frontal attack on an overbearing publicity also has its own aspect of opportunism, insofar as it has smoothed the way toward recuperating the reputations of conservative political leaders who themselves are convicted conspirators. These twice "born-again" Christian right leaders notably include Oliver North and (former Nixon aide) Charles Colson, whom Dobson hosted on *Focus on the Family* in two of the broadcast series discussed below and who both hosted popular radio talk shows of their own in the 1990s. The schema of evangelical-conservative discursive strategy here is thus convoluted, to say the least: departing from traditional conspiratorialism, the Christian right underscores the urgency of its demands for a less invasive public sphere (in part) by selectively intensifying publicity's intrusiveness (in league with an independent counsel of whom very little accountability is required and who thus acts as a sort of official conspirator); the Christian right also thereby redeems the careers of leaders whose bona fide intrigues have previously been exposed by the same forces of publicity the movement excoriates—and these individuals, having experienced a private/spiritual rebirth, are then reborn publicly as media figures.

As I have emphasized throughout the foregoing chapters, however, Christian right radio can be interpreted as something other than an instrument serving leaders' strategic attempts to manipulate their followers. Indeed, to concentrate exclusively on this mode of analysis creates the risk that cultural critique itself may gravitate toward conspiracy theory, though this unfortunate conclusion by no means necessarily follows from approaches centered on strategy. Nonetheless, as the preceding examination of Focus's "compassionate professionals" along with the prior discussion of Adorno's theory of dialectical criticism suggested, we need to pay close attention to those elements of Christian right culture that might preserve a degree of autonomy from political instrumentalisms by virtue of their rootedness in historical tradition and their composition as unified, coherent aesthetic forms. For these features of Christian right culture may harbor both additional dynamics of ideology (that is, cultural elements reinforcing the political-economic status quo) and unsuspected moments of protest against the powers that be.

In the case of North's and Colson's 1990s appearances with Dobson on *Focus on the Family*, strategically advantageous denunciations of the culture of publicity are woven into the fabric of a distinctive narrative of salvation. Both North and Colson confirm their identities as "born again" Christians through enduring persecution by the mainstream media. This indicates one aspect of the political significance of the narrative itself: it serves as a vehicle to convey tactically useful and consequential ideas. As in the case of the shows featuring Focus's compassionate professional, however, so likewise in these broadcasts the political import of this redemption narrative can be conceptualized in less instrumentalist, less purely strategic terms. Doing so depends on taking a more extensive look at this narrative's composition to identify how it strives toward a coherence and integrality, developing a traditional form by pursuing certain aspects of its immanent dynamics. (Here, let us recall Adorno's explication of this approach to cultural criticism in "Cultural Criticism and Society" and *Philosophy of Modern Music*, explored in chapter 1, along with my criticism above of his contention that "mass-cultural" products admitted no analysis along these lines.) And doing this requires that we at least provisionally consider in earnest the claim of this narrative to transcend political necessity, to embody a vision of the good life that remains true to a distinctive religious heritage while addressing contemporary experiences. Perhaps, like the warring aspects of Focus's compassionate professional, the contradictions within Focus's figure of the "Christian" politician do not merely evince the fundamental constructedness and strategic purposefulness of Christian right narratives. They may also maintain a more substantively robust and multivalenced relationship to society as a whole in the post-Fordist era, as well as to the more specific characteristics of political representation, publicity, and accountability in this society.

"Ollie" North: The National Defender as Ordinary Dad

Shortly after the dismissal of charges against Oliver North in 1991 for his alleged misconduct in the Iran-Contra affair, North and his wife, Betsy, joined Dobson in Focus's broadcasting studio. The recording of this conversation was subsequently broadcast nationwide on *Focus on the Family* (after editing), and Focus still distributes a popular cassette tape of the series. Initially, the most striking aspect of this broadcast series is its stated premise: not to debate the legitimacy or illegitimacy of North's actions as a White House staffer but rather to show, in Trout's words, that "despite all of his responsibilities, all of his involvements in the government, he's a *family* man, he's a *father*" whose family members went through a protracted trauma and survived it because of their commitments to God and each other.[7] Dobson picks up the cue: "Mike, that's a very important point. Focus on the Family *delimits* itself to family-related issues. We're not interested in Iran-Contra, we're not interested in international politics, we don't get *into* that sort of thing. . . . we're interested in the *family* aspect of what's happened to these people, and we're also interested in their personal lives and their relationship with the Lord."[8] The shows emphasize North's identity as an ordinary individual who should be judged in terms of his private persona and home life, rather than his public conduct, in a plethora of ways. Most obviously, Dobson includes Betsy North in the conversation and encourages her to describe what the scandal was like for her and for the Norths as a family. Strangely, Dobson blurs historical fact by speaking as though accusations had been made against Oliver and Betsy North alike: "Ollie and Betsy lived through a *nightmare*," he declares, "and have just recently had their names totally cleared—they've been exonerated, there are no more charges against them."[9] The odd, offhand suggestion that Betsy North was suspected of colluding in her husband's misdeeds receives no further comment, but it is symptomatic of a central dynamic of Focus's narrative of Oliver North's trial. It epitomizes how the series as a whole construes the central conflict in the trial as North's struggle to hold together his private life in the face of brutal adversity, a struggle joined in Christian solidarity by his wife and kids.

As a "family man"—or, as North puts it, "the husband of one and the father of four"—North is thus made to seem a very humble and ordinary person. *Focus on the Family* places him on a level with Dobson's listeners.

His modest familiarity is vigorously flagged, in particular, by the names that Dobson and Betsy North use to address and refer to him. On *Focus on the Family*, "Lieutenant Colonel Oliver North" is transformed into the unpretentious chum "Ollie" for Dobson and Trout. The listener is moreover treated to a rare peek into the Norths' intimate life as a couple, discovering that Betsy has a special, affectionate name for her man that it seems no one else uses, "Larry." In describing the Iran-Contra hearings themselves, the Norths remember the family's daily routines in ways solidifying "Ollie's" identity as a private person defined by his spousal and parental roles, just as the men who populate Focus's imaginary are supposed to give family matters higher priority than anything else in their lives except their faith. "Ollie" jokes about having been "the most photographed commuter in America" and having "put in some long hours" at the office preparing to give testimony. In turn, "Betsy" recalls having to get up extra early to feed the ponies, take care of the children, and "fix [her] hair" before making the drive downtown.[10]

Besides invoking these images of mundane, middle-class life, the broadcasts further establish North's basic equality with the audience by emphasizing the significance of the congressional investigation for North's "walk with the Lord." On Dobson's program, the congressional probe becomes the culminating event in a series of lifelong tests of North's Christian faith. Set in the context of North's avowal that Jesus saved him from injury and death in a series of crises (a teenage automobile crash, combat in Vietnam, and a jeep accident during preparations for military intervention in Lebanon), North's recollections of his testimony before Congress are transfigured into a testimony to God's grace. North's subjection to the Iran-Contra inquiry is thus represented as being no different in its basic meaning from the trials endured by other evangelicals who are trying to stay on the straight and narrow path. North declares this outright when Dobson prompts him to describe the inspirational purpose of his new book, *Under Fire*:

The purpose, Jim, is to hopefully encourage people. I mean, there's a lot about our travail that could be perceived by some as very *discouraging*, and yet what I would like people to take away from it is a sense that first of all, everybody goes through *something* like this in their lives. Thankfully, for most of us, it's not that public, it doesn't become a front page issue. But every family faces some terrible ordeal of one kind or another, everybody is under fire at some point—whether it's a relationship between a husband and wife, or . . . family conflict of the kinds of things [*sic*] that you do so well at explaining and helping people through, or whether it's a matter of how we approach the government. My hope is that people will read this book and take from it some encouragement that they're not alone. *We* weren't alone. We were every minute of it sustained by the prayers of tens of thousands of people. . . . We could never have done it by ourselves.[11]

The probation of North's faith in the Iran-Contra investigation is thus linked to the testing of his family's ability to stay together in the face of the investigation's relentless pressures.[12] Indeed, North refigures the investigation as a test of the mettle of the entire national evangelical community. And North, in turn, places himself on equal footing with his fellow believers, whose trials of faith have been no less grueling—and no less momentous, in cosmic terms—than his own, even if fewer people have known about them.

Focus on the Family furthermore gives the leveling of North with Dobson's audience an expressly political bent by stressing North's identity as an ordinary American citizen. Dobson reminds North (and the listening audience) that with the conclusion of the investigation, North is once again free to exercise his basic political rights:

> Dobson: Ollie, you are totally cleared, your trials are over, you're no longer charged with anything, you can even *vote*, is that right?
> North: Got the vote back![13]

The triumphant confirmation of North's reenfranchisement is repeated toward the beginnings of both the first and second broadcasts in the program series. Later in the second show, North justifies his decision to "take the Fifth Amendment" as simply seeking the benefit of "a constitutional protection that we all enjoy." These apparently unnoteworthy moments in the broadcast series serve a notable purpose, for they signal that North is equal to ordinary Americans not only by virtue of his commitments to family and faith but also because he participates in politics and articulates demands to the state in the same manner as does every other citizen: by casting a ballot and invoking his constitutional rights.

Focus on the Family emphasizes not only North's equality with Dobson's listeners, however, but also his stature as an admirable, responsible, and powerful political leader. Notwithstanding Dobson's and Trout's initial disavowals of any interest in political affairs, eventually Dobson invites North to justify his deception of Congress, and North eagerly complies:

> Dobson: Ollie, I know that *one* reason that you were not entirely candid and in fact lied to the congressional committee that came over to the White House was that you were trying to protect men in the field, men in other countries whose lives would have been endangered if that information was public. . . .

North: One of the things that I found most difficult about all of this was being placed in a situation where, having been told very specifically that this will never be revealed—there's secrets within secrets, there's lives at risk—then being pointedly asked about that kind of information by people who we knew would leak it [*sic*]. It sounds so simple today to look back at a world that has changed dramatically in the last several years, and yet there were *many* lives at risk. . . .

Dobson: When you began shredding information and you were later accused of withholding documents from Congress, within that information was life and death data that not only *could* have resulted in the death of someone in another country but *did*. General Alvarez, as I understand it, in Honduras, may have been assassinated because of information released by this process.

North: Indeed. General Alvarez worked with our government for a number of years in supporting the Nicaraguan resistance and is dead today, machine-gunned by opponents of that policy.[14]

This conversation thus attempts to legitimize misleading Congress on the grounds of national security in the cold war world. It is noteworthy, in addition, that North's deception is justified on the basis of his personal concern for the individual lives of his (and the nation's) allies in the global struggle against communism. As Dobson's initial comment suggests, North's actions become understandable and defensible above all because he is "Ollie," someone known intimately by his comrades "in the field" and Dobson's listeners alike. North may have exercised prodigious, even extraordinary, power. But it is power that seems fundamentally accessible to the ordinary American because North himself is a "regular guy"—a "family man," a Christian, a voting citizen, a dependable friend. Moreover, it is power that "the American people" have authorized, according to North, for they demonstrated this during Iran-Contra by deluging him with supportive letters, prayers, and financial donations.[15] On *Focus on the Family*, North thus represents a distinctly democratic ideal of the political leader who is both a humble man of the people and expressly commissioned by the people to act on their behalf.

In general, then, North's comments on Dobson's program invoke a traditional evangelical narrative of redemption, reworking it so that certain political implications are brought to the fore. North is the believer who finds salvation by taking the road of humility. His comments thus resonate with powerful biblical currents, with countless stories of Jesus, the prophets, and the apostles humbling themselves in order to do the work of God. Defining features of evangelical Protestantism, moreover, provide the traditional backdrop against which Focus's presentation of North as the humble Christian likely makes sense to the listening audience. Above all, evangelicalism dispenses with all pretentiousness and ostentation in religious worship, language, and song. It emphasizes the spiritual accessibility of God by making its rituals and routines accessible to common tastes and styles. In the eras of the Great Awakenings, this meant abandoning "high church" protocol for more emotional and spectacular collective demonstrations of piety. In contemporary evangelical "megachurches," in turn, the services are "simple, even spartan"; "the melodies are simple, rather folksy, and everyone seems to know the words." From the pulpit of a large evangelical church in southern California, the preacher takes a "workmanlike" approach to biblical texts, reviewing the rise and fall of ancient Hebrew dynasties "as a sports fan would study box scores." "People are coming here," another young pastor declares, because they hear God's call and they "like coming to a place where they can wear Levi's, shorts, tennis shoes, bare feet, whatever, and sit and listen to some guy teach the Word of God in a way that they can understand it."[16] This pastor has put his finger on the signature theological and cultural egalitarianism of American evangelical Protestantism. Focus, in turn, develops the narrative of salvation through humility such that it addresses (and finesses) the problem of the interrelationship between the religious egalitarianism characteristic of evangelicalism and the more broadly shared ideal of political egalitarianism, which remains the credo of the modern national security state. The narrative figure of the humble leader, epitomized by North, seems to reconcile his privileged possession of classified knowledge and vast power with his identity as a man of the people acting according to their will.

Pressures stemming from internal tensions within this narrative, however, make the harmonious countenance of Focus's figure of the humble leader no less prone to faults and fissures than that of the compassionate professional. In the first place, a number of comments signaling North's elite and exceptional status simply do not cohere entirely with the shows' stress on his equality with Focus's listeners. Describing his appearances before the House investigating committee, for instance, North casually recalls that there were thirty secret service agents assigned to protect him from an unspecified "terrorist threat." Somehow, he adds with wonderment, a compassionate supporter was still able to thrust a card with an uplifting biblical verse into his hands, and the verse gave him courage throughout the proceedings.[17] The point of this story is not only to call attention to North's spiritual bond with ordinary people of good faith but also to remind the listener of just how important a person North actually is. Toward this end, North also describes his testimony in the Iran-Contra hearings as "one of the most extraordinary ordeals in the *history of this republic!*"[18] Such hyperbole ratchets up the level and the significance of the "adversity" North has endured, setting him distinctly apart from the vast majority of other citizens and baldly contradicting his claim that "everybody goes through something like this in their lives."[19]

North's image of humility is likewise both promoted and undercut by the constant references to North's status as a prominent figure in the national media. Consider, for example, North's account of the reporters who staked out his home when the Iran-Contra scandal hit the papers:

> They were there by the time I'd open the door in the morning at six. . . . They would first of all litter the landscape with wrappings from Seven-Eleven or whatever fast-food place they'd stopped at on the way out with coffee cups and the like. The roadway in front of our house is a single lane little road that dead-ended down the road about two hundred meters from where we lived, very quiet little country setting [sic]. And these guys showed up the first time in the morning of the 26th of November and they were there every single day for seven months except one day. They were there Christmas, they were there Easter, they were there Passover, they were there Lent. . . . I guess their religious holiday was the one day they weren't there and that was New Year's Day.[20]

The contrast could not be more stark between the clean-living Norths and the ill-mannered media correspondents, who display a thorough contempt for "family values"—including a nutritious breakfast at home, well-groomed lawns, an avoidance of stimulants and alcohol, and an active religious life. North's recollection of being hounded by the media thus helps establish the patina of the Norths as a normal, middle-class family, and of North himself as a humble citizen. However, it also fosters a keen sense of Oliver North as a man of great consequence, someone who is distinctly unlike Dobson's ordinary listeners.

North's account of the media stakeout of his family home furthermore contradicts the narrative's handling of the idea of publicity. As the ideal, humble leader, public exposure works in North's favor, allowing him to spread his "encouraging" message far and wide. Indeed, publicity is vital to North's fulfillment of this role, just as public testimonies to God's saving grace and public displays of faith are core elements of evangelical religion. Thus we hear Dobson proudly and approvingly say to North: "You're going to be on tour, you're going to be on television, you're going to be in the news for days to come."[21] Publicity, the narrative seems to say initially, helps establish the equality of the humble leader with all other believers and hasten the redemption of individual souls and the world at large. Yet in the next breath North and Dobson condemn the agencies of publicity by caricaturing the media as a pack of bloodhounds who are the inveterate enemies of the average family symbolized by the Norths—fully outfitted with country-suburban home, pickup truck, kids, and ponies.

This alternate, condemnatory stance toward the forces of publicity has ominous consequences for the political dimension of the narrative. For it dematerializes the bonds of accountability between leaders and ordinary citizens. Just like the Norths' family home, the Reagan White House where North organized covert, legally proscribed support to Nicaraguan rightists comes to be understood as a properly private domain, a realm into which the agents of publicity in the media and the Congress have no right to intrude. Under these circumstances, the people's authorization of the leader's actions in their name can only be symbolic, diffuse, and after-the-fact. The sense in which North "represents" the demos is thus fraught with tensions and ambiguities on *Focus on the Family*, ambiguities encapsulated in North's repeated references to the letters, prayers, and donations sent to him by citizens of goodwill during the trial. On the one hand, North comes across as the servant of the people, one who carries out their expressed will. On the other hand, his authority seems to have more of a plebiscitary character: he "represents" the people by symbolizing their unity and paternalistically acting according to his estimate of their best interests; and the fountain of his legitimacy as a leader is not so much their declared intentions but more their general "faith" in his capacities to act for the good of the public. Throughout the broadcast series, North stresses that during his trials he never lost the conviction that so long as he remained "faithful" to Christian values, he would ultimately be vindicated of any wrongdoing. He also emphasizes, however, that he was able to persevere because of the strength he gained from the millions who retained their "faith" in him. At one point, North offers the following exegesis of the U.S. Marine Corps's motto, semper fidelis (always faithful), as a way of characterizing his personal attitude during his "ordeal":

> "Semper fidelis" . . . What it means to me is faithfulness to God, faithfulness to our families, and faithfulness to those truly traditional values that made this country what it is. In Romans 8:28 it says, it's *His plan*, it does *not* say you'll understand it. It does *not* say that you're gonna grasp the fullness of what it is He has in mind. It says, if you're faithful, if you're faithful, it'll be carried out. Faithfulness is essential to all of what we've gotta do.[22]

This embrace of soldierly obedience, in the certainty that whoever has determined the "plan" to be followed has good reasons for their judgment of what must be done, reasons that need not and quite possibly cannot be understood by ordinary folk, becomes the obligation of "the American people" in the second, competing political imaginary that North's narrative evokes.

In this aspect of the narrative, in turn, North's justification of his actions in Iran-Contra acquires a more authoritarian tone: he is not just "Ollie," not just a leader among equals, but rather the rightful claimant to broadly discretionary authority and the public's unquestioning deference. There remains, however, a tertiary agency mediating the relations between the humble leader's not-so-humble alter ego and the people. Into the vacuum created by the withdrawal of the mainstream media and the Congress into Satan's camp steps none other than God "Himself." Interestingly, North does not profess to have always acted properly as steward of the public interest in the Reagan White House. However, he contends that his improprieties violated God's will rather than the people's trust:

North: There's no doubt that I made mistakes. I'm a mortal just like everybody else, I made some very serious mistakes, I admitted those mistakes that I made during the hearings, I admitted them again in my own trial. . . . I have always known where I was going, not because I was a good person or because of my work or because of my efforts or my energy—it's because He died to save me. And I know that He has forgiven me for the errors in judgment and the mistakes that I made. . . . Dobson: You know what's interesting to me, the Bible says "for all have sinned and fallen short of the glory of God"—*all* of us, *none* of us is without sin and without blame. And yet the grace of God somehow reaches us. And yet when a person is in a very public role, and his misdeeds are very widely publicized, some people think that they *cannot be forgiven*, and reinstated, that the Lord cannot *reach* them somehow.[23]

Here once again, the conversation insists on North's fundamental parity with Dobson's audience members. Just like them, he is prone to sin and urgently needs God's forgiving grace along with a spirit of repentance. Yet the political implications are manifestly contradictory: the message of egalitarianism and accountability to the public interest is mingled with the unmistakably authoritarian propositions (1) that the Christian leader is ultimately accountable only to God for his actions in the name of the collective, and (2) that his political responsibility to other citizens consists in gratefully receiving their plebiscitary acclaim along with their prayers that he act wisely, recognize his misdeeds when they occur, and duly repent of these wrongs as personal sins.

Focus's narrative of the humble leader is thus contradictory throughout. On the one hand, North seems to exemplify an ordinary citizen who is the equal of all by virtue of his private commitments to faith, family, and friends, along with his political status as a voter and possessor of constitutional rights. He is a citizen, moreover, who loses none of these qualities when he exercises state authority at the highest levels and gains widespread exposure in the public sphere. North thus emblematizes what would appear to be the thoroughly democratic, egalitarian character of American political institutions, along with their consonance with and roots in the cultural egalitarianism of evangelical Protestantism. On the other hand, *Focus on the Family* depicts North as a plebiscitary leader who wields command over a populace to which he is superior because he has endured exceptional travails and maintains fidelity to divine purposes that he is specially capable of discerning. Publicity becomes not a mode by which power is democratically shared, but an impertinent, blasphemous, and order-threatening trespass on the sacred domain of the ruler. The final status of North as a model of redemption through humility thus remains unresolved: he gestures simultaneously toward leaders' humble solidarity with ordinary people, and toward the degrading obeisance of the common folk to their betters, as the way of salvation. Fighting for precedence over the egalitarian impulses of the evangelical redemption narrative, in other words, is a fundamentalist strain emphasizing submission to divine authority as the path of Christ—and the foundation of authentic democracy.

Like the compassionate professional, the embattled narrative of the humble leader resurfaces periodically in other broadcasts as an organizing structure of *Focus on the Family*. Exploring several other shows in which this narrative emerges will thus help tease out its peculiar features before confronting the analytical, dialectical questions that concern us: Why would listeners who allow themselves the genuine wish for equality that the program expresses, and the experience of equality that the program provides in a virtual manner, then acquiesce to the program's simultaneous denial of that hope? Under what historical circumstances would this forced resolution of the narrative's contradictions seem acceptable? In Adornian terms, what is the social physiognomy of the humble leader's shifting countenance? In what ways, that is, do the heteromorphous faces of this narrative figure reflect, reproduce, and perhaps protest against social antagonisms? We shall return to these questions after encountering a few more of Focus's humble leaders.

"Chuck" Colson: Renunciate of Power, Warrior for Democracy

The North series rearticulates the traditional evangelical narrative of salvation through humility in terms that address the extraordinary accumulation of power in the contemporary state, highlighting the relationship between publicity and democratic authority. In doing so, it predictably alights now and again on a historical touchstone in which controversies concerning the legitimacy of state power and the public's capacity to scrutinize its leaders reached a particularly acute crisis: the Watergate scandal. Watergate obliquely enters the picture when North notes the repeated coincidence of troubles in his family life with "dark decades" in the nation's history, clearly meaning Iran-Contra in one case and evoking the memory of Watergate by mentioning that he and Betsy had contemplated divorce in 1974–75.[24] Here, Watergate serves as a convenient parallel to Iran-Contra, as depicted on *Focus on the Family*: it confirms the sense that when the Congress and the press challenge executive authority, families fall apart and God's purposes are thwarted. Dobson, in turn, draws explicitly on the residual trauma of Watergate to buttress the authoritarian counterstrain in the narrative of the humble leader. In Iran-Contra, Dobson laments, Congress was determined "to *revisit* Watergate and *this* time . . . do it right." Dobson suggests that like another well-known guest in Focus's studio, former Nixon aide Charles Colson, North was stymied in his attempts to carry out his patriotic duties and assaulted in his private life by the voracious appetite of the publicity apparatus.[25] Yet a review of an appearance by Colson on *Focus on the Family* shows that Colson's narrative, like North's, is actually self-contradictory rather than consistently authoritarian. In fact, both are versions of the tangled narrative of the humble leader that pervades a number of Focus's broadcasts.

Like the North series, the Colson broadcasts actively foster the sense that Dobson's guest and the audience are cut from the same Christian cloth. Dobson and Colson begin by chuckling sadly over many people's persistent tendency to stigmatize Colson as a Watergate villain, when for the past twenty years his life has been defined by his "personal encounter with Jesus Christ" and his "continued walk with the Lord." Colson then narrates the story of his salvation, the catalyst for which was a witness from another believer and the enormously popular evangelical book by C. S. Lewis, *Mere Christianity*, given to him by this individual. After being "alone with the Lord for the first time in [his] life," Colson recalls, he understood that "the truth of God is in every one of us, the image of God is impressed into us."[26]

Colson's story of being drawn toward the path of faith not only emphasizes his private as opposed to his public persona. It also dramatically marks him as an ordinary evangelical Christian—someone who is just like Dobson's listeners, and someone who resembles them precisely because he has "come to Christ" in exactly the same manner that countless other, evangelical noncelebrities have, with the aid of Lewis's book and a nudge from another believer. Colson's affirmation of the basic spiritual resemblance of all individuals underscores this affinity. In addition, his unashamed admission that he wept profusely in "calling out to God" for the first time is right in line with common evangelical expectations and experiences regarding the emotional loss of control that accompanies being saved. Colson moreover accentuates his equal status with other believers by emphasizing his mortality at another point in the broadcast series, remembering how sure he was that he would soon "see Jesus face to face" at a critical moment during his surgery for stomach cancer.[27]

But how can these moments of connection with Dobson's listeners, these attempts to put himself on a level with them, be reconciled with Colson's auspicious experience as a member of a president's inner circle? Colson achieves this by folding his career history into his broader background as a man who once futilely sought fulfillment from passing rather than eternal things, but has now renounced the former. As Nixon's main "hatchet man," Colson enjoyed a fat salary, the influence stemming from his reputation for toughness, luxury "toys" such as a yacht, and other perks of high executive office. These gratifications were not only meaningless in themselves, Colson insists, but also part of a pattern of living sinfully: What Colson regrets most about having worked for Nixon is "not the things you read about in Watergate, but the hatred and the envy and the pride and the bitterness and the pride [sic] and the covetousness. If I didn't know for *certain* that Jesus died for those sins on the cross," he adds, "I could not live with myself today."[28] Having recognized his sins for what they truly were and become born again, Colson attests, he has left "the years of power" behind and humbly embraced life as an ordinary person. More than this, Dobson emphasizes, Colson now breaks bread with the most downtrodden of people in the most undesirable of places. As Dobson puts it, the prisoners whom Colson encounters these days through his organization, Prison Fellowship Ministries, are "broken down-and-outers who can offer nothing in return but affection and love." To see them, Colson must travel to "Third World" countries and enter out-of-the-way spaces permeated by "the smell of excrement" and the threat of violence. But these hardships are mere trifles, according to Colson, since they do not diminish in the least the satisfaction he receives from his intimate, personal, and loving contact with other human beings.[29]

Colson's narrative, like North's, thus mobilizes distinctly egalitarian currents of Christian thought. Indeed, Colson's egalitarianism is even more far-reaching than North's, since he asserts his basic solidarity with not only ordinary middle-class Americans but also the world's most destitute and dejected persons. His is a story of redemption through humility, even self-sacrifice. And this experience of being humbled and associating with the oppressed enables him to offer knowing, sympathetic "encouragement . . . to a lot of people who are going through some *extremely* tough times."[30] Colson's chief ally in this discipline of self-giving, significantly, is media publicity, which to him operates in a fundamentally democratizing capacity. A genuine luminary within the evangelical subculture, Colson nonetheless envisions his role more as that of a communicator who provides information and public services than as an authority figure who issues commands. He avers that his daily radio news commentary *Break-Point*, for instance, simply tries "to equip the believer to think 'Christianly' about issues" and "current events." He and Dobson marvel at the capacity of radio broadcasting to set off "multiplying effects" far beyond their own control in the studio:

> Dobson: Isn't it fun when you realize you're just a li'l *peanut* in the grand scheme of things? I was in Miami last week and a woman told me that she did *not* know Jesus Christ, and she was working around her house, she was sweeping, and Mike, you and I said, "now, whoever's out there, put down your broom and *listen* to this" (all laugh), and it hit her right between the eyes. And it really is interesting how the Lord can tailor-make what we do here in the studio.
> Colson: That's the wonderful thing about it, because we know it's not us but it's God who's working.
> Trout: We've said that you've been the Chairman of the Board [of Prison Fellowship Ministries] since 1984—the ministry started quite a bit before that.
> Colson: The ministry started in the year that I got out of prison— actually, we started working in the prisons in 1975 and then we incorporated in 1976, and then I became Chairman and another became President—because that's a big job, to run it, and my job is to go out and to preach and to write books and to now, thank you, go on the radio.[31]

Colson thus sharply circumscribes his own agency, stressing that someone else has the "big job" of running the company and that he and his associates, including Dobson, are in any case simply instruments of the divine will, just as anyone else can be. The best sort of leadership, Colson and Dobson imply, reflects an awareness that all are on an equal plane before God. And it does this by setting a positive example and facilitating other people's independent decisions to do right—not by barking orders. Media publicity, moreover, provides vital support for the humble leader's endeavors.

At the same time, in Colson the figure of the humble leader once again incorporates a dimension of formidable power in the secular world. *Focus on the Family* makes it plain that Colson has traveled in elite circles before and continues to do so today. The believer whose witness inspired Colson's conversion was, in worldly terms, no ordinary person—he was chairman of the board of the military contracting behemoth Raytheon, for which Colson had been serving as a high-ranking attorney. When Dobson and Colson describe the White House perks that Colson claims he eventually sacrificed—such as the yacht, personal helicopter service, and proximity to the Oval Office—they do so in tantalizing detail, creating the sense that Colson is clearly at home with the trappings of great authority. Colson may have given up the boat and moved his office out of the White House after Watergate and his conversion, but he has not forfeited his rarified access to the halls of power. Indeed, it seems that his network has expanded to become worldwide in scope. The inmates Colson has met through Prison Fellowship Ministries often turn out to be foreign dignitaries rather than ordinary criminals or impoverished debtors:

> A fellow in a prison was converted in Ethiopia in the prison. During five years in prison he led thirty-two hundred people to Christ. They built a church, the Marxist government is overthrown, and he now is ministering to the guards, five hundred of whom have now come to Christ, and they've built a church among the guards! . . . I got a letter a few months ago, Jim, from the President of Zambia. He was just elected—the first freely elected president, they threw out the Marxist government, President Kowandi who'd been a terrible dictator was out—and I got this wonderful, warm letter from him, I had no idea why, just thanking me for Prison Fellowship, encouraging me, and hoping I would do well. Well, when I got to Korea I discovered that the president had been a prisoner and in prison had been led to Christ by Prison Fellowship volunteers; and when he got out his *marriage* was in trouble and Prison Fellowship volunteers worked with him and his wife and got their marriage back together; and now he's the President of the country.[32]

Colson's power in the political world thus seems ironically to have grown, not diminished, with his embrace of Christian humility and his relinquishing of official duties. Colson drives this point home with the following elaboration of his experiences in Korea:

> Today I was just in Korea, for example, and we had our conference of Prison Fellowship international convocation [*sic*]—people congregated from all over the world. I met men from Russia and eastern Europe who had been converted reading my books, and a whole delegation got off a bus at the conference center in Korea—Russians—and they came rushing up to me. One of them was a city councilman in St. Petersburg, another one was a journalist from Moscow, another one was an Orthodox priest who'd been in prison—many of them came rushing up to me and started embracing me and kissing me on both

cheeks. All I could think of was, I spent most of my life—a Marine Lieutenant during the Korean War—learning how to kill communists. I was in the Senate during the big arms buildup in the fifties, working on the defense budget. I was in the White House with four years of briefings on missile tonnage and megatonnage and throw weight, and how we're going to have a nuclear standoff, and listening to the intelligence summaries coming in every day from the Soviet Union. All my life fighting the cold war, and now suddenly God has brought an *end* to that, and look at the marvelous and mysterious ways—what could never be done politically—these men are now standing on a street corner embracing me and kissing me on both cheeks, telling me how my book *Loving God* had transformed their lives, and you tell *me* which gives you the greatest thrill![33]

As in the North broadcasts, the clear message here is that the leader's Christian humility and fundamental equality with all human beings is perfectly compatible with—indeed, conducive to—his possession of prodigious political influence, even though this influence may not operate through conventional political channels. Moreover, Colson not only claims to have led ordinary Russians toward a new commitment to democracy, he also evokes the sense that his own position as a leader has been legitimized through democratic means. Circulating at the conference in Korea, Colson essentially plays the role of "Ollie," for he is both of the people and evidently authorized by them to lead on their behalf. The mediation of a public sphere through which *Loving God* has been disseminated, in turn, crucially certifies the democratic character of Colson's authority. The concluding image of beatitude, picturing a startled Colson in the exuberant arms of a public official, a priest, and a journalist, exquisitely encapsulates the harmonious reconciliation of humility and power, of intimacy and publicity, that Colson's version of the narrative of the humble leader effectuates.

As in the North series, however, egalitarian and authoritarian elements are densely interwoven in the telling of this narrative. Colson's description of his adoring reception in Korea, for example, equivocates on its own democratic implications. On the one hand, the physical embrace of Colson and the anonymous Russians vividly confirms Colson's status as a man of the people. On the other hand, the mode by which "the people" authorize Colson as their leader is plainly not "democratic" in any way that involves a sense of his enduring accountability to them for his actions in their name. Although the humble leader is depicted as the equal—even the intimate friend—of his followers, his authority seems to be founded on the vague and predominantly affective acclaim of a plebiscite.

Dobson, in turn, helps Colson develop the vision of this plebiscitary arrangement as a historically concrete and morally compelling alternative to the contemporary institutional structure of U.S. political society, by clarifying the irremediable perdition of the latter:

On one side you have the media, the entertainment industry, the Congress and the court system and the White House, you have the professions—are *all* on the other side. On the side of traditional Christianity there are only two, only two centers of power—the Church and the family. Now we've known the *family* was threatened, but until recently I haven't fully understood the degree to which the *Church* is being assaulted by *hell itself.*[34]

In response to this onslaught of Satan's forces, Colson proposes not so much that citizens pray for the leaders of institutions that retain their fundamental legitimacy, as the North series suggests by celebrating the trial's conclusion in North's favor. Instead, Colson urges that devoted Americans mobilize within a wholly distinct public realm: here, "the Church" refers to the assemblage of believers, churches, and other evangelical institutions that is mystically united but also able to act as a social and political collectivity. Building up the Church, according to Colson, requires above all generating loyalty and obedience to the Church's leaders:

The Church is on the frontlines and the Church is being assaulted, the Church is being beleaguered. The pastors need our support and our help, and the lay people need to get behind their pastor and make that Church a living, vital organization in their community. . . . When a church lacks the proper sense of *"koinonia"*—fellowship, a bonding together, a real sense of accountability and a real sense of discipline— then it always breaks down into power fights and factions. We refuse to respect the pastor's authority. Now, I think the pastor's gotta have authority over that church, because *he* is the one ordained by God to speak to that congregation on God's behalf. He needs to be *accountable* to the church and *held* to account, but clearly tht pastor needs authority. In the church that I worship in, . . . the pastor, when he came, . . . had a covenant with twenty-five points, and he wanted it agreed to between the members of the church and himself. And it's *excellent* because it spells out exactly what's expected. And that's what the churches need to do. We are tearing pastors apart in this country . . . and it's shocking.[35]

Colson's insistence that pastors must be "held to account" for their actions in the name of the congregation resonates with the egalitarian current in the narrative. Nonetheless, the countercurrent reasserts itself in several ways. First, Colson prioritizes the pastor's need for "authority," his caveat concerning "accountability" notwithstanding. In Colson's ideal model of clergy-laity relations, moreover, the pastor offers a "covenant" to his parishioners (which they appear obligated to accept), rather than working out mutual expectations through dialogue and a more "contractual" agreement to which both sides are equal parties. Furthermore, Colson's remarks lean much more heavily toward rebuking and shaming listeners for rebelling against pastoral "authority" and even "tearing pastors apart" than toward provoking a critical regard for church leaders. As a model for the mobilization of ordinary individuals against oppressive and sinful institutional forces, then, this notion of the Church embodies a brand of democracy that is highly compromised, to say the least.

In addition, when Colson specifies the process he endorses for holding pastors accountable to "the Church," this mechanism turns out to be far from democratic. Instead of a general and public parish review, Colson advocates the pastor's private supervision by an elite circle of peers:

> One of the things that I talk about in the book [*The Body*, 1993] and feel very strongly about is the accountability that is necessary in the Christian life. I know you've done it, Jim, and I've done it—I've gone to certain members of my board and I tell them, "Doesn't matter what area of my life, it's open to you, you come in, you look at my books, you ask me questions. . . ." [Ideally, pastors and selected board members] sit around in a circle and they have seven questions and they ask one another these questions. They go down the list and it's all of the obvious temptations—"Have you lied?" and sexual immorality—and they finally get to the last one, [which] is, "Have you just lied to me?" (Both laugh) But they hold one another to account in that way. And I think that is *extremely* important, because I don't trust myself. And I know how easily pride affected me once before in my life and could again at this moment or twenty minutes from now, and so I have a group that I hold myself totally accountable to—as a matter of fact I will make no decision unless they unanimously agree to it, that's a major decision.[36]

Not only is a very limited segment of the collective empowered to scrutinize the pastor's conduct, and not only is the pastor's probation clearly meant to occur behind closed doors. Holding the pastor accountable blurs the distinction between the pastor's private morality and his faithful or unfaithful execution of church affairs. Indeed, the former ultimately appears to be the more pressing point of evaluation—this much is suggested when Colson and Dobson repeatedly refer to statistics showing the disturbing frequency with which pastors engage in "inappropriate sexual behavior with someone in their present church."[37] Colson's widely popular early nineties book about rejuvenating the Church is titled *The Body*, and it is quite literally the corporeal containment of the pastor that here guarantees the rectitude of the Church—not the critical mediation of a religious-public sphere or any other more democratic institution for ensuring accountability.

Meanwhile, Colson casts ordinary parishioners in the role of soldiers in the Church's pastor-led "cosmic struggle" against evil:

> We should look at our churches *exactly* the way you look at Marine Corps training for combat because that's what it *is*! It's the *church*, the body of believers, who *meet* together for worship and study, for the proclamation of the Word, for the administration of the sacraments, *and* for the equipping of believers in the world. That is *how* we are *preparing* today for the spiritual combat in which we live, and we should take it every bit as seriously as soldiers in the Marines preparing to go to war.[38]

Colson's theory of the Church thus forms the centerpiece of the manifestly authoritarian counterstrain that undermines the egalitarian, democratic sensibility of the narrative. As in the North series, here the institutional mediations between the public and its leader are spiritualized, inasmuch as the legitimacy of every major institution of the government and the public sphere is denied, and the leader's authority comes to rest on a plebiscitary and emotionalistic admiration for the leader's private virtue. But here these mediations then rematerialize in hierarchical form, in the Church, reinvigorated as the army of God whose captain is commissioned through the monitoring of his private virtue and bodily integrity by a cloistered elite.

These aspects of the narrative, in turn, provide an amply secure basis for *Focus on the Family* to clear Colson's name of any wrongdoing as one of the leading architects of Nixon's dirty tricks. Colson echoes North when he justifies his illegal conduct as a public official by appealing to his privileged knowledge of military secrets and his obligation to protect the lives of his comrades-in-arms:

> Dobson: You told me privately a number of years ago that if you could have actually presented all the evidence that you had at your disposal, you would never have been convicted, you would never have gone to prison, and in order to keep a state secret you accepted that seven months. . . . Tell the story of what you *could not tell*, at that time.
> Colson: Well, the problem was that I didn't go to prison for Watergate, I went to prison for the Ellsberg break-in at the psychiatrist's office.

And the reason that they broke in was that they were very concerned about the papers that he had stolen from the government.[39]

Dobson: Pentagon papers.

Colson: The Pentagon Papers, and others—national security memoranda—and was disseminating to the media [*sic*]. And one of them turned up at the Russian delegation in the United Nations, several of them turned up on the desks of U.S. senators, many of them made their way into the newspapers, but we didn't know all the papers yet [*sic*]. Now, breaking into a psychiatrist's office was a stupid, dumb thing, and I did not know about it in advance, but I was part of a conspiracy to *defame* Ellsberg and that's what I pleaded guilty to. If, however, the court had allowed, or if we had been willing to testify, what was *in* the Pentagon Papers—sequestered during the trials and protected, never released, but that we were fearful *would* be released— I think it would have been exculpatory, possibly even exonerating of what we did to attempt to expose Ellsberg, because *in* the Pentagon Papers were the names of CIA agents operating abroad at that moment, so lives would have been in *instant* jeopardy. We had names of people who were CIA cover [*sic*] agents operating in the Soviet Union—they were *in* those papers that Ellsberg had. We had reason to be alarmed for *lives*! Not only that, but in there was intelligence of conversations taking place, recorded conversations, taking place among Soviet officials from their limousines while they were driving around in the Kremlin [*sic*]. We had such sophisticated listening devices in our satellites that we could actually monitor and listen to their phone conversations. But those transcripts—if they had been *released*—would have let the Russians know, the Soviets know, that we were actually listening to their radio communications in Moscow and would have been *devastating* to our national security effort. So we all discussed it at the time and agreed that regardless of the consequences to our case, we would never disclose that. We went before the judge and told him these things and he said, "All of those things have to be protected and can't be used." But of course, if they had been used would [*sic*] have largely helped us—certainly with the jury—would have helped us greatly.

Dobson: And yet as you said it was God's will that you *went* to prison— He *used* that in your life.

Colson: I look back now and realize that had I fought the case I would have won. . . . But, no, God had a *plan* for my life.[40]

Resonances of North's condemnations of Congress and the media are plainly audible in this conversation. Once again, the highest echelons of executive authority are figured as a realm where privileges of privacy hold sway, although here the model for the privatization of executive power in the national security state is supplied not by the image of the family home but rather by the figure of the pastor in the militarized church. Colson converts the question of his actions' consistency with the will and interest of the public into their harmony with the divine "plan" for his life. This plan led him to prison—not as punishment for wrongdoing, however, but rather to fulfill God's purposes both that "national security" not be further jeopardized by additional leaks and that Colson find his destiny as a minister to prisoners. Colson's fidelity to God's plan is the measure of his fitness to lead, just as it is for the pastor; and God lays active responsibility for the future of the country solely on Colson and his fellow "elders" of the national security state, just as the pastors and their select peers are the trustees of the Church.

These features of the narrative subsist in sharp and unresolved tension with the humble leader's claim to power that is expressly and democratically authorized by the public. The ordinary citizens with whom Colson otherwise wants to confirm his equal status, in turn, must content themselves with the satisfactions of hearing tidbits of previously classified information, marveling at the CIA's technological ingenuity (eavesdropping on "Marxist dictators" in their limousines—what will they think up next!), and wondering over the mysterious ways of God. They are not to judge their leaders, however, as this is solely the prerogative of God and a select few of "His" agents. Finally, the fact that the Ellsberg break-in—the theft of confidential patient files from a psychologist's office—provides the context for Focus to exonerate Colson underscores an additional, discomfiting irony: with the triumph of privacy over publicity, the public apparently forfeits its own rights to privacy even as their leaders' sacred domain is sealed off from all public scrutiny. In sum, internally contradicting the classically evangelical narrative of redemption through humility in the Colson broadcasts is a fundamentalist logic according to which salvation is dispensed according to obedience—and, if necessary, outright humiliation—before authority.

"The Freshmen": Calling the People to Their Knees

This chapter began by noting that Focus's denunciations of an overweaning publicity undoubtedly serve the opportunistic interests of convicted conspirators turned spokespersons for the Christian right. I have argued, however, that the aspersions cast on the agencies of publicity have political implications going beyond these strategic aims, inasmuch as they internally disturb a narrative describing a particular, traditionally rooted notion of the mutual sustenance given one another by evangelical Christianity and democratic politics. This argument gains additional fortitude when we consider that the narrative of the humble leader not only structures Dobson's conversations with former conspirators who need to have their names cleared but also undergirds episodes of *Focus on the Family* featuring politicians whose status as exemplary leaders is more likely to be already undisputed among Focus's listeners.

In January 1995, Focus broadcast a recording of a roundtable discussion with seven newly elected Republicans in the U.S. House of Representatives along with Gary Bauer, then head of the Family Research Council (FRC). The large number of guests in this broadcast precludes Dobson from asking each one to tell her or his story of personal salvation in as much detail as North and Colson are able to do. Nevertheless, Dobson prompts them to declare openly their evangelical commitments to the Christian faith.[41] He thus clearly intends to make the panelists come alive to his listeners as ordinary individuals, to convey a keen sense of the former's common experience and equal standing with the latter.

In introducing the panelists, moreover, Dobson draws out details signaling that these representatives are quite different from the smooth "insiders" that usually gravitate toward the Capitol. Rather, it seems easy to relate to them on a personal level, mainly because (the show stresses) they all have "real lives" outside Washington, D.C. In particular, they have private work lives that establish multiple possible points of connection with the listening audience. Steve Largent and J. C. Watts of Oklahoma are former football players undoubtedly familiar to most listeners who follow NFL and NCAA sports, and Largent is also a hunting buddy of Dobson's. Ron Lewis "was a pastor in a little community back in Kentucky" and "owned a Christian bookstore." Tom Coburn, also from Oklahoma, is a private physician like so many of Dobson's friends and radio guests. Dobson thus develops the notion that these misfits within the national governing elite are private individuals with normal jobs, just like their (and his) constituents.

Moreover, according to Dobson, these members of "the freshman class" on Capitol Hill value life as private citizens incomparably more than their places of governmental privilege. They demonstrate this by disavowing legislative careerism, as Dobson explains: "They feel the Lord has sent them there for a limited amount of time—almost none of them profess to wanting a career in government. They have come there to make an impact, to do what they can, and then return to private life."[42] Each guest in turn confirms Dobson's declaration that she or he has entered public life not out of personal ambition but from a sense of God's call to contribute to the common good. The discussants thus come across as bucking the status quo in Congress, which they see as encouraging members to hoard power and money in a manner symbolized by a little-known cache of "several million dollars worth of historic art" in the (formerly Democratic) majority whip's office, a hidden trove to which Dobson pointedly refers at the start of the broadcast. Denying that his guests have been "bought by special interests," Dobson asserts that the freshmen Republicans are free to legislate responsibly—that is, in ways responsive to both the biddings of their personal principles and the common sense of their constituents. And they can be trusted, they contend, because they know they are ordinary people who are no different from those who live in their districts—people who expect to have to work for their pay, and people with a humility borne of deep Christian faith.[43]

This is not to say, however, that "the freshmen" minimize or trivialize their power as U.S. representatives. In metaphorical terms: having stumbled on the treasures concealed in the majority whip's office, "the freshmen" respond not by handing over the (ill-gotten?) goods to the people but by appropriating them for Republicans—by moving in and taking charge. They are fully aware of their ability to initiate widespread political and social change, as a comment by Tennesseean Zach Wamp illustrates:

> I think Ronald Reagan said, paraphrasing, that the great decisions of this country are not made in Washington, D.C.—they're made around family *dinner* tables every night across this country. Until moms and dads meet their responsibility we *cannot* really restore American civilization as we once knew it. We can turn the direction of the *government* around. . . . But this—if this is truly going to be what it *deserves* to be, we have to *light* the fire in Washington and it *has* to make its way to the American dinner table.[44]

Wamp's statement deftly manages to affirm the ultimate, nation-making power of individual families and ordinary "moms and dads" while staking a bold claim to the power and responsibility of government to instigate civic renewal. In a similar vein, Bauer calls on the other panelists to actively shape public opinion in the context of invoking the theme of democratic self-rule: "This was an experiment in liberty under God. The founders knew that *only* a virtuous people could remain free, and if this new freshman class can get *that back* in the public mind, that will be more powerful than any legislation that's passed."[45] Bauer's remark seems to imply recognition of the fact that the Republicans' claimed "mandate" to implement the Contract with America (along with the Christian Coalition's Contract with the American Family) was unlikely to translate into many new statutes. Nevertheless, his and Wamp's comments also illustrate the fact that, for "the freshmen," professing Christian humility in no way necessitates abdicating the reins of power. Quite to the contrary, Dobson's guests evoke an image of humble leadership that reconciles substantial civil authority to an egalitarian identification with the ordinary, working citizen. The panelists personify the ideal of the amateur legislator who relies on her common-sense knowledge of her constituency's and the nation's interests, and whose effectiveness and judiciousness presume no intellectual or moral distinctions between those who govern and those who are governed. As a corollary, we should note that "the freshmen" not only affirm the value of publicity, of free and open communication and deliberation, but moreover have in a sense *become* the agents of publicity by committing themselves to congressional service. In religious vocabulary, in turn, they join North and Colson in giving the traditional evangelical narrative of salvation through humility a particular, updated casting by attempting to establish the consonance of this redemptive path with the energetic deployment of worldly power.

Once more, however, the strains on this narrative's coherence are severe and debilitating. When Dobson and Bauer characterize the other panelists as "a different breed of Congressman and Congresswoman," they hint that "the freshmen" possess an especially pure, American character making them essentially superior to other residents of the United States. The idea that these individuals are peers of Dobson's listeners is further belied by the specific attributes of their occupational lives, which include levels of fame, prestige, and authority not commonly shared by most citizens. The gap separating Dobson's guests from his listeners widens and deepens when the former begin to reiterate North's and Colson's condemnations of publicity. Coburn, for instance, explains that only a united expression of outrage from his clients was able to prevent damage from being done by opponents who tried to "smear" him "with the 'religious right extremist' kind of label": "I had a reputation for being a Christian physician, and so when the attacks came during the campaign I had this wonderful defense of all my patients—about 10,000 of them—they stood up and said, 'That's not right, he's not a radical, he represents us!' So it was a wonderful experience."[46] As in the broadcast series discussed above, so likewise here the righteous indignation and enthusiasm of the plebiscite is counterposed to the destructive recklessness of the status quo public sphere. Spontaneous plebiscitary acclaim, moreover, supplants critical scrutiny in the public sphere as the basis of legitimate government. These dynamics blatantly contradict the egalitarian dimension of the narrative of the humble leader as manifested in the testimonies of "the freshmen."

The broadcast suggests, however, that citizens still may turn to prayer as a way of mediating the authority of public officials. Indeed, the congressional roundtable program promotes the image of the nation at prayer, in which the primary responsibilities of citizenship are met even more aggressively than the Colson or North broadcasts. The representatives' professions of faith, and their hosts' frequent reminders that the guests are "deeply committed Christians," in one sense suggest their equality with the listener. In another sense, however, these and other statements foster the impression that as confessing believers these legislators speak for God in politics, have received their public authority directly from God, and are accountable to God rather than to the public for their actions in the name of the state. Trout, for instance, calls the guests' election to Congress "an answer to prayer." Helen Chenoweth-Hage of Idaho recalls that Tom De-Lay's first response after hearing that he had been elected majority whip was to exclaim: "to God be the glory"; to Chenoweth-Hage, this exemplified "tremendous leadership." Indiana Representative Mark Souder declares that his fellow roundtable participants "owe nothing to other people" for their November victories. Instead, he says, "they owe it to God, they owe it to the people in their districts," thus implying that he has been elected because a majority of his constituents heeded God's express wishes. By extension, for Souder, responsible citizenship must mean praying for God's will to become known and for political leaders to obey divine commands. Dobson and Bauer make this notion of the prayerful citizen explicit in the following exchange:

> Bauer: These individuals are going to be under incredible pressure from Washington . . . and the only way we can stop that is if all those good folks will stand behind these members and others of the other party who are standing for the right values, encourage them, stay involved on the local level—and I think if we do that we have a chance of really accomplishing something.
> Dobson: And *pray* for them, too.
> Bauer: Absolutely.
> Dobson: *That* is the key to everything.[47]

The issue here clearly is not how citizens can keep reins on their officials' exercises of public power but rather how citizens can best support their leaders and help them find the strength to follow God's commands. For Dobson, reports that citizens are increasingly turning to prayer to meet the latter need indicate that a "real American renewal" is in the offing: "That *is* the thing that excites me the most, is that people *are* praying all across this country. We have done several radio programs on that recently, and my wife's office at the National Day of Prayer, and with Campus Crusade and the other Christian organizations that are all reflecting this— people are on their *knees* and that is affecting this city!"[48] Dobson is specifically referring to the program aired on the previous day in which

Campus Crusade for Christ president Bill Bright explains that he recently decided to undergo a forty-day fast after being struck by God's promise to Solomon in II Chronicles 7:14. Bright paraphrases this verse as follows: "If my people called by my name will humble themselves, pray, and seek my face, turn from their wicked ways, then will I hear from heaven, forgive their sins, and heal their life."[49] According to Bright, reading this verse led him to convene a summit meeting of the "leaders of the evangelical movement across the country" in December 1994 to pray that the nation would experience a "great revival" of faith. Dobson, Bright, and their wives tearfully share their feelings of wonder at God's greatness in bringing such a gathering to fruition. In the following day's program, in turn, Chenoweth-Hage cites this same scriptural verse:

> I knew that if I just lived His will every day and sought His strength, that the prayers that were going up around the nation would result in a change. I didn't know what it was, I didn't know whether I would win or not, but I did know that II Chronicles 7:14 really works. And our Father has proposed a contract to us there, and the American people across this nation began to live out the first part of that contract, and we began to see God begin to have the potential, if we abide in Him, in healing our land.[50]

Considered jointly, these two broadcasts thus furnish a complete vision of the responsible citizenry. "Called to prayer" by Dobson and other evangelical leaders, the nation repents of its sins and thereby becomes "sensitive to the leading of the Lord moment by moment," as Dawnette Bright, former Chair of the Christian right–sponsored National Day of Prayer, puts it.[51] The penitent American people then elects candidates who stand for God's purposes and beseeches God that those leaders will be similarly attuned to divine guidance. The narrative of redemption through humility still has an underlying presence, but the harmonization of egalitarian theological and political dynamics has been interrupted by an authoritarian, fundamentalist vision of the evangelical polity.

Other aspects of these broadcasts resonate with patterns identified above in the Colson and North series, although they are not quite as pronounced in these other shows. Dobson's and Bright's picture of an exclusive convocation of evangelical elites, along with Dobson's references to the proliferation of Bible study groups among members of Congress, call to mind Colson's recommendations that church leaders and their peers engage in mutual supervision of their moral conduct. Furthermore, when Dobson admonishes the freshman representatives in closing to "keep your lives clean," he echoes the notion established in the North and Colson broadcasts that the legitimacy of government servants' official actions derives from their personal morality.[52] Together with these features of the broadcast, the more developed image of the nation at prayer, led by officials who view their public service as nothing more or less than "an act of obedience" to God's direct orders and who expect a similar sort of compliance with their own decisions from their constituents, generates an authoritarian countercurrent within the narrative of the humble leader, troubling the egalitarian strain that the program nonetheless vigorously sets in motion.

Strategy, Social Physiognomy, and Focus's Humble Leader

In the shows featuring Oliver North, Charles Colson, and "the freshmen," *Focus on the Family* tells the stories of public officials' exercise of power and relations with ordinary citizens in a distinctive way. These individuals' accounts of their political lives are always already highly personal, even intimate, narratives of their relationships with God, their families, and fellow believers. But it is evident that these stories are not simply about family life per se, notwithstanding Dobson's and Trout's declarations to this effect at the beginning of the North broadcast series.

The broadcasts discussed above clearly accomplish a good deal of valuable advertising and public relations for the Christian right's leaders in the spheres of electoral politics and government. In the most straightforward sense, these episodes of *Focus on the Family* promote deference to the national security apparatus at a time when its legitimation needs have abruptly increased because of the end of the cold war and enthusiasm for the legislative agenda pursued by the ultraconservative faction of House Republicans. The North series may also have given an early boost to North's 1994 campaign for the U.S. Senate. Dobson's broadcasts, moreover, dovetail strategically with other media projects of the Christian right and new right: North began broadcasting his own radio talk show in the mid-1990s; Colson has operated through a variety of evangelical conservative media, with his radio program *BreakPoint* and his multiple best-selling books; and conservative House Republicans have for several years used congressional facilities to produce television shows and interviews, such as the Republican National Committee's *Rising Tide* (transmitted on Paul Weyrich's National Empowerment Television network) and the House Republican Study Committee's *Talk Right*.[53] These various media efforts reinforce one another's messages and bolster each other's audiences, yielding obvious benefits for conservative politicians.

The politics of Focus's episodes featuring the figure of the humble leader can also be conceptualized, with the help of Foucault and cultural studies, as a process of identity constitution. Focus helps generate a mode of citizenship that simultaneously operates along the dimensions of belief, emotion, and the body. This type of citizenship is enacted when commitment to the "straight" family norm is affirmed as the highest form of ethical obligation; when the individual lets her- or himself be overwhelmed by feelings of indignation at the violation of private family space, or of elation, anguish, and ecstasy at the memory of saving contact with the divine presence; and when the body assumes the submissive posture of prayer, "on its knees," in the company of other citizens. In these ways, Dobson's broadcasts resonate with influential, critical-theoretical conceptions of U.S. citizenship at the end of the twentieth century: for example, with Lauren Berlant's idea of the "infantile" citizen who requires the paternalistic protection of the patriarchal state, a mode of citizenship that is gender-coded feminine and symbolized here by Betsy North; or with Lawrence Grossberg's notion of the sentimental citizen, for whom the mere fact of emotional investment in something that "matters" comprises both the formal and substantive entirety of political commitment.[54] Moreover, when listeners to *Focus on the Family* begin increasingly tuning in to additional Christian right media, their habits of media consumption enmesh them in comfortable webs of everyday practices that constitute who they are, as Christians and as citizens.

But these dynamics of power do not exhaust the political implications of the broadcasts discussed above. Analyses of strategic, discursive effects can be complemented and brought into critical perspective when we attend for a moment to these shows' tradition-infused, yet contemporary, narrative coherence. This is the unexplored analytical standpoint to which Adorno's theory of dialectical cultural criticism alerts us: the approach that does not reduce all aspects of cultural phenomena to implements of strategy but rather attempts to discern their composition as a whole. The embattled nature of this whole can then serve as a window into society's antagonisms, Adorno suggests; in turn, this process of interpretation can bring to light any "negative" potencies the phenomenon possesses with respect to these antagonisms. As we have seen, the broadcasts considered in this chapter do indeed possess the characteristic of narrative integrality, and our criticism of the narrative of the humble leader has found it to be rent with acute contradictions. What, then, is the social physiognomy of Focus's janus-faced figure of the humble leader?

Answering this question requires that we take stock of the current vigor of the institutions that are supposed to ensure the reconciliation of egalitarian values with the power and privilege of public office. That is, to define the humble leader's social physiognomy it is necessary to examine how well the mechanisms of democratic accountability are functioning in the United States today. We must furthermore determine the relationships between patterns of political accountability—or the lack of it—and the overarching conditions of post-Fordist political-economic transformations.

Corruption and the Accountability Crisis

Accountability and the Banality of Scandal. Watergate, Iran-Contra, and the string of investigations of President Clinton are only the most spectacular among a multitude of ethics investigations that have occurred since the early 1970s. Not only presidents and "presidents' men" but also members of the House and Senate and nominees to the Supreme Court have been increasingly subject to these probes. The list of explorations of alleged official skulduggeries during the 1990s alone is dizzyingly long, including Whitewater, "Troopergate," "Travelgate," and the Paula Jones case, as well as inquiries into Vice President Al Gore's 1996 campaign fund solicitations, House Speaker Newt Gingrich's publishing improprieties, Senator Bob Packwood's sexual harassment of his employees, and U.S. Supreme Court then nominee Clarence Thomas's conduct toward Anita Hill. Despite the appearance generated by these scandals that public officials are increasingly subject to ever-greater scrutiny of their conduct by the public and other officials, in many ways democratic accountability in the United States is becoming more and more tenuous. Indeed, the proliferation of ethics scandals may be more accurately interpreted as a symptom of declining accountability than as evidence that accountability has reached a new intensity. This much is suggested, in particular, when we consider the roots of recent ethics probes in the U.S. Senate and House of Representatives.

In Congress, there have been increasing numbers of ethics scandals and multiplying attempts to regulate members' behavior according to ethical standards since the mid-1970s.[55] Most worrisome is the fact that these scandals do not reflect the proliferation of "individual" offenses, such as bribe taking—that is, misuses of public office for purely private gain. Rather, they indicate the growth of what Dennis Thompson calls "institutional corruption," a phenomenon that "encompasses conduct that under certain conditions is a necessary or even desirable part of institutional duties."[56] A particularly common kind of institutional corruption is the routine combination of fundraising and constituent service in congressional offices, and the progressive integration of these functions into a unified and normalized process. (These comprised the main forms of wrongdoing in the Keating Five scandal, which offers a vivid example of this type of corruption.) Arguably, senators and representatives should earnestly devote themselves to seeking reelection, since their desire for reelection presumably motivates them to carry out their duties in ways satisfactory to their constituents. Absent the public financing of campaigns, moreover, and setting aside for the moment the issue of gross imbalances between corporate and other interests in the provision of campaign funds, it seems logically appropriate that campaign donations trigger some degree of favorable response in members' policymaking decisions. But when institutional convention sanctions the ever-more tightly synthesized granting of access in exchange for campaign donations, in a political environment where money has assumed such extraordinary influence over members' electoral prospects, it can reasonably be concluded that a certain kind of corruption has developed. And the collective, diffuse character of this corruption, the fact that it is "more systematic and more pervasive" than isolated cases of individual corruption, suggests that these tendencies are eroding the accountability of national representative institutions in general.[57]

The changing nature of campaign finance itself bears much of the blame for the diminution of representatives' accountability to the public. The number of corporate political action committees (PACs) has grown exponentially since the early 1970s, and these PACs' "receipts, expenditures, and contributions to congressional candidates have increased significantly" over the same time period.[58] Candidates' and officeholders' intensifying pursuit and spending of PAC funds constrain citizens' options for holding officials accountable through voting by allowing incumbents to conduct early, preemptive campaigns and diminishing the prospects (and thus the likely candidacies) of challengers who do not seek or receive the support of PACs.[59] Indeed, senators and members of Congress now need to raise money perpetually in order to compete effectively in the next election. The average successful candidate for a House seat must raise $6,730 every week; this figure tops $10,000 for challengers, who do not yet enjoy the substantial material and less tangible benefits of congressional office.[60] A comparable dynamic holds in presidential politics, where the explosion of "soft money" contributions has rendered obsolete existing campaign finance regulations. Nearly one-half of all soft money contributions to the two major parties in 1995–96 arrived in bundles of $100,000 or more, and soft-money spending by corporations outdistanced similar expenditures by labor unions by a ratio of more than 15 to 1.[61] In a society with a high degree of economic inequality, such as the United States today, these conditions translate into atrophied accountability to wealthy individuals and private corporations and little accountability to the rest of the population.

Trends within the legislative apparatus suggest, moreover, that politicians victorious at the polls face additional insulation from broad public accountability once they settle into their posts. Since at least the mid-1960s, Congress has reshaped its institutional structure along lines established by the executive branch. Specifically, Congress has delegated much of its policy-determining authority to administrative agencies and professionalized the work of committee and member staffs. Theodore J. Lowi argues that, in the process, a particular kind of knowledge has gained importance for legislators: "professional" knowledge, which approaches the constituency as an amalgam of groups whose interests are defined according to their congruence with the functional requirements and technical capacities of the federal bureaucracy, has replaced "amateur" (or "constituency") knowledge, which relies on "informal" perceptions to gauge the "concrete" needs of a geographically and socially integral constituency. For Lowi, dependence on a different sort of knowledge means the production of a different type of law: law that establishes vague objectives and sloughs off onto administrative bodies the responsibility for designing policies to achieve those goals, rather than setting specific "rules" defining legal and illegal forms of conduct. In short, as the rule of law is abandoned by Congress, an accountability crisis mounts.[62]

In addition, interest groups' "increased formal penetration . . . into the bureaucracy (advisory committees), the presidency (White House group representatives), and the Congress (caucuses of members)" compounds the accountability deficit further still.[63] The nesting of interest groups in intragovernmental policy processes first gained the concentrated attention of political scientists in the late 1960s. This phenomenon was later accelerated by "congressional reforms that opened up the legislative process during the 1970s [and] provided a much larger number of access points for today's lobbyists."[64] The evolving aggregation of interest groups' discretion over federal legislation has shown no signs of abating in the 1990s, as the intimate involvement of pharmaceutical firms, insurance companies, and physicians in health care reform initiatives illustrated.[65] And interest groups' broader sway over the substance of public policy carries with it biases toward social groups with greater financial, educational, technological, and organizational resources, further detracting from the degree of accountability on which most citizens (but particularly female, nonwhite, and poor or working-class Americans) can depend.[66]

The expansion in regulation and complexification of policy processes that has hastened Congress's abdication of its legislative responsibilities, in turn, has nurtured a transformation of the professional norms among legislators. The increasing quantity of federal regulations and the spread of procedural obstacles to passing legislation have multiplied opportunities for members who seek to maximize their services to interest groups. Accordingly, congressional service has become more attractive (because it is potentially more lucrative) to individuals who aim to work in legislative posts for limited periods, capitalizing thereafter on the "rent-seeking" relationships with interest groups cultivated while in Washington. By contrast, individuals who aspire to careers in public service comprise a declining proportion of the House and Senate memberships.[67] Pace the vitriol vented against "career politicians" by conservative term limits advocates, those who intend to make public service a career are likely to be more attuned to their responsibilities to the public than officials whose goals are much more self-consciously and thoroughly private and pecuniary. The proliferation of "rent-seeking" behaviors, moreover, reinforces the trend toward deeper institutional corruption in Congress, thus adding to the accountability crisis indirectly as well as directly.

Post-Fordism and the Commodification of Politics. This amalgam of structural changes in the U.S. state—the rising frequency of scandal and institutional corruption, the exploding power of money in elections, the growth of rent-seeking behavior in the legislature, and the lapse of the rule of law in Congress—can be interpreted as a set of dimensions of the more general transition to a post-Fordist political economy. In particular, the organizational forms (PACS), strategic emphases (support for paid advertising), and fundraising technologies (direct mail) characteristic of the current campaign finance environment have not only fueled scandal, rent-seeking behavior, and interest group penetration of policy processes. They have also provided the central means by which the defection of key sectors of business and the working class from the Fordist grand compromise among corporations, labor, and the state has been carried out in the realms of elections and public policymaking.

Based geographically in the Sun Belt, the new right capitalized financially on the rapid economic growth of this region during the 1960s–1990s. The industrial interests represented by this Republican faction—above all, interests in natural resource exploitation, real estate speculation, certain branches of high technology, and service industries—have had little economic incentive to cooperate with organized labor or to accede to extensive government regulation. The new right has gained additional, crucial financial strength, moreover, while cultivating a patchwork of mass constituencies and a corps of grassroots activists, by pursuing single-issue campaigns centered on a variety of causes, especially opposition to property taxes, racial integration, gun control, and abortion. Meanwhile, institutional innovations such as the increasing adoption of direct primaries have been another component, along with direct mail and single-issue campaigning, of the spread of "plebiscitary mechanisms that maximize the impact of large inputs of money and advertising" and that have been conducive to the growing power of the new right.[68]

The new right's financial juggernaut has established the standard of competition in recent decades to which the Democratic party and individual Democratic candidates (as well as old-guard Republicans) have been compelled to adjust. The development of this rightist financial-electoral power base, moreover, signals not just a transformation of the prior systems of campaign finance and partisanship per se but more broadly the disintegration of core political aspects of the Fordist regimes of accumulation and regulation. These include steadfast party allegiances among voters; business and white working-class support for the Democratic program of welfare state expansion, state regulation of labor-management relations, and demand-led economic growth; political candidates' financial reliance on a stable party system dominated by New Deal Democrats and eastern-establishment Republicans; this system's greater insulation of policy processes from the individualistic entrepreneurialism of rent-seeking political actors; and electoral rules and conventions safeguarding the power of the major parties and the traditionally dominant factors within them.

Politically, then, the societal transition to post-Fordism has spelled out a mounting crisis of democratic accountability. To be sure, it would be unreasonable to romanticize the degree of accountability characteristic of the declining system. The Fordist arrangement centralized policymaking power among small cadres of corporate, labor, and government elites. It confined labor activism mostly to the lodging of individual grievances, and it relied on a culture of partisanship that tended to be intellectually shallow and characterized by low rates of political participation, rates that were especially small among women and minorities. The lack of accountability of major party, government, corporate, and labor officials to the demands of African Americans and women provided an important impetus for the civil rights, Black Power, student, antiwar, environmental, and women's movements in the 1950s–1970s. The glory days of the Fordist regimes of accumulation and regulation, in short, were hardly a panacea of democracy.

Nevertheless, it would be difficult to argue that the onset of post-Fordist conditions have exercised a democratizing influence in terms of promoting the accountability of political leaders to ordinary citizens. The effect has rather been the opposite: post-Fordism's advance in society at large has both driven and presupposed a restructuring of electoral and legislative processes in line with new modes of campaign finance, and these changes have drastically constricted the power of average citizens to hold public officials accountable for their actions in the name of the nation. At the same time, those paths toward democratization that were in significant ways contingent on the maintenance of Fordist practices and institutions, such as the enfranchisement of southern blacks and their incorporation into major party politics as claimants within the Democratic welfarist coalition, have been cut off.[69]

Finally, the technological advances characteristic of post-Fordism, especially in communications technologies, and the intensified atmosphere of economic competition among large corporations have exacerbated the political accountability deficit by fueling financial and organizational transformations in the media industry, changes that have centralized power in the public sphere. The long-term reduction in the number of independent news sources, the rise in the number of localities served by only one newspaper, and the concentration of media ownership by a few large corporations has been documented and criticized since the 1940s by presidential commissions, Supreme Court justices, critical theorists, and alternative media activists alike. These trends have vastly escalated in recent years, as the 1990s takeovers of major television networks by Disney and Westinghouse spectacularly illustrated. The financial mergers, buyouts, and reorganizations of media companies have threatened the diversity of news coverage by making the major news outlets less disposed to publicize information that might compromise the profits of other subsidiaries owned by their parent corporations. In addition, heightened competition among media companies, public hostility toward the media, and these firms' increasing reliance on public relations professionals have all strengthened the media's orientation toward business interests rather than "social and journalistic values."[70] Furthermore, regulatory changes such as the Reagan administration's abandonment of the fairness doctrine and the Clinton administration's deregulation of cable television have reinforced the priority of the bottom line for media organizations.

The media, moreover, lend to the current accountability crisis its peculiar confusion concerning the distinction between the public and the private. To return briefly to an earlier theme: a large part of the reason why the proliferation of scandals makes it seem as though public officials are being held accountable for their actions more than ever before, despite the many signs of deteriorating accountability, is that scandals regularly generate disorientation regarding the difference between public and private concerns. The unearthing of intimate secrets involving personal relationships often gives the impression that efforts to hold officials accountable have become downright excessive, or at any rate have lost sight of their proper object. The bewilderment over the difference between issues of public import and purely private incidents was especially pronounced in the investigation of President Clinton's relationship with Monica Lewinsky. But it also has antecedents going back to Richard Nixon's claims that his tapes recorded private conversations and were the private property of the president.

In general, scandals effectuate accountability in ways conducive to confusion over the public/private distinction, and they do this because they are so individually focused. That is, scandals invariably personalize the trespass of the public trust, bringing to light incidents that inevitably involve both personal moral failings and betrayals of official responsibilities in one and the same action or set of actions. As a result, public discourse becomes devoted not merely to evaluating whether a particular action was wrong but rather to distinguishing between public and private matters. This has the perverse effect, in turn, of expanding the verbiage about seemingly private affairs, since these matters must be thoroughly specified so that their separateness from other, "public" matters can be firmly established. In short, then, as accountability wanes in the electoral and legislative spheres, substitutionary attempts to stimulate accountability through ethics scandals inflate personal conduct in private relationships into an ever-larger basis for judging the legitimacy of officials' actions in the name of the public—regardless of all the earnest attempts to segregate private from public issues, and indeed precisely because of the intensification of these labors. Under post-Fordism, economic globalization proceeds apace with political hyperpersonalization.

Post-Fordist Contradictions: Applauding the Participatory Republic.
Ironically, the systematic erosion of accountability in the electoral, legislative, and public spheres has coincided with developments in media programming formats and electoral campaign strategies that seem to be on the verge of making politics more participatory—indeed, more democratic—than has been the case in recent memory. As the media industry has become more concentrated financially, the styles and formats of electronically mediated political communication burst into a new multiplicity during the 1990s. Moreover, the "new media," such as radio and television talk shows, television news magazines, MTV, and computer networks, appear to offer expanded opportunities for ordinary citizens to engage in political expression and deliberation. In turn, political leaders including the president and members of Congress, not to mention the hosts of these new media fora themselves, are actively cultivating the sense among the public that a renaissance of participatory democracy is currently underway.

Historically, evoking a sense of identity with ordinary Americans has always been a vital aspect of political leaders' strategies to legitimate their authority in this country.[71] But the populist component of leaders' legitimation took on a new urgency and centrality as the twentieth century drew to a close. The presidential campaign of 1992 was a watershed event in this regard. With the air of leading a populist revolt against the entrenched and corrupted power of the traditional news media, Bill Clinton and Ross Perot charted new directions in political candidates' participation in "soft" media shows: Clinton played the saxophone on the Arsenio Hall show and chatted with young people on MTV's *Rock the Vote*; Perot famously announced his candidacy on CNN's *Larry King Live*. These were only the most memorable and vivid of many instances in the campaign that collectively helped generate a populist tone both more pronounced and qualitatively different from its abundant precedents in earlier campaigns. In addition to exploiting television talk shows and news magazines, talk radio, and MTV, all the major presidential candidates widely distributed economic plans (following Paul Tsongas's lead in the Democratic primary), documents that far exceeded conventional issue papers in their detail and length. Perot's bar charts and long, content-heavy infomercials on the national budget projected a similar confidence in the capacities of ordinary individuals to sort through complex policy questions. Democratic candidate Jerry Brown financed his campaign by asking voters to call an 800-number to make donations. And Clinton conducted "electronic town meetings" in which he spontaneously answered questions from the audience, a practice that the new administration continued after the election.[72] Meanwhile, the popularity of talk radio exploded on the political right as Rush Limbaugh and his local-market clones gained vast audiences, billing themselves as the facilitators of "democracy in action," as arenas for ordinary people to have authentic and honest political conversations with one another.[73]

There was a common message underlying these innovations, despite their disparate "ideological" emphases in terms of public policy. Only that political leader was worthy of support who exposed himself to greatly intensified scrutiny by the "real" public (not just the elites who read the *New York Times*), actively sought personal and intimate conversations with average citizens, stressed in both word and deed his trust in the people's rational judgment, and energetically engaged in the interactivity distinguishing the new media from traditional media. Indeed, precisely this was the deeper current of ideology that encompassed the broad political spectrum from Limbaugh to Clinton, the underlying harmony among their evidently antagonistic discourses.

The actual democratizing effects and potential of the shift toward the new media have been much debated, and there are persuasive arguments and empirical evidence that electronic populism has so far produced little in the way of enduring and consequential participatory norms. Interview shows may offer voters more leisurely encounters with candidates than ads and soundbites on the news, but they are likely to provide the same kinds of information as these other sources, with an even greater emphasis on personality traits and private life.[74] And while citizens' expectation levels regarding the participatory quality of political discourse have been raised, anticipations that their increased political expression will have a substantive impact on policy have been disappointed, since the "soft" media are even more directly keyed to the imperatives of commercial success than are traditional news media.[75] Use of the Internet, hailed by Newt Gingrich and others as the supposed cornerstone of a new era of direct democracy, remains limited in extent (especially compared to older media like television), socioeconomically exclusive, and highly unrepresentative in terms of users' partisanship.[76]

Regardless of the many ways that the much-heralded spring of electronic participatory democracy actually falls short of what candidates and talk show hosts claim for it, however, the crucial point here is that it has emerged as a pervasive stream of ideology in an era of declining democratic accountability. The former serves to legitimate the latter, to deflect questions that might expose the latter to critical examination. We see vivid examples of this ideological relationship in the trajectory of events in two major sex scandals involving President Clinton. When Clinton's affairs with Gennifer Flowers and Monica Lewinsky were exposed, the possibility of recognizing these incidents as the lipstick traces of the accountability crisis was quickly defused by events that seemed to verify the advent of the new participatory-democratic age—the New Hampshire electronic town meeting convened by the Clinton '92 campaign and Congress's release of the Starr report over the Internet (followed by the broadcasting of Clinton's videotaped testimony before the grand jury, Linda Tripp's tapes of her conversations with Lewinsky, and the impeachment hearings). In both cases, the marvel of historically unprecedented opportunities for citizen involvement in national processes of deliberation and adjudication, made possible by technological and media-formatting innovations, was significantly juxtaposed with the most visible (though also the most superficial) symptoms of the structural deficit in accountability. The former was bound to discourage critical reflection on whether the latter might represent anything more ominous than the individual sexual indiscretions of Bill Clinton. We might also note that Democrats and Republicans alike, albeit in different contexts, proved willing to sponsor these events, indicating the common benefit that this ideological dynamic yields to mainstream leaders who take publicly antagonistic stands in relation to one another, but who are jointly responsible for the withering of accountability. The inconsistency between the ideology of electronic populism and the draining of accountability from electoral, legislative, and media processes thus remains an abiding contradiction within the general political economy of the United States today.

What is the relationship of *Focus on the Family* to this general ideological dynamic of the post-Fordist United States? Dobson and his guests, along with the reporters and interviewees on Focus's daily political news broadcast *Family News in Focus*, frequently chastise the government for being deaf to the demands of the public, a public imagined in terms that code fundamentalist "family values" as mainstream. Taking either of these shows at face value leads one quickly to the conclusion that the government is radically out of touch with ordinary citizens (at least the imputed majority of them), who see homosexuality as perverse, abortion as murder, and school prayer as essential to the common culture. In short, Focus's cries that public policy is being held hostage by gay activists, Planned Parenthood, and the American Civil Liberties Union rely on the underlying theme that government's accountability to the demos has reached a nadir.

On the most immediate level, Dobson's conversations with Oliver North, Charles Colson, and the congressional roundtable participants confirm this sense that accountability in the nation's core political institutions is sorely lacking. For North and Colson, interviewed before the Republican takeover of Congress in 1994, it is the U.S. House of Representatives and the media that have most egregiously abdicated their responsibilities to the public. A bit more optimism about the possibility of legislation in accordance with the will of the people naturally emerges in the remarks of the House lawmakers in early 1995. Still, the later broadcast offers no wholesale reappraisal of Congress's responsiveness to the public—after all, these officials had run for Congress by running against Congress (as the saying goes in congressional studies) and recognized the persistent minority status of their faction within the Republican party and the House. Moreover, in a sense "the freshmen" keep the discourse of accountability loss going simply by shifting its institutional focus. Thus when Dobson denounces liberals for ignoring the true interests of teenage and poor Americans in formulating sex education and welfare policies, his comments resonate with countless broadcasts by Focus and other Christian right media organizations in the 1990s that accused the Clinton administration of flouting accountability expectations. No matter which branch harbors the leading offenders, in sum, in each of these shows the mere mention of "Washington" calls up a host of resentments at public officials' apparently near-total insulation from the people's demands and criticisms.

However, if we peer behind the most explicit content of *Focus on the Family* and consider the program's narrative continuities in light of the post-Fordist sources of the accountability crisis, it becomes evident that Dobson's shows tell a more complicated story about the status of democracy in the United States today. The self-contradictory narrative of the humble leader in one respect radicalizes the sense that accountability has been forfeited, provoking a far deeper pessimism about democratic possibilities than that implied in castigating "the liberals" supposedly running the Clinton administration. For when North, Colson, and the freshman Republicans are exalted to the status of the plebiscitary leader whose accountability is to God rather than to the public; when ordinary citizens are told to remain "on their knees" in pious and unquestioning obedience; and when the forces of publicity are demonized as blasphemous trespassers on the sacred, properly private domain of power—in these dimensions of the narrative of the humble leader, *Focus on the Family* reflects the structural deterioration of accountability that increasingly defines representative government and the public sphere under post-Fordist conditions.

Yet *Focus on the Family* registers not only this historical tendency but moreover the contradiction-riddled attempt to assimilate it to democratic expectations. As we have seen, vying for primacy with the narrative figure's authoritarian visage is this figure's egalitarian aspect—the face (and voice) of "Ollie," who has "got the vote back"; of "Chuck," who gets saved by joining the millions of other readers of *Mere Christianity*; and of "Tom" (Coburn), who cherishes his regular job and private life. It is the countenance, in short, of the leader who is on a level with his or her constituents, knows them well because she or he interacts with them constantly (often through electronic media), and at once symbolizes and effectuates their active participation in self-government. In this respect, Focus's figure of the humble leader manifests the imprint of the populist ideology currently redirecting public attention away from the accountability deficit. Thus, the sociopolitical contradiction between the new populist ideology and the actual decay of democratic accountability finds expression in the constitutive tensions of Focus's narrative of the humble leader.

Focus's narrative of the compassionate professional not only expresses but moreover fosters the trend toward a decidedly compassionless system of health and human services by cultivating cynicism and exclusionary thinking among Dobson's audience. In like manner, the narrative of the humble leader actively reinforces the accountability crisis even as the former reflects the latter in its compositional structure. Those who listen regularly to *Focus on the Family* and accept the program's forced reconciliation of the humble leader's warring aspects are so much the more likely to deny that populist democracy is antithetical to the maintenance of the current rules of campaign finance, the decline of careerism in Congress, the delegation of legislative discretion to interest groups, and the centralization of financial power in the media industry. This is perhaps why so many evangelical conservatives find it possible to lambaste "Washington" as the lair of usurpers while energetically throwing themselves into conventional lobbying activities and electioneering for candidates who oppose campaign finance reform, support industrial deregulation, and deride the public service norms traditionally attached to legislative office.

And yet the fissures within Focus's narrative of the humble leader persist, along with the clash between ideology and institutional tendencies in post-Fordist America. The dialectical character of this narrative's relationship to social conditions, as Adorno reminds us, consists in the former's simultaneous expression, reinforcement, and *negation* of the latter's antagonisms in the fault lines of its structural composition. In reproducing the contradictions of the present political economy within Christian right culture, *Focus on the Family* negatively bears witness to the lack of genuine reconciliation in U.S. society today—here, in particular, the deepening failure of political institutions to realize growing participatory-democratic aspirations. The narrative of the humble leader thus exudes a faint, negative-utopian sigh, making it possible for the listener to refuse the lure of the narrative's false reconciliation and thereby come to a critical knowledge of society through the unlikely doorway of Christian right radio.

Thinking negative-dialectically about *Focus on the Family* also requires that narrative analysis somehow stimulate critical reflection on social theory. Such intellectual exertion provides an important safeguard against social theory's possible slippage into any form of conspiracy theory. Precisely how might a recognition of the dialectical relationship between *Focus on the Family*'s narratives of the compassionate professional and the humble leader enable social theory to avoid certain categorial reifications or uncritical assumptions? Once again, let us delay answering this question until the dialectical criticism of *Focus on the Family*'s narrative-forms has been taken a step further and we have filled in a few more key features of the program's social physiognomy.

5

Christian Victims in the Backlash Society

Far from concealing suffering under the cloak of improvised camaraderie, the culture industry takes pride in looking it in the eye like a man and acknowledging it, however great the strain on self-control. The pathos of composure justifies the world which makes it necessary. . . . Tragedy made into a carefully calculated and accepted aspect of the world becomes a blessing. It is a safeguard against the reproach that truth is not respected, whereas it is really being adopted with cynical regret.—Max Horkheimer and Theodor W. Adorno, *Dialectic of Enlightenment*, 1944

Redemption, Stereotype, and Narrative

As the preceding chapters have demonstrated, *Focus on the Family* often spotlights figures of authority: men with professional status, men of political renown—in short, men of substantial power. Inasmuch as these individuals model specific paths of salvation and social action for Dobson's listeners, it is intended that the latter imitate the former, and this dynamic seems to posit an essential similarity between speaker and listener. At the same time, Dobson, North, and the other guests discussed above are clearly marked as exceptional leaders who appear to have a legitimate claim on the deference of Focus's ordinary constituents.

Often, however, *Focus on the Family* brings into the studio individuals whose life experiences and social credentials are a good deal nearer to those of most listeners. Dobson regularly lends his microphone to ordinary people who claim that their own stories of personal travail and triumph prove the reality of divine, saving grace and its complementarity with the Christian right's political causes.

Individual testimonies to redemption are a thoroughly stereotyped feature of evangelical conservative media culture. *Focus on the Family* follows the well-worn trail blazed by Pat Robertson, whose enormously popular television talk show *The 700 Club* features a daily segment in which a believer narrates the tale of her or his descent into a life of perdition, followed by a miraculous rescue and conversion effected by Jesus Christ. Robertson and Dobson alike, in turn, call on a formula for publicly announcing the evangelical gospel that stretches back into nineteenth-century revivalism, a formula perfected by fire-and-brimstone preachers such as Dwight L. Moody. Perhaps more than any other revivalist, Moody routinized the public "witness" to salvation of ordinary Christians as one component of a highly professionalized strategy of accumulating saved souls and ministry dollars. Like *Focus on the Family*, Moody's emotional festivals of prayer, confession, and jubilation juxtaposed testimonies from socially prominent individuals (for Moody, respected Chicago businessmen) with the witnessing of more humble folk (often Irish American laborers).[1] These standardized confessionals functioned as potent instrumentalities within Moody's overall, systematized schema for "producing" revivals in ways that relied explicitly on industrial techniques to maximize attendance, enthusiasm, and financial yield.[2] Standardizing the ritual of the personal testimony, moreover, enabled the formal structure of the revivals to reinforce the ideological message that Moody explicitly articulated: that "there is no difference" in God's eyes between "the rich and the poor" in terms of their sinfulness, their suffering in the world, and their need of Christ's saving touch.[3]

On the logic of Horkheimer and Adorno's theory of the culture industry, we might contend that Dobson's redeployment of this standardizing technique on *Focus on the Family* has similar ideological effects today. The ceaseless bombardment of listeners with salvation stories conveyed in highly personalized tones but identical in all of their basic rhythms and motifs, we might argue, generates intensely conformist pressures. Evangelicals are induced to consume the broadcasts, videos, and printed publications spawned by Focus on the Family and other Christian right media companies to satisfy cravings created and coordinated by those very organizations. The device of standardization, ironically extended to that very experience claiming the most radical of disjunctures with everyday relations of power—the experience of spiritual salvation—ensures that felt moments of religious transcendence are utterly closed off from any hope for a historical transcendence of social domination. The equal conformity of all to the electronic "altar calls" of the contemporary Christian right media thus inoculates from critical consciousness the bitter socioeconomic and political inequalities proliferating under post-Fordist conditions.

This argument, however, exaggerates the degree to which the testimonies to God's miracles on *Focus on the Family* have become amalgamated to and indistinguishable from the false "miracle of [social] integration" conjured by the culture industry.[4] Dobson's guests certainly traffic in stereotypes. But their narratives nonetheless retain an aspect of structural coherence and integrality, along with a place within a historically continuous, religious tradition. When ordinary people—noncelebrities and nonspecialists—address listeners of *Focus on the Family*, a particularly vivid sign of this narrative contiguity and continuity is the striking prominence of the traditional Christian theme of forgiveness in their comments. Forgiving those who have done them harm takes on both spiritual and social significance for these individuals. It "puts them right" in God's eyes, and it is the spark that kindles a commitment to social and political activism oriented toward the transformation of society. The act of forgiveness thus becomes a source of power in two senses. Moreover, its incorporation into this narrative generates a set of complementary answers to abiding theological questions concerning (1) the individual's role (as distinct from God's efficacy) in bringing about her own salvation, and (2) the relationship between the redemption of the individual and that of the world.

But is the narrative of Focus's forgiving victim, like those of the compassionate professional and the humble leader, beset by contradictions that belie its claim to map out an unobstructed road to redemption in today's society? And if so, then what might these contradictions in the narrative reveal about conflicts pervading U.S. society as a whole in the post-Fordist era? More fundamentally: precisely what sort of relationship does this narrative maintain vis-à-vis the historical circumstances in which it has come to be? Adorno's theory suggests that when inconsistencies of aesthetic form are exposed as expressions of the superficial and false reconciliation of social antagonisms, a negative force preserved within the cultural object is thereby liberated—even though the object cannot help but legitimate these same ruptures by making them appear natural and inevitable. Does such a contestative force emanate from Focus's narrative of the forgiving victim, compelling us to see its relationship to social antagonisms as not merely ideological but additionally dialectical, comprising both affirmative and negative impulses?

Margy Mayfield: Forgiving Violence against Women

One of the most popular audiotapes in Focus's catalogue is the testimony of Margy Mayfield, an evangelical homemaker who tells how she was abducted by a rapist-murderer but later set free after persuading her captor to accept Jesus' saving grace. In a recorded public address, Mayfield describes being kidnapped in a K-Mart parking lot by an armed man who, she says, "had been on the FBI ten-most-wanted list . . . for the last ten years, . . . had raped and brutally murdered women all over the country, and was known for his intense hate for women." Ignorant of her attacker's history and buoyed by "the spirit of God" that becomes "mighty" within her, Mayfield realizes immediately that this man's soul is the site of a spiritual battle in which her Christian influences are needed. She knows this because, on the one hand, the man (Stephan Morin) appears to be possessed by "satanic" forces: he is "crying and shaking." On the other hand, he mentions having spontaneously wandered into a church earlier that day even though he "didn't know what to do," and this signals to Mayfield that God has already been reaching out to him prior to their encounter. Mayfield places her hands on her assailant, not heeding his warnings that he will shoot her if she does not stay sitting on her hands in her car, and declares her "authority over every demonic force" within the man in the name of Jesus. Mayfield then "witnesses" to Morin, announcing to him that accepting Jesus can save him from eternal damnation. Telling him that she is not afraid of him because "perfect love casts out fear," she gives him cash from her electronic teller and drives with him to a nearby town without attempting to escape. Mayfield finally inspires her would-be brutalizer to beg Jesus for mercy, become "born again" right there in the car, and proclaim his intention to give up a life of crime and instead to "tell people about Jesus Christ." Morin then lets Mayfield go free and soon afterward gives himself up to the police. He eventually is executed for the murder he had committed just prior to abducting Mayfield, but spends his final days evangelizing in prison and dies "with a testimony on his lips."[5]

Margy Mayfield is a paradoxical sort of crime victim, at once both utterly helpless and in complete control of the situation. The model after which Mayfield's character is fashioned is none other than Jesus himself. In this story, Mayfield follows Jesus' example and fulfills his commandments in starkly literal terms. Her narrative evokes numerous parallels with biblical passages: Jesus spending time in the company of prostitutes and thieves, dismissing their wrongdoings as irrelevant if they will only turn and love God; Jesus commanding his disciples to offer their coat to a robber who demands only their shirt, and to walk ten miles with the highwayman who would force them to walk only one mile with him; Jesus carrying his cross for the crucifiers. Laying hands on the man who has threatened to kill her if she moves, Mayfield personifies courageous fidelity to Jesus' admonitions that anyone who seeks to save her life will lose it, and that people must love their enemies.[6] Mayfield thus models the ethical attitude of radical, Christlike forgiveness for Focus's audience.

Her story seems intended to provide listeners with living proof that unwavering adherence to Christ's difficult law of love is possible—and, more fundamentally, that embracing the most extreme powerlessness is precisely and paradoxically the way to be filled with the most awesome power.

Mayfield's spiritual power emboldens her not simply to accomplish the incredible feat of catalyzing Morin's conversion but also to begin working with a new intensity to spread the gospel. As a result of her successful response to God's call, Mayfield becomes a certain kind of activist—a distinctly evangelical activist, inasmuch as her efforts are centrally devoted to helping other people become "born again," but also an activist on behalf of women. In the recorded epilogue to her main presentation on *Focus on the Family*, Mayfield explains that she was called on one last time to "minister" to Morin in prison shortly before his execution, to reassure him that his salvation and God's promises were genuine. Mayfield's new labor on behalf of the gospel is thus in one sense intimate and interpersonal. But in addition, her extraordinary experience turns her into a public figure, a fact that Focus emphasizes by broadcasting her remarks in a public speech (complete with enthusiastic audience reactions) rather than inviting her into the studio for a conversation with Dobson. Moreover, Mayfield acquires the aura of an activist by virtue of the insertion of her speech into the context of Focus's programming list, in the midst of a two-week span in which featured guests or speakers included national conservative leaders Phyllis Schlafly (who criticized the Clinton health reform plan), George Gilder (who lambasted federal welfare programs), and Richard Glasow (who decried attempts to make RU-486, an abortion-stimulating pill, available in the United States). Mayfield is no rabble-rouser on behalf of the death penalty—she is far too nice and too much the traditional "woman" to be an outspoken advocate for such state-sponsored violence. Nevertheless, she comes across as a certain type of *feminist* activist, for she presents herself as a woman who has encountered and successfully resisted misogyny and masculinist violence. Mayfield's salvation through forgiveness, in other words, is crucially linked to her "missionary work" as a public critic of hatred and violence against women.

The story of Margy Mayfield is thus fundamentally structured as a narrative of redemption, and it concerns her own salvation (and that of the world) just as much as, or even more than, that of Morin. This narrative, additionally, underscores Mayfield's individual agency in recognizing a trial of her faith, overcoming her terror, and responding to the harshest cruelty and gravest danger in an uncompromising spirit of forgiveness. Furthermore, the narrative binds Mayfield's personal salvation inextricably to the redemption of society by having her encounter with Morin catalyze her new, self-conscious role as an activist and public persona, a role that again highlights her agency in bringing about the fulfillment of God's promises.

Yet the narrative also sharply undercuts the sense of Mayfield's personal agency that it itself generates. Mayfield's forgiving response to her situation of peril seems jarringly automatic, even mechanical. Her comments evince little sense that she has actually had to struggle in any way to find within her heart the capacity for forgiveness. By her account, neither self-interested thinking, nor retaliatory violence, nor the tiniest hint of malice so much as occurs to her as a possibility when she is with Morin. Even Jesus lost his patience and became enraged on occasion: before uttering his final words of forgiveness while hanging on the cross, he overturned the tables of the money changers, called the Pharisees "vipers," and agonized in the garden of Gethsemane.[7] As arduous as it would be to follow Jesus' example, to emulate Mayfield would be a more formidable task, for as a model of compassionate forgiveness she is even less prone to human distractions than the Christian savior.

Dobson concludes the program by marveling at what he views as Mayfield's unparalleled demonstration of "faith in action." This faith, however, ultimately does not demand that Mayfield strive against selfish impulses to resolve a conflict between the needs of self and other, as the Christian Scriptures acknowledge the believer must by emphasizing their heroes' (often unsuccessful) confrontations with base, self-centered desires. (Think of Peter denying any acquaintance with Jesus after the latter's arrest.) On *Focus on the Family*, instead, faith means total submission to the divine power that breaks into the profane realm, takes control of the believer, and renders those desires temporarily inoperative:

> 'Course he assured me not to try anything funny. But I wasn't about to, you know, it wasn't even in my heart to try anything like that, because the compassion of Jesus Christ just overwhelmed me. I had a lot of compassion for this man that goes—when you walk in the Spirit of God it goes against your natural mind. Your natural mind is repulsed, almost, by this individual, but the love of God is a love that knows no barriers, it is beyond the sense realm, beyond the reason realm, it goes beyond that. It's the capacity to love the unlovable and to go beyond feeling or reason.[8]

Superficially, these remarks of Mayfield seem to describe the victorious struggle of spiritual consciousness to overcome the "natural mind's" imperatives, which presumably include anger at Morin, fear of Morin, and the desire to escape from Morin. But Mayfield harbors none of these perfectly understandable thoughts and emotions. Indeed, she explicitly disavows even the slightest itch to try to outsmart Morin and regain her freedom. Instead, Mayfield curiously describes her "natural" response to Morin as being "repulsed" by someone whom she numbers as one of "the unlovable." What is lost here in this subtle but crucial shift is any sense that her relationship to Morin is interpersonal. Acknowledging anger, fear, and a yearning to escape from Morin might not yet be Christlike forgiveness, but it would at least concede to Morin a degree of respect for his human individuality and agency. Lacking this core of interpersonal respect—something akin to that which Hegel termed "recognition"—the forgiveness proffered by Mayfield seems ineffably hollow. Forgiveness becomes not an act of resolutely recognizing the God-beloved humanity of the other even when the other acts inhumanely, but rather an experience of being spiritually anesthetized against feeling disgust at the other's essential inhumanity.

More generally, the narrative of salvation through forgiveness that animates Mayfield's comments sharply equivocates on the role and character of individual agency in the attainment of redemption. Rather than reconciling autonomous will and divine command, Mayfield's actions seem simply to collapse the former into the latter. Consequently, forgiveness becomes merely a matter of following orders. The only impediment Mayfield faces to doing so is the possibility that she might panic and thereby become incapable of carrying out her mission; the question of her possible unwillingness to do so almost never arises. Mayfield's sure step falters only once: she suddenly feels afraid when she telephones her husband to tell him she is all right, wondering when she will see her family again. Even here, however, her fear seems not so much for her own safety as for the well-being of her family. And this terror is quickly expurgated by a moment of self-discipline in which Mayfield takes "authority over the spirit of fear" and resolves not to "try to play God" but to follow God's directives concerning "exactly what to do." The central conflict in this narrative of salvation, then, is not whether the individual will make God's bidding her own will but whether she will perform reliably, remaining "calm" and sticking to God's "plan" instead of losing her grip. Self-control, not self-determination, is what is vitally at stake here. Dobson remarks approvingly that Mayfield "kept her wits about her," "kept her confidence," and "kept her cool"—and in the end, that is the definitive content of her "faith in action."[9] Mayfield's testimony thus transmutes the ethical problem of responding to victimization with forgiveness into the technical problem of maintaining a calm disposition and effectively fulfilling commands.

Finally, Mayfield's story backpeddles on its promise of social transformation in two ways. First, the narrative reinstates narrow self-preservation as the fruit of faith even though superficially it debunks this value. In the absence of any substantively ethical dilemma for the protagonist, the lesson of the narrative devolves on her eventual success in protecting herself from harm through her technical capacity to act in the way that she has been "programmed" by God. Mayfield admonishes her listeners: "When you're walking with the spirit of God, you obey *Him*, because if you *don't* you might end up *dead*. I could have ended up dead, trying anything."[10] The transcendent necessity compelling Mayfield to be "obedient to the spirit of God" thus ends up being directed toward the fulfillment of natural necessity.[11] More precisely, transcendent and natural necessity become fused into a single entity: the execution of God's "plan" results in simply a more durable kind of self-preservation than that which is available on earth. And this fusion of ends carries with it a fusion of means, comprising the second way in which the narrative undercuts its own socially transformative zeal. For self-preservation requires Mayfield's unwavering and unquestioning submission to masculine authority, whether wielded (aggressively and dangerously) by Morin or (lovingly yet imperiously) by God "Himself." Over and against the figure of active and confident feminine and feminist power that Mayfield otherwise represents, the narrative warns women never to try any "funny stuff"—above all, by asserting any fundamental autonomy from and critique of patriarchy.

Raleigh Washington: Forgiving Racism

Other citizen activists featured on *Focus on the Family* emphasize more strongly and explicitly their commitments to social and political causes. Raleigh Washington furnishes Focus's version of the veteran, African American civil rights activist who continues to work toward "racial reconciliation" and outreach to impoverished urban communities. In a joint appearance on Dobson's program with his white coauthor Glen Kehrein, Washington explains how his activism against racism is rooted in his personal experiences in the armed forces. Washington's promising military career was cut short when a racist white general made false accusations against him, leading to his discharge without retirement benefits. Despite this wrenching injustice, however, Washington claims that he "had no bitterness" because of "the joy of [his] salvation" and the growing "call on [his] life to ministry." As a result of his forgiving spirit, Washington attests, God provided him with a lawyer who worked on his case for nine years without pay and eventually secured Washington's retirement pay.[12]

Washington also recalls an evening in 1960 when he went out for dinner in Lawrence, Indiana, with several white fellow servicemen but was refused service in a series of white-only restaurants. The men were finally allowed to eat dinner at the fourth (and most expensive) place they tried. According to Washington, after being denied service at the first few establishments he had offered to go his own way and let his three friends eat in peace. One of the others, however, a soldier named Lou Taglia, insisted that they stay together and eventually even paid for Washington's meal. Washington reminisces: "When I remember Lawrence, I don't remember all of the racism I faced. I remember the love of one man, Lou Taglia, who made a difference. And that's what Christ has done—his death at Calvary—he's died to break down the dividing wall of hostility, and if white brothers and sisters will go out of their way intentionally and express love, it will erase an awful lot of sin."[13] For Washington, the humiliations of enduring racist hatred have thus only made him stronger. He is more appreciative of the power of individual, ethical decision and more determined than ever to work toward widespread social change through public venues such as his publications and appearance on *Focus on the Family* with Kehrein. As in Mayfield's testimony, the significance of Calvary is archetypical for the figure of the forgiving victim, represented here by Washington, who paradoxically gleans an enduring and salvific power from circumstances of extreme powerlessness. The power of ethical decision demonstrated here is not only Taglia's but also Washington's, inasmuch as it is the power to forgive "bitter" injustice—this links the two anecdotes together. This power at once attests to, helps effect, and springs from the individual's personal salvation while nurturing a consciousness in that person of the need to contribute actively to the world's redemption.

Once again, however, the question of the hero's ethical agency remains a deeply troubled and ambiguous aspect of this narrative of salvation. In both the conflict with the general and the Lawrence episode, Washington's role in the eventual triumph over racism is curiously passive. Washington does not describe having to *overcome* feelings of "bitterness" and resentment toward the general or the racist restaurateurs. Instead, these feelings are simply erased by the intervention of the spirit of forgiveness sent from God, just as the more concrete (although also divinely inspired) interventions of the attorney and Lou Taglia conveniently, almost magically, spirit away the material deprivations that Washington otherwise would have suffered. In what, then, does Washington's attitude of forgiveness consist if it does not require him to confront the injustices done to him along with his natural feelings of anger about them, even as a matter of memory after the moment of crisis has passed? Absent these elements, it cannot involve acknowledging these deeds as the actions of other, morally responsible human beings. Washington's forgiveness thus cannot be seen as an interpersonal act, an act that answers injury with a steadfast recognition of one's own and the other's common, sanctified humanity. Instead, forgiveness here implies simply an acquiescent adjustment to circumstances, an almost reflexive resolve to keep things calm so that God's orchestration of events, feelings, and memories can proceed unimpeded. In short, it forfeits the character of ethical choice and assumes that of technical prudence, thus reiterating the core narrative contradiction present in Mayfield's story.

Washington's remarks likewise undermine their own call to social activism and pledge of societal change. Closure is brought to each of his two stories of racist conflict in a way that emphasizes the fulfillment of Washington's personal interests but ignores those of African Americans more broadly. In both anecdotes, the solution to racism is unremittently individualistic, depending on private legal action and the private charity of people like the lawyer and Taglia. Military norms might remain racist and Lawrence's restaurants might stay segregated—but at least Washington ends up with income security and a fine meal, to boot. This feature of the narrative mutes and confuses Washington's exhortation toward collective action for the cause of "racial reconciliation" while reinstating self-preservation as the hero's ultimate goal over against the narrative's conflicting admonition to follow Christ's example of forgiveness by abnegating the concern for self-preservation. Additionally, just as Mayfield's successful completion of her pseudofeminist mission within God's overarching "plan" demands that she never transgress masculine authority, so again here the salvation narrative of the forgiving victim hinges on obedience to a seemingly intransigent order of social subordination. Washington remains silent and compliant in the face of racism, moving on when the restaurant owners tell him to do so, attempting to defuse conflict rather than provoke it, and relying exclusively on the goodwill of well-intentioned whites to rectify other whites' abuses.

Gianna Jessen and Heidi Huffman: Forgiving Abortion

Mayfield's story of abduction and Washington's account of racism elicit indignation on the part of Dobson's listeners and then channel this sense of moral affront toward evangelism and social activism on behalf of women and African Americans. However, no testimonies to injustice, suffering, and brutality have persistently sparked more righteous anger among the Christian right's constituents, or provided such keenly effective motivation to political involvement, than those dealing with abortion. Media culture has served as a primary vehicle for kindling outrage over abortion since the movement's genesis in the 1970s, when the films *Silent Scream* and *Whatever Happened to the Human Race?* with their grisly scenes of dead fetuses and mangled baby dolls, were viewed with horror by evangelicals across the nation. Since that time, fury over abortion has continued to galvanize the movement's supporters. And in nineties Christian right media like *Focus on the Family*, the stories are just as gory, the outrage just as palpable, and the imperative to take action just as vehement as they were two decades ago.

New layers of complexity, however, heighten the sophistication and multiply the meanings of discussions of abortion on *Focus on the Family*, in comparison with older antiabortion texts in Christian right media. Most notably for our purposes, Focus weaves its account of abortion atrocities into the narrative of the forgiving victim, the basic motifs of which we have seen illustrated by the broadcasts featuring Mayfield and Washington. The result is an especially captivating rendition of this narrative's appeal to redemption through forgiveness and power through weakness— and an excruciatingly vivid display of the narrative's core contradictions.

Gianna Jessen is a renowned activist and symbol for the Christian right and, more narrowly, the antiabortion movement. She appears at public conventions that spotlight leaders from diverse reaches of the right, stunning audiences with her story of how, as a fetus, she survived her mother's attempt to have an abortion and how she has steadily overcome the physical disabilities caused by the abortive procedure and grown up to become a young leader in the fight against abortion. In one of Dobson's broadcast series, transmitted shortly before the twenty-second anniversary of *Roe v. Wade* in early January 1995, Jessen talks about her life, along with Heidi Huffman, another "abortion survivor," and the two girls' mothers. The series begins with a lengthy account by Tina Huffman, Heidi's mother, of her attempt to secure an abortion as a pregnant, unmarried teenager. As so many other abortion narratives in the Christian right media do, Tina Huffman's story depicts abortion as a heinous deed that occurs in mysterious and threatening back rooms and is perpetrated by evil "abortionists." The latter seem obsessively to crave satisfaction from extracting fetuses from the womb and from preventing pregnant women from learning what is ostensibly the awful truth: that the abortion will cause them to die, to become sterile, or to suffer interminable physical and emotional pain. The following passage typifies the overall mood of this portion of the broadcast, its portrayal of abortion providers as individuals with the basest motivations, and its account of abortion as quite literally a "walk through the valley of death":

Dobson: Did *anybody* sit down and tell you, "you're gonna regret this for the rest of your life, this is a very serious thing you're doing, you're killing a baby"—did anybody talk to you like that?

Huffman: No. I had no knowledge of abortion, I had no knowledge of fetal development, I didn't know anything—only that it would end an unplanned pregnancy.

Dobson: And you were very distressed to be pregnant.

Huffman: Yes, and you're fearful. And, see, there's this power and influence, and that was the only *influence* that I was receiving, was abortion. Every—not one person said, "have you considered adoption," or this, keeping the baby—not one person said that. So I headed off to this abortion clinic on April 4th in South Carolina with a friend of mine, and walked into this abortion clinic and looked around. And I saw all these girls in there, there was a lot of teenagers in there, and you know, not one man was sitting there. (Huffman begins to cry.)

Dobson: Mmm, you were alone. (sadly)

Huffman: (crying) I'm sorry, I tell this *over and over.*

Dobson: You really would not apologize for those tears *here*, of all places, Tina, because we understand where you've been.

Huffman: (regaining control) But, they said "bring $150 in cash only," they didn't take a Visa or Mastercard, and I gave them my money. And I had to sign these consent forms, and there's all these little bitty lines, and so you know, you don't take time to read it all. And you're taken back into this room where all these girls are lined up, and you know, they don't tell you, "Well, there's a possibility you could die from a legal abortion, or we could botch it, you could become *sterile* from a first-trimester abortion. Nothing was said—they didn't even tell me the procedure of the abortion. And they gave me a Valium, and I was taken into this room, and the abortionist and a nurse were there and it was suction-curettage abortion. And complications set in during it.[14]

Shortly thereafter, when Huffman's persistent hemorrhaging convinces "a local gynecologist" that the abortion has indeed been "botched," Huffman attempts (on this male physician's bidding) to initiate legal proceedings against the "abortion clinic." But as the listener has no doubt already guessed, the clinic has meticulously covered its tracks and claims to have "misplaced her files," thus immunizing itself from litigation. A happy ending to Huffman's trials is already in view, however, since the gynecologist assumes that Huffman will now carry her pregnancy to term rather than advising her once again to try "killing the baby." Relieved of the nefarious "power and influence" of those who thirst for abortion, Huffman complies with the doctor's orders that she report back "week after week for testing, amniocentesis, and things." Despite a complicated pregnancy, an induced premature labor, and an emergency C-section, in which doctors discover that "a majority of the amniotic fluid was gone," the infant is born and survives. Heidi's live birth and survival, the delivering physician declares, is "a miracle" for which "there's no medical explanation."[15]

This part of the broadcast series reiterates numerous themes common to antiabortion narratives over the past few decades, themes probably familiar even to those who have given the Christian right's denunciations of abortion only passing notice. Abortion providers appear as pure villains; contesting their vile "influence" is the occasional, moral physician (patterned after the image of Focus's compassionate professional); women who seek abortions seem to exercise no independent judgment about how to handle their pregnancies, and suffer terrible mistreatment; the fetus, in turn, is subjected to unspeakable (though explicitly and precisely described) tortures. Yet as the series proceeds, it becomes clear that Focus's version of this "classic" tale of abortion's horror has an idiosyncratic and novel twist. Analysts of the Christian right sometimes speculate that the effectiveness of antiabortion rhetoric can be attributed to the fact that this discourse invites the listener to identify with the helplessness and peril of the fetus.[16] On *Focus on the Family*, this dynamic doubtless attains a new intensity when, as it were, the fetus actually speaks. Even more important than the simple fact that the fetus's living voice is finally heard, however, is what the fetus says and how it says it. Miraculously given the chance to speak, the fetus articulates a message of forgiveness geared toward energizing a broad social movement against abortion.

Heidi Huffman and Gianna Jessen, with the aid of Dobson's prompting, each stress that they have forgiven their mothers for trying to have them aborted, without reservation. For example, the following exchange takes place between Dobson and Jessen (who is adopted):

Dobson: Gianna, have you met your biological mother?
Jessen: No, I haven't. . . . But let me say that I have *forgiven her totally* for what she's done because I've been forgiven on the cross.
Dobson: You're not angry at her?
Jessen: Not at *all*, I have totally forgiven this woman.
Dobson: If she were sitting here, what would you say to her?
Jessen: I would say, "I forgive you for what you've done," and ask her if she knows the Lord, ask her what was going on, what were her circumstances, just talk to her and just find out a little bit.[17]

Jessen and Heidi Huffman subsequently stress that they have forgiven not only their own mothers but also the "angry" members of "proabortion" forces. On occasion, they say, these women have even declared to their faces that they would have wanted their mothers' abortions to have succeeded. Jessen recalls her reaction to one such incident: "I wasn't hurt by that because I knew where she was coming from, and so that was okay. And so later, afterwards, I went up and I gave her a hug and I said, 'Well, have a nice day!' just to let her know that it was okay that she felt differently than I did, but that didn't change what God had called me to do."[18] Like Mayfield and Washington, both Jessen and Huffman thus display a boundless and startling capacity to forgive their apparent persecutors. And even more acutely than these other featured guests on *Focus on the Family*, their remarks weave a story of how the greatest moral and practical fortitude can be drawn from situations of the most extreme powerlessness and forsakenness.

Jessen's and Huffman's striking ability to forgive attests to the fact that they have not only been born, but born again. Their personal salvation, in turn, is bound up with the redemption of society, for the consciousness of God's active, saving intervention in their lives impels them toward political action in the public sphere as leaders of a nationwide, grassroots movement for social change. Dobson's guests relate a series of anecdotes describing how they have "travel[ed] the nation" from Milwaukee to Colorado Springs, and even journeyed overseas to Ireland, to address "prolife gatherings." Gianna Jessen, especially, has a winning and vivacious manner of speaking that resonates with precocious self-confidence and warmth, and this makes her sound like a leader whose place in the public eye is natural and fitting. Notwithstanding Jessen's precocity, however, *Focus on the Family* more fundamentally fosters the impression that Gianna Jessen and Heidi Huffman are young activists who are fighting for the rights of the young—for children, that is, since after all that is what fetuses in the womb are, for Dobson's constituents.

It is also crucial to recognize that the broadcast series contextualizes the individual actions of Dobson's guests within a more far-reaching and broadly participatory movement to end abortion. The primary institutional nexus of this antiabortion movement, as Dobson, his guests, and members of the studio audience stress, is the rapidly expanding network of "crisis pregnancy centers." These local, quasi-clinical organizations are operated by evangelicals who offer counseling that dissuades women with unwanted pregnancies from seeking abortions and informs them about services to help them cope with the difficulties of carrying their pregnancies to term. About midway through the series, Tina Huffman tells how she was once approached by a woman after a public speaking engagement who confessed that she had heard her speak previously and had "hated" her for making her feel guilty about having "aborted [her] son at four months through a saline abortion." Now, however, this woman does "volunteer work for a crisis pregnancy center," having "repented of what [she] had done" and successfully undergone "postabortion counseling" herself. Dobson takes up this cue to advertise the work of crisis pregnancy centers, subtly shifting the focus of the conversation from the personal ordeals of his guests to the prospect of collective action:

> Sitting in our gallery today are a lot of people that represent crisis pregnancy centers, and those are some of my favorite people in the whole world because there are about four thousand of those centers in the United States, there are a number of 'em in Canada, and every day they're saving babies, every day they're doing this *marvelous* work. And yet they take so much flak, and they get so criticized and ridiculed, and prime-time America assaults them and all these other national broadcasts assault them. And all they're doing is trying to care for these frightened young women who are pregnant and don't know what to do, and they're bringing babies into the world. Focus on the Family has a *ministry* here, one of our fifty-four, fifty-five—how many ministries do we have now?—that reaches out to crisis pregnancy centers. We just allocated another $100,000 to try to help them financially and other ways, because most of them struggle to try to *stay afloat.* They're staffed by volunteers, busy people who are just trying to give their time. So, there are about twenty or thirty members of crisis pregnancy centers that are sitting out in our gallery—let me invite you all, or anybody else who wants to, to come to the microphone and talk to these courageous people and especially these two young women here that—I haven't known you very long, but I love you, you know that!

Dobson's comments have a similar resonance to psychologist Joseph Nicolosi's references to the proliferation of therapy outlets for "recovering homosexuals" (see chapter 3): in both cases Dobson and his guests foster the notion that a national movement for change is underway linking intellectuals, professionals, and thousands of ordinary citizens. And like this earlier broadcast series, the series featuring Jessen and Huffman makes this sense of grassroots enthusiasm tangible through the format of the broadcast, which incorporates the questions of an excited studio audience into the show and explicitly calls attention to the fact that it is doing this.

It must be recalled that all this outpouring of activist spirit is originally attributable to the attitude of Christlike forgiveness assumed by Dobson's guests, according to the structure of the narrative. Gianna Jessen's and Heidi Huffman's forgiving behavior, however, evinces the same vacuousness and insubstantiality that we have seen in the cases of Mayfield and Washington. Indeed, as victims within the womb, Jessen and Huffman prototypically represent this feature of Focus's figure of the forgiving victim. For in the cases of these girls (as fetuses), an interpersonal, intersubjective relationship of mutual respect between the tormented and her tormenter is obviously, quite literally impossible. The fetus simply cannot experience helplessness, anger at the perpetrator of violence, and a desire for liberation from danger in an ethically mature manner—not, at least, in a way that incorporates self-reflection and moral "recognition" of the other. In addition, the fetus's forgiveness of the mother seems all the more ephemeral and meaningless, given the total lack of moral agency that *Focus on the Family* ascribes to the mothers. (By contrast, the girls are eerily silent regarding whether or not they forgive the "abortionists," who appear to bear the greatest degree of moral choice in these catastrophes.) The structural impossibility for the girls, as fetuses, to forgive their mothers does not apply in the incidents when "proabortion" activists level attacks at the show's protagonists, but the disconcertingly effortless model of forgiveness reasserts itself nonetheless. The disturbingly impersonal quality of Jessen's forgiveness of her accosters is nowhere more transparent than in the chilling cheerfulness of her response to one of the abortion defenders she describes: when this woman tells Jessen she wishes she were dead, Jessen responds, "Have a nice day!"

Likewise, the girls' narratives cement the position of the forgiving victim as one in which active resistance ironically depends on passive compliance with dominant relations of social power—here, parental and masculine authority. As in the series of "false memory syndrome" (also analyzed in chapter 3), so in these shows one unmistakable aspect of the message is that children must never harbor anger or resentment toward their parents, no matter what extremes of suffering the former may have endured at the hands of the latter. In turn, the shows' repeated characterizations of the mothers as "frightened young women" who are desperately confused, utterly ignorant about their own bodies, and incapable of autonomously deciding how to handle their unwanted pregnancies reveal another respect in which *Focus on the Family* undercuts the promise of social transformation: by reinforcing traditional views of women as "the weaker vessel." Finally, as in the broadcasts featuring Mayfield and Washington, the pledge of a renewed world is betrayed by the eventual reinstallment of individual self-preservation as the telos of the narrative. The fetus can only resist being aborted by virtue of its physical instincts for survival. Indeed, it cannot do otherwise than to obey its natural drive for self-preservation. This fact lends an odd ring to Dobson's admiring comments that Huffman is "a survivor" and Jessen "a fighter," as though they were somehow morally responsible for having lived through the attempts to have them aborted. Once again, divine and natural necessity become inseparable in Focus's narrative of the forgiving victim. The sheer survival of the protagonists becomes the motivation for their faith, the root of their forgiveness, and the main point of their stories, displacing the narrative's competing concern with the collective renewal of society.

On the Instrumentality of Forgiveness and Its Limits

Although the stories of Margy Mayfield, Raleigh Washington, and Gianna Jessen and Heidi Huffman counsel passivity and acquiescence in the face of white, masculine, and parental authorities, there is no doubt that they also invigorate active support for the policy agenda of the Christian right. Mayfield's saga attempts to derail any empathy with Morin that might cause the listener to question his subjection to capital punishment by casting Morin as "repulsive," one of "the unlovable" in society. Indeed, Morin's execution is mentioned merely as an afterthought, and the moral and legal conundra posed by capital punishment are bracketed out of the conversation by its incorporation into the deadly efficient economy of salvation, which defines the execution as part of the price Morin must pay for eternal life. The story of Raleigh Washington is about overcoming racism not just through friendship, but more specifically through the fabled camaraderie of American soldiers. As such, this story helps to foster the militarism that has been a pronounced feature of the Christian right since the dawn of the cold war (indeed, since World War I).[19] This broadcast concludes, in turn, by denouncing efforts to address racism through public policy, in particular affirmative action but also, more generally, any measures recommended by "the politically correct ideology on campuses today" (by which Dobson apparently means hate crime policies and multicultural/diversity education initiatives).[20] Meanwhile, the spotlighting of articulate and personable children who survived attempts to have them aborted as fetuses is nothing short of brilliant as a political strategy to drive home the message that abortion is not just the taking of potential human life but rather the murder of innocent babies. In sum, the tales of Focus's forgiving victims evidently and ingeniously serve the instrumental needs of the Christian right to cultivate affectively intense and cognitively specific enthusiasm for a wide range of the Christian right's issues.

At the same time, these shows can be seen as instrumentalities within Focus's operations as the flagship enterprise of the Christian right's culture industry. The protagonist's fall into a perilous situation and consequent, miraculous rescue, followed by her or his "witnessing" to God's grace, is a refrain that *Focus on the Family* repeats over and over, and for the regular listener the differences among the individual broadcasts inevitably begin to blur. The astonishment that the program invites the listener to feel at the hero's final deliverance from Satan's forces thus can never be quite as genuine or heartfelt as it is supposed to be, for the outcome is always known in advance. As Horkheimer and Adorno write, "the culture industry perpetually cheats its consumers of what it perpetually promises," and precisely in doing so ensures the consumer's unending appetite for its cotton-candy products.[21] That is, the very hollowness of these characters' experiences of redemption through forgiveness, as described on *Focus on the Family*, keeps Dobson's constituents tuning in and sending in "requested donations" to purchase the organization's tapes, videos, and books.

Yet surely neither the aesthetic nor the political ramifications of the narrative continuities binding together the broadcast series discussed in this chapter are exhausted by the observation that *Focus on the Family* continually mobilizes instrumentally advantageous stereotypes and other devices of product standardization. Nor is this narrative's political significance restricted to its discharges of stimuli that help fashion favorable attitudes toward the Christian right's policy stands. Additional and unsuspected dimensions of the politics of Focus's forgiving victim come into view when we examine this figure's complete "physiognomy" instead of assessing its individual features in isolation from one another. As we have seen, Adorno encourages us to do the former. The elaboration of the stories of Mayfield, Washington, and Jessen and Huffman has sketched exactly such a physiognomy, with its characteristically paradoxical and compositionally interrelated traits: power gleaned from powerlessness, ethically empty forgiveness, and activist commitment mingled with deference to traditional authority. Returning once again to Adorno's theory of social physiognomy prompts the question: how might the unsuccessful strivings of this narrative figure to achieve unity and coherence offer a textual analogue to society's constitutive inconsistencies? And what sort of negative force, if any, do these persistent narrative antagonisms exude vis-à-vis social antagonisms?

These questions can be answered by "listening" to these stories of redemption through forgiveness yet again, but this time in the context of a historical account of the recent progress toward equality and respect—or lack thereof—for women, African Americans, and children. Answers to the questions above can be solidified, in turn, by situating this account of changing gender, racial, and generational power relations within an analysis of the post-Fordist political economy. When these steps are taken, we may discern that these editions of *Focus on the Family* have as much (or more) to do with fundamental questions concerning the status of women, racial minorities, and children in U.S. society as with the narrower issues of capital punishment, defense spending, and abortion, or even with Christian salvation. We may also discover with no little surprise, however, that Focus's disposition toward women's, blacks', and children's power is significantly more complex than is commonly assumed.

The third quarter of the twentieth century witnessed unprecedented and far-reaching achievements for African Americans and women in attaining new levels of political and social power. The civil rights movement brought about the enforcement of legal recognition of blacks' equal humanity and citizenship within American society, culminating in the victorious struggle for reenfranchisement and pressing beyond voting rights on behalf of measures to redress the pervasive economic inequalities between blacks and whites. Galvanized in part by experiences of persistent sexism within the civil rights and antiwar movements, and preserving the commitments to grand social change that these prior movements nourished, the women's movement of the late 1960s and early 1970s fought successfully to reduce discrimination in employment and education, advance political participation, and secure abortion rights for women. Both the civil rights and women's movements had significant implications for children, especially those of poor or low-income parents whose abilities to provide their young ones with financial support, fulfillment of other basic needs, and higher quality education were significantly strengthened by the antipoverty programs, antidiscrimination efforts, and education reforms that emerged partly in response to these movements.

More recently, however, what appeared earlier to be a steady and irrepressible upsurge in the social and political power of women, African Americans, and children has tailed off and, in many respects, even been reversed. The backlash against women's, blacks', and children's empowerment has taken tangible shape in public policy shifts in the areas of welfare, affirmative action, education, and a host of other components of the welfare state.

The Consequences of Welfare "Reform." In the expansion of poor relief in the 1960s, roughly eight hundred thousand families became new recipients of Aid to Families with Dependent Children (AFDC).[22] Most of the families helped by AFDC were headed by single women, and although AFDC did not raise most of their incomes above the poverty line, it significantly increased their incomes and made them "less poor" than they would have been otherwise.[23] The impact of AFDC on poverty steadily diminished, however, from the end of the 1960s until the program's abolition in 1996. Frances Fox Piven and Richard A. Cloward note that, for AFDC, "benefits lost 42 percent of their purchasing power between 1970 and 1990. By 1990, the maximum benefit was less than half the poverty level in a majority of states, and less than a third of that level in a quarter of the states; for a family of three, the daily per capita benefit in the median payment state was $4.00. (And as the nation entered recession in 1990, the pace of AFDC cuts actually accelerated.)"[24] Even the indexing of food stamp benefits to inflation in 1972 did not prevent the overall purchasing power of AFDC families from declining "by about 27 percent between 1972 and 1990." Simultaneously, moreover, eligibility criteria were made more restrictive and more cumbersome to satisfy over this time period. The result was that the percentage of (officially) poor children receiving AFDC benefits declined by 25 percent, from a historic high of 80.5 percent in 1973 to 59.9 percent in 1990.[25]

The welfare overhaul legislation passed by Congress and signed by President Bill Clinton in 1996 capped a twenty-five-year progression toward the diminution in the value and reach of AFDC benefits by eliminating the program altogether and replacing it with a federal block grant to state antipoverty agencies. Among other provisions, the welfare overhaul act ended the federal entitlement to financial assistance for the eligible poor and required that adults who receive welfare benefits begin paid employment within two years of their entry onto the relief rolls. Since its passage, this legislation has combined with similar reforms at the state and local levels to generate major reductions in the welfare rolls.[26] Very soon, moreover, similar effects are likely to be felt from the act's prohibition on the use of federal funds for aid to adults who have been on welfare for over five years.

As the repeal of AFDC and the intensification of work requirements have cut the number of people receiving assistance, they have also subjected those who remain on the rolls to new forms of discipline that in most cases detract from their residue of personal autonomy and fail to enhance their prospects of long-term, stable, satisfying, and sufficiently remunerative employment. The state-level "experiments" with welfare-to-work programs that have been much celebrated by liberal and conservative policymakers and policy analysts alike since the early 1970s have by and large accumulated a very weak record of success in these terms. To be sure, job training initiatives in some states have produced positive outcomes for some welfare recipients. On the whole, however, the success of these policy innovations has been impeded by the simple lack of sufficiently rewarding employment opportunities in the recent labor market for those on public assistance.[27] Indeed, by ensnaring welfare clients within an increased tangle of bureaucratic requirements, demanding (in most cases) that they perform tasks that neither utilize the work skills they possess nor permit them to develop more marketable skills, and subjecting them to "complete lack of control over their work lives" and to the stigmatization of fellow workers, workfare programs arguably diminish the capacity of those who participate in them to attain lasting financial self-sufficiency.[28]

In its report on the president's decision to sign the welfare overhaul legislation passed by Congress in the summer of 1996, *Congressional Quarterly Weekly Report* included a photograph of Jesse Jackson, Patricia Ireland (president of the National Organization for Women), and Eleanor Smeal (of the Feminist Majority) leading a protest outside the White House.[29] The picture illustrated the recognition by prominent progressives in the United States that although welfare "reform" was of significance for all citizens, it was of particular consequence for African Americans and women; a quotation on the same page from Senator Paul Wellstone noted that it would also have an especially pronounced effect on the lives of children. Those whom the new structure of the poverty relief system aims to force into the competitive labor market (a rather misleading objective, since the vast majority of welfare recipients already perform paid jobs, supplementing their meager earnings with meager public benefits[30]) are predominantly women. Poor women are putatively disempowered when policymakers scale back or eliminate the programs that previously enhanced these women's economic and political capacities by increasing their incomes, providing stability in the midst of difficult life circumstances, and even furnishing a basis for the mobilization of the welfare rights movement.[31] These changes also disproportionately and negatively affect the economic and political power of African Americans, who are represented among the nation's poor in a proportion nearly double to their percentage of the total population (despite the fact that, contrary to persistent stereotypes, African Americans make up a majority of neither the poor nor the population of persons on welfare). And in addition, the legislation marked a recession in the public commitment to improving the lives of poor children, who make up over 40 percent of people in poverty while comprising less than one-quarter of the nonpoor population.[32]

It should be noted, finally, that the recent welfare overhaul is in one sense only an especially pronounced example of the overall reduction in the size and reach of the welfare state over the past twenty-five years. And aside from offering government assistance to enhance the life prospects and political potency of women and African Americans, welfare state programs have also been vital sources of employment for black Americans, serving as a key engine of the growth of the black middle class.[33] The elimination of public sector jobs, in turn, has particularly acute and adverse implications for the job prospects of those who have disproportionately depended on government employment opportunities.

The Roll-Back of Affirmative Action. Meanwhile, systematic efforts to expand educational and employment opportunities throughout the economy for racial and ethnic minorities and women have been scaled back over the last two decades through a combination of federal administrative actions (and inaction), judicial decisions, and grassroots conservative mobilizations. It seems a very long time, indeed, since a Republican president placed his support behind a plan to boost minority hiring in government construction projects by defining high, numerical targets and setting specific timetables, as Richard Nixon did in endorsing the Philadelphia Plan in 1969. Affirmative action continued to receive strong support from federal officials and business leaders during the 1970s, and even though the U.S. Supreme Court's 1978 decision in *Regents of the University of California v. Bakke* "made it clear that numerical preferences without evidence of prior discrimination would not be allowed, . . . it also gave supporters of affirmative action and institutions looking for guidance encouragement by allowing the consideration of race among other criteria for admission." Nevertheless, in repudiating precisely the sorts of numerical goals set by the Nixon administration, and in failing to establish the necessity of any government mechanisms to compel institutions not engaging in race-conscious admissions procedures to change their behavior, the Court in *Bakke* began seriously reining in the momentum that had previously built up toward increasingly far-reaching federal affirmative action policies.[34]

The 1980s witnessed a number of major leaps forward for opponents of affirmative action. Under Ronald Reagan, who had won the White House running on an agenda that was emphatically averse to affirmative action, the federal Office of Federal Contract Compliance sharply and deliberately reduced its efforts to monitor the hiring of women and minorities by federal contractors and to pursue complaints against contractors.[35] A series of Supreme Court decisions promised more enduring changes in the structure of affirmative action. During the 1980s, the Supreme Court (1) narrowed the scope of allowable federal action against educational institutions found to have violated antidiscrimination provisions in Title IX of the Civil Rights Act (in *Grove City College v. Bell*); (2) precluded the protection of minority workers in company layoffs (in *Wygant v. Jackson Board of Education*); (3) prohibited policies setting aside certain percentages of government contracts for minority businesses, finding affirmative action unacceptable "unless it was introduced explicitly as a remedy for documented past discrimination" (in *Croson v. City of Richmond*); and (4) relocated the burden of proof for establishing discrimination or the lack thereof from alleged violators to those claiming to have suffered discrimination (in *Wards Cove Packing Co., Inc. v. Atonio et al.*). Affirmative action also experienced a few significant victories in this decade, when the Court ruled (in *Johnson v. Transportation Agency, Santa Clara County*) that "ignoring minor differences in test/interview performance in the hiring process did not constitute grossly unequal hiring practices in the name of affirmative action," and when Congress restored the pre–*Grove City* status quo in the Civil Rights Restoration Act of 1988 (which passed over Reagan's veto).[36] Nonetheless, the trend against affirmative action was clearly established in these years, and its long-term viability was promoted through the ideological recomposition of the federal judiciary and bureaucracy by the Reagan administration. In broader terms, the 1980s saw an end to the historic alignment of the presidency and the federal judiciary with many of the more progressive elements of the civil rights movement, and thus the dissolution of the most crucial institutional bases of support for the movement's objectives.[37]

More moderate Republican and Democratic presidential leadership in the 1990s consolidated rather than challenged the secular decline of federal support for affirmative action. The Civil Rights Act of 1991, backed by President Bush, enhanced the power of women to combat sexual harassment through "provisions for victims of sexual harassment to receive damages." The act also mandated that a federal commission be established to study the "glass ceiling" phenomenon. However, the act did not specifically take issue with or reverse the decisions rendered by the Supreme Court during the previous decade. The Clinton administration, in turn, faced an intensification of antiaffirmative action rhetoric by the right and responded by backing away from affirmative action even further. When Lani Guinier, Clinton's initial nominee for assistant attorney general for civil rights, was derided by conservative Republicans as a "quota queen" (on the basis of her legal scholarship advocating experimentation with proportional representation to enhance the efficacy of minorities' voting rights), Clinton withdrew her nomination. And when the Supreme Court in 1995 (in *Adarand Constructors, Inc. v. Peña*) rejected a federal policy granting bonuses to prime contractors who subcontracted with "socially disadvantaged individuals," further narrowing the scope of permissible federal action to combat racial discrimination and reinforcing the principle that affirmative action may occur only as a remedy for "identifiable discrimination against specific persons," instead of as a matter of regular policy,[38] Clinton used the language of affirmative action's foes to announce his support for the decision and to instruct federal agencies to comply with it: "Affirmative action has to be made consistent with our highest ideals of personal responsibility and merit. . . . [This means n]o quotas in theory or practice; no illegal discrimination of any kind, including reverse discrimination; no preference for people who are not qualified for any job or other opportunity; and as soon as a program has succeeded, it must be retired."[39] Far beyond the beltway, but with potentially significant implications for future federal policy, voters in California and Washington state passed nearly identical ballot initiatives in 1996 and 1998, respectively, that proscribed any preferential treatment on the basis of race, gender, or ethnicity by the governments of those states.[40] These have been the most drastic attacks on affirmative action yet, and they have further energized the already vibrant movement to end all preferential treatment through federal legislation and additional state legislative enactments. (This was especially true in the case of Washington, where affirmative action opponents had feared that a loss in this state with a relatively low minority population would have boded ill for the success of similar measures in states with more substantial numbers of African Americans and other minorities.)

Clinton's statement in response to the ruling in *Adarand* invited the optimistic supposition that affirmative action might have been losing friends in the 1990s because it had "succeeded" and was no longer necessary. But the Glass Ceiling Commission convened by President Bush, "in examining the top, highest-paying corporate jobs, found that women and minorities, rather than getting preferences, are still largely excluded; at least 95 percent of these jobs are still occupied by white males."[41] It is true that, since the early 1960s, blacks have moved into the medical, legal, and social work professions in unprecedented numbers. Still, "the largest number and percentage of jobs for educated African Americans . . . have been in the local, state, and federal government."[42] Within government, moreover, blacks tend disproportionately to occupy clerical and other low-skill positions while remaining seriously underrepresented in legislative posts and within the faculties of public higher educational institutions. Women maintain a "particularly weak presence in state legislatures," and for both women and blacks underrepresentation within these bodies appears causally linked with disproportionately low levels of participation in public university faculties.[43] Moreover, as in the case of African Americans, "the benefits of affirmative action have not reached the majority of employed women, who remain concentrated in low-paying, female-intensive fields." Even though the percentage of women in professional, managerial, and administrative positions climbed from under 20 percent in 1970 to over 30 percent in 1991, working-class women in blue-collar occupations continued to face sex discrimination in employment opportunities.[44]

Women have achieved some significant gains through the comparable worth movement, which has fought the persistently lower pay standards in occupations with predominantly female workforces relative to occupations in which men comprise most of the workforce. Twenty-one states and a host of municipalities have adopted comparable worth policies, although with widely varying levels of commitment and only in certain regions (the Northeast, the West Coast, and the northern Midwest); and empirical research has demonstrated the positive effects of these initiatives. Moreover, an important Supreme Court decision in 1981 (*County of Washington v. Gunther*) "held that sex discrimination suits filed under Title 7 of the Civil Rights Act were not limited to claims of unequal pay for equal work," opening the door to litigation challenging wage levels in sex-segregated occupations. However, this decision left major issues unresolved, in particular whether the standard of proof establishing discrimination required the plaintiff to demonstrate direct, individual "disparate treatment" as opposed to more indirect, statistically demonstrable "disparate impact." In the absence of a ruling on this issue, lower courts have consistently required the stricter standard of proof. In addition, the federal government has never instituted comparable worth policies, which like affirmative action have not recovered from serious setbacks during the Reagan and Bush administrations. Meanwhile, the ratio of female to male earnings for full-time workers has only improved slightly since the 1970s, rising from the notorious 0.59 figure denounced by the early women's movement to about 0.70.[45]

In short, institutionalized racism and sexism remain very much present realities in the United States. The capacity of affirmative action and comparable worth by themselves to change this situation fundamentally is, to be sure, debatable.[46] Yet the continuing excision of affirmative action policies from the legal repertoire of government antidiscrimination efforts, along with the apparent impasse reached by the comparable worth struggle, cannot but intensify these injustices.

Education: Plessy *Redux.* One crucial reason why affirmative action policies, even of the most far-reaching kind, arguably offer an insufficient basis for achieving educational and economic equality is that social disadvantages often become firmly established during childhood through the U.S. educational system. The 1954 Supreme Court recognized this problem in its landmark decision in *Brown v. Board of Education. Brown* declared segregated schools to be "inherently unequal" and provided the legal basis for later initiatives to foster social equality by desegregating schools. Neither *Brown* nor the *Brown II* decision a year later specified standards for what "desegregation" meant or how the *Brown* mandate was to be implemented. However, the Johnson administration's energetic action pursuant to the Civil Rights Act of 1964 prompted historic change in southern schools by denying federal funding to segregated schools and bringing litigation against these institutions. The Court subsequently clarified the standards for achieving desegregation, ordering in 1968 (in *Green v. County School Board of New Kent County*) that "schools must dismantle segregated dual (or segregated) systems 'root and branch' and that desegregation must be achieved with respect to facilities, staff, faculty, extracurricular activities, and transportation." Three years later, in *Swann v. Charlotte-Mecklenberg Board of Education*, the Court affirmed busing as a legitimate strategy to overcome school desegregation based in segregated housing patterns.[47] Thus, large-scale federal efforts to remedy discrimination in education complemented its similarly groundbreaking support for antipoverty programs and affirmative action during this same era.

Like affirmative action and welfare, however, the desegregation of public education has faced a mounting backlash since the early 1970s. The tide of federal activism began to turn with the election of Richard Nixon, whose administration deliberately slowed the pace of desegregation enforcement. Nixon also commenced the reconstitution of the federal judiciary by conservative Republican presidents, a change so dramatic that by 1995, 60 percent of federal judges had been appointed by Nixon, Reagan, or Bush (after extensive ideological vetting by the Justice Department and the White House). But the Supreme Court began to reverse its posture toward desegregation much earlier. The 1974 decision in *Milliken v. Bradley* precluded city-suburban desegregation in the north "unless plaintiffs could demonstrate that the suburbs or the state took actions that contributed to segregation in the city." Since northern metropolitan areas, by and large, had not maintained officially segregated schools within the same school district, *Milliken* thus effectively nullified the impact of *Brown* in the north.[48] Of course, desegregation supporters could still take heart from victories in the south, where desegregation advanced during the 1970s. Indeed, schools became somewhat less segregated in the 1980s, as the effects of local desegregation strategies endured.[49] Local governments were nonetheless fighting against a powerful wave of federal opposition to desegregation, as the Reagan administration completely defunded educational and public relations aspects of desegregation programs and filed no new desegregation lawsuits.[50] In sum, by the 1980s, desegregation—like welfare and affirmative action—had decisively lost its support in the executive and judicial branches of the federal government. Meanwhile, congressional action failed to counter presidential and judicial antagonism to desegregation, producing only one major piece of legislation to advance desegregation (the Emergency School Aid Act of 1973), and then repealing this law in the Omnibus Budget Reconciliation Act of 1981.[51]

In the 1990s, the Supreme Court deployed its authority to chart acceptable paths for school districts throughout the country to return to segregation. A series of key decisions has redefined desegregation measures, earlier intended to catalyze a lasting and vigilant commitment to desegregation, as temporary slaps on the wrist after which the reinstating of segregated education becomes acceptable. In *Missouri v. Jenkins* (1995), the Court ruled that "equalization remedies should be limited in time and extent and that school districts need not show any actual correction of the education harms of segregation."[52] In other words, without needing to produce any evidence of higher academic achievement by minorities or changes in "discriminatory attitudes" by whites—indeed, even in situations where racist attitudes and scholastic achievement gaps may have increased—school districts once found to be discriminatory are now permitted to resume segregationist practices. And once a school district has obtained "unitary status, the courts presume any government action creating racially segregated schools to be innocent, unless a plaintiff proves that the school officials intentionally decided to discriminate. This burden of proof is nearly impossible to meet, as contemporary school officials can easily formulate plausible alternative justifications." *Jenkins* and other recent cases have thus rendered obsolete the vision and substance of *Brown*, which recognized racism as a deeply entrenched phenomenon that is a normal and institutionally anchored dynamic within American society, rather than an exceptional behavior of errant individuals. More ominously, however, *Jenkins* seems even to contradict the "separate but equal" principle formulated in *Plessy v. Ferguson* (1896), since the current Court ascribes no obligation to local school districts to maintain any level of equality among resegregated schools.[53]

Educational segregation continues to relegate vast numbers of black and other minority children to bitterly dissatisfying and unmotivating experiences in school, and to lifelong inequalities relative to the white majority. Recent statistics confirm the viability of Jonathan Kozol's stark and graphic descriptions of squalor and desperate need in urban schools across the country in his popular book *Savage Inequalities* (1991). Kozol documented the mountain of hardships faced by children, teachers, and administrators in these largely minority-populated schools, including above all insufficient instructional materials, inadequate physical plant facilities, and horrendous sanitation problems.[54] These difficulties of urban schools are rooted in the financial structure of public education in the United States, according to which (1) schools are funded primarily on the basis of local property taxes, and (2) the federal government subsidizes unequal funding of public education by making the payment of property taxes and mortgage payments deductible expenses.[55] It is well-known, of course, that in spite of these problems the gap in educational achievement between black and white students has narrowed since the 1970s. Blacks' standardized test scores have steadily risen, as has the percentage of blacks enrolling in postsecondary education, and dropout rates for blacks have fallen. Yet black dropout rates remain double the rates of whites, and blacks' test scores still lag significantly behind those of whites, with the gap increasing dramatically in reading, mathematics, and science as students move from elementary to secondary schools.[56] The gap in college enrollment after high school graduation has actually increased since the early 1970s; and even though the percentage of blacks enrolling in college has risen by twelve percentage points, this figure still stood at only 57 percent in 1997, eleven points beneath the level for whites.[57] Meanwhile, barely half (51.3 percent) of the Hispanic population has completed high school, in comparison to figures of 66.7 percent for blacks and 80.5 percent for all non-Hispanics; and only 9.7 percent of Hispanics have finished four or more years of college, against figures of 11.5 percent for blacks and 22.3 percent for non-Hispanics.[58] A higher percentage of minority enrollment in public schools still correlates with lower spending per pupil, as does lower median household income—and as Kozol points out, even "equal funding for unequal needs is not equality."[59] Decades of research has shown that key factors spurring educational achievement are moderately small school size, small class size, a challenging curriculum, and qualified teachers. Substantial research also demonstrates that when minority students receive comparable resources to those enjoyed by whites the former perform on par with the latter. But today, as in the past, "minority children are much less likely than white children to have any of these resources," and as a consequence experience persistently high dropout and illiteracy rates and low achievement levels.[60]

Post-Fordism and the Backlash: Structure and Ideology

The weakening social position of minorities, women, and children is vividly revealed at flashpoints in recent political history like the Welfare Reform Act of 1996, Washington state's Initiative 200, and *Missouri v. Jenkins*. And the special vitriol that conservatives seem to reserve for their attacks on welfare, affirmative action, and the public schools lends these issues a further capacity to encapsulate the essence of the current backlash. Nevertheless, the declining power of these historically subordinated groups is also evident in policy developments in a host of other government and corporate policy areas, including (but not limited to) child care, legal aid, housing programs, the carceral system, voting rights, and capital investment. The fact that racial minorities, women, and children are losing power on a plethora of fronts throughout society suggests that this phenomenon belongs to a more general structural transformation of U.S. society. And indeed, the racist, sexist, and antichild backlashes can be seen as fundamental to the advance of post-Fordism in the state and economy, and thus as integrally interconnected and structurally based, rather than as singular problems that could be effectively addressed in isolation from one another or in the absence of broader, more systemic change.

The civil rights, black power, welfare rights, Chicano, and women's movements were similar mobilizations, in one sense, in that they were expressions of discontent among groups who generally had been excluded from the Fordist compromise and wanted full participation in the benefits conceded to more privileged workers by large corporations and the state.[61] The expansions of poverty relief, affirmative action, and school desegregation efforts in the late 1960s and early 1970s exemplified the genuine successes that these movements achieved in this regard, at least for a brief time. Unfortunately, the buildup of these forces' momentum coincided with the hastening transition toward post-Fordist conditions of accumulation, production, and consumption in the 1970s. Not only did this transition undermine the very social compact (and the Democratic Keynesian/welfarist coalition that was its main political anchor) to which blacks, Latinos, women, and the poor sought entry; it furthermore introduced new labor market conditions that spelled an even deeper entrenchment of social inequalities based on race, ethnicity, and sex. David Harvey writes: "The labour market has . . . undergone a radical restructuring. Faced with strong market volatility, heightened competition, and narrowing profit margins, employers have taken advantage of weakened union power and the pools of surplus (unemployed or underemployed) labourers to push for much more flexible work regimes and labour contracts."[62] The post-Fordist labor market divides into "core" and "periphery" groups. For the former—by far the smaller of these groups—"flexibility" may well translate into more autonomous, highly skilled, and personally meaningful work, as the more optimistic celebrants of "flexible specialization" promise. The latter, by contrast, are expected to perform low-skill work with maximum adaptability to new production systems oriented toward rapid responses to continually changing market conditions, without the rewards of high wages, permanent contracts, decent benefits, or promotion prospects.[63] Despite the penetration of more secure and lucrative occupations by small percentages of women and minorities, "the new labour market conditions have for the most part re-emphasized the vulnerability of disadvantaged groups." This is particularly true for women, who have been actively recruited "into burgeoning low-wage sectors of the economy."[64] And the most vulnerable of all are the predominantly immigrant and Third World women who end up working in the "patriarchal" labor systems that are reemerging in the post-Fordist economy: forms of production such as sweatshops that operate informally, in domestic or underground contexts, often under the arbitrary authority of a "mafia-like" boss, performing work under subcontracting arrangements with transnational corporations:

Not only do the new labour market structures make it much easier to exploit the labour power of women on a part-time basis, and so to substitute lower-paid female labour for that of more highly paid and less easily laid-off core male workers, but the revival of subcontracting and domestic and family labour systems permits a resurgence of patriarchal practices and homeworking. This revival parallels the enhanced capacity of multinational capital to take Fordist mass-productions systems abroad, and there to exploit extremely vulnerable women's labour power under conditions of extremely low pay and negligible job security. The Maquiladora programme that allows US managers and capital ownership to remain north of the Mexican border, while locating factories employing mainly young women south of the border, is a particularly dramatic example of a practice that has become widespread in many of the less developed and newly-industrializing countries (the Philippines, South Korea, Brazil, etc.).[65]

Under the altered structural conditions of post-Fordism, in sum, women's and minorities' earlier ambitions of assimilation into social strata enjoying higher standards of living have become increasingly anachronistic, running counter to basic dynamics of the labor market.

The long-term, mounting opposition in all branches of the federal government and in public opinion to welfare, affirmative action, and school desegregation described in the previous section coheres with this reorganization of the labor market in readily apparent ways. The elimination or drastic reduction of welfare benefits; the subjection of poor relief recipients to the "dramaturgy" of ritual degradation staged by "welfare-to-work" programs; the rollback of affirmative action, driven rhetorically by leaders who scapegoat women and minorities for the declining economic prospects of white working-class men; and the shutdown of aspirations toward higher education and social advancement for black and Latino children in resegregated public schools, while "big-city bureaucrats" and "big (teachers') unions" are demonized to explain these students' low rates of achievement—all of these grand shifts in public policy work together to discipline the least privileged sectors of the working class into conformity with the new, harsher norms of the post-Fordist economy. These policy transformations have been all the more convenient, both economically and politically, (1) as partial remedies to the fiscal strain generated by the postwar state's massive, decades-long subsidization of production in the private monopoly sector through "welfare and warfare" expenditures alike;[66] and (2) as concessions to the leading forces of grassroots politics in the post-Fordist era, "the revanchist middle strata" organized at various points since the early 1970s into antibusing coalitions, taxpayers' associations, homeowners' movements, and antiaffirmative action campaigns—and, of course, Christian right groups.[67]

The ideological politics of post-Fordism, however, do not simply involve a reassertion of traditional (that is, bourgeois-liberal, individualist, sexist, racist, and ageist) values. Rather, the earlier successes of minorities' and women's social movements have powerfully shaped contemporary justifications of the revoking of welfare, affirmative action, and desegregation programs. In the aftermath of these movements, many leading intellectuals and politicians have felt compelled to characterize the repeal of AFDC, the banning of race- and sex-conscious hiring and admissions policies, and the effective nullification of *Brown* as the culmination rather than the repudiation of the civil rights and women's movements.

Paeans to *Brown* reliably appear in the nation's news sources with the passage of each major anniversary of this decision. *Brown* is invariably characterized as a watershed event, a turning point in history after which no return to the dark ages of (or preceding) *Plessy* is conceivable, let alone practically possible. As Gary Orfield and colleagues write:

> Ignoring the past, we have come to think of segregation as no more relevant to contemporary American educational policy than 1890s' debates about "free silver" or the 1930 Smoot-Hawley tariff are to contemporary economic policy. . . . We celebrate *Brown* and Martin Luther King, Jr. in our schools, even when these very schools are still almost totally segregated by race and poverty. Millions of African American and Latino students learn the lessons of *Brown* while they sit in segregated schools in collapsing cities, where almost no students successfully prepare for college.[68]

Brown's supposedly lasting viability is paid tribute not only by public school students, but moreover by the very federal judges whose opinions have cleared the path toward legal and speedy resegregation. Ironically, this celebration of *Brown* legitimizes discourses of education "reform" that downplay racial inequality as a problem yet to be solved. Thus the proponents of vouchers and charter schools perversely refigure the legacy of the civil rights movement as a release from the moral obligation to consider race as the central category of social inequality, consequent to the movement's ostensibly irreversible victories. At the same time, these "reformers" imply that the shift away from race-conscious rhetoric and policy portends the achievement of unprecedented degrees of equality and, furthermore, the "empowerment" of blacks and Latinos. Petitions to the courts for "unitary status" normally promote themselves not as resegregationist initiatives but rather "as new educational improvement programs or efforts to increase parental involvement."[69] Moreover, the rhetoric of "local control," which has guided Supreme Court decisions since *Milliken* and has become especially pronounced in the 1990s, and that of "choice," which is perpetually invoked by the voucher and charter school "reform" movement, suggest that the termination of the desegregation project will infuse new power into minority communities.

Likewise, national leaders have touted the slashing of antipoverty programs as a new and long overdue form of emancipation for poor individuals and communities. Recent Republican and Democratic presidents have echoed one another in characterizing federal welfare programs as "a new kind of bondage" (Reagan, speaking to the National Association for the Advancement of Colored People in 1981) and as "trapping generation after generation in dependency" (Clinton, announcing his intention to sign the 1996 welfare reform act).[70] Within this discursive context, rescinding poverty relief cannot but acquire an aura of setting the captives free and unleashing their power to contribute to the productivity of the nation and their local communities. At the same time, the rhetoric of welfare reform insists that those who are being transported from welfare to work undergo strict monitoring and supervision. In one sense, this undermines the theme of liberation. In another sense, however, it similarly guarantees the production of a newly empowered subject—though a subject whose power develops gradually according to distinctly Foucauldian processes rather than springing forth exuberantly following the elimination of the repressive state apparatus. At least in theory, the disciplinary rigor of welfare-to-work programs "increases the skill of each individual, coordinates these skills, accelerates movements . . . [and] tends to increase aptitudes, speeds, output and therefore profits."[71] Echoes of Foucault resound, for example, in the following excerpt from a *Washington Post* story about welfare-to-work initiatives in the D.C. area, published several months after the repeal of AFDC:

> The bustling kitchen inside the Marriott at Metro Center in downtown Washington is a laboratory for welfare reform. Amid goat cheese and smoked salmon and the clamor of pots and pans, head chef Dennis Marcinik tries to mold jobless men and women into capable cooks. . . . Preparing the unskilled, dependent poor can be done, but it is rarely easy. Often, it requires the boss to become almost uncomfortably intimate with the lives of workers. . . . "At one point, we were buying them alarm clocks to make sure they got to work on time," said Janet Tully, who manages Marriott's six-year-old job training program, widely considered a model for corporate welfare-to-work efforts.[72]

But whether the emphasis is on emancipation or discipline, one crucial, common element in discourses of welfare reform is clear: the intensified powerlessness of the poor before state and market institutions alike is recast as their attainment of newfound power.

There has been no more vivid or more explicit example of the ideological inversion of the aspirations of the civil rights movement by its opponents, however, than the antiaffirmative action initiatives recently passed by West Coast voters. Washington's Initiative 200 declared: "This Act shall be known and cited as the Washington State Civil Rights Act," following the lead of California two years previously. It moreover elided the distinction between "preferential treatment" and "discrimination" in its initial and most widely read lines, which articulated the purpose of the act as "prohibiting government entities from discriminating or granting preferential treatment based on race, sex, color, ethnicity, or national origin."[73] The initiative's chief supporting organization topped its Web page with the slogan "equal justice under law." An uplink to a "welcome message" brought to the screen the assurance that the measure would "affirm the principle that every individual should be protected from race discrimination in this country," along with the affirmation that fighting racial discrimination "in the early '60s . . . was exactly the right thing to do." This message then added: "The vision behind this campaign is of an America that looks beyond race—not dwells on it."[74] Racism (and sexism) are thus to be overcome by their suppression from public conversation. According to the dominant contemporary ideology of "civil rights," empowerment in the future can only result from disempowerment in the present.

The new "civil rights" ideology thus amounts to an epochal transvaluation of values in the United States. And on the most immediate level, it sharply contradicts the structural dynamics of post-Fordism in the state and the private sector, even as it quietly facilitates these structural shifts. This ideological transformation is driven even further for women by the recent promotion of backlash feminism in the mainstream media—in which *Time* magazine anoints the mooning and waiflike Ally McBeal heiress to a putative tradition extending back to Gloria Steinem, Betty Friedan, and Susan B. Anthony, and which place Katie Roiphe's self-absorbed snips at other feminists for taking the fun out of sex at Harvard on par with serious critiques of women's underemployment, underpayment, and continuing vulnerability to rape, sexual harassment, and domestic abuse.

What is it that makes such "postfeminist feminism" and the inverted "civil rights" ideology so apparently popular? In part, as we have seen, it is the inviting promise that previously untapped sources of power for women, minorities, and children await our eager exploitation of them. However, it is also partly the desire to "look beyond" past injustices. In certain core respects, that is, the attractiveness of the new "civil rights" and feminist ideologies consists in the allure of forgiving and forgetting as a disposition that seems not only psychologically unburdening but also morally responsible. In the early years of the civil rights movement, participants in nonviolent demonstrations demanded of themselves a constant attitude of forgiveness toward their attackers, forging power out of this unwavering commitment to recognize the latter's humanity even when reciprocal treatment was brutally denied. Today, the call to forgive has become at once less explicit, disconnected from resistance, and far more vast, diffuse, and depersonalized in its scope. Yet it resonates profoundly in admonitions to "look beyond" racism and sexism, as well as in the construction of this envisioning as the authentic, contemporary way to preserve the civil rights heritage. It reverberates, moreover, in the stories of Margy Mayfield, Raleigh Washington, and Gianna Jessen and Heidi Huffman, and it is to these stories that we will now return.

The Dialectics of Forgiveness

Focus on the Family promotes clear and conservative positions on the issues of welfare, affirmative action, and educational reform. Focus invites opposition to public welfare programs of all kinds, on the grounds that such programs assault American families by overtaxing them, encourage teenage girls to have babies out of wedlock, and undermine what it considers to be the divinely and naturally established role of men as providers for families.[75] Dobson notes that interracial "anger and hostility" persists despite the passage of "affirmative action laws," and for Washington this proves that "governmental programs" cannot "solve the problem" of racial discrimination.[76] And *Focus on the Family* provokes nothing short of terror over recent federal efforts to reform educational standards like the Goals 2000 program, which Focus's educational policy manager Linda Page characterizes as a "frightening" brand of "engineering" and which Dobson calls a "grab for power" by a federal elite that wants to "gain control of the minds and hearts and souls of children" and "a steamroller that will absolutely run over you and your kids, if you're not wary." (Instead, Page supports the notion of "home rule school districts so that the power goes back to local communities.")[77] In short, when Focus addresses these policy issues directly it unequivocally and passionately applauds the backlash.

Core elements of Focus's narrative of the forgiving victim, in turn, securely buttress its more overt ideological work on behalf of the backlash. Margy Mayfield's resolve to submit to masculine authority, Raleigh Washington's passive reliance on the goodwill of whites to help him negotiate the insults and other hardships caused by racism, and the utter helplessness of Gianna Jessen and Heidi Huffman as fetal near-victims of abortion express in narrative form the acquiescence that post-Fordist society demands of women, minorities, and children in the face of newly exploitative labor conditions and advancing governmental indifference to poverty and inequality. These individuals' stubborn refusal to *name* the injustices they suffer reflects the silence demanded of women, minorities, and children today by educational and welfare "reforms" and "civil rights" initiatives that putatively weaken their social position. And their mechanistic reflexes of forgiveness mime precisely the sort of compliant pardon for the continuing history of racism and patriarchy that fulfills the new imperative to "look beyond" and not "dwell on" these forms of oppression: a pardon, that is, that reifies the lack of mutual, interpersonal recognition between the victim and the perpetrator of harm rather than attempting to overcome it by confronting the latter with his or her moral responsibility for the damage caused. The advent of post-Fordism has witnessed the demobilization of the civil rights and women's movements, in point of fact eliminating major opportunities for women, blacks, and Latinos to act collectively to achieve power and equality and increasingly leaving individualized, self-preservationist behavior as the only viable response to the brutalities imposed by the emergent political economy. This aspect of the social totality, too, finds vivid expression in Focus's narrative of the forgiving victim, when the narrative's call for social transformation recedes behind the securing of the hero's individual safety and survival, by virtue of which—and only by virtue of which—the narrative finally attains closure.

At the same time, post-Fordist contradictions between social structure and ideology are reproduced in Focus's narrative of redemption through forgiveness. The experiences of Mayfield, Washington, Jessen, and Huffman, as related on *Focus on the Family*, underscore the key claims of the new "civil rights" and "postfeminist" discourses. Focus's forgiving victim miraculously finds power in circumstances of the most extreme powerlessness, and this is precisely what resegregationist logic tells minority children in dilapidated urban schools, what the opponents of affirmative action promise women and minorities whose exclusion from employment and educational opportunities continues, and what the advocates of welfare "reform" say to the poor who face destitution in the aftermath of service cutbacks. The inverted discourses of "civil rights" and "postfeminism," furthermore, piously affirm that the historic, twentieth-century movement for equality and social justice triumphantly marches on. This enthusiasm, too, gains expression in the activist fervor of Focus's forgiving victims, as they galvanize grassroots efforts to punish (to death) the perpetrators of violence against women, to work (as private individuals) toward "racial reconciliation," and to fight for the rights and lives of ("unborn") children. The crucial point, however, is that these moments of the narrative persist in unresolved tension with the narrative's competing current—where powerlessness is not the root of power but simply submission, where social transformation collapses into self-preservation, and where forgiveness is merely forgetfulness. The "social physiognomy" of Focus's internally embattled narrative of the forgiving victim is the antagonistic structure of post-Fordist society.

The endurance of these narrative contradictions vouchsafes the dialectical character of *Focus on the Family*'s relationship to the social totality. On the one hand, the narrative of the forgiving victim reproduces and reinforces the trends in public policy and the labor market discussed above that are substantially reducing the power of women, minorities, and children in the current phase of capitalist development. On the other hand, it preserves what Adorno referred to as an indelible "truth-content" inasmuch as its passionate but failed "striving toward identity" and harmony bears witness to the false reconciliation of social contradictions under post-Fordist conditions. The narrative thus indicts the political and socioeconomic status quo—if only negatively—and the contortion that this effects in its simultaneous legitimation of dominant political-economic tendencies yields an otherwise unnoticeable, tiny, but ineliminable recess in which critical thought can nestle.

But precisely what does this critique of *Focus on the Family*, along with the analyses formulated in the two preceding chapters, yield in terms of new insight for social theory under post-Fordism? And how might these experiments in social physiognomy inform cultural-political practices oriented toward the transformation of the conditions of social domination specific to post-Fordism and refracted in the narrative structures of *Focus on the Family*? Does recognizing the negative-utopian moments in Focus's narratives of the compassionate professional, the humble leader, and the forgiving victim simply offer reminders that hope is possible even when the movement of history seems to do nothing but dash hopes? Or can listening to *Focus on the Family* and critically understanding its dialectical energies contribute something more substantial to social theory and transformational social practice?

6

Negative Dialectics and Political Practice

Visiting the "Stations" of the Cross

The Catholic tradition known as "the stations of the cross" invites the believer to "accompany" Jesus symbolically along the way of his trial and execution through a dramatic reenactment. Plaques with painted or sculpted scenes of Jesus' final hours are hung in chronological order on the walls of the church, which prompts the individual, who walks from one to another along the interior perimeter of the building, to remember each stage of the passion. At one "station," for example, the believer is reminded of the mocking of Jesus at his trial. Further on, she sees a representation of Jesus stumbling beneath the weight of the cross he carries for himself. Sometimes a priest leads the procession, which often occurs during Lent, especially during Holy Week. But the ritual can take place at any time of year, and is often conducted by individuals or groups of lay persons without any clerical leadership. The progression from station to station may include the reading of "devotions" (that is, prayers) or the singing of songs; or it may be silently meditative.

By performing the stations of the cross, the believer learns through imitative behavior the path of redemption. The ritual unites visual images, bodily movement, and sometimes music and/or written texts to stir emotion, provoke reflective thought, and catalyze spiritual experience. This practice is in a basic sense educative, and its pedagogy employs sensory appeals to generate a narrative. These appeals not only convey the narrative to the individual but moreover draw the individual into the narrative as a participant. The materiality of the images and rhythms of motion, in particular, make the road to Golgotha seem more tangible, and make the believer's personal implication in this road more vivid. These effects probably become even more pronounced in some recent, characteristically post–Vatican II adaptations of the ceremony that supplement or replace the images of Jesus with contemporary photographs of individuals suffering from poverty and other forms of injustice. Other experimental versions take the pilgrim outside the church to visit homeless shelters and food banks—the "stations of the cross" frequented daily by millions of poor people in the contemporary United States.[1] Thus whether it occurs inside churches or around neighborhoods, walking among the stations of the cross in liturgical solidarity with Jesus is meant to generate a sense of solidarity with fellow believers and, above all, with persons who suffer from need, deprivation, and violence.

The expansion of evangelical-Protestant conservative radio has made possible a wide range of alternative journeys between different "stations" of the cross. By these "journeys" I mean, of course, the actions of tuning in to a "Christian" radio station and listening to the sequence of programs—one of which will invariably be Focus on the Family—or simply of station hopping and hearing the radio lock on to a succession of signals, several of which in any given trip around the dial are bound to radiate from evangelical broadcasters. These peregrinations, like those in the Catholic tradition, involve learning about the path to salvation and tend to concentrate on the pain and death endured by Jesus. They also may be usefully conceptualized, in part, as rituals, to the extent that radio listening assumes a regularized, patterned form and in turn becomes incorporated into daily or weekly routines. Like progressive Catholics, moreover, evangelicals have sought to diversify and multiply the narratives related on their route among the "stations of the cross," interposing contemporary human subjects into the traditional and overarching biblical narrative about Jesus himself to accentuate various specific aspects of "Christlike" behavior. As we have seen, this is precisely how Focus's narratives of the compassionate professional, the humble leader, and the forgiving victim are constituted. Evangelicals also parallel these Catholics in relocating the stations of the cross into what are commonly seen as secular spaces.

Yet there are obvious and important distinctions between the Catholic practice of the stations of the cross and this loosely defined evangelical alternative. Christian right radio condenses and constricts the sensory stimuli to learning the way of redemption. The intervention of spoken text is dramatically intensified while the elements of the visual and the kinesthetic are eliminated: here, the pedagogy relies only on textual narrative, perhaps along with the occasional musical interlude. This substantially augments the power of the institution formulating the narrative, even though the dispersion of the practice itself into an infinity of locations throughout society would seem to detract from this sort of institutional authority. The effect of "Christian" radio's adaptation of the ritual on this practice's capacity to make the passion of Jesus seem tangible and personally consequential is similarly ambiguous. On the one hand, the points of possible contact between the narrative of salvation and worldly experience multiply beyond counting, for they are as numerous as the spaces into which radios can be placed and turned on. On the other hand, the replacement of bodily movement and visual image within the practice itself by the more abstract motions of the ear and mind, as these faculties adjust to each new frequency and program, removes the immediate, material, and mimetic component of the ritual. This cannot but make the believer's encounter with the narrative more passive and more abstract. Such passivity and abstractness are underscored, moreover, by the elimination of the intentionally communal context for visiting the "stations of the cross." These qualities of the experience are enhanced, moreover, by the fact that a commodity-exchange relationship ultimately may substitute for this context of community, if the listener responds to the eager solicitations of her "suggested donations" in return for a tape or book. Of course, the commodity reintroduces an element of materiality into the experience. But its presence is delayed until well after the experience has ended. Indeed, it appears suddenly and unpredictably one day in the mail, and this accentuates its disjuncture from the preceding, figurative journey among the "stations of the cross" positioned along the FM and AM bands. "A commodity," Marx wrote, is "a very strange thing, abounding in metaphysical subtleties and theological niceties."[2] Fetishizing the commodities dispensed by "Christian" radio stations heightens the metaphysical quality of the theological praxis of visiting the "stations of the cross," in comparison to the traditional ritual.

Navigating Christian right radio's "stations of the cross" thus allows the story of Jesus' life, suffering, and death to resonate with injustice in today's world in ways that are at once more highly tenuous and more comprehensively directed by those who design the programming, relative to the traditional practice of Catholic devotion and its nontraditional variants. Nevertheless, the analysis of Focus on the Family in the preceding chapters demonstrates that, these conditions notwithstanding, narrative structures of Christian right radio consistently preserve negative-utopian moments that illuminate the grave injustices perpetrated by post-Fordist society. To be sure, the commodity fetishism and other abstract(ing) qualities of the Christian right's version of the "stations of the cross" undoubtedly make these moments harder for even the dedicated listener to discern, not to mention the casual user of the radio's "search" button. But the possibility always remains that one or more of these scarce but searing moments will present itself to the listener, given the right time and place—maybe on the trip home from a visit to the primary care physician who has just denied permission to see a nonnetwork specialist; or en route to an interview for a job in some field traditionally considered "women's work"; or on the morning after yet another election day that breaks records for campaign spending.

These opportunities are likely to be rare, however, and even when they arise the ideological force of the narratives' reflection of social contradictions is by no means absent. In other words, simply because instances of utopian negativity survive within Focus's otherwise legitimationist narratives does not mean that supporters of single-payer health care, publicly financed campaigns, and school desegregation can happily expect that, sooner or later, evangelicals will spontaneously start joining their ranks. What these negative-utopian glimmerings emphasize, however, is that Christianity—perhaps even evangelical Christianity—can still provide a meaningful and effective "idiom" for provoking radical consciousness on the grounds of cultural experience. And different narrative constructions within this "idiom" may be able to do a much better job of this than those furnished by *Focus on the Family* are ever likely to do.

Critical Theory and Emancipatory Practice

Adorno's theory has often and justly been criticized for its uncertain and excessively mystical connection to political practice, as was discussed in chapter 1. Overly preoccupied with aesthetic solutions to the "metatheoretical" question of how thought could become self-reflective, Adorno lacked sufficient sensitivity to the basic Marxian insight that theory's critical character could only be certified through practical struggle with and against sociohistorical forces. In a recent and influential study, Stephen T. Leonard has argued persuasively that this problem manifested itself in Adorno's (and many of his Frankfurt School colleagues') unwillingness to identify any "idioms" in which social groups grounded in particular historical situations could reason their way toward a radical political understanding of their experiences and their attempts to contest domination. Leonard summarizes the problem with trenchant clarity:

> The attempt to ground critical theory without reference to a practical context—an addressee—makes critical theory bankrupt in its own terms. Without the identification of historically situated individuals to whom it is addressed, and for whom it might serve as a means of "enlightenment and emancipation," a critical theory becomes nearly indistinguishable from those forms of theory which, in Marx's words,

"have only *interpreted* the world" when "the point" should be "to *change* it" (*MER*: 145). Without a practical dimension, critical theory cannot achieve its own stated aim of helping those who suffer from domination and unfreedom to understand the sources of their oppression, and emancipate themselves from that oppression. It is not enough to claim that one is committed to the emancipation of those who suffer from unwarranted and unnecessary domination. For such a theory must also be committed to understanding its own origin in specific, historically situated struggles, and it must be committed to understanding its verification as being tied to the self-emancipating actions of those to whom it is addressed.[3]

Leonard contends that Adorno and other "modernist" critical theorists recognized that the proletariat had not proven to be the universal subject of history as Marx had predicted, but were unwilling to relinquish their commitment to universal reason as the epistemological model for revolutionary consciousness. They thereby precluded critical theory's living engagement with specific political struggles, cutting off the vital nourishment of its roots. According to Leonard, however, more recent forms of critical theory have hewn much more closely to the spirit of Marx's famous eleventh thesis on Feuerbach. In particular, Leonard finds that the intellectual movements of dependency theory, Paolo Freire's critical pedagogy, liberation theology, and feminism have reinvigorated critical theory by virtue of their more strenuous attempts to formulate theory in the context of collective, social-transformational practices.[4] In this view, Adorno and his colleagues are to be credited with having advanced the critique of knowledge that claims to be transhistorically objective, but faulted for their attempt to perpetuate a historically unsubstantiated faith in universal reason, a faith that demanded theory's self-defeating seclusion from actual politics.[5]

Leonard is certainly correct to criticize the ill-fated severance of Adorno's theory from its sources of validation in concrete political struggles. But he overlooks the possibility, explored in this book, of redeploying a distinctly Adornian attentiveness to the dialectical potencies of cultural artifacts in new and politically productive ways. As the foregoing analysis of *Focus on the Family* shows, it is possible to reconstruct an Adornian method of cultural interpretation that brings to the surface negative-utopian features constituted in relation to particular constellations of historical circumstances, rather than simply in anticipation of a hazier and more transcendentalist notion of the redemption of the world. Specifically, it demonstrates that these moments manifest themselves in evangelical conservative narrativizations of post-Fordist experiences, namely

the disjunctures between communitarian ideology and exclusionary practices in the health and human services state-industrial complex; between
egalitarian-populist ideology and declining accountability in an electoral
system awash in cash; and between new "antiracist and feminist" ideologies and the deepening disempowerment of minorities and women.
The critique of *Focus on the Family* has helped us see these social contradictions as opportunities for political engagement, moreover, and to
identify those broad segments of society that experience these contradictions as populations favorably positioned to be recruited into organized,
progressive-populist efforts to challenge them politically. In other words,
the dialectical criticism of *Focus on the Family* reveals several locations
within the social totality where a remarkably intense amount of ideological "work" is being done. This indicates that these may be points
of instability within the superficially harmonious orchestration of post-
Fordism's contradictions, points at which political challenges might be
strategically well focused. Such efforts would comprise precisely those
"specific, historically situated struggles" that, as Leonard rightly insists,
alone can vouchsafe any truth that critical theory claims to expound.

Lastly, and perhaps most importantly, the dialectical criticism of *Focus
on the Family*'s dominant narratives invites speculation that struggles for
social welfare rights, democratic electoral reforms, and justice and equality for women and minorities could be activated at least in part through the
"idiom" of American evangelicalism. Critical theory must indeed search
for a popular idiom in which to make itself comprehensible, to cultivate
responsiveness to the negative-utopian elements in Christian right radio,
and thereby to contribute to radical political practices. This critique of
Dobson's program demonstrates that far from being either wholly incorporated into the culture industry or entirely splintered into a postmodern
pastiche of free-floating signs, evangelicalism in the United States today
remains a living tradition—even in its media forms. It should then be
possible for cultural radicals to work within its distinctive idiom, bringing
it to a new and more critical level of development in terms of both its
intrinsic qualities and its relation to historical conditions. If this can indeed be done, then critical theory will have found a new mode of articulation in which to be constructed, communicated, and validated.

Precisely how might evangelicalism, which the new right so readily and
efficiently commandeers, counterintuitively provide intellectual and political radicalism with a new voice? Let us remember Adorno's pinpoint-
ing of the aesthetic qualities that most decisively determine the political
content of a cultural object: "The moment in the work of art which enables it to transcend reality . . . does not consist in the harmony achieved,
of the dubious unity of form and content, the internal and the external,

the individual and society, but rather in those features in which discrepancy appears, in the necessary failure of the passionate striving toward identity."[6] If the aim is to resist identity, then the challenge would be that of devising new narratives within the evangelical idiom that accentuate with the utmost acuteness and severity their own theological contradictions. For this would enable them to call attention to the structural contradictions of society, whereas attempting to force their own internal contradictions under cover would likewise consign social contradictions to invisibility beneath a falsely reconciled appearance. Narratives of this sort could perhaps take the following specific form: they could thematize *failures of coherence* between striving for personal salvation and working toward the salvation of all the world, rather than insisting on the inevitable compatibility between the individual and social aspects of salvation, as does Focus on the Family.

One example of a text that does this, though from a theological perspective that is more liberal-Protestant than evangelical-Protestant, is a popular paperback by David Hilfiker, a physician who has lived out his Christian commitment by providing medical services to very poor residents of Washington, D.C. In 1982, Hilfiker moved to the District to begin practicing what he now calls "poverty medicine," after having spent seven years building a successful practice in a small town in Minnesota. Hilfiker writes that he has understood his "journey" among the ill and poor in Washington "both as a struggle against injustice on behalf of those abandoned by the rest of us and as a search for [his] own spiritual center." Initially, Hilfiker notes, he was optimistic that his local actions as part of a nondenominational "Christian spiritual community" would call forth a broader political response to the needs he witnessed:

> Was it not possible for us to call the medical profession back to its traditional responsibility to the poor? If we, through our speeches and writings, told the story of inner-city pain to a broad enough audience, it might turn individual compassion into social compassion, which would then translate into political action. Equal opportunity was a fundamental American promise: Surely, then, it was possible to offer the citizens of the American inner city at least basic medical care![7]

But Hilfiker eventually recognizes that fundamental changes in the priorities of the medical profession, the health industry in general, and public policy are unlikely to happen in the near future. And he realizes, and emphasizes in his book, that his personal path in imitation of Christ is radically disjoined from the transformation of society because of the structural dynamics of this society's operation. In a certain sense, then, Hilfiker offers a testimony to the impossibility of a fully actualized Christian redemption, given contemporary social conditions. Thus in its very structure this narrative accentuates its own self-contradictoriness—and in the process brings to light that of society.

It might be argued that evangelicalism in the United States has dramatically differed from (theologically) liberal Protestantism in ways that make the invocation of a similar narrative within evangelicalism singularly improbable. And it is true that abiding currents of premillennialist pessimism about human beings' capacities to reform society would keep many evangelicals from entertaining the grand hopes for social change that Hilfiker expresses. Additionally, those evangelicals who are strongly influenced by the fundamentalist, quasi-Baconian dogmatism that posits the inevitable harmony among God's purposes, the forces of nature, and social history would consider simply heretical the notion that social conditions could ever thwart the fulfillment of God's plan. However, by no means do all evangelicals today adhere strictly to assumptions like these. Recent decades have actually witnessed a gradual growth in attitudinal and behavioral diversity within the evangelical subculture, and this increases the possibilities for cross-fertilization between liberal and evangelical domains. Political movements for emancipation, notably of slaves and women, have relied heavily on traditional evangelical narratives in different epochs of the United States's past, and it is neither inconceivable nor wholly unlikely that the idiom of evangelicalism could once again furnish a means of building cooperation between radical intellectuals and popular struggles. Indeed, the ongoing vitality of the Sojourners spiritual-political community in Washington, D.C., since the late 1960s, along with more recent organizing efforts by progressive evangelicals involved with Evangelicals for Social Action, suggests the enduring possibility of a rearticulation of the claims of critical theory within the idiom of evangelicalism.

Regardless of the difficulty or ease with which more self-consciously negative-utopian narratives like Hilfiker's could emerge some day within evangelicalism, however, the dialectical criticism of *Focus on the Family* also intimates that Christian idioms, more broadly, could offer a venue for critical theory's revitalizing connection to a context of practical struggle. For the themes of salvation through compassion, humility, and forgiveness are certainly not the property of evangelical Christians alone. Leonard has pointed out the opportunities for critical theory's self-development and political involvement that Latin American liberation theology provides. Communities in the United States where liberation theology has been influential, particularly certain Catholic and African American churches, would likely offer similar prospects for critical theorists interested in cultivating solidarity with popular struggles. By suggesting that significant political value could be gained from the construction of new, more self-evidently negative-utopian narratives within the idioms of these communities, this book's venture in critical theory takes a first step toward building such solidarity—fully aware, however, that conclusively determining the desirability and practicality of this suggestion would require listening in a focused way to liberation theologians' concerns, and engaging in extended dialogue with these theorists and the activists and believers for whom they speak.

In addition, decoding the social physiognomy of *Focus on the Family* indicates that Christian-progressive efforts on behalf of social justice and democracy have much to gain by developing narratives specifically intended for dissemination through electronic and commercial media. This would mean, in other words, multiplying, diversifying, and heightening the tensions among the "stations of the cross" on the radio dial as well as within other media contexts. To be sure, as we have seen, learning the path of salvation through radio listening alters and in some ways constricts the possibilities for drawing critical, political lessons from religious-cultural practices, in comparison to some traditional liturgies. And it is clear that the standardization and stereotyping that would inevitably accompany any attempt to expand "Christian left" media would measurably detract from the radical potential of such cultural initiatives. In response to this concern, some consolation might be derived from the fact that no network of media-popularized counternarratives approaching the financial and organizational vastness of the Christian right media is even conceivable, let alone a practical possibility, in the foreseeable future. But, of course, insulation from the deradicalizing effects of cultural production for transmission to mass audiences comes at the price of the relatively limited, overall impact of these innovations. Nevertheless, the crucial point is that if narratives in the electronic spheres are indeed capable of manifesting the dialectical forces that have been discerned here in *Focus on the Family*, then the strategic possibilities of this realm for progressives ought not to be overlooked or dismissed.

The argument here, in sum, is that understanding the politics of Christian right popular culture invites a practical response that is centrally concerned with the production of new forms of religious-cultural expression and oriented by a radical critique of the post-Fordist state and economy. Taking this stand contrasts markedly with the currently predominant mode of political response to the Christian right by its critics. Liberal theoretical assumptions largely define the terrain on which the Christian right is presently challenged. The main organizations that do battle with the Christian right in Congress and in state houses across the country raise typically liberal complaints about the movement. Thus, for example, People for the American Way primarily opposes the movement's willingness to compromise the freedom of speech in the latter's campaigns to remove sexually explicit materials from school classrooms and public libraries. The American Civil Liberties Union, in turn, charges the movement with undermining church-state separation. And Planned Parenthood relies on the liberal discourse of rights when it denounces Christian right attempts to roll back women's "reproductive rights."

Major religious organizations antagonistic to the Christian right have likewise tended to criticize the movement on chiefly liberal grounds. The Unitarian Universalist Association (UUA), long an institutional bulwark of the secular-humanist spirituality that evangelical conservatives condemn, proposed in the mid-1990s that member churches study and respond to a resolution titled *Challenging the Radical Right.* This resolution describes the Christian right as "radical" in the threat that it poses to the continuing vitality of core liberal values: free "intellectual and artistic expression," tolerance among a "multicultural" citizenry that includes many persons living in "nontraditional families," and an accurately informed electorate.[8] The fastest growing organization of religious groups challenging the Christian right is The Interfaith Alliance (TIA), a group that first received national attention when it sparred with the Christian Coalition in thirty-six states during the 1996 elections (and imitated one of its tactics) by distributing alternative, moderate-progressive "voter guides" to religious communities.[9] Operating both as a national interest group and as a coalition of grassroots chapters, TIA exhorts its constituents to fight for the preservation of "mainstream" political values, especially "our civil and religious liberties," from the "radical right's" onslaught of "extremism," "hatred," and "intolerance."[10]

These political responses to the Christian right are not so much misguided as seriously incomplete. To be sure, censorship in the classroom and on the Internet perniciously restrains individual liberty and the development of a communicatively engaged and respectful public. These values, however, are being far more deeply undermined by the political and economic forces associated with post-Fordism, broadly speaking, than by the Christian right alone. Like liberal critiques of the Christian right, this analysis of *Focus on the Family* embraces a concern for the cultivation of ethically autonomous individuality. Indeed, the discouragement of such individuality is one of the most disturbing elements in Focus's narratives of the compassionate professional, the humble leader, and the forgiving victim. But individual, ethical autonomy depends on historically specific, social-structural conditions for its realization, as the interpretation of Dobson's program demonstrates. Today, the attainment of at least a marginally more robust, autonomous individuality—by health care and human service providers and their clients, elected officials and their constituents, and women, minorities, and children—demands radical challenges to post-Fordist tendencies in the health industry, the electoral system, and the welfare state.

There are signs that liberal religious organizations opposed to the Christian right understand to some degree this theoretical deficit in the liberal perspective. In Washington state in 1998 TIA strongly supported a ballot initiative to raise the minimum wage and opposed Initiative 200. The study materials accompanying the UUA's earlier resolution speculate that "the shattered American dream" and "job insecurity" are "primary contributors to the rise of the Radical Religious Right."[11] These attempts to draw links between critical analysis of the Christian right and critique of the political economy could be greatly strengthened in the future, furnishing the starting points for a radical deepening of the liberal response to the movement.

At the same time, religious communities critical of the Christian right are uniquely positioned to develop a progressive response to the movement beyond the boundaries carefully observed by liberals: they can elaborate and enrich the cultural component of political opposition to the movement, and to the broader historical conditions of its emergence. Liberalism, as a rhetorical and institutional mode of contesting the Christian right's power, stakes too much on legal principles and not enough on generating competing narratives. Whether liberal critics invoke the freedom of speech, religious disestablishment, or reproductive rights, arguments grounded on technical rules are unlikely to win enough support to challenge the Christian right effectively on a popular, grassroots level. For even if the well-established idiom of liberal individualism provides these critics with a mode of address that resonates widely throughout the contemporary political culture, this idiom is by its nature resistant to being used in the composition of narratives that define moral purposes and commitments. An effective political response to the Christian right and its constitutive, post-Fordist context needs to include rather than bracket out moral narrative, especially narratives composed in the manner exemplified by Hilfiker's testimony. Religious idioms can supply prodigious resources for such ventures in cultural politics, experiments for which liberalism is simply incapable of providing a conceptual, historical, and practical-communal foundation. Critical theory, in turn, can provide this process of experimental narrative composition with both social-theoretical guideposts and a critical awareness of culture's dialectical potencies.

Adorno reminds us, however, that engagement in political practice as such can no more guarantee critical theory's self-reflectivity than can the aesthetic search for negative-utopian moments of transcendence. If critical theory is to declare its solidarity with any particular, historically situated struggle, it must at the same time resolutely refuse to instrumentalize itself in the service of that struggle entirely. Adornian critical theory contributes something additional and distinctive to these endeavors by continuing to insist that thought's self-reflectivity depends also on moments in which it "grants precedence" to a cultural object and then allows the criticism of cultural experience to reflect back on social theory. This is the meaning of negative dialectics, and it is what we have done in this study by devoting concentrated attention to our cultural object, *Focus on the Family*, and then letting its social physiognomy provoke new considerations about how political forces to transform post-Fordist conditions might be mobilized, and how critical theory itself might be communicated, constructed, and verified in the process of doing this by entering practical contexts of American Christianity. But commitment to political struggles must never mean wholesale identification with them. In a more positive sense: Adornian thinking suggests the particular need for continuing intellectual work to develop cultural traditions on their own terms and within their own idioms, rather than simply accommodating their traditions to radical political objectives. Thus, for instance, alternative stagings (by church communities) and soundings (on the radio) of the "stations of the cross" that lead pilgrims into the abodes of hunger and poverty must never abandon their distinctly liturgical and theological form and aims—they must always strive to be more than efforts to recruit volunteers. For it is precisely by manifesting the failure of a passionately desired coherence—between church and world, between individual redemption and social reality—that religious culture opens itself to world-transforming engagement with critical theory and radical practices.

Appendix A

Complete Listing of *Focus on the Family*

Broadcasts Selected for Research

Method and Criteria for Selecting Broadcasts

A total of seventy-eight broadcasts of *Focus on the Family* were selected for this project. From April 1994 through April 1995, I listened regularly to evangelical conservative radio and consulted the listings available in the monthly magazine, *Focus on the Family*. I later ordered several additional tapes of broadcasts aired prior to April 1994 from Focus on the Family. The broadcasts I selected for special consideration were chosen to reflect the diversity of the program's material in these terms:

the wide range of public policy issues important to Focus;
the variety of family problems and individual psychological maladies addressed by Dobson and his guests;
the varying degrees to which different broadcasts make Focus's evangelistic religious commitment explicit;
the diverse range of formats employed on the program (for example, professional panels, personal testimonies, prerecorded speeches before live audiences, and dramas); and
the different types of guests featured on the program (for example, ordinary believers, national politicians, and popular evangelical speakers).

As explained in the introduction, most of the seventy-eight broadcasts selected exhibited one of the three major narrative structures analyzed in detail in chapters 3–5, although not every show did so. Carrying out an "immanent critique" of *Focus on the Family* necessitated the detailed, microscopic consideration of a more limited number (twenty-one) of shows. The table below includes information concerning the narrative forms displayed in not only these shows but also those broadcasts not closely examined. A review of this information indicates that the narrative of the "compassionate professional" is manifested on *Focus on the Family* more frequently than those of the "humble leader" and the "forgiving victim." This suggests that those contradictions of post-Fordism expressed in the contradictions of Focus's narrative of the "compassionate professional" (specifically, as chapter 3 argues, the growing exclusivity of health care and social services, the diminishing ethical autonomy of professionals in these fields, and the declining quality of health and social services even for those who can access them) furnish especially effective points of departure for the construction of alternative narratives and political alliances aimed at radicalizing evangelicalism and enriching activism on the left with the popular idioms of Christianity.

A word must be said about those shows that bore negligible traces, or none at all, of the three major narratives. The featured guests on these shows displayed certain regularities in their occupations and styles of communication: they were most commonly preachers (18–19 July 1994; 30–31 January 1995), popular evangelical speakers (16 November 1994; 7–8, 14–15 December 1994; 6 February 1995), or public affairs experts (11–12, 13 July 1994; 2–3 August 1994; 20 February 1995; 11–12 April 1995). Sustained examination of these broadcasts might well have uncovered the existence of additional narrative structures and thus enhanced this interpretation of *Focus on the Family*. However, this study does not claim to provide an exhaustive account of the politics of *Focus on the Family*. As my introductory comments on postmodernist, Foucauldian, Gramscian, and social-movement approaches to the Christian right indicate, different theoretical frameworks can shed light in various ways on the Christian right's cultural politics. For present purposes, it is particularly important to emphasize that there are almost certainly narrative dynamics unexplored in this book that help to constitute the politics of *Focus on the Family*. These modes of narrativity, and the broadcasts making use of them, would likely offer fruitful material for future research.

Inventory of Broadcasts Selected

Editions of *Focus on the Family* analyzed in detail in chapters 3–5 are printed in boldface type. Narrative structures are coded as follows: CP = compassionate professional; HL = humble leader; FV = forgiving victim. Titles/roles of guests and speakers are those that were most current at the time of the broadcasts.

Date	Title	Guest(s)	Topic(s)	Narrative
2–3 February 1989	Pornography Kills	Ted Bundy	pornography	CP, FV
23–25 October 1991	**A Visit with Lt. Col. and Mrs. Ollie North**	**Oliver North, Betsy North**	**faith, family, national security**	HL
14–15 January 1993	**Being Light in the Darkness**	**Charles Colson**	**spiritual rebirth, cultural change, national security**	HL
26 February 1993	Physician-Assisted Suicide	Rita Marker, David Llewellyn, Joni Tada Erickson (physicians)	euthanasia	CP
21 June 1993	Medical Ethics in the '90s	Kerby Anderson (physician)	euthanasia, abortion, genetics	CP
19–20 July 1993	Reclaiming Our Culture	Charles Colson	cultural change	HL
19–21 April 1994	**Hope for the Homosexual**	**Joseph Nicolosi, "Allen Smith"**	**homosexuality**	CP
5 July 1994	It Is Well	Drama	faith, poverty	—
6 July 1994	The Family around the World: Japan	Cornelius Iida (Japanese interpreter for presidents Carter and Reagan)	Japanese families	—
7 July 1994	How to Beat Burnout	Paul Meier (psychologist), Frank Minirth (psychologist), Don Hawkins (pastor)	overwork, masculinity	CP
11–12 July 1994	Men and Marriage	George Gilder (economist)	sexuality, welfare, masculinity, crime	—
13 July 1994	(title not available)*	Richard Glasow (dir., Natl. Right to Life Educational Trust Fund), Rob Gregory (*Family News in Focus*, FOTF), Tom Minnery (v.p. of Public Policy, FOTF)	RU-486 (abortion pill)	—
14–15 July 1994	**Spiritual Warfare: The Story of Stephan Morin**	**Margy Mayfield**	**faith, violence against women**	FV
18–19 July 1994	I, Isaac, Take You, Rebekah	Ravi Zacharias (pastor)	sexuality, marriage	—
20–21 July 1994	How to Fall in Love with Your Kids	Joe White (dir., Kanikuk and Kanikomo summer camps)	parenting adolescents	CP

Date	Title	Guest(s)	Topic(s)	Narrative
22 July 1994	(title not available)*	Phyllis Schlafly (pres., Eagle Forum)	health care reform	—
25 July 1994	Educating Our Children	James Dobson (no guest)	federal education policy	CP
26 July 1994	Resisting Temptation	Ted Engstrom (pres. emeritus, World Vision)	male sexuality	CP
27 July 1994	**What Is Intelligence?**	**James Dobson (no guest)**	**intellectual development**	**CP**
28–29 July 1994	**Can You Raise Your Child's I.Q.?**	**James Dobson (no guest)**	**intellectual development**	**CP**
1 August 1994	Preparing for Adolescence, pt. 3	James Dobson (no guest)	adolescent sexual development	CP
2–3 August 1994	A Jewish Perspective on the Cultural War	Don Feder (columnist, *Boston Herald*), Michael Medved (cohost, *Sneak Previews*)	entertainment, the media, the Holocaust	—
4 August 1994	Five Things I Know about People	John Maxwell (pastor)	communication, faith	—
31 August 1994	Straight Talk to Men and Their Wives	James Dobson (no guest)	fatherhood, masculinity	CP
1 September 1994	Back to School	anonymous parents and children	the first day of school	—
16 November 1994	Learning to Communicate	Gary Smalley, John Trent (popular evangelical speakers)	gender differences	—
30 November 1994	(title not available)*	James Dobson (no guest)	faith, salvation	—
1 December 1994	Welcome to Focus	Don Hodel (fmr. U.S. Sec. of Interior), Barbara Hodel (wife of D. Hodel)	spiritual rebirth, family trauma, government service	HL
6 December 1994	The Pain of Illiteracy	John Corcoran (literacy activist), Kathy Corcoran (wife of J. Corcoran)	illiteracy, education	FV
7–8 December 1994	Hiding Places	Patsy Clairmont (popular evangelical speaker)	women's emotional health	—
13 December 1994	Christian Child Rearing	Paul Meier (psychologist)	child discipline	CP
14–15 December 1994	God Isn't Dead	Gert Behanna (popular evangelical speaker)	marriage, spiritual rebirth	—
16–17 December 1994	**Harmony in the Inner City**	**Glen Kehrein, Raleigh Washington**	**racial reconciliation**	**FV**

Date	Title	Guest(s)	Topic(s)	Narrative
27 December 1994	Bill Bennett on America	William Bennett (fmr. U.S. "drug czar," fmr. U.S. Sec. of Educ.)	cultural and moral degeneration	—
10–11 January 1995	The Empty Nest	panel of mothers	children leaving home	—
12–13 January 1995	Christian Men and Sexuality	Archibald Hart (prof., Dean of Grad. School, Fuller Theol. Seminary)	male sexuality, masculinity	CP
16 January 1995	**A Call to Prayer**	**Bill Bright (pres., Campus Crusade for Christ), Dawnette Bright (fmr. chair, Natl. Day of Prayer), Shirley Dobson (chair, Natl. Day of Prayer)**	**prayer, national revival, repentance**	HL
17 January 1995	**(title not available)***	**Gary Bauer (pres., Family Res. Council), Helen Chenoweth (U.S. House of Reps., R-ID), Tom Coburn (USHR, R-OK), Steve Largent (USHR, R-OK), Ron Lewis (USHR, R-KY), Mark Souder (USHR, R-IN), Zach Wamp (USHR, R-TN), J. C. Watts (USHR, R-OK)**	**faith and government service**	HL
18–20 January 1995	**A Matter of Life**	**Gianna Jessen, Diana DePaul, Heidi Huffman, Tina Huffman**	**abortion**	FV
23 January 1995	Walk on the Moon	Charles Duke (U.S. astronaut)	marriage, spiritual rebirth	HL
30–31 January 1995	Becoming a Man of God	John Maxwell (pastor)	masculinity, sexuality, faith	—
6 February 1995	You Gotta Have a Sense of Humor	Dennis Swanberg (pastor, popular evangelical speaker)	parenting	—
9 February 1995	Parenting Isn't for Cowards, Pt. 6	James Dobson (no guest)	parenting adolescents	CP
16–17 February 1995	**Repressed Memories**	**Paul Meier (psychologist),**	**false memory syndrome**	CP

Date	Title	Guest(s)	Topic(s)	Narrative
		Paul Simpson (psychologist), David Gatewood (clin. supr. of counseling, FOTF)		
20 February 1995	(title not available)*	Gary Bauer (pres., Family Res. Council)	United Nations Convention on the Rights of the Child	—
22–23 February 1995	Rekindling the Torch of Liberty	Alan Keyes (fmr. U.S. Amb. to the U.N., 1996 Repub. pres. cand.)	abortion	—
24 February 1995	Parenting Isn't for Cowards, pt. 9	James Dobson (no guest)	spirituality and parenting	CP
2 March 1995	Managing Your Home and Time	Emilie Barnes (popular evangelical speaker)	home organization	—
6 March 1995	One Fearless Child, One Faithful Family	Bill Koch (father), Pam Koch, Victoria Koch (daughter)	coping with illness-related family trauma	CP
23 March 1995	Tilly	Drama	abortion	—
11–12 April 1995	Goals 2000: History Redefined	Michelle Easton (fmr. appointee, U.S. Depts. of Educ., Justice; Clair Luce Policy Institute), Linda Page (mgr. of educ. policy, FOTF)	federal education standards	—
25 April 1995	Life on the Edge: The Myth of Safe Sex	Joe McIlhaney (physician)	sexual abstinence, sexually transmitted disease	CP
18 May 1995	Life on the Edge: Pornography: Addictive, Progressive and Deadly	Ted Bundy	pornography	CP, FV
10–11 January 1996	Bill McCartney: A Man after God's Heart	Bill McCartney (pres., Promise Keepers)	masculinity, spirituality	HL

*In trying to ascertain the titles of five broadcasts several years after they were transmitted, I was informed by Focus that copies of these broadcasts had not been kept in Focus's archives and that these shows' titles were therefore unavailable. In four of the five cases, that is because these shows were not regularly scheduled but rather preempted scheduled broadcasts so that a political topic of special current interest could be addressed. In the fifth case, Dobson preempted a regularly scheduled broadcast to do a show on the meaning of faith and the nature of God. (This broadcast also included a rare, direct exhortation from Dobson to "unsaved" listeners in his audience that they become "born again" at that moment. Such calls to be redeemed are highly uncharacteristic of Dobson, who is not a preacher.)

Appendix B

Itinerary for Research Visit to

Colorado Springs, 21–25 February 1996

21 February 1996

Interviews at Focus on the Family
Alan Crippen, Senior Fellow, Institute for Family Studies
John Eldredge, Director, Public Policy Seminars and Research

Recording sessions of "Focus on the Family" observed
1. Guest: Larry Burkett, home financial adviser
    Topic: women leaving the workplace to reassume traditional family roles
2. Guests: Thomas Lacona, Professor, SUNY Cortland; Joseph McIl-
              haney, gynecologist; Amy Stevens, Manager of Youth Cul-
              ture, Focus on the Family
    Topic: combining character education with education about sexual abstinence

Organizing meeting for Food for Thought, held at
First United Methodist Church of Colorado Springs
(See discussion below.)

22 February 1996

Interviews at Focus on the Family
Jeannie Crooks, Research Coordinator, Correspondence Department
Clarence Shuler, Director, Black Family Ministries
Russell Freeman, International Media Coordinator
Mark Fugleberg, Producer, *Family News in Focus* radio program

Recording session of "Focus on the Family" *observed*
Guest: Rob Parsons, Director, Care for the Family (U.K. affiliate of Focus on the Family)
Topic: balancing fatherhood and work responsibilities

Class observed at Focus's Institute for Family Studies
Course: "Leadership and Family Studies"
Teacher: Michael Rosebush, Ph.D.
Topic: pornography, male sexuality, and marriage
Speaker: Gene McConnell, National Coalition for the Protection of Children and Families

(As of 1996, Focus's Institute for Family Studies (IFS) offered a semester-long internship and academic program for approximately thirty college students at a time. The students received full college credit for their work at Focus on the Family (sixteen credit hours for four courses). Many came from small evangelical Christian colleges, but some students were from larger universities, including Baylor University and Oklahoma State University. The IFS had a staff of four faculty, three of whom held or were completing Ph.D.'s.)

23 February 1996

Interviews at Focus on the Family
Paul Hetrick, Vice President for Public Relations
Tom Hess, Editor, *Citizen* magazine
Caia Mockaitis, Public Policy Information Manager
Jim Daly, Director, International Division
Larry Burtofft, Public Policy
John Fuller, Producer, *Focus on the Family* radio program
Mark Maddox, Senior Director of Public Policy
Christine Fallentine, Staff Development Coordinator

Interview at Citizens Project
Meagan Day, staff (See discussion below.)

Telephone Interview
Harvey Joyner, Minister, Unitarian Universalist Congregation of Colorado Springs, and local activist on issues of tolerance, free speech, and gay rights.

24 February 1996

Class observed at Focus's Institute for Family Studies
Course: "The Family and the Contemporary Philosophical Climate"
Teacher: Greg Jesson, M.A. (dissertation then in progress)
Topic: proving the existence of God

25 February 1996

Interview
Amy Divine, Board of Directors, Citizens Project; cofounder of Citizens Project and Food for Thought (See discussion below.)

A Further Note on Theory and Practice: Progressives and the Christian Right in Colorado Springs, February 1996

Readers of this book may find of interest a citizens' undertaking that emerged in response to the climate of intolerance that grew in Colorado Springs during the early 1990s. Tensions in Colorado Springs mounted following Focus on the Family's relocation to that area and the subsequent magnet effect that Focus's move exerted on many other evangelical conservative, parachurch organizations. These stresses were further exacerbated by controversy over the state anti–gay rights ballot initiative that won passage in 1992, Colorado's Amendment 2—an initiative publicly supported by Dobson, Focus on the Family, and many evangelical conservative leaders who were familiar faces in Focus's media projects, notably Promise Keepers founder Bill McCartney.

   In the midst of this turmoil, some citizens in Colorado Springs formed Citizens Project. Defining itself as "a grassroots organization in the Pikes Peak region dedicated to upholding the traditional American values of pluralism, freedom of religion and separation of church and state," Citizens Project began publicizing and contesting the agenda of the Christian right in its newsletter *Freedom Watch*. Some of the individuals involved in this venture of strategic opposition to the Christian right, however, also initiated a program called Food for Thought geared toward fostering communication and understanding between partisans and opponents of the Christian right, and between evangelicals and other religious persons. Members were sought from a wide range of religious, racial, and cultural backgrounds and with a diversity of theological, moral, political, and economic views. They agreed to participate in a series of "dialogue dinners" of eight to ten individuals with differing social and religious ideas. The explicit goal of these gatherings was to nurture understanding, respect, self-criticism, and common ground—to cultivate a genuine "dialogue of the extremes"—while sharing food.

Food for Thought attracted not only liberals and progressives but also a fair number of leaders and ordinary individuals from evangelical conservative communities—including a Focus on the Family vice president and a writer for Focus's *Citizen* magazine. According to organizers, the "face to face" contact and "challenging of stereotypes" that Food for Thought generated contributed to a peaceful and cooperative resolution in a highly publicized conflict over sex education in local schools. "The more we do things like Food for Thought, the more I realize how much evangelical support there is for our positions"—such was the experience of local progressive activist and Citizens Project and Food for Thought cofounder Amy Divine.[1]

The practical reflections in the conclusion of this book concentrate on the development of new types of media communications based on the critical reworking of Christian idioms to contest *Focus on the Family* on its own terrain, as it were. Nonetheless, organizations like Food for Thought provide a "face to face" context for the creation of alternative social/spiritual narratives offering additional and exciting possibilities for the construction of populist coalitions that defy commonly presupposed left/right binary oppositions. Such activities should be of great interest to critical theorists who are concerned not only with reinvesting critical theory in concrete political struggles but moreover with critically evaluating the legacies of Jürgen Habermas and other theorists of "communicative action" and "communicative ethics," for whom person-to-person, intersubjective communication is the primary ground of social emancipation. With regard to the foregoing analysis of *Focus on the Family*, I would simply point out that communicative efforts such as those undertaken by participants in Food for Thought probably stand to gain something valuable from incorporating an awareness of the negative-utopian moments that subsist in the narratives of Christian right radio. For by virtue of these moments, Christian right narratives already resonate with progressives' concerns for universal health care, adequate provision for social service needs, far-reaching campaign finance reform, and an authentic revitalization of movements to empower minorities, women, and children.

Notes

Introduction

1 *Day One*, ABC, 21 September 1995.

2 Gustav Niebuhr, "Advice for Parents and for Politicians: Religious Group Speaks to Family Issues and to the Right," *New York Times*, 30 May 1995, A12.

3 Michael J. Gerson, "A Righteous Indignation," *U.S. News and World Report*, 4 May 1998, 20. Also see the *New York Times's* coverage of Dobson's speech several months earlier before the conservative Council for National Policy, in which Dobson threatened to "abandon the Republican Party," taking "as many people with [him] as possible," if Republican leaders in Congress did not make more progress on issues of particular concern to the Christian right, especially homosexuality and sex education. See Laurie Goodstein, "Conservative Christian Leader Accuses Republicans of Betrayal," *New York Times*, 12 February 1998, A22.

4 "GOP Leaders, Religious Conservatives Agree on Goals," *Seattle Times*, 9 May 1998, A3.

5 See Mark J. Rozell and Clyde Wilcox, "Conclusion: The Christian Right in Campaign '96," in *God at the Grass Roots, 1996: The Christian Right in the American Elections*, ed. Mark J. Rozell and Clyde Wilcox (Lanham, Md.: Rowman and Littlefield, 1997), 255–69. The development of Christian right PAC activity was particularly prevalent in Texas during the 1996 campaign season. See John M. Bruce, "Texas: A Success Story, at Least for Now," in Rozell and Wilcox, *God at the Grass Roots, 1996*, 43.

6 Goodstein, "Conservative Christian Leader Accuses Republicans of Betrayal."

7 For a precise and critical elaboration of this model of power, see Steven Lukes, *Power: A Radical View* (London: Macmillan, 1974), esp. 11–15.

8 See Nancy Tatom Ammerman, *Bible Believers: Fundamentalists in the Modern World* (New Brunswick, N.J.: Rutgers University Press, 1987); Steve Bruce, *The Rise and Fall of the New Christian Right* (New York: Oxford University Press, 1988), 39–45; Sara Diamond, *Roads to Dominion: Right-Wing Movements and Political Power in the United States* (New York: Guilford, 1995); Jerome L. Himmelstein, "The New Right," in *The New Christian Right: Mobilization and Legitimation*, ed. Robert C. Liebman and Robert Wuthnow (Hawthorne, N.Y.: Aldine, 1983), 13–29; James Davison Hunter, *American Evan-*

gelicalism: Conservative Religion and the Quandary of Modernity (New Brunswick, N.J.: Rutgers University Press, 1983), 118–19; James Davison Hunter, *Evangelicalism: The Coming Generation* (Chicago: University of Chicago Press, 1987), 6–7; Robert C. Liebman, "The Making of the New Christian Right," in Liebman and Wuthnow, *New Christian Right*, 234–35; George M. Marsden, *Understanding Fundamentalism and Evangelicalism* (Grand Rapids, Mich.: William B. Eerdmans, 1991), 74–75, 95, 103.

9   See Diamond, *Roads to Dominion*, 3–4.

10 See especially Bruce, *Rise and Fall of the New Christian Right*. Matthew Moen generally concurs with the judgment that the Christian right did not enjoy any major policy successes during the Reagan administration, but he insightfully draws attention to the movement's substantial progress in gaining power on Capitol Hill. For Moen, this advancement can be discerned in the increasing number of movement-sponsored bills and amendments introduced, committee and subcommittee testimonies offered, and hearings scheduled, as well as the displacement of liberal concerns from the congressional agenda. By thus expanding the definition of "success," especially for organizations like the Moral Majority and Christian Voice, which were newcomers to national politics, Moen shows that the movement's achievements during the 1980s were in some important ways "impressive." See Matthew C. Moen, *The Christian Right and Congress* (Tuscaloosa: University of Alabama Press, 1989), esp. 141–47.

11 For admirably specific analyses of state-by-state trends in Christian right political activism during the 1990s, see Rozell and Wilcox, *God at the Grass Roots, 1996*, along with Mark J. Rozell and Clyde Wilcox, eds., *God at the Grass Roots, 1994: The Christian Right in the 1994 Elections* (Lanham, Md.: Rowman and Littlefield, 1995).

12 See Bruce, *Rise and Fall of the New Christian Right*; Steve Bruce, "The Inevitable Failure of the New Christian Right," in *The Rapture of Politics*, ed. Steve Bruce, Peter Kivisto, and William H. Swatos Jr. (New Brunswick, N.J.: Transaction, 1995); Steven Gardiner, "Through the Looking Glass and What the Christian Right Found There," in *Media, Culture, and the Religious Right*, ed. Linda Kintz and Julia Lesage (Minneapolis: University of Minnesota Press, 1998), 141–58; Theodore J. Lowi, *The End of the Republican Era* (Norman: University of Oklahoma Press, 1995); Matthew C. Moen, "From Revolution to Evolution: The Changing Nature of the Christian Right," in Bruce, Kivisto, and Swatos, *Rapture of Politics*, 123–35; Rozell and Wilcox, *God at the Grass Roots, 1996*; and Clyde Wilcox, "Premillennialists at the Millennium," in Bruce, Kivisto, and Swatos, *Rapture of Politics*, 21–39.

13 See Diamond, *Roads to Dominion*, 237–41.

14 Ibid., 4.

15 Ibid., 7.

16 Karl Marx, "Anti-Church Movement—Demonstration in Hyde Park," in *Karl Marx and Friedrich Engels on Religion* (New York: Schocken, 1964), 127–34.

17 Karl Marx, "A Contribution to the Critique of Hegel's Philosophy of Right: Introduction," in *Early Writings*, tran. Rodney Livingstone and Gregor Benton (New York: Vintage, 1975), 244.

18 See Julia Lesage, "Christian Media," in Kintz and Lesage, *Media, Culture, and the Religious Right*, 31.

19 Stuart Hall, *The Hard Road to Renewal: Thatcherism and the Crisis of the Left* (London: Verso, 1988), 47–48.

20 Ibid., 51, 55.

21 Lauren Berlant, *The Queen of America Goes to Washington City: Essays on Sex and Citizenship* (Durham, N.C.: Duke University Press, 1997), 97.

22 Ibid., 65–71.

23 Linda Kintz, *Between Jesus and the Market: The Emotions That Matter in Right-Wing America* (Durham, N.C.: Duke University Press, 1997). See esp. 4–5, 55–57.

24 See Kintz and Lesage, *Media, Culture, and the Religious Right*.

25 Kintz, *Between Jesus and the Market*, 48–49.

26 See Lawrence Grossberg, *We Gotta Get Out of This Place: Popular Conservatism and Postmodern Culture* (New York: Routledge, 1992); Hall, *Hard Road to Renewal*; Dick Hebdige, *Subculture: The Meaning of Style* (New York: Routledge, 1994).

27 See Antonio Gramsci, *Selections from the Prison Notebooks*, ed. and trans. Quintin Hoare and Geoffrey Nowell Smith (New York: International, 1971), 144–57, 180–82.

28 The broadcasts selected were chosen to reflect diversity in each of the following dimensions: the full range of public policy issues important to Focus; the variety of family problems and individual psychological difficulties addressed by Dobson and his guests; the varying degrees to which different shows made Focus's religious commitment explicit; the diverse range of formats and rhetorical styles made use of on *Focus on the Family* (e.g., professional panel discussions, personal testimonies, prerecorded speeches to live audiences, and dramas); the wide variety of guests featured on the program (including ordinary believers, public officials, professionals in various fields, and popular evangelical speakers).

29 Meryem Ersoz, "Gimme That Old-Time Religion," in Kintz and Lesage, *Media, Culture, and the Religious Right*, 216–17.

30 Among the guests featured on the broadcasts listed in appendix A, for example, there were professional experts who lacked the quality of Christlike, universal love that characterizes the figures of the "compassionate professional" analyzed in chapter 3 (*Focus on the Family*, "Physician-Assisted Suicide," 26 February 1993; *Focus on the Family*, "Medical Ethics in the '90s," 21 June 1993; *Focus on the Family*, "Men and Marriage," 11–12 July 1994). Conversely, in other shows Dobson spoke with guests who seemed to demonstrate great compassion but possessed only quasi-professional credentials or no aura of professionalism at all (*Focus on the Family*, "How to Fall in Love with Your Kids," 20–21 July 1994; *Focus on the Family*, "Managing Your Home and Time," 2 March 1995). Some political leaders heard on Dobson's program did not emphasize their lives as private individuals, as did the "humble leaders" discussed in chapter 4 (*Focus on the Family*, [title not available], 22 July 1994; *Focus on the Family*, "Bill Bennett on America," 27 December 1994; *Focus on the Family*, "Rekindling the Torch of Liberty," 22–23 February 1995). And some of those portrayed as victims on *Focus on the Family* responded to their mistreatment by victimizing others, rather than by manifesting the forgiveness characteristic of Focus's "forgiving victim" figures, analyzed in chapter 5 (*Focus on the Family*, "Pornography Kills," 2–3 February 1989; *Focus on the Family*, "Men and Marriage," 11–12 July 1994). Appendix A lists all the broadcasts selected and notes the narrative structure that is most evident in each one.

31 See Michel Foucault, "Nietzsche, Genealogy, History," in *The Foucault Reader*, ed. Paul Rabinow (New York: Pantheon, 1984), 76–97.

32 The American Civil Liberties Union and People for the American Way typify this predominantly liberal response of political activists. In the academic literature critical of the Christian right, see especially Isaac Kramnick and R. Laurence Moore, *The Godless Constitution: The Case against Religious Correctness* (New York: W. W. Norton, 1996); and Lowi, *End of the Republican Era*.

33 John W. Kennedy, "Mixing Politics and Piety," *Christianity Today*, 15 August 1994, 42. The 1994 *Broadcasting and Cable Yearbook*, an industry publication, ranked "Christian" stations seventh. More recently, the *Washington Post* placed stations with religious formats fourth "behind country music, news talk and adult contemporary music." See Ersoz,

"Gimme That Old-Time Religion," 212; and Caryle Murphy, "They're Finding God on the Radio," *Washington Post*, 27 May 1997, A1, A8.

34 Kennedy, "Mixing Politics and Piety," 42. *Broadcasting and Cable Yearbook* again supplies the more conservative estimate. However, the *Washington Post* joins *Christianity Today* in citing the figure of 1,600 stations, based on another (secular) broadcast industry publication. See Ersoz, "Gimme That Old-Time Religion," 212; Murphy, "They're Finding God on the Radio," A8.

35 Kennedy, "Mixing Politics and Piety," 42.

36 James L. Guth, John C. Green, Lyman A. Kellstedt, and Corwin E. Smidt, "Onward Christian Soldiers: Religious Activist Groups in American Politics," in *Interest Group Politics*, 4th ed., ed. Allan J. Cigler and Burdett A. Loomis (Washington, D.C.: Congressional Quarterly, 1995), 60.

37 Gerson, "Righteous Indignation," 22. Gerson further notes that every week twenty-eight million people hear Dobson's radio broadcasts or see Focus's television clips.

38 Focus on the Family, "Focus on the Family Tour Information" (brochure) (Colorado Springs: Focus on the Family, n.d.).

39 Mike Ward, "Focus on the Family Group Plans to Move," *Los Angeles Times*, 15 June 1990, B3.

40 *Focus on the Family*, "Parenting Isn't for Cowards, Pt. IX," 24 February 1995.

41 James Dobson, *Dare to Discipline* (Wheaton, Ill.: Tyndale House, 1970), 225–26.

42 Ibid., 98–99.

43 Ibid., 27.

44 Consider, for example, the following passages: "In my opinion, spankings should be reserved for the moment a child (age ten or less) expresses a defiant "I will not!" or "You shut up!" When a youngster tries this kind of stiff-necked rebellion, you had better take it out of him, and pain is a marvelous purifier. . . . You have drawn a line in the dirt, and the child has deliberately flopped his big hairy toe across it. Who is going to win? Who has the most courage? Who is in charge here?" (Dobson, *Dare to Discipline*, 27). "Nothing brings a parent and child closer together than for the mother and father to win decisively after being defiantly challenged. . . . It is not necessary to beat the child into submission; a little bit of pain goes a long way with a young child. However, the spanking should be of specific magnitude to cause the child to cry genuinely. After the emotional ventilation, the child will often want to crumple to the breast of his parent, and he should be welcomed with open, warm, loving arms. At that moment you can talk heart to heart" (ibid., 35).

45 Rolf Zettersten, *Dr. Dobson: Turning Hearts toward Home* (Dallas: Word, 1989), 90. Also see Gerson, "Righteous Indignation," 22.

46 Focus on the Family, "James C. Dobson, Ph.D.: Biographical Information" (Colorado Springs: Focus on the Family, January 1996); Zettersten, *Dr. Dobson*, 84–85, 96–98, 113–15.

47 For example, as Eithne Johnson astutely points out, the video series "extends the product over separate viewings" and is usually advertised in ways that "emphasize the importance of repeated viewings," thereby ironically heightening its attractiveness as a commodity through appeals to the evangelical inclination "to see religion as a personal process to be lived, instead of a product to be passively consumed." Video series also reconfigure the relationship between market exchange and enjoyment of the product, since they are purchased before they are viewed, and this eliminates the necessity of interrupting the narrative flow with appeals for donations. See Eithne Johnson, "The Emergence of Christian Video," in Kintz and Lesage, *Media, Culture, and the Religious Right*, 191–210.

48 Ward, "Focus on the Family Group Plans to Move"; Focus on the Family, "Focus on

the Family Tour Information." Also see Gerson, "Righteous Indignation," 22. On the role of Colorado Springs as a leading geographic nexus of Christian right activity, see Marc Cooper, "God and Man in Colorado Springs," *The Nation*, 2 January 1995, 9–12.

49　Focus on the Family, "The Ministries of Focus on the Family" (Colorado Springs, Focus on the Family, 8 November 1995).

50　Gerson, "Righteous Indignation," 23.

51　Focus on the Family, "Annual Report: 1994" (Colorado Springs: Focus on the Family); Laura Sessions Stepp, "The Empire Built on Family and Faith," *Washington Post*, 8 August 1990, C1. The figures for IFE represent the corporation's 1993 total operating revenues; see Razelle Frankl, "Transformation of Televangelism: Repackaging of Christian Family Values," in Kintz and Lesage, *Media, Culture, and the Religious Right*, 186. Also see Gerson, "Righteous Indignation," 23.

52　Niebuhr, "Advice for Parents and for Politicians."

53　For each program, approximately two hours of discussion are prerecorded and then edited down to thirty minutes. My comments in this section are based on my research visit to Focus on the Family's Colorado Springs headquarters, 21–24 February 1996, during which I interviewed senior staff members, visitors, and student interns, and observed the recording of three editions of *Focus on the Family*.

54　Niebuhr, "Advice for Parents and for Politicians."

55　These data stem from an internal study of individuals on Focus's mailing list, which was conducted in 1992 and provides the most recent publicly available information concerning the demographics of Focus's membership. The study also showed that the majority of Focus's constituents are women in their thirties and forties, and that 86 percent of the constituents are Protestants (Niebuhr, "Advice for Parents and for Politicians").

56　Dobson's use of television has been limited to his appearances on talk shows in the late 1960s and early 1970s, a brief experiment with television in the first years of Focus on the Family, and the recent production of several ninety-second spots designed for secular broadcasting contexts. In these spots, Dobson is seen alone in an office or hallway of a house and speaks directly to the camera about the importance of building family "traditions," establishing mutual "respect" and "accountability" within marriage, and helping children to "compensate for disadvantages." The spots involve no elaborate filming techniques, and Dobson refrains entirely from mentioning the evangelical Christian background of his advice. Focus representatives informed me that these spots have been successfully distributed to and broadcast on many stations around the country, but they did not provide specific figures detailing how widely they are being shown.

57　Mike Davis, *Prisoners of the American Dream: Politics and Economy in the History of the US Working Class* (New York: Verso, 1986), 219.

58　See Davis, *Prisoners of the American Dream*, 158–62, for historical background on the new right's innovations in political technologies and organizational forms, emphasizing the growth of direct mail, paid advertising, and ballot initiative campaigns.

59　Stepp, "Empire Built on Family and Faith." According to the biography of Dobson written by a former executive vice president of Focus, listeners bombarded the White House with some eighty thousand letters in several days asking for Dobson to be appointed to the committee (Zettersten, *Dr. Dobson*, 150).

60　Focus on the Family, "James C. Dobson, Ph.D."

61　Russell Chandler, "Evangelical Broadcaster Seeks 'Pro-Family' Lobby," *Los Angeles Times*, 4 March 1989, sec. 2, 6.

62　Caia Mockaitis, Public Policy Information Manager, Focus on the Family, interview by author, Colorado Springs, 23 February 1996.

63 These figures come from inventory sheets indexing Focus's issues packets, social research briefs, and youth culture reports, updated in January–February 1996.

64 Mark Fugleberg, Producer, *Family News in Focus*, Focus on the Family, interview by author, Colorado Springs, 22 February 1996.

65 Tom Hess, Editor, *Citizen* magazine, Focus on the Family, interview by author, Colorado Springs, 21 February 1996; Jeannie Crooks, Correspondence Research Coordinator, Focus on the Family, interview by author, Colorado Springs, 21 February 1996. Focus's web page can be accessed at www.family.org.

66 See Guth et al., "Onward Christian Soldiers"; James L. Guth and Oran P. Smith, "South Carolina Christian Right: Just Part of the Family Now?" in Rozell and Wilcox, *God at the Grass Roots, 1996*, 15–31; Focus on the Family, *Physician*, January–February 1996, 16; Mark J. Rozell and Clyde Wilcox, "Virginia: When the Music Stops, Choose Your Faction," in Rozell and Wilcox, *God at the Grass Roots, 1996*, 99–114; Corwin E. Smidt and James M. Penning, "Michigan: Veering to the Left?" in Rozell and Wilcox, *God at the Grass Roots, 1996*, 115–34.

67 Focus on the Family, "Family Policy Councils" (brochure) (Colorado Springs: Focus on the Family, n.d.).

68 In addition, the *Washington Post* has called the FPCs "Focus-organized coalitions," and the *Los Angeles Times* reported that the project of forming FPCs in all fifty states was "launched" by Focus in 1989. See Chandler, "Evangelical Broadcaster Seeks 'Pro-Family' Lobby"; Stepp, "Empire Built on Family and Faith."

69 John Eldredge and Greg Jesson, *Community Impact Curriculum* (Colorado Springs: Focus on the Family, May 1993).

70 See Julia Lesage, "Christian Media," in Kintz and Lesage, *Media, Culture, and the Religious Right*, 21–49.

71 See Julia Lesage, "Christian Coalition Leadership Training," in Kintz and Lesage, *Media, Culture, and the Religious Right*, 295–325.

72 According to Focus's policy administrators, whom I interviewed in my visit to Colorado Springs in February 1996, no thorough follow-up or monitoring of the committees had been carried out or was planned. These individuals explained that Focus terminated the CIS program in 1995 because they had communicated their message in all the locations where it made sense to do so, and there was no particular need to revisit the same places to repeat the same presentation (Alan Crippen, Senior Fellow, Institute for Family Studies, Focus on the Family, interview by author, Colorado Springs, 21 February 1996; John Eldredge, Director, Public Policy Seminars and Research, Focus on the Family, interview by author, Colorado Springs, 21 February 1996).

73 Sara Diamond, "Focus on Some Families," *Z Magazine*, July–August 1994, 29–33.

1 Adorno on Mass Culture and Cultural Criticism

1 Karl Marx, "Concerning Feuerbach," in *Early Writings*, trans. Rodney Livingstone and Gregor Benton (New York: Vintage, 1975), 423.

2 See Susan Buck-Morss [Benjamin Snow, pseud.], "Introduction to Adorno's 'The Actuality of Philosophy,' " *Telos* 10, no. 1 (spring 1977): 113–19.

3 Theodor W. Adorno, "Kulturkritik und Gesellschaft," in *Prismen: Kulturkritik und Gesellschaft* (Frankfurt am Main: Suhrkamp, 1955), 15–16; Adorno, "Cultural Criticism and Society," in *Prisms*, trans. Samuel Weber and Shierry Weber (Cambridge: MIT Press, 1983), 26. This book makes use of the standard, currently available translations of Adorno's writings. However, I have also consulted the original German texts and made numerous

alterations to the extant translations, to generate what I take to be clearer ways of expressing Adorno's meaning. My notes and bibliography thus provide references to both the original texts and the standard English translations, for those of Adorno's writings from which I have drawn direct quotations.

4 Adorno, "Kulturkritik und Gesellschaft," 16; "Cultural Criticism and Society," 26–27.

5 Ibid., 18–19; ibid., 28. Frankfurt School historian Martin Jay locates Adorno's cultural criticism within a "strain" of Marxism that "follows the lead of Engels" in assuming that the "objective social content of a work . . . might well be contrary to the avowed desires of the artist and might express more than his class origins." This approach to aesthetic criticism is contrasted to that which was "derived primarily from the writings of Lenin and codified by Zhdanov at the first Soviet Writers' Congress in 1934." The Leninist approach, according to Jay, "finds merit only in those works displaying unabashed political partisanship" and "ultimately culminated in the sterile orthodoxy of Stalinist socialist realism." The most important influence on "Adorno's reception of Marx," however, was Georg Lukács's book *History and Class Consciousness.* As Susan Buck-Morss puts it, Lukács "maintained that the commodity structure, whose mysteries Marx had dispelled in the first chapter of *Kapital,* permeated every aspect of bourgeois society, including the very patterns of bourgeois thought." Adorno relied extensively on Lukács's notion that reification and exchange value were integral to the formation of all cultural objects under the conditions of late capitalism. He rejected, however, "Lukács' equation of truth with proletariat class consciousness" because to do so, in Adorno's view, entailed sacrificing the "intellectual independence" necessary to genuine social transformation. See Susan Buck-Morss, *The Origin of Negative Dialectics: Theodor W. Adorno, Walter Benjamin, and the Frankfurt Institute* (New York: Free Press, 1977), 25–32; Martin Jay, *The Dialectical Imagination: A History of the Frankfurt School and the Institute of Social Research, 1923–1950* (Boston: Little, Brown, 1973), 173; Georg Lukács, *History and Class Consciousness: Studies in Marxist Dialectics,* trans. Rodney Livingstone (Cambridge: MIT Press, 1971).

6 Adorno, "Kulturkritik und Gesellschaft," 25; "Cultural Criticism and Society," 33.

7 See Theodor W. Adorno, *The Jargon of Authenticity,* trans. Knut Tarnowski and Frederic Will (Evanston, Ill.: Northwestern University Press, 1973).

8 See Theodor W. Adorno, *Negative Dialektik,* in *Gesammelte Schriften 6,* ed. Rolf Tiedemann (Frankfurt am Main: Suhrkamp, 1973), 184–87; Adorno, *Negative Dialectics,* trans. E. B. Ashton (New York: Continuum, 1973), 180–86.

9 Adorno, *Negative Dialektik,* 191; *Negative Dialectics,* 191. Adorno elaborates: "The reconciled condition would not annex the alien, with philosophical imperialism. Instead, its happiness would lie in the fact that the alien, in the nearness it is granted, remains what is distant and different, beyond the heterogeneous and beyond that which is one's own" (ibid., 192; ibid., 191).

10 Adorno, "Kulturkritik und Gesellschaft," 23; "Cultural Criticism and Society," 32.

11 Adorno, "Kulturkritik und Gesellschaft," 18–19; "Cultural Criticism and Society," 28–29. The word *ambivalent,* which I employ here, following the translators of the English version of *Prismen,* is a poor substitute for the idea Adorno is attempting to convey. Adorno uses the adjective *doppelschlägtige,* which is derived from the musical term *Doppelschlag,* meaning an ornament such as a trill or grace note. Beyond simply expressing the notion of wavering commitment, Adorno may also be attempting to accentuate social theory's predisposition to contextualize cultural criticism and cultural phenomena historically, just as the musical ornament aurally contextualizes the main note by briefly sounding the notes just above or below it.

12 Adorno, "Kulturkritik und Gesellschaft," 24–25; "Cultural Criticism and Society," 32–33.

13   Ibid., 19; ibid., 29.

14   Ibid., 25; ibid., 33.

15   Ibid., 19; ibid., 28–29.

16   Max Horkheimer and Theodor W. Adorno, *Dialektik der Aufklärung: Philosophische Frag-
     mente* (Frankfurt am Main: Fischer, 1969), 139; Horkheimer and Adorno, *Dialectic of
     Enlightenment*, trans. John Cumming (New York: Continuum, 1972), 131.

17   Adorno, "Kulturkritik und Gesellschaft," 23; "Cultural Criticism and Society," 32.

18   Theodor W. Adorno, "Veblens Angriff auf die Kultur," in *Prismen*, 81; Adorno, "Veblen's
     Attack on Culture," in *Prisms*, 85.

19   Adorno, "Kulturkritik und Gesellschaft," 23–24; "Cultural Criticism and Society," 32.

20   See Jay, *Dialectical Imagination*, 222–23; Theodor Adorno, "Scientific Experiences of a
     European Intellectual in Migration," trans. Donald Fleming, in *The Intellectual Migra-
     tion: Europe and America, 1930–1960*, ed. Donald Fleming and Bernard Bailyn (Cam-
     bridge, Mass.: Harvard University Press, Belknap Press, 1969), 338–70.

21   See Rolf Wiggershaus, *The Frankfurt School: Its History, Theories, and Political Signifi-
     cance*, trans. Michael Robertson (Cambridge: MIT Press, 1994), 302–26.

22   Axel Honneth, *The Critique of Power: Reflective Stages in a Critical Social Theory*, trans.
     Kenneth Baynes (Cambridge: MIT Press, 1991), 72.

23   Friedrich Pollock, "State Capitalism: Its Possibilities and Limitations," in *The Essential
     Frankfurt School Reader*, ed. Andrew Arato and Eike Gebhardt (New York: Continuum,
     1982), 72–78. This essay was originally published in English in *Studies in Philosophy and
     Social Sciences*, the journal of Adorno and his colleagues at the Institute for Social Re-
     search during the early phase of their residence in the United States.

24   Ibid., 92.

25   Horkheimer and Adorno, *Dialektik der Aufklärung*, 128; *Dialectic of Enlightenment*, 120.

26   Ibid., 168; ibid., 159.

27   Ibid., 171; ibid., 162.

28   Ibid., 130, 141–42; ibid., 122, 133–34.

29   Ibid., 131; ibid., 123.

30   Ibid., 145; ibid., 137.

31   Ibid., 131; ibid., 123.

32   Ibid., 170–71; ibid., 161–62.

33   Ibid., 148, 171; ibid., 139, 161–62.

34   Ibid., 128–29; ibid., 121.

35   Adorno, "Kulturkritik und Gesellschaft," 21–22; "Cultural Criticism and Society," 31.

36   Horkheimer and Adorno, *Dialektik der Aufklärung*, 133–34; *Dialectic of Enlightenment*,
     125–26.

37   Theodor W. Adorno, *Philosophie der Neuen Musik*, in *Gesammelte Schriften 12*, ed. Rolf
     Tiedemann (Frankfurt am Main: Suhrkamp, 1975), 18, 65; Adorno, *Philosophy of Modern
     Music*, trans. Anne G. Mitchell and Wesley V. Blomster (New York: Continuum, 1973), 9,
     64.

38   Ibid., 57; ibid., 55.

39   Ibid., 59; ibid., 57.

40   Ibid., 52–55; ibid., 48–51.

41   Ibid., 59–60; ibid., 57–58.

42   See Theodor Adorno, *In Search of Wagner*, trans. Rodney Livingstone (New York: Verso,
     1991).

43   Adorno, *Philosophie der Neuen Musik*, 68; *Philosophy of Modern Music*, 68.

44   Ibid., 61; ibid., 59.

45   Ibid., 127–74; ibid., 135–217.

46   See Mike Davis, *City of Quartz: Excavating the Future in Los Angeles* (New York: Vintage, 1992), 46–54; John Docker, *Postmodernism and Popular Culture: A Cultural History* (Cambridge: Cambridge University Press, 1994); Andrew Ross, *No Respect: Intellectuals and Popular Culture* (New York: Routledge, 1989).

47   Neither Jürgen Habermas nor Axel Honneth questions Adorno's ultimate adherence to the most pessimistic articulation of his theory of the culture industry. See Jürgen Habermas, *The Theory of Communicative Action*, vol. 1, trans. Thomas McCarthy (Boston: Beacon, 1984), 370–72; and Honneth, *Critique of Power*, 33–34, 36, 77–81.

48   For critical analyses arguing that in some of these writings Adorno modifies the relentlessly denunciatory stance toward mass culture that characterizes *Dialectic of Enlightenment*, see Miriam Hansen, "Mass Culture as Hieroglyphic Writing: Adorno, Derrida, Kracauer," *New German Critique* 56 (spring–summer 1992): 43–73; Gertrud Koch, "Mimesis und Bilderverbot in Adornos Ästhetik: Ästhetische Dauer als Revolte gegen den Tod," *Babylon* 6 (1989): 36–45; Thomas Y. Levin, "For the Record: Adorno on Music in the Age of Technological Reproducibility," *October* 55 (1990): 23–47.

49   Buck-Morss, *Origin of Negative Dialectics*, 265n.

50   Ibid., 108.

51   Ibid.

52   Ibid., 109.

53   Jay, *Dialectical Imagination*, 186.

54   The most pointed criticisms of this nature came from the American critic Edward Shils, who in 1957 accused Adorno of failing to grasp the "democratic essence of American mass culture" (Buck-Morss, *Origin of Negative Dialectics*, 108–9; see also Edward Shils, "Daydreams and Nightmares: Reflections on the Criticisms of Mass Culture," *Sewanee Review* 65 [autumn 1957]: 587–608).

55   Theodor W. Adorno [Hektor Rottweiler, pseud.], "Über Jazz," *Zeitschrift für Sozialforschung* 5, no. 2 (1936): 237.

56   See, for example, the essays "How to Look at Television," *Quarterly of Film, Radio, and Television* 8, no. 3 (spring 1954): 213–35; and "Transparencies on Film," trans. Thomas Levin, *New German Critique* 24–25 (1981–82): 199–205. The only two exceptions to this pattern were Adorno's studies of the radio addresses of the American fundamentalist and anti-Semite Martin Luther Thomas, which I will examine in the next chapter, and his analysis of the *Los Angeles Times* astrology column. Adorno never readied either of these studies for publication, though both have been published in the *Gesammelte Schriften*. See "The Psychological Technique of Martin Luther Thomas' Radio Addresses," in *Gesammelte Schriften 9.1: Soziologische Schriften II*, ed. Susan Buck-Morss and Rolf Tiedemann (Frankfurt am Main: Suhrkamp, 1975), 7–141; and "The Stars Down to Earth," *Gesammelte Schriften 9.2: Soziologische Schriften II*, ed. Susan Buck-Morss and Rolf Tiedemann (Frankfurt am Main: Suhrkamp, 1975), 7–120.

57   Adorno, "Über Jazz," 237–38.

58   Honneth, *Critique of Power*, 72.

59   See James O'Connor, *The Fiscal Crisis of the State* (New York: St. Martin's, 1973); Claus Offe, *Contradictions of the Welfare State*, ed. John Keane (Cambridge: MIT Press, 1984).

60   Honneth, *Critique of Power*, 73, 315.

61   Ibid., 75–76.

62   See Adorno, *Negative Dialektik*, 41–42, 149–51; *Negative Dialectics*, 30–31, 146–48.

63   Adorno, "Kulturkritik und Gesellschaft," 25; "Cultural Criticism and Society," 34.

64   Ibid., 25; ibid., 34.

65 Ibid., 24; ibid., 32–33.

66 Ibid., 26; ibid., 34.

67 Ibid., 26; ibid., 34.

68 Adorno, *Negative Dialektik*, 354–56; *Negative Dialectics*, 361–63.

69 Adorno, "Kulturkritik und Gesellschaft," 20; "Cultural Criticism and Society," 29.

70 For especially trenchant and influential critiques of Adorno's neglect of practical ques-
    tions (one by a former student of Adorno's), see Hans-Jürgen Krahl, "The Political Contra-
    dictions in Adorno's Theory," *Telos* 21 (fall 1974): 164–67; Stephen T. Leonard, *Critical
    Theory in Political Practice* (Princeton, N.J.: Princeton University Press, 1990).

71 Theodor W. Adorno, *Minima Moralia: Reflexionen aus dem beschädigten Leben*, in *Ge-
    sammelte Schriften 4*, ed. Rolf Tiedemann (Frankfurt am Main: Suhrkamp, 1980), 16, 27;
    Adorno, *Minima Moralia: Reflections from Damaged Life*, trans. E. F. N. Jephcott (New
    York: Verso, 1978), 18, 26.

72 Regarding these contradictions, such as the declining profitability of capital and the grow-
    ing unacceptability of the barriers to accumulation posed by rigid structures of "mass
    production" and "mass consumption," see Michel Aglietta, *A Theory of Capitalist Regula-
    tion: The US Experience*, trans. David Fernbach (London: New Left, 1979); O'Connor,
    Fiscal Crisis of the State; Offe, *Contradictions of the Welfare State*; Michael J. Piore and
    Charles F. Sabel, *The Second Industrial Divide: Possibilities for Prosperity* (New York:
    Basic, 1984).

73 See Theodor W. Adorno, "Studies in the Authoritarian Personality," in Buck-Morss and
    Tiedemann, *Gesammelte Schriften 9.1*, 143–509; "Psychological Technique of Martin
    Luther Thomas' Radio Addresses," in Buck-Morss and Tiedemann, *Gesammelte Schriften
    9.1*, 7–141. Both of these texts are discussed in detail in chapter 2. See also Theodor
    W. Adorno, "Anti-Semitism and Fascist Propaganda," in *Gesammelte Schriften 8: Soziolo-
    gische Schriften I*, ed. Rolf Tiedemann with Gretel Adorno, Susan Buck-Morss, and Klaus
    Schultz (Frankfurt am Main: Suhrkamp, 1972), 397–407; Theodor W. Adorno, "Freudian
    Theory and the Pattern of Fascist Propaganda," in Tiedemann with Adorno, Buck-Morss,
    and Schultz, *Gesammelte Schriften 8*, 408–33.

2 Adorno's Critique of Christian Right Radio in the New Deal Era

 1 Max Horkheimer and Theodor W. Adorno, *Dialektik der Aufklärung: Philosophische Frag-
    mente* (Frankfurt am Main: Fischer, 1969), 168–69; Horkheimer and Adorno, *Dialectic of
    Enlightenment*, trans. John Cumming (New York: Continuum, 1972), 159–60.

 2 Ibid., 130; ibid., 122.

 3 Theodor W. Adorno, "The Radio Symphony: An Experiment in Theory," in *Radio Re-
    search 1941*, ed. Paul F. Lazarsfeld and Frank N. Stanton (New York: Duell, Sloan and
    Pearce, 1941), 110–39.

 4 T. W. Adorno, "A Social Critique of Radio Music," *Kenyon Review* 7, no. 2 (spring 1945):
    208–17.

 5 Horkheimer and Adorno, *Dialektik der Aufklärung*, 168; *Dialectic of Enlightenment*, 159.

 6 See Theodor W. Adorno, "Anti-Semitism and Fascist Propaganda," in *Gesammelte
    Schriften 8: Soziologische Schriften I*, ed. Rolf Tiedemann with Gretel Adorno, Susan
    Buck-Morss, and Klaus Schultz (Frankfurt am Main: Suhrkamp, 1972), 397–407; Adorno,
    "Freudian Theory and the Pattern of Fascist Propaganda," in Tiedemann et al., *Gesam-
    melte Schriften 8*, 408–33.

 7 Theodor W. Adorno, *Negative Dialektik*, in *Gesammelte Schriften 6*, ed. Rolf Tiedemann

(Frankfurt am Main: Suhrkamp, 1973), 184–87; Adorno, *Negative Dialectics*, trans. E. B. Ashton (New York: Continuum, 1973), 180–86.

8 See the discussion of previous scholarship on this issue in chapter 1.

9 "Reading Adorno in reverse, from *Dialectic of Enlightenment* backwards to the Wagner essay of 1937/38," Andreas Huyssen argues convincingly that "the framework for [Adorno's] theory of the culture industry was already in place *before* his encounter with American mass culture in the United States." Nevertheless, while in this analysis of Wagner Adorno indeed developed "the pivotal categories of fetishism and reification, ego-weakness, regression and myth" that would later comprise the theoretical matrix for the critique of the culture industry, a number of reflections on the specific and concrete techniques employed by the culture industry appear to have been worked out at least partially in the Thomas study, as I demonstrate below. See Andreas Huyssen, "Adorno in Reverse: From Hollywood to Richard Wagner," *New German Critique* 29 (spring–summer 1983): 37.

10 For a precise clarification of the different functions of these metaphors within Adorno's cultural theory, and a reflection on their relationships to the "perverted" and "utopian" forms of mimetic behavior, see Miriam Hansen, "Mass Culture as Hieroglyphic Writing: Adorno, Derrida, Kracauer," *New German Critique* 56 (spring–summer 1992): 43–73.

11 Rolf Wiggershaus, *The Frankfurt School: Its History, Theories, and Political Significance*, trans. Michael Robertson (Cambridge: MIT Press, 1994), 351–80.

12 Ibid., 358.

13 Ibid.

14 Martin Jay, *The Dialectical Imagination: A History of the Frankfurt School and the Institute of Social Research, 1923–1950* (Boston: Little, Brown, 1973), 139.

15 Leo Lowenthal and Norbert Guterman, *Prophets of Deceit: A Study of the Techniques of the American Agitator*, 2d ed. (Palo Alto, Calif.: Pacific, 1970), 7.

16 Ibid., 13–14.

17 Ibid., 15.

18 Ibid., 15–16.

19 Ibid., 29–30.

20 Ibid., 35–37.

21 Ibid., 47–48.

22 Ibid., 64.

23 Ibid., 100, 115–17.

24 Ibid., 117.

25 Ibid., xiii.

26 Ibid., 140.

27 ibid., 45.

28 In his introduction to the book, Horkheimer notes that *Prophets of Deceit* "places under the microscope certain phenomena that may seem negligible at first sight" and thereby "gains diagnostic insight into the latent threat against democracy" (Lowenthal and Guterman, *Prophets of Deceit*, xii–xiii).

29 Theodor W. Adorno, "Studies in the Authoritarian Personality," in *Gesammelte Schriften 9.1: Soziologische Schriften II*, ed. Susan Buck-Morss and Rolf Tiedemann (Frankfurt am Main: Suhrkamp, 1975), 158.

30 Ibid., 151.

31 Ibid., 156.

32 Ibid., 151.

33 Ibid., 160–61.

34 Ibid., 333.

35 Ibid., 158.

36 Ibid., 310–16.

37 Ibid., 362.

38 Ibid., 434–39.

39 Ibid., 346.

40 In addition, Adorno never makes good on the suggestion noted above that the study uncovers common features among the respondents that break down the high-scorer/low-scorer typology. Although Adorno indicates that high and low scorers alike exhibit a predisposition against "utopianism" and an instrumentalist attitude toward religion, for example, in both of these cases Adorno argues that low scorers hold these views for more critical and rational reasons than do high scorers (Adorno, "Studies in the Authoritarian Personality," 388–90, 442–43).

41 Jay writes that the essay "Elements of Anti-Semitism" in *Dialectic of Enlightenment* furnished "the general analysis of the objective dimension of anti-Semitism that informed the Institut's thinking while it conducted its empirical probes of the subjective side of the problem. It was expressed, however, only in German or in private correspondence. As a result, one side of Adorno's methodological division was lost to public view, leaving in its place what seemed to some like psychological reductionism and the abandonment of Critical Theory's stress on the totality." Notwithstanding *The Authoritarian Personality*'s apparent compromise of critical theory's foundational principles, one of the most influential criticisms of the study was Edward Shils's argument that the book failed to examine authoritarian attitudes among ideologically leftist subjects, and thus (ironically) that it was too dogmatically left wing. Shils picked up on something important, for as we have seen, Adorno's endorsement here of a rationalism/irrationalism binary when contrasting political radicalism and fascism did indeed undercut his more characteristic disposition to expose failures of critical reasoning—as we have seen, specifically *dialectical* reasoning—on the left (Jay, *Dialectical Imagination*, 234, 247–50).

42 Lowenthal and Guterman, *Prophets of Deceit*, 1–4.

43 Theodor W. Adorno, "The Psychological Technique of Martin Luther Thomas' Radio Addresses," in *Gesammelte Schriften 9.1: Soziologische Schriften II*, ed. Susan Buck-Morss and Rolf Tiedemann (Frankfurt am Main: Suhrkamp, 1975), 11.

44 Ibid., 11–12.

45 Ibid., 12.

46 Some readers may justly wonder here why I do not provide a synopsis of the piece and its conclusions. The exceedingly fragmented character of the study makes such an endeavor not only uncommonly laborious but also misleading: the study is simply not organized in the hierarchical manner that the task of summarizing presupposes. That is, it is not built around any central thesis established through subordinate arguments and/or corollary points. Instead, the study congeals as an agglomeration of reiterated exercises in critical reflection that one by one—but without any teleological purpose, and thus with no logical beginning or end—decode individual aspects of Thomas's rhetoric. Since this chapter is above all concerned with methodological issues, however, it makes more sense at any rate to concentrate on rendering Adorno's method with precision than to review the study's content in its entire scope.

47 Adorno, "Psychological Technique of Martin Luther Thomas' Radio Addresses," 19–20.

48 Ibid., 30.

49 Ibid.

50 Ibid., 52–55.

51 Ibid., 38.

52 Ibid., 39–40.
53 Ibid., 52–56.
54 Ibid., 74.
55 Ibid., 76.
56 Ibid., 12.
57 Horkheimer and Adorno, *Dialektik der Aufklärung*, 152; *Dialectic of Enlightenment*, 144.
58 Adorno, "Psychological Technique of Martin Luther Thomas' Radio Addresses," 18.
59 Horkheimer and Adorno, *Dialektik der Aufklärung*, 148–49; *Dialectic of Enlightenment*, 139–41.
60 Adorno, "Psychological Technique of Martin Luther Thomas' Radio Addresses," 50–51.
61 Horkheimer and Adorno, *Dialektik der Aufklärung*, 156–57; *Dialectic of Enlightenment*, 147–48.
62 Adorno, "Psychological Technique of Martin Luther Thomas' Radio Addresses," 80–84.
63 Horkheimer and Adorno, *Dialektik der Aufklärung*, 129; *Dialectic of Enlightenment*, 121.
64 Adorno, "Psychological Technique of Martin Luther Thomas' Radio Addresses," 86.
65 Ibid.
66 Three of the study's sections, including "The Religious Medium" (sec. 3), deal with speech devices grouped together by reason of their common content, while the other two (secs. 1 and 4) address Thomas's "self-characterization" and his use of scapegoat figures ("ideological bait"). The remaining section (2) is entitled "Thomas' method," but is not essentially different in its approach to the material than the other parts of the study. That is, with the exception of a few preliminary comments, it simply continues the catalogue and analysis of Thomas's "tricks."
67 Adorno, "Psychological Technique of Martin Luther Thomas' Radio Addresses," 88–90.
68 Ibid., 105–10.
69 Ibid., 110–13.
70 Ibid., 86.
71 In his subsequent contribution to *The Authoritarian Personality*, Adorno almost explicitly identified religion as merely a subdivision of the culture industry. To Adorno, religion had completely lost its distinctive substance, leaving only "neutralized residues" that merely reinforced the social authority of the administrated market. On an individual level, Adorno argued, religious doctrine was "'consumed' in a haphazard way as a 'cultural good.'" Adorno contended that concern for the "specific content" of such doctrine had been replaced in the twentieth century by the mechanical acceptance of the doctrine's "formal constituents" that "are apt to be congealed into mere formulae." On the level of the community, Adorno added, religion's "preservation in a noncommittal ideological form" had transformed it into a "social cement" useful to "the maintenance of the *status quo*" (Adorno, "Studies in the Authoritarian Personality," 431–35).
72 Horkheimer and Adorno, *Dialektik der Aufklärung*, 176; *Dialectic of Enlightenment*, 167.
73 Adorno, "Psychological Technique of Martin Luther Thomas' Radio Addresses," 61.
74 Adorno, "Radio Symphony."
75 Adorno, "Psychological Technique of Martin Luther Thomas' Radio Addresses," 36–37, 58–59.
76 Ibid., 81–83.
77 Ibid., 41, 73, 99.
78 Ibid., 52, 109.
79 Ibid., 51, 137.
80 Ibid., 93, 117–19.
81 Ibid., 96, 101, 138.

82 Ibid., 45, 51.

83 Ibid., 48, 111, 139.

84 Ibid., 103, 109, 129.

85 Ibid., 67, 100, 138.

86 Ibid., 52.

87 David Stoesz and Howard Jacob Karger, *Reconstructing the American Welfare State* (Lanham, Md.: Rowman and Littlefield, 1992), 10.

88 Ibid., 10–11. See also Frances Fox Piven and Richard A. Cloward, *Regulating the Poor: The Functions of Public Welfare*, 2d ed. (New York: Vintage, 1993), 45–119.

89 See Mike Davis, *Prisoners of the American Dream: Politics and Economy in the History of the US Working Class* (New York: Verso, 1986), 52–73.

90 Frances Fox Piven, "Welfare and the Transformation of Electoral Politics," *Dissent* 43, no. 4 (fall 1996): 65.

91 Ibid., 63.

92 Randall Balmer, *Mine Eyes Have Seen the Glory: A Journey into the Evangelical Subculture in America* (New York: Oxford University Press, 1993), 269.

93 See Michel Aglietta, *A Theory of Capitalist Regulation: The US Experience*, trans. David Fernbach (London: New Left, 1979), 111–22, 151–61, 179–98; Giovanni Arrighi, *The Long Twentieth Century: Money, Power, and the Origins of Our Times* (New York: Verso, 1994), 4–13, 269–300; Davis, *Prisoners of the American Dream*, 182–95; David Harvey, *The Condition of Postmodernity: An Enquiry into the Origins of Cultural Change* (Oxford: Basil Blackwell, 1989), 125–40; Michael J. Piore and Charles F. Sabel, *The Second Industrial Divide: Possibilities for Prosperity* (New York: Basic, 1984), 49–132.

94 See Aglietta, *Theory of Capitalist Regulation*, 122–30, 161–69; Arrighi, *Long Twentieth Century*, 300–324; Davis, *Prisoners of the American Dream*, 195–230; Harvey, *Condition of Postmodernity*, 141–72; Piore and Sabel, *Second Industrial Divide*, 194–280.

95 Harvey, *Condition of Postmodernity*, 159–60.

96 For a useful discussion of these continuities, see especially Harvey, *Condition of Postmodernity*, 189–97.

3 Christian Professionals and the Fraying Fabric of Health and Human Services

1 There are notable exceptions to this tendency in the history of evangelicalism, however. See the account of social mission among black evangelicals in contemporary Mississippi in Randall Balmer, *Mine Eyes Have Seen the Glory: A Journey into the Evangelical Subculture in America* (New York: Oxford University Press, 1993), 176–92. See also the discussion of the social activism enjoined by various elements of the nineteenth-century Holiness movement in George M. Marsden, *Fundamentalism and American Culture: The Shaping of Twentieth-Century Evangelicalism: 1870–1925* (New York: Oxford University Press, 1982), 80–93.

2 See Lawrence Grossberg, *We Gotta Get Out of This Place: Popular Conservatism and Postmodern Culture* (New York: Routledge, 1992).

3 Anonymous, *Primary Colors: A Novel of Politics* (New York: Warner, 1996). For a focused discussion of the cultural politics of the film *Primary Colors*, see Paul Apostolidis, "Action or Distraction? Cultural Studies in the USA," in *Political Theory and Cultural Studies*, ed. Jodi Dean (Ithaca, N.Y.: Cornell University Press, forthcoming).

4 Focus's earliest audio- and videotape products often took this format, for example the 1977 audio and video series *Focus on the Family.*

5 *Focus on the Family*, "What Is Intelligence?" 27 July 1994.

6   *Focus on the Family*, "Can You Raise Your Child's I.Q.?" 28 July 1994.

7   Ibid., 28–29 July 1994.

8   *Focus on the Family*, "What Is Intelligence?"

9   Ibid.

10   The role of "the nuclear family" as "the most important educational delivery system," according to Dobson's interpretation of the Harvard study, was also among the study's "conclusions that correlated perfectly with the values you find in scripture" and "validated" Dobson's messages "for 15 years here in this broadcast" (*Focus on the Family*, "Can You Raise Your Child's I.Q.?" 28 July 1994).

11   Ibid. I have used italics here and in other quotations from *Focus on the Family* to convey a sense of the speaker's cadence of speech.

12   Ibid.

13   Ibid.

14   Dobson's discussion of intelligence per se provides another example of his fusion of the physiological, the social, and the spiritual into a totality of truth. Asked by Trout to define "intelligence," Dobson at first articulates a rather jumbled conception that includes technical adeptness in following linguistic and mathematical rules, the capacity to achieve personal goals through actions conforming to given cultural norms, and successful performance in institutionalized systems for measuring intellectual ability such as school curricula and IQ tests. Dobson immediately qualifies this definition, however, claiming that these attributes represent only "the outward manifestation of intelligence as defined in this culture." According to Dobson, intelligence is "really" a complex biological phenomenon involving electrochemical interactions among "a network of billions of cells" in the cerebral cortex. For Dobson, this supposedly more authentic intelligence is simultaneously accessible to biological investigation and something utterly mysterious—perhaps even a bit frightening. For scientific research, he claims, the phenomenon is "just fearfully and wonderfully *new*!" "It almost staggers us to even contemplate what goes on in the human brain," he marvels. For Dobson, the physiological thus becomes the mystical and radiates the social: apparently without tension or contradiction, the three systems of order are consolidated into one, the only appropriate attitude toward which is apparently awe and wonder (*Focus on the Family*, "What Is Intelligence?").

15   *Focus on the Family*, "Can You Raise Your Child's I.Q.?" 28 July 1994.

16   Ibid.

17   Ibid.

18   Dobson and his guests vividly forge the chain of equivalence between blackness, urban dwelling, drug use, crime, and antisocial attitudes in a two-broadcast series featuring conservative culture critic George Gilder (*Focus on the Family*, "Men and Marriage," 11–12 July 1994). See also the discussion of race in *Focus on the Family*, "Harmony in the Inner City," 16 December 1994.

19   *Focus on the Family*, "Can You Raise Your Child's I.Q.?" 29 July 1994.

20   Ibid., 28 July 1994. Dobson further undercuts his own valorization of professional-scientific knowledge when he relates the story of how his simple question concerning the true essence of intelligence exposed the ultimate ignorance of his neurophysiology professor.

21   See Marsden's excellent discussion of the strong influence on fundamentalism of the philosophy of "common-sense realism," an early, Scottish Enlightenment epistemology that asserted a strict, cosmological unity of "truth" (meaning at once scientific "fact" and the morally "good") in opposition to "error" (Marsden, *Fundamentalism and American Culture*, 55–56, 110–16). For studies of contemporary fundamentalism that confirm the persistence of this dualism, see Nancy Tatom Ammerman, *Bible Believers: Fundamental-*

ists in the Modern World (New Brunswick, N.J.: Rutgers University Press, 1987); James Barr, *Fundamentalism* (Philadelphia: Westminster, 1978); Martin E. Marty and R. Scott Appleby, eds., *Fundamentalisms Observed* (Chicago: University of Chicago Press, 1991); and Martin E. Marty and R. Scott Appleby, *The Glory and the Power: The Fundamentalist Challenge to the Modern World* (Boston: Beacon, 1992).

22 *Focus on the Family*, "Repressed Memories," 16 February 1995.

23 Ibid.

24 Ibid.

25 Ibid., 17 February 1995.

26 Ibid., 16 February 1995.

27 Ibid., 17 February 1995.

28 Ibid.

29 Meier is a psychiatrist and the "co-founder of the Minirth-Meier New Life Clinics," a large and well-known evangelical counseling institution; Simpson practices psychology privately and has worked as a "case manager for Child Protective Services in Tucson, Arizona"; Gatewood serves as the Clinical Supervisor of Counseling for Focus on the Family (*Focus on the Family*, "Repressed Memories," 17 February 1995).

30 Ibid.

31 Ibid.

32 Ibid., 16 February 1995.

33 Ibid.

34 Ibid.

35 Ibid.

36 Ibid.

37 Ibid., 17 February 1995.

38 *Focus on the Family*, "Hope for the Homosexual," 19 April 1994.

39 See Paul E. Johnson, *A Shopkeeper's Millennium: Society and Revivals in Rochester, New York, 1815–1837* (New York: Hill and Wang, 1978); Marsden, *Fundamentalism and American Culture.*

40 *Focus on the Family*, "Hope for the Homosexual."

41 Ibid.

42 Ibid.

43 Ibid., 20 April 1994.

44 Ibid., 19–21 April 1994.

45 Ibid., 21 April 1994.

46 Ibid.

47 Ibid., 19–21 April 1994.

48 Ibid., 20–21 April 1994.

49 At the same time, lesbians and bisexuals are also positioned alongside gay men as outsiders, but by different discursive means: same-sex desire among women is simply ignored by the conversants, for the most part; and Nicolosi asserts that bisexuality is merely a fiction opportunistically manufactured by gay political activists (ibid., 21 April 1994).

50 Ibid., 20–21 April 1994.

51 Ibid., 21 April 1994.

52 Ibid., 20 April 1994.

53 Ibid.

54 Theodor W. Adorno, *Philosophie der Neuen Musik*, in *Gesammelte Schriften 12*, ed. Rolf Tiedemann (Frankfurt am Main: Suhrkamp, 1975), 32; Adorno, *Philosophy of Modern Music*, trans. Anne G. Mitchell and Wesley V. Blomster (New York: Continuum, 1973), 25.

55 National Center for Health Statistics (NCHS), *Health, United States, 1993* (Hyattsville, Md.: Public Health Service, 1994), 225.

56 Katharine R. Levit, Helen C. Lazenby, Bradley R. Braden, and the National Health Accounts Team, "National Health Spending Trends in 1996," *Health Affairs* 17, no. 1 (January–February 1998): 42.

57 Mitchell F. Rice, "Health Care Reform, Managed Competition, and the Urban Medically Underserved," *Journal of Health and Social Policy* 8, no. 4 (1997): 32–33.

58 Levit et al., "National Health Spending Trends in 1996," 36, 46.

59 NCHS, *Health, United States, 1993*, 49; Henry J. Aaron and Robert D. Reischauer, " 'Rethinking Medicare Reform' Needs Rethinking," *Health Affairs* 17, no. 1 (January–February 1998): 71; Kenneth E. Thorpe, "The Health System in Transition: Care, Cost, and Coverage," *Journal of Health Politics, Policy and Law* 22, no. 2 (April 1997): 352. See also Emily Friedman, "The Uninsured: From Dilemma to Crisis," in *Beyond Crisis: Confronting Health Care in the United States,* ed. Nancy F. McKenzie (New York: Meridian, 1994), 23; and Joel S. Weissman and Arnold M. Epstein, *Falling through the Safety Net: Insurance Status and Access to Health Care* (Baltimore, Md.: Johns Hopkins University Press, 1994), 2, 31.

60 Robin M. Weinick, Margaret E. Weigers, and Joel W. Cohen, "Children's Health Insurance, Access to Care, and Health Status: New Findings," *Health Affairs* 17, no. 2 (March–April 1998): 127–36; Weissman and Epstein, *Falling through the Safety Net,* 35–41.

61 Monika Zechetmayr, "Native Americans: A Neglected Health Care Crisis and a Solution," *Journal of Health and Social Policy* 9, no. 2 (1997): 29–47.

62 See Jacob S. Hacker and Theda Skocpol, "The New Politics of U.S. Health Policy," *Journal of Health Politics, Policy and Law* 22, no. 2 (April 1997): 315–38.

63 Sara Rosenbaum, Kay Johnson, Colleen Sonosky, Anne Markus, and Christ DeGraw, "The Children's Hour: The State Children's Health Insurance Program," *Health Affairs* 17, no. 1 (January–February 1998): 75–89.

64 Raymond J. Baxter and Robert E. Mechanic, "The Status of Local Health Care Safety Nets," *Health Affairs* 16, no. 4 (July–August 1997): 9.

65 Linda E. Fishman and James D. Bentley, "The Evolution of Support for Safety-Net Hospitals," *Health Affairs* 16, no. 4 (July–August 1997): 31.

66 Peter J. Cunningham and Ha T. Tu, "A Changing Picture of Uncompensated Care," *Health Affairs* 16, no. 4 (July–August 1997): 167; see also Joyce M. Mann, Genn A. Melnick, Anil Bamezai, and Jack Zwanziger, "A Profile of Uncompensated Hospital Care, 1983–1995," *Health Affairs* 16, no. 4 (July–August 1997): 223–32.

67 Fishman and Bentley, "Evolution of Support for Safety-Net Hospitals," 45. Rice notes: "Public hospitals operated by state and local governments are being closed, leased, or privatized with increasing frequency. . . . Inner-city hospital emergency rooms and trauma centers are closing with increasing frequency." The latter trend is especially ominous, since "the hospital emergency room is the primary route to physician and health services for the urban medically underserved" (Rice, "Health Care Reform, Managed Competition, and the Urban Medically Underserved," 42).

68 Fishman and Bentley, "Evolution of Support for Safety-Net Hospitals," 45. See also Baxter and Mechanic, "Status of Local Health Care Safety Nets," 19–21.

69 Richard G. Frank, Chris Koyanagi, and Thomas G. McGuire, "The Politics and Economics of Mental Health 'Parity' Laws," *Health Affairs* 16, no. 4 (July–August 1997): 110–11.

70 Jeffrey A. Buck and Beth Umland, "Covering Mental Health and Substance Abuse Services," *Health Affairs* 16, no. 4 (July–August 1997): 120.

71 See William Goldman, Joyce McCulloch, and Roland Sturm, "Costs and Use of Mental Health Services before and after Managed Care," *Health Affairs* 17, no. 2 (March–April 1998): 40–52; Ching-to Albert Ma and Thomas G. McGuire, "Costs and Incentives in a Behavioral Health Carve-Out," *Health Affairs* 17, no. 2 (March–April 1998): 53–69. Ma and McGuire do not in fact address the issue of whether those in need of services are deprived of them by introducing managed care in mental health care provision, although they show that doing so reduced costs for the state of Massachusetts.

72 Frank, Koyanagi, and McGuire, "Politics and Economics of Mental Health 'Parity' Laws," 117.

73 The Domenici-Wellstone amendment to the Kassebaum-Kennedy health care reform bill, which mandated health insurance "portability," "prohibits different treatment of mental health care in lifetime caps and annual reimbursement ceilings. It only affects plans that already have mental health benefits and does not mandate inclusion of mental health coverage in the benefit package. Plans that now have mental health coverage may drop coverage entirely. . . . [The amendment further] allows health plans to continue to place annual day and visit limitations on covered services and to use higher levels of cost sharing for mental health care than for other services" (Frank, Koyanagi, and McGuire, "Politics and Economics of Mental Health 'Parity' Laws," 109).

74 See Hacker and Skocpol, "New Politics of U.S. Health Policy."

75 For more information regarding these policy changes, see Hacker and Skocpol, "New Politics of U.S. Health Policy," 322–26. Hacker and Skocpol's comparison of the failures of national health reforms under the Truman and Clinton administrations points to several specifically political impediments to further progressive reform today, in particular the lack of a liberal policymaking consensus and the power and unity of the new right in Congress and as a social movement. These changes in the landscape of party strength, elite thinking, and public opinion are of course also distinguishing characteristics of the post-Fordist moment.

76 For a detailed examination of these strategies of competition, see Paul B. Ginsburg, "The Dynamics of Market-Level Change," *Journal of Health Politics, Policy and Law* 22, no. 2 (April 1997): 363–83.

77 For a discussion of the role of technocratic ideology in managed care, defined as the notion that "standardized medical practice through knowledge gleaned from aggregated measures, disciplined through the 'logic' of the marketplace, will control costs while it maintains quality," a notion drawing on "scientific credibility," see Gary S. Belkin, "The Technocratic Wish: Making Sense and Finding Power in the 'Managed' Medical Marketplace," *Journal of Health Politics, Policy and Law* 22, no. 2 (April 1997): 509–32.

78 Paul Starr, *The Social Transformation of American Medicine* (New York: Basic, 1982), 20–27, 203–18, 249–56, 331–34, 420.

79 Ibid., 428.

80 Norman Ginsburg, *Divisions of Welfare: A Critical Introduction to Comparative Social Policy* (London: Sage, 1992), 134; Starr, *Social Transformation of American Medicine*, 447. John B. McKinlay and John D. Stoeckle, moreover, point to the erosion of physicians' prerogatives concerning "gatekeeping" functions such as the dispensation of drug prescriptions, the growing proportion of salaried physicians, and even increasing interest among physicians in unionization as indicators of physicians' dwindling autonomy. See John B. McKinlay and John D. Stoeckle, "Corporatization and the Social Transformation of Doctoring," in MacKenzie, *Beyond Crisis*, 271–84. In a related vein, Barbara Ehrenreich contends that medicine, like many other professions, is currently experiencing a process of "class polarization," in which one group is merging with "the corporate elite" while "another

layer . . . sediments toward the white-collar end of the working class." Whether the trajectory of a given medical professional's mobility is upward or downward, however, that individual is likely to experience diminished economic and social autonomy as a result of her or his increasing interdependence with or subordination to corporate decision makers (Ehrenreich, *Fear of Falling: The Inner Life of the Middle Class* [New York: Pantheon, 1989]).

81 Deborah A. Stone, "The Doctor as Businessman: The Changing Politics of a Cultural Icon," *Journal of Health Politics, Policy and Law* 22, no. 2 (April 1997): 546–52. See also Ginsburg, "Dynamics of Market-Level Change," 372; John K. Inglehart, "Physicians as Agents of Social Control: The Thought of Victor Fuchs," *Health Affairs* 17, no. 1 (January–February 1998): 90–96.

82 See Stone, "Doctor as Businessman," 538.

83 Stone argues, furthermore, that managed care does not merely avoid ethical issues but indeed encourages ethically repugnant conduct. This is because managed care creates incentives for a physician to deny clinically necessary care to her patients by making her income contingent on the purchaser's (e.g., an HMO's) expenses for that doctor's patients. Practices such as income withholding and the granting of bonuses thus generate a system of payments that "converts each sick patient, even each illness, into a financial liability for the primary care doctor. . . . Sick patients become adversaries rather than occasions for compassion and intimacy." More broadly, Stone trenchantly criticizes the "cultural transformation" that has inverted the previous assumption that doctors' pecuniary interests and clinical judgments had to be kept completely segregated from one another, fostering the new idea that ethical practice positively requires doctors to act like entrepreneurs in the health care market (Stone, "Doctor as Businessman," 542–51).

84 Ginsburg, *Divisions of Welfare*, 136–37; Judith Havemann, "Welfare Reform Incorporated: Social Policy Going Private," *Washington Post*, 7 March 1997, A1, A14.

85 Michael B. Fabricant and Steve Burghardt, *The Welfare State Crisis and the Transformation of Social Service Work* (Armonk, N.Y.: M. E. Sharpe, 1992), xiii–xiv.

86 See Robert H. Miller and Harold S. Luft, "Does Managed Care Lead to Better or Worse Quality of Care?" *Health Affairs* 16, no. 5 (September–October 1997): 7–25.

87 Stone, "Doctor as Businessman," 552–54.

88 For example, see "Text of President Clinton's Announcement on Welfare Legislation," *New York Times*, 1 August 1996, A10. Clinton characterized the end of federal welfare entitlements as a set of provisions to mend a "broken" system, giving America "a chance we haven't had before to break the cycle of dependency" and offering states "powerful performance incentives to place people in jobs" and "the capacity to create jobs" through employer subsidies. Then presidential candidate Bob Dole echoed these thoughts, emphasizing that the legislation would give "states the flexibility to design programs that best meet the needs of the people they serve." See Robert Dole, "Dole's Statement on Measure," *New York Times*, 1 August 1996, A10.

89 See Alain Lipietz, *Towards a New Economic Order: Postfordism, Ecology, and Democracy* (New York: Oxford University Press, 1992).

90 Ibid., 43–46.

91 Rodham Clinton does this, for instance, by foregrounding divorce as the source of a wide range of social problems including poverty and mental illness. She goes so far as to quote William Bennett's statement to the Christian Coalition that "in terms of damage to the children of America, you cannot compare what the homosexual movement . . . has done to what divorce has done to this society." Rodham Clinton's cryptic disclaimer that one can "welcome" Bennett's statement even while not agreeing with all of his remarks rather weakly undercuts the sense here that there is something basically wrong with being gay

or lesbian, and that the problem has to do with a transgression of the conventional family norm. This sense certainly coheres with her subsequent statement that "every society needs a critical mass of families that fit the traditional ideal, both to meet the needs of most children and to serve as a model for other adults who are raising children in difficult settings" (Hillary Rodham Clinton, *It Takes a Village, and Other Lessons Children Teach Us* [New York: Simon and Schuster, 1996], 39–41, 50).

92 Clinton, *It Takes a Village*, 13–14. See Robert D. Putnam, "Bowling Alone: America's Declining Social Capital," *Journal of Democracy* 6, no. 1 (January 1995): 65–78.

93 Clinton, *It Takes a Village*, 74–75, 126.

94 Ibid., 76–83.

95 Ibid., 312.

96 See Bruce Frohnen, *The New Communitarians and the Crisis of Modern Liberalism* (Lawrence: University Press of Kansas, 1996), 153–55.

97 See Clinton, "Text of President Clinton's Announcement on Welfare Legislation," A10.

98 In general, however, the leading voices of the new right in public officialdom have sustained the paradigm of liberal productivism advanced by Reaganism, with its emphases on militant patriotism, material prosperity through scientific and technological advances, successful competition in the global economy, dismantling the welfare state, devolution of federal authority, and fiscal conservatism. See Newt Gingrich, *To Renew America* (New York: HarperCollins, 1995).

99 Donald W. Light, "The Rhetorics and Realities of Community Health Care: The Limits of Countervailing Powers to Meet the Health Care Needs of the Twenty-first Century," *Journal of Health Politics, Policy and Law* 22, no. 1 (February 1997): 105–45.

100 *Focus on the Family*, [title not available], 22 July 1994.

4   Christian Politicians and the Decline of Democratic Accountability

1 Leo Lowenthal and Norbert Guterman, *Prophets of Deceit: A Study of the Techniques of the American Agitator*, 2d ed. (Palo Alto, Calif.: Pacific, 1970), 24.

2 Ibid., 25–26.

3 See James A. Aho, *The Politics of Righteousness: Idaho Christian Patriotism* (Seattle: University of Washington Press, 1990); Michael Barkun, *Religion and the Racist Right: The Origins of the Christian Identity Movement* (Chapel Hill: University of North Carolina Press, 1997).

4 My remarks here concerning *The 700 Club* are based on my daily monitoring of the program for one month (July 1994).

5 Curtis Harris, President, American Academy of Medical Ethics, from an audiotape excerpt aired on *Focus on the Family*, [title not available], 13 July 1994; James Dobson, on *Focus on the Family*, "Hope for the Homosexual," 19 April 1994; *Focus on the Family*, [title not available], 20 February 1995.

6 Focus on the Family, *Family News from Dr. James Dobson* (Colorado Springs: Focus on the Family, September 1998).

7 *Focus on the Family*, "A Visit with Lt. Col. and Mrs. Ollie North," 23 October 1991.

8 Ibid.

9 Ibid.

10 Ibid.

11 Ibid., 24 October 1991.

12 North drives home the point that the Iran-Contra hearings were a "trial" not only of his own religious commitment but moreover of his family's strength by referring to an image

that gave him sustenance throughout his "ordeal." This is a picture that ronce hung over a fellow marine's desk showing "a white water raft and great turmoil . . . and the family clinging to the side of this raft as they're going down this raging river, and the caption underneath that says, 'God doesn't promise you a smooth passage, just a safe delivery'" (*Focus on the Family*, "A Visit with Lt. Col. and Mrs. Ollie North," 24 October 1991).

13 Ibid.

14 Ibid., 25 October 1991.

15 Ibid., 23–25 October 1991.

16 Randall Balmer, *Mine Eyes Have Seen the Glory: A Journey into the Evangelical Subculture in America* (New York: Oxford University Press, 1993), 16, 21.

17 *Focus on the Family*, "A Visit with Lt. Col. and Mrs. Ollie North," 23–24 October 1991.

18 Ibid., 23 October 1991.

19 Ibid., 24 October 1991.

20 Ibid.

21 Ibid., 23 October 1991.

22 Ibid.

23 Ibid., 25 October 1991.

24 Ibid., 23 October 1991.

25 Ibid., 24–25 October 1991.

26 *Focus on the Family*, "Being Light in the Darkness," 14 January 1993.

27 Ibid.

28 Ibid.

29 Ibid.

30 Ibid.

31 Ibid., 15 January 1993.

32 Ibid.

33 Ibid., 14 January 1993.

34 Ibid., 15 January 1993.

35 Ibid.

36 Ibid.

37 Ibid.

38 Ibid., 14 January 1993.

39 Ellsberg, a former Pentagon official, had leaked to the press a set of classified documents that came to be known as the Pentagon Papers. These files described actions of U.S. armed forces in Vietnam that had been systematically hidden from the public.

40 *Focus on the Family*, "Being Light in the Darkness," 14 January 1993.

41 *Focus on the Family*, [title not available], 17 January 1995.

42 Ibid.

43 Ibid.

44 Ibid.

45 Ibid.

46 Ibid.

47 Ibid.

48 Ibid.

49 *Focus on the Family*, "A Call to Prayer," 16 January 1995.

50 *Focus on the Family*, [title not available], 17 January 1995.

51 *Focus on the Family*, "A Call to Prayer," 16 January 1995; *Focus on the Family*, [title not available], 17 January 1995.

52 *Focus on the Family*, "A Call to Prayer," 16 January 1995; *Focus on the Family*, [title not available], 17 January 1995.

53 See Julia Lesage, "Christian Media," in *Media, Culture, and the Religious Right*, ed. Linda Kintz and Julia Lesage (Minneapolis: University of Minnesota Press, 1998), 21–49.

54 See Lauren Berlant, *The Queen of America Goes to Washington City: Essays on Sex and Citizenship* (Durham, N.C.: Duke University Press, 1997); Lawrence Grossberg, *We Gotta Get Out of This Place: Popular Conservatism and Postmodern Culture* (New York: Routledge, 1992), 263–79.

55 Dennis F. Thompson, *Ethics in Congress: From Individual to Institutional Corruption* (Washington, D.C.: Brookings Institution, 1995), 1.

56 Ibid., 7–8, 31–32.

57 Ibid., 31–32.

58 M. Margaret Conway and Joanne Connor Green, "Political Action Committees and the Political Process in the 1990's," in *Interest Group Politics*, 4th ed., ed. Allan J. Cigler and Burdett A. Loomis (Washington, D.C.: Congressional Quarterly, 1995), 158–61.

59 Conway and Green, "Political Action Committees and the Political Process in the 1990's," 165–66.

60 Dan Clawson, Alan Neustadtl, and Mark Weller, *Dollars and Votes: How Business Campaign Contributions Subvert Democracy* (Philadelphia: Temple University Press, 1998), 2.

61 Ibid., 114–16. See also Anthony Corrado, "Financing the 1996 Elections," in *The Elections of 1996*, ed. Gerald Pomper (Chatham, N.J.: Chatham House, 1997), 135–71.

62 Theodore J. Lowi, "Toward a Legislature of the First Kind," in *Knowledge, Power, and the Congress*, ed. William H. Robinson and Clay H. Wellborn (Washington, D.C.: Congressional Quarterly, 1991), 9–36. Lowi argues that this accountability crisis is symptomatized by the heightening of "voter frustration" and alienation, the "explosion" of litigation and the "rise of court-made rights," and the saddling of the presidency with extraordinary, contradictory, and unfulfillable expectations. Regarding this crisis of the presidency, see Theodore J. Lowi, *The Personal President: Power Invested, Promise Unfulfilled* (Ithaca, N.Y.: Cornell University Press, 1985); and Mark Silverstein, "Watergate and the American Political System," in *The Politics of Scandal: Power and Process in Liberal Democracies*, ed. Andrei S. Markovits and Mark Silverstein (New York: Holmes and Meier, 1988), 15–37.

63 Burdett A. Loomis and Allan J. Cigler, "Introduction: The Changing Nature of Interest Group Politics," in *Interest Group Politics*, 5th ed., ed. Allan J. Cigler and Burdett A. Loomis (Washington, D.C.: Congressional Quarterly, 1998), 1.

64 Ibid., 26–27.

65 Burdett A. Loomis and Allan J. Cigler, "Introduction: The Changing Nature of Interest Group Politics," in Cigler and Loomis, *Interest Group Politics*, 4th ed., 24–25. On the secular trend toward the delegation of policymaking power by legislators to interest groups, see Theodore J. Lowi, *The End of Liberalism: The Second Republic of the United States* (New York: Norton, 1979).

66 Burdett A. Loomis and Eric Sexton provide evidence of the procorporate tilt of influence in Congress by analyzing the predominance of corporate advertising, especially advertising by defense contractors, in the major periodicals read by Capitol Hill staff and other elites in the policymaking processes—*National Journal* and *Congressional Quarterly Weekly Report*. See Burdett A. Loomis and Eric Sexton, "Choosing to Advertise: How Interests Decide," in Cigler and Loomis, *Interest Group Politics*, 4th ed., 194–210.

67 Glenn Parker, *Congress and the Rent-Seeking Society* (Ann Arbor: University of Michigan Press, 1996); see esp. 86–90.

68 Mike Davis, *Prisoners of the American Dream: Politics and Economy in the History of the US Working Class* (New York: Verso, 1986), 158–62.

69 See ibid., 256–300.

70 Michael Gurevitch and Jay G. Blumler, "Political Communications Systems and Demo-
    cratic Values," in *Democracy and the Mass Media: A Collection of Essays*, ed. Judith
    Lichtenberg (New York: Cambridge University Press, 1990), 279–81; Judith Lichtenberg,
    "Foundations and Limits of Freedom of the Press," in Lichtenberg, *Democracy and the
    Mass Media*, 122–23; Carl Sessions Stepp, "Access in a Post-Social Responsibility Age," in
    Lichtenberg, *Democracy and the Mass Media*, 189–90.
71 See Edwin Diamond and Robert A. Silverman, *White House to Your House: Media and
    Politics in Virtual America* (Cambridge: MIT Press, 1997), 15–31.
72 See ibid., 2–11.
73 See ibid., 140–45.
74 See Marion R. Just, Ann N. Crigler, Dean E. Alger, Timothy E. Cook, Montague Kern, and
    Darrell M. West, *Crosstalk: Citizens, Candidates, and the Media in a Presidential Cam-
    paign* (Chicago: University of Chicago Press, 1996), 142–47.
75 See Richard Davis and Diana Owen, *New Media and American Politics* (New York: Ox-
    ford University Press, 1998), 23, 151–52, 162–63.
76 See Diamond and Silverman, *White House to Your House*, 164; Davis and Owen, *New
    Media and American Politics*, 127–28.

5 *Christian Victims in the Backlash Society*

1   Dwight L. Moody, *Moody: His Words, Work, and Workers*, ed. Rev. Charles H. Fowler
    (New York: Nelson and Phillips, 1878), 518–31.
2   See George M. Marsden, *Fundamentalism and American Culture: The Shaping of Twen-
    tieth-Century Evangelicalism, 1870–1925* (New York: Oxford University Press, 1982), 32–
    39.
3   Dwight L. Moody, *The Best of D. L. Moody*, ed. Wilbur M. Smith (Chicago: Moody Bible
    Institute, 1971), 79–87, 97–111.
4   Max Horkheimer and Theodor W. Adorno, *Dialektik der Aufklärung: Philosophische Frag-
    mente* (Frankfurt am Main: Fischer, 1969), 163; Horkheimer and Adorno, *Dialectic of
    Enlightenment*, trans. John Cumming (New York: Continuum, 1972), 154.
5   *Focus on the Family*, "Spiritual Warfare: The Story of Stephan Morin," 14–15 July 1994.
6   John 19:17; Luke 7:34–50, 15:1–7; Matt. 5:38–48, 10:39, 16:25–26, 27:39–49, 28:16–20; in
    The New English Bible, with the Apocrypha, gen. ed. Samuel Sandmel (New York: Oxford
    University Press, 1976).
7   Matt. 21:12–13, 23:33, 26:36–41; in *The New English Bible*.
8   *Focus on the Family*, "Spiritual Warfare: The Story of Stephan Morin," 14 July 1994.
9   Ibid., 14–15 July 1994.
10 Ibid., 15 July 1994.
11 Ibid., 14 July 1994.
12 *Focus on the Family*, "Harmony in the Inner City," 16 December 1994.
13 Ibid.
14 *Focus on the Family*, "A Matter of Life," 18 January 1995.
15 Ibid.
16 See Linda Kintz, *Between Jesus and the Market: The Emotions That Matter in Right-Wing
    America* (Durham, N.C.: Duke University Press, 1997), 263–71.
17 *Focus on the Family*, "A Matter of Life," 18 January 1995.
18 Ibid., 19 January 1995.
19 See Sara Diamond, *Roads to Dominion: Right-Wing Movements and Political Power in
    the United States* (New York: Guilford, 1995); Marsden, *Fundamentalism and American
    Culture*.

20 *Focus on the Family*, "Harmony in the Inner City," 16 December 1994.

21 Horkheimer and Adorno, *Dialektik der Aufklärung*, 148; *Dialectic of Enlightenment*, 139.

22 Frances Fox Piven and Richard A. Cloward, *Regulating the Poor: The Functions of Public Welfare*, 2d ed. (New York: Vintage, 1993), 183.

23 See Rebecca Blank, *It Takes a Nation: A New Agenda for Fighting Poverty* (Princeton, N.J.: Princeton University Press, 1997), 136–40.

24 Piven and Cloward, *Regulating the Poor*, 372.

25 Piven and Cloward note, moreover, that "the campaign to drive the rolls down succeeded much more than these figures suggest because the official poverty line increasingly underestimated the extent of poverty" (*Regulating the Poor*, 379).

26 In New York City alone, the welfare rolls declined by over 30 percent between 1995 and 1998, as 363,000 poor people were removed from the welfare system. See Vivian S. Toy, "Tough Welfare Rules Used as Way to Cut Welfare Rolls," *New York Times*, 15 April 1998, A10, A24.

27 See Blank, *It Takes a Nation*, 173–76; Mary E. Hawkesworth, "Workfare and the Imposition of Discipline," *Social Theory and Practice* 11, no. 2 (summer 1985): 163–81; Piven and Cloward, *Regulating the Poor*, 382–95.

28 See Hawkesworth, "Workfare and the Imposition of Discipline," 171–72.

29 Jeffrey L. Katz, "After Sixty Years, Most Control Is Passing to States," *Congressional Quarterly Weekly Report*, 3 August 1996, 2196.

30 Blank, *It Takes a Nation*, 148.

31 See Piven and Cloward, *Regulating the Poor*, 320–30.

32 Blank, *It Takes a Nation*, 15–21.

33 James Jennings, "Introduction: New Challenges for Black Activism in the United States," in *Race and Politics: New Challenges and Responses for Black Activism*, ed. James Jennings (New York: Verso, 1997), 7.

34 Sunita Parekh, *The Politics of Preference: Democratic Institutions and Affirmative Action in the United States and India* (Ann Arbor: University of Michigan Press, 1997), 126–27.

35 Ibid., 128–29.

36 Ibid., 129–37.

37 Ibid., 129–30, 143.

38 See Bryan K. Fair, *Notes of a Racial Caste Baby: Color Blindness and the End of Affirmative Action* (New York: New York University Press, 1997), 147.

39 Quoted in Christopher Edley Jr., *Not All Black and White: Affirmative Action, Race, and Other American Values* (New York: Hill and Wang, 1996), 38.

40 The antiaffirmative action movement gained added momentum in 1996, moreover, when a federal appeals court prohibited the University of Texas School of Law from applying any race-conscious admissions policies.

41 Michael Goldfield, *The Color of Politics: Race and the Mainsprings of American Politics* (New York: New Press, 1997), 340.

42 Ibid., 322.

43 John W. Critzer and Kul B. Rai, "Blacks and Women in Public Higher Education: Political and Socioeconomic Factors Underlying Diversity at the State Level," *Women and Economics* 19, no. 1 (1998): 19–39.

44 Linda Blum, *Between Feminism and Labor: The Significance of the Comparable Worth Movement* (Berkeley: University of California Press, 1991), 4, 28–33; Elaine Sorensen, *Comparable Worth: Is It a Worthy Policy?* (Princeton, N.J.: Princeton University Press, 1994), 6.

45 Sorensen, *Comparable Worth*, 5–20.

46 See Christopher Jencks and Meredith Phillips, "The Black-White Test Score Gap," *Brookings Review* 16, no. 2 (spring 1998): 24–27; Orlando Patterson, "Affirmative Action: Opening Up Workplace Networks to Afro-Americans," *Brookings Review* 16, no. 2 (spring 1998): 17–23; Susan Welch and John Gruhl, *Affirmative Action and Minority Enrollments in Medical and Law Schools* (Ann Arbor: University of Michigan Press, 1998).

47 Gary Orfield, Susan E. Eaton, and the Harvard Project on School Desegregation, *Dismantling Desegregation: The Quiet Reversal of* "Brown v. Board of Education" (New York: New Press, 1996), xxi–xxii, 8–9.

48 Ibid., xxii, 13.

49 Ibid., 18.

50 Ibid., 16–18.

51 Ibid., 25.

52 Ibid., xxiii.

53 Ibid., xxiii, 1–4, 19–20.

54 More systematic empirical research bears out Kozol's general claims: see Linda Darling-Hammond, "Race and Education: Unequal Opportunity," *Brookings Review* 16, no. 2 (spring 1998): 28–32.

55 Jonathan Kozol, *Savage Inequalities: Children in America's Schools* (New York: Crown, 1991), 55.

56 Jencks and Phillips, "Black-White Test Score Gap"; U.S. Department of Education, National Committee for Educational Statistics, *NAEP 1996: Trends in Academic Progress: Achievements of US Students in Science, Math, Reading, and Writing* (Washington, D.C.: U.S. Department of Education); U.S. Department of Education, National Committee for Educational Statistics, *Dropout Rates in the United States: 1996* (Washington, D.C.: U.S. Department of Education).

57 U.S. Department of Commerce, Bureau of the Census, *Current Population Surveys: October 1996* (Washington, D.C.: U.S. Department of Commerce).

58 Peter Skerry, "E Pluribus Hispanic?" in *Pursuing Power: Latinos and the Political System* (Notre Dame, Ind.: University of Notre Dame Press, 1997), 22.

59 Darling-Hammond, "Race and Education"; Kozol, *Savage Inequalities*, 54; U.S. Department of Commerce, Bureau of the Census, *1990 Census School District Special Tabulations* (Washington, D.C.: U.S. Department of Commerce); U.S. Department of Education, National Committee for Educational Statistics, *Common Core of Data: School District Fiscal Data, 1993–1994* (Washington, D.C.: U.S. Department of Education).

60 Darling-Hammond, "Race and Education," 28–32.

61 David Harvey, *The Condition of Postmodernity: An Enquiry into the Origins of Cultural Change* (Oxford: Basil Blackwell, 1989), 138.

62 Ibid., 150.

63 Ibid., 150–51. Mike Davis concurs with Harvey, describing the emergence of "occupational income/status extremes unmediated by substantial middle ranges" under post-Fordism, and specifically linking this phenomenon to the "explosion of exchanges in fictional capital" in the 1980s. Davis emphasizes, however, that "low-wage employment, far from being a mere 'periphery' to a high-wage core, has become the job growth–pole of the economy." See Mike Davis, *Prisoners of the American Dream: Politics and Economy in the History of the US Working Class* (New York: Verso, 1986), 208–9, 215.

64 Davis, *Prisoners of the American Dream*, 209.

65 Harvey, *Condition of Postmodernity*, 152–55. Davis similarly observes that "the accelerated formation of this *borderlands economic system* since the late 1960s has become integral to the new accumulation patterns characterized by a co-ordinated expansion of low-wage employment and middle-strata affluence" (*Prisoners of the American Dream*, 221).

66 See Davis, *Prisoners of the American Dream*, 198; James O'Connor, *The Fiscal Crisis of the State* (New York: St. Martin's, 1973), 23–24.

67 Davis, *Prisoners of the American Dream*, 211–12, 222. For an analysis of the populist power mobilized by the homeowners' movement in Los Angeles, see Mike Davis, *City of Quartz: Excavating the Future in Los Angeles* (New York: Vintage, 1992), 153–219.

68 Orfield et al., *Dismantling Desegregation*, 23.

69 Ibid., 24.

70 William J. Clinton, "Text of President Clinton's Announcement on Welfare Legislation," *New York Times*, 1 August 1996, A10.

71 Michel Foucault, *Discipline and Punish: The Birth of the Prison* (New York: Vintage, 1979), 210.

72 Jon Jeter, "Efforts to Move Poor from Welfare to Work Going Slowly in Area," *Washington Post*, 6 March 1997, A1, A18.

73 State of Washington, Office of the Secretary of State, *1998 Online Voters Guide for the General Election—November 3, 1998*, 18 November 1998.

74 I-200 PRO, *Yes on I-200: The Washington State Civil Rights Initiative Web Page*, 18 November 1998.

75 *Focus on the Family*, "Men and Marriage," 11–12 July 1994.

76 *Focus on the Family*, "Harmony in the Inner City," 16 December 1994.

77 *Focus on the Family*, "Goals 2000: History Redefined," 11 April 1995.

6 Negative Dialectics and Political Practice

1 I am grateful to Kathy Morefield for information about traditional and nontraditional versions of the stations of the cross.

2 Karl Marx, *Capital: Volume One*, trans. Ben Fowkes (New York: Vintage, 1977), 163.

3 Stephen T. Leonard, *Critical Theory in Political Practice* (Princeton, N.J.: Princeton University Press, 1990), 50.

4 See Leonard, *Critical Theory in Political Practice*, 96–248.

5 Ibid., 41–53.

6 Max Horkheimer and Theodor W. Adorno, *Dialektik der Aufklärung: Philosophische Fragmente* (Frankfurt am Main: Fischer, 1969), 139; Horkheimer and Adorno, *Dialectic of Enlightenment*, trans. John Cumming (New York: Continuum, 1972), 131.

7 David Hilfiker, *Not All of Us Are Saints: A Doctor's Journey with the Poor* (New York: Ballantine, 1994), 40–41.

8 Unitarian Universalist Association of Congregations, *Challenging the Radical Right* (Boston: Unitarian Universalist Association of Congregations, June 1995).

9 John C. Green, "The Christian Right and the 1996 Elections: An Overview," in *God at the Grass Roots, 1996: The Christian Right in the American Elections*, ed. Mark J. Rozell and Clyde Wilcox (Lanham, Md.: Rowman and Littlefield, 1997), 8.

10 Herbert D. Valentine, letter to membership (Washington, D.C.: Interfaith Alliance, 1995).

11 Unitarian Universalist Association of Congregations, *Challenging the Radical Right*, 4.

Appendix B

1 Amy Divine, cofounder of Food for Thought and Citizens Project, Board of Directors of Citizens Project, interview by author, Colorado Springs, 25 February 1996. My remarks on local politics in Colorado Springs also draw on conversations with Meagan Day (Citizens Project's sole staff member in February 1996) and other activists in Colorado Springs.

Note to Appendix B

Bibliography

Aaron, Henry J., and Robert D. Reischauer. "'Rethinking Medicare Reform' Needs Rethinking." *Health Affairs* 17, no. 1 (January–February 1998): 69–71.

Adorno, Theodor W. "Anti-Semitism and Fascist Propaganda." 1946. In *Gesammelte Schriften 8: Soziologische Schriften I*, ed. Rolf Tiedemann with Gretel Adorno, Susan Buck-Morss, and Klaus Schultz, 397–407. Frankfurt am Main: Suhrkamp, 1972.

———. "Cultural Criticism and Society." In *Prisms*, trans. Samuel Weber and Shierry Weber, 19–34. Cambridge: MIT Press, 1983.

———. "Freudian Theory and the Pattern of Fascist Propaganda." 1951. *Gesammelte Schriften 8: Soziologische Schriften I*, ed. Rolf Tiedemann, 408–33. Frankfurt am Main: Suhrkamp, 1972.

———. "How to Look at Television." *Quarterly of Film, Radio, and Television* 8, no. 3 (spring 1954): 213–35.

———. *In Search of Wagner*. 1952. Trans. Rodney Livingstone. New York: Verso, 1991.

———. *The Jargon of Authenticity*. 1964. Trans. Knut Tarnowski and Frederic Will. Evanston, Ill.: Northwestern University Press, 1973.

———. "Kulturkritik und Gesellschaft." 1955. In *Prismen: Kulturkritik und Gesellschaft*, 7–26. Frankfurt am Main: Suhrkamp, 1955.

———. *Minima Moralia: Reflections from Damaged Life*. Trans. E. F. N. Jephcott. New York: Verso, 1978.

———. *Minima Moralia: Reflexionen aus dem beschädigten Leben*. 1951. In *Gesammelte Schriften 4*, ed. Rolf Tiedemann. Frankfurt am Main: Suhrkamp, 1980.

———. *Negative Dialectics*. Trans. E. B. Ashton. New York: Continuum, 1973.

———. *Negative Dialektik*. 1966. In *Gesammelte Schriften 6*, ed. Rolf Tiedemann, 7–412. Frankfurt am Main: Suhrkamp, 1973.

———. *Philosophie der Neuen Musik*. 1949. In *Gesammelte Schriften 12*, ed. Rolf Tiedemann. Frankfurt am Main: Suhrkamp, 1975.

———. *Philosophy of Modern Music*. Trans. Anne G. Mitchell and Wesley V. Blomster. New York: Continuum, 1973.

———. "The Psychological Technique of Martin Luther Thomas' Radio Addresses." 1943. In *Gesammelte Schriften 9.1: Soziologische Schriften II*, ed. Susan Buck-Morss and Rolf Tiedemann, 7–141. Frankfurt am Main: Suhrkamp, 1975.

———. "The Radio Symphony: An Experiment in Theory." In *Radio Research 1941*, ed. Paul F. Lazarsfeld and Frank N. Stanton, 110–39. New York: Duell, Sloan and Pearce, 1941.

———. "Scientific Experiences of a European Intellectual in Migration." 1969. Trans. Donald Fleming. In *The Intellectual Migration: Europe and America, 1930–1960*, ed. Donald Fleming and Bernard Bailyn, 338–70. Cambridge, Mass.: Harvard University Press, Belknap Press, 1969.

———. "A Social Critique of Radio Music." *Kenyon Review* 7, no. 2 (spring 1945): 208–17.

———. "The Stars Down to Earth." 1953. In *Gesammelte Schriften 9.2: Soziologische Schriften II*, ed. Susan Buck-Morss and Rolf Tiedemann, 7–120. Frankfurt am Main: Suhrkamp, 1975.

———. "Studies in the Authoritarian Personality." 1950. In *Gesammelte Schriften 9.1: Soziologische Schriften II*, ed. Susan Buck-Morss and Rolf Tiedemann, 143–509. Frankfurt am Main: Suhrkamp, 1975.

———. "Transparencies on Film." 1967. Trans. Thomas Levin. *New German Critique* 24–25 (1981–82): 199–205.

———. [Hektor Rottweiler, pseud.] "Über Jazz." *Zeitschrift für Sozialforschung* 5, no. 2 (1936): 235–57.

———. "Veblens Angriff auf die Kultur." 1955. In *Prismen: Kulturkritik und Gesellschaft*, 68–91. Frankfurt am Main: Suhrkamp, 1955.

———. "Veblen's Attack on Culture." In *Prisms*, trans. Samuel Weber and Shierry Weber, 73–94. Cambridge: MIT Press, 1990.

Aglietta, Michel. *A Theory of Capitalist Regulation: The US Experience.* Trans. David Fernbach. London: New Left, 1979.

Aho, James A. *The Politics of Righteousness: Idaho Christian Patriotism.* Seattle: University of Washington Press, 1990.

Ammerman, Nancy Tatom. *Bible Believers: Fundamentalists in the Modern World.* New Brunswick, N.J.: Rutgers University Press, 1987.

Anonymous. *Primary Colors: A Novel of Politics.* New York: Warner, 1996.

Apostolidis, Paul. "Action or Distraction? Cultural Studies in the USA." In *Political Theory and Cultural Studies*, ed. Jodi Dean. Ithaca, N.Y.: Cornell University Press, forthcoming.

Arrighi, Giovanni. *The Long Twentieth Century: Money, Power, and the Origins of Our Times.* New York: Verso, 1994.

Balmer, Randall. *Mine Eyes Have Seen the Glory: A Journey into the Evangelical Subculture in America.* New York: Oxford University Press, 1993.

Barkun, Michael. *Religion and the Racist Right: The Origins of the Christian Identity Movement.* Rev. ed. Chapel Hill: University of North Carolina Press, 1997.

Barr, James. *Fundamentalism.* Philadelphia: Westminster, 1978.

Baxter, Raymond J., and Robert E. Mechanic. "The Status of Local Health Care Safety Nets." *Health Affairs* 16, no. 4 (July–August 1997): 7–23.

Belkin, Gary S. "The Technocratic Wish: Making Sense and Finding Power in the 'Managed' Medical Marketplace." *Journal of Health Politics, Policy and Law* 22, no. 2 (April 1997): 509–32.

Berlant, Lauren. *The Queen of America Goes to Washington City: Essays on Sex and Citizenship.* Durham, N.C.: Duke University Press, 1997.

Blank, Rebecca. *It Takes a Nation: A New Agenda for Fighting Poverty.* Princeton, N.J.: Princeton University Press, 1997.

Blum, Linda. *Between Feminism and Labor: The Significance of the Comparable Worth Movement.* Berkeley: University of California Press, 1991.

Bruce, John M. "Texas: A Success Story, at Least for Now." In *God at the Grass Roots, 1996: The*

Christian Right in the American Elections, ed. Mark J. Rozell and Clyde Wilcox, 33–50. Lanham, Md.: Rowman and Littlefield, 1997.

Bruce, Steve. "The Inevitable Failure of the New Christian Right." In *The Rapture of Politics*, ed. Steve Bruce, Peter Kivisto, and William H. Swatos Jr., 7–20. New Brunswick, N.J.: Transaction, 1995.

——. *The Rise and Fall of the New Christian Right*. New York: Oxford University Press, 1988.

Buck, Jeffrey A., and Beth Umland. "Covering Mental Health and Substance Abuse Services." *Health Affairs* 16, no. 4 (July–August 1997): 120–26.

Buck-Morss, Susan. [Benjamin Snow, pseud.] "Introduction to Adorno's 'The Actuality of Philosophy.'" *Telos* 10, no. 1 (spring 1977): 113–19.

Buck-Morss, Susan. *The Origin of Negative Dialectics: Theodor W. Adorno, Walter Benjamin, and the Frankfurt Institute*. New York: Free Press, 1977.

Chandler, Russell. "Evangelical Broadcaster Seeks 'Pro-Family' Lobby." *Los Angeles Times*, 4 March 1989, 116ff.

Clawson, Dan, Alan Neustadtl, and Mark Weller. *Dollars and Votes: How Business Campaign Contributions Subvert Democracy*. Philadelphia: Temple University Press, 1998.

Clinton, Hillary Rodham. *It Takes a Village, and Other Lessons Children Teach Us*. New York: Simon and Schuster, 1996.

Clinton, William J. "Text of President Clinton's Announcement on Welfare Legislation." *New York Times*, 1 August 1996, A10.

Conway, M. Margaret, and Joanne Connor Green. "Political Action Committees and the Political Process in the 1990s." In *Interest Group Politics*, 4th ed., ed. Allan J. Cigler and Burdett A. Loomis, 155–73. Washington, D.C.: Congressional Quarterly, 1995.

Cooper, Marc. "God and Man in Colorado Springs." *The Nation*, 2 January 1995, 9–12.

Corrado, Anthony. "Financing the 1996 Elections." In *The Elections of 1996*, ed. Gerald Pomper, 135–71. Chatham, N.J.: Chatham House, 1997.

Crippen, Alan. Senior Fellow, Institute for Family Studies, Focus on the Family. Interview by author. Colorado Springs, 21 February 1996.

Critzer, John W., and Kul B. Rai. "Blacks and Women in Public Higher Education: Political and Socioeconomic Factors Underlying Diversity at the State Level." *Women and Economics* 19, no. 1 (1998): 19–39.

Crooks, Jeannie. Correspondence Research Coordinator, Focus on the Family. Interview by author. Colorado Springs, 21 February 1996.

Cunningham, Peter J., and Ha T. Tu. "A Changing Picture of Uncompensated Care." *Health Affairs* 16, no. 4 (July–August 1997): 167–75.

Darling-Hammond, Linda. "Race and Education: Unequal Opportunity." *Brookings Review* 16, no. 2 (spring 1998): 28–32.

Davis, Mike. *City of Quartz: Excavating the Future in Los Angeles*. New York: Vintage, 1992.

——. *Prisoners of the American Dream: Politics and Economy in the History of the US Working Class*. New York: Verso, 1986.

Davis, Richard, and Diana Owen. *New Media and American Politics*. New York: Oxford University Press, 1998.

Day One. ABC, 21 September 1995.

Diamond, Edwin, and Robert A. Silverman. *White House to Your House: Media and Politics in Virtual America*. Cambridge: MIT Press, 1997.

Diamond, Sara. "Focus on Some Families." *Z Magazine*, July–August 1994, 29–33.

——. *Roads to Dominion: Right-Wing Movements and Political Power in the United States*. New York: Guilford, 1995.

Dobson, James. *Dare to Discipline.* Wheaton, Ill.: Tyndale House, 1970.

Docker, John. *Postmodernism and Popular Culture: A Cultural History.* Cambridge: Cambridge University Press, 1994.

Dole, Robert. "Dole's Statement on Measure." *New York Times,* 1 August 1996, A10.

Edley, Christopher, Jr. *Not All Black and White: Affirmative Action, Race, and Other American Values.* New York: Hill and Wang, 1996.

Ehrenreich, Barbara. *Fear of Falling: The Inner Life of the Middle Class.* New York: Pantheon, 1989.

Eldredge, John. Director, Public Policy Seminars and Research, Focus on the Family. Interview by author. Colorado Springs, 21 February 1996.

Eldredge, John, and Greg Jesson. *Community Impact Curriculum.* Colorado Springs: Focus on the Family, May 1993.

Ersoz, Meryem. "Gimme That Old-Time Religion." In *Media, Culture, and the Religious Right,* ed. Linda Kintz and Julia Lesage, 211–25. Minneapolis: University of Minnesota Press, 1998.

Fabricant, Michael B., and Steve Burghardt. *The Welfare State Crisis and the Transformation of Social Service Work.* Armonk, N.Y.: M. E. Sharpe, 1992.

Fair, Bryan K. *Notes of a Racial Caste Baby: Color Blindness and the End of Affirmative Action.* New York: New York University Press, 1997.

Fishman, Linda E., and James D. Bentley. "The Evolution of Support for Safety-Net Hospitals." *Health Affairs* 16, no. 4 (July–August 1997): 30–47.

Focus on the Family. "Annual Report: 1994." Colorado Springs: Focus on the Family.

———. *Family News from Dr. James Dobson.* Colorado Springs: Focus on the Family, September 1998.

———. "Family Policy Councils" (brochure). Colorado Springs: Focus on the Family, n.d.

———. "Focus on the Family Tour Information" (brochure). Colorado Springs: Focus on the Family, n.d.

———. "James C. Dobson, Ph.D.: Biographical Information." Colorado Springs: Focus on the Family, January 1996.

———. "The Ministries of Focus on the Family." Colorado Springs: Focus on the Family, 8 November 1995.

———. *Physician.* January–February 1996.

Foucault, Michel. *Discipline and Punish: The Birth of the Prison.* New York: Vintage, 1979.

———. "Nietzsche, Genealogy, History." In *The Foucault Reader,* ed. Paul Rabinow. New York: Pantheon, 1984.

Frank, Richard G., Chris Koyanagi, and Thomas G. McGuire. "The Politics and Economics of Mental Health 'Parity' Laws." *Health Affairs* 16, no. 4 (July–August 1997): 108–19.

Frankl, Razelle. "Transformation of Televangelism: Repackaging of Christian Family Values." In *Media, Culture, and the Religious Right,* ed. Linda Kintz and Julia Lesage, 163–89. Minneapolis: University of Minnesota Press, 1998.

Friedman, Emily. "The Uninsured: From Dilemma to Crisis." In *Beyond Crisis: Confronting Health Care in the United States,* ed. Nancy F. McKenzie, 23–37. New York: Meridian, 1994.

Frohnen, Bruce. *The New Communitarians and the Crisis of Modern Liberalism.* Lawrence: University Press of Kansas, 1996.

Fugleberg, Mark. Producer, *Family News in Focus,* Focus on the Family. Interview by author. Colorado Springs, 22 February 1996.

Gardiner, Steven. "Through the Looking Glass and What the Christian Right Found There." In *Media, Culture, and the Religious Right,* ed. Linda Kintz and Julia Lesage, 141–58. Minneapolis: University of Minnesota Press, 1998.

Gerson, Michael J. "A Righteous Indignation." *U.S. News and World Report*, 4 May 1998, 20–29.

Gingrich, Newt. *To Renew America*. New York: HarperCollins, 1995.

Ginsburg, Paul B. "The Dynamics of Market-Level Change." *Journal of Health Politics, Policy and Law* 22, no. 2 (April 1997): 363–83.

Ginsburg, Norman. *Divisions of Welfare: A Critical Introduction to Comparative Social Policy*. London: Sage, 1992.

Goldfield, Michael. *The Color of Politics: Race and the Mainsprings of American Politics*. New York: New Press, 1997.

Goldman, William, Joyce McCulloch, and Roland Sturm. "Costs and Use of Mental Health Services before and after Managed Care." *Health Affairs* 17, no. 2 (March–April 1998): 40–52.

Goodstein, Laurie. "Conservative Christian Leader Accuses Republicans of Betrayal." *New York Times*, 12 February 1998, A22.

"GOP Leaders, Religious Conservatives Agree on Goals." *Seattle Times*, 9 May 1998, A3.

Gramsci, Antonio. *Selections from the Prison Notebooks*. Ed. and trans. Quintin Hoare and Geoffrey Nowell Smith. New York: International, 1971.

Green, John C. "The Christian Right and the 1996 Elections: An Overview." In *God at the Grass Roots, 1996: The Christian Right in the American Elections*, ed. Mark J. Rozell and Clyde Wilcox, 1–14. Lanham, Md.: Rowman and Littlefield, 1997.

Grossberg, Lawrence. *We Gotta Get Out of This Place: Popular Conservatism and Postmodern Culture*. New York: Routledge, 1992.

Gurevitch, Michael, and Jay G. Blumler. "Political Communications Systems and Democratic Values." In *Democracy and the Mass Media: A Collection of Essays*, ed. Judith Lichtenberg, 269–89. New York: Cambridge University Press, 1990.

Guth, James L., John C. Green, Lyman A. Kellstedt, and Corwin E. Smidt. "Onward Christian Soldiers: Religious Activist Groups in American Politics." In *Interest Group Politics*, 4th ed., ed. Allan J. Cigler and Burdett A. Loomis, 55–76. Washington, D.C.: Congressional Quarterly, 1995.

Guth, James L., and Oran P. Smith. "South Carolina Christian Right: Just Part of the Family Now?" In *God at the Grass Roots, 1996: The Christian Right in the American Elections*, ed. Mark J. Rozell and Clyde Wilcox, 15–31. Lanham, Md.: Rowman and Littlefield, 1997.

Habermas, Jürgen. *The Theory of Communicative Action*, vol. 1. Trans. Thomas McCarthy. Boston: Beacon, 1984.

Hacker, Jacob S., and Theda Skocpol. "The New Politics of U.S. Health Policy." *Journal of Health Politics, Policy and Law* 22, no. 2 (April 1997): 315–38.

Hall, Stuart. *The Hard Road to Renewal: Thatcherism and the Crisis of the Left*. London: Verso, 1988.

Hansen, Miriam. "Mass Culture as Hieroglyphic Writing: Adorno, Derrida, Kracauer." *New German Critique* 56 (spring–summer 1992): 43–73.

Harvey, David. *The Condition of Postmodernity: An Enquiry into the Origins of Cultural Change*. Oxford: Basil Blackwell, 1989.

Havemann, Judith. "Welfare Reform Incorporated: Social Policy Going Private." *Washington Post*, 7 March 1997, A1, A14.

Hawkesworth, Mary E. "Workfare and the Imposition of Discipline." *Social Theory and Practice* 11, no. 2 (summer 1985): 163–81.

Hebdige, Dick. *Subculture: The Meaning of Style*. New York: Routledge, 1994.

Hess, Tom. Editor, *Citizen* magazine, Focus on the Family. Interview by author. Colorado Springs, 21 February 1996.

Hilfiker, David. *Not All of Us Are Saints: A Doctor's Journey with the Poor*. New York: Ballantine, 1994.

Himmelstein, Jerome L. "The New Right." In *The New Christian Right: Mobilization and Legitimation*, ed. Robert C. Liebman and Robert Wuthnow, 13–29. Hawthorne, N.Y.: Aldine, 1983.

Honneth, Axel. *The Critique of Power: Reflective Stages in a Critical Social Theory*. Trans. Kenneth Baynes. Cambridge: MIT Press, 1991.

Horkheimer, Max, and Theodor W. Adorno. *Dialectic of Enlightenment*. Trans. John Cumming. New York: Continuum, 1972.

——. *Dialektik der Aufklärung: Philosophische Fragmente*. 1944. Frankfurt am Main: Fischer, 1969.

Hunter, James Davison. *American Evangelicalism: Conservative Religion and the Quandary of Modernity*. New Brunswick, N.J.: Rutgers University Press, 1983.

——. *Evangelicalism: The Coming Generation*. Chicago: University of Chicago Press, 1987.

Huyssen, Andreas. "Adorno in Reverse: From Hollywood to Richard Wagner." *New German Critique* 29 (spring–summer 1983): 8–38.

I-200 PRO. *Yes on I-200: The Washington State Civil Rights Initiative Web Page*. 18 November 1998.

Inglehart, John K. "Physicians as Agents of Social Control: The Thought of Victor Fuchs." *Health Affairs* 17, no. 1 (January–February 1998): 90–96.

Jay, Martin. *The Dialectical Imagination: A History of the Frankfurt School and the Institute of Social Research, 1923–1950*. Boston: Little, Brown, 1973.

Jencks, Christopher, and Meredith Phillips. "The Black-White Test Score Gap." *Brookings Review* 16, no. 2 (spring 1998): 24–27.

Jennings, James. "Introduction: New Challenges for Black Activism in the United States." In *Race and Politics: New Challenges and Responses for Black Activism*, ed. James Jennings. New York: Verso, 1997.

Jeter, Jon. "Efforts to Move Poor from Welfare to Work Going Slowly in Area." *Washington Post*, 6 March 1997, A1, A18.

Johnson, Eithne. "The Emergence of Christian Video." In *Media, Culture, and the Religious Right*, ed. Linda Kintz and Julia Lesage, 191–210. Minneapolis: University of Minnesota Press, 1998.

Johnson, Paul E. *A Shopkeeper's Millennium: Society and Revivals in Rochester, New York, 1815–1837*. New York: Hill and Wang, 1978.

Just, Marion R., Ann N. Crigler, Dean E. Alger, Timothy E. Cook, Montague Kern, and Darrell M. West. *Crosstalk: Citizens, Candidates, and the Media in a Presidential Campaign*. Chicago: University of Chicago Press, 1996.

Katz, Jeffrey L. "After Sixty Years, Most Control Is Passing to States." *Congressional Quarterly Weekly Report*, 3 August 1996, 2190–96.

Kennedy, John W. "Mixing Politics and Piety." *Christianity Today*, 15 August 1994, 42–47.

Kintz, Linda. *Between Jesus and the Market: The Emotions That Matter in Right-Wing America*. Durham, N.C.: Duke University Press, 1997.

Kintz, Linda, and Julia Lesage, eds. *Media, Culture, and the Religious Right*. Minneapolis: University of Minnesota Press, 1998.

Koch, Gertrud. "Mimesis und Bilderverbot in Adornos Ästhetik: Ästhetische Dauer als Revolte gegen den Tod." *Babylon* 6 (1989): 36–45.

Kozol, Jonathan. *Savage Inequalities: Children in America's Schools*. New York: Crown, 1991.

Krahl, Hans-Jürgen. "The Political Contradictions in Adorno's Theory." *Telos* 21 (fall 1974): 164–67.

Kramnick, Isaac, and R. Laurence Moore. *The Godless Constitution: The Case against Religious Correctness*. New York: W. W. Norton, 1996.

Leonard, Stephen T. *Critical Theory and Political Practice*. Princeton, N.J.: Princeton University Press, 1990.

Lesage, Julia. "Christian Coalition Leadership Training." In *Media, Culture, and the Religious Right*, ed. Linda Kintz and Julia Lesage, 295–325. Minneapolis: University of Minnesota Press, 1998.

——. "Christian Media." In *Media, Culture, and the Religious Right*, ed. Linda Kintz and Julia Lesage, 21–49. Minneapolis: University of Minnesota Press, 1998.

Levin, Thomas Y. "For the Record: Adorno on Music in the Age of Technological Reproducibility." *October* 55 (1990): 23–47.

Levit, Katharine R., Helen C. Lazenby, Bradley R. Braden, and the National Health Accounts Team. "National Health Spending Trends in 1996." *Health Affairs* 17, no. 1 (January–February 1998): 35–51.

Lichtenberg, Judith. "Foundations and Limits of Freedom of the Press." In *Democracy and the Mass Media: A Collection of Essays*, ed. Judith Lichtenberg, 102–35. New York: Cambridge University Press, 1990.

Liebman, Robert C. "The Making of the New Christian Right." In *The New Christian Right: Mobilization and Legitimation*, ed. Robert C. Liebman and Robert Wuthnow, 234–35. Hawthorne, N.Y.: Aldine, 1983.

Light, Donald W. "The Rhetorics and Realities of Community Health Care: The Limits of Countervailing Powers to Meet the Health Care Needs of the Twenty-first Century." *Journal of Health Politics, Policy and Law* 22, no. 1 (February 1997): 105–45.

Lipietz, Alain. *Towards a New Economic Order: Postfordism, Ecology, and Democracy*. New York: Oxford University Press, 1992.

Loomis, Burdett A., and Allan J. Cigler. "Introduction: The Changing Nature of Interest Group Politics." In *Interest Group Politics*, 5th ed., ed. Allan J. Cigler and Burdett A. Loomis, 1–32. Washington, D.C.: Congressional Quarterly, 1998.

——. "Introduction: The Changing Nature of Interest Group Politics." In *Interest Group Politics*, 4th ed., ed. Allan J. Cigler and Burdett A. Loomis, 1–31. Washington, D.C.: Congressional Quarterly, 1995.

Loomis, Burdett A., and Eric Sexton. "Choosing to Advertise: How Interests Decide." In *Interest Group Politics*, 4th ed., ed. Allan J. Cigler and Burdett A. Loomis, 194–210. Washington, D.C.: Congressional Quarterly, 1995.

Lowenthal, Leo, and Norbert Guterman. *Prophets of Deceit: A Study of the Techniques of the American Agitator*. 2d ed. Palo Alto, Calif.: Pacific, 1970.

Lowi, Theodore J. *The End of Liberalism: The Second Republic of the United States*. 2d ed. New York: Norton, 1979.

——. *The End of the Republican Era*. Norman: University of Oklahoma Press, 1995.

——. *The Personal President: Power Invested, Promise Unfulfilled*. Ithaca, N.Y.: Cornell University Press, 1985.

——. "Toward a Legislature of the First Kind." In *Knowledge, Power, and the Congress*, ed. William H. Robinson and Clay H. Wellborn, 9–36. Washington, D.C.: Congressional Quarterly, 1991.

Lukács, Georg. *History and Class Consciousness: Studies in Marxist Dialectics*. Trans. Rodney Livingstone. Cambridge: MIT Press, 1971.

Lukes, Steven. *Power: A Radical View*. London: Macmillan, 1974.

Ma, Ching-to Albert, and Thomas G. McGuire. "Costs and Incentives in a Behavioral Health Carve-Out." *Health Affairs* 17, no. 2 (March–April 1998): 53–69.

Mann, Joyce M., Genn A. Melnick, Anil Bamezai, and Jack Zwanziger. "A Profile of Uncompensated Care, 1983–1995." *Health Affairs* 16, no. 4 (July–August 1997): 223–32.

Marsden, George M. *Fundamentalism and American Culture: The Shaping of Twentieth-Century Evangelicalism: 1870–1925*. New York: Oxford University Press, 1982.

——. *Understanding Fundamentalism and Evangelicalism*. Grand Rapids, Mich.: William B. Eerdmans, 1991.

Marty, Martin E., and R. Scott Appleby, eds. *Fundamentalisms Observed*. Chicago: University of Chicago Press, 1991.

——. *The Glory and the Power: The Fundamentalist Challenge to the Modern World*. Boston: Beacon, 1992.

Marx, Karl. "Anti-Church Movement—Demonstration in Hyde Park" (25 June 1855). In *Karl Marx and Friedrich Engels on Religion*, 127–34. New York: Schocken, 1964.

——. *Capital: Volume One*. Trans. Ben Fowkes. New York: Vintage, 1977.

——. "Concerning Feuerbach." In *Early Writings*, trans. Rodney Livingstone and Gregor Benton, 421–23. New York: Vintage, 1975.

——. "A Contribution to the Critique of Hegel's Philosophy of Right: Introduction." In *Early Writings*, trans. Rodney Livingstone and Gregor Benton, 243–57. New York: Vintage, 1975.

McKinlay, John B., and John D. Stoeckle. "Corporatization and the Social Transformation of Doctoring." In *Beyond Crisis: Confronting Health Care in the United States*, ed. Nancy F. McKenzie, 271–84. New York: Meridian, 1994.

Miller, Robert H., and Harold S. Luft. "Does Managed Care Lead to Better or Worse Quality of Care?" *Health Affairs* 16, no. 5 (September–October 1997): 7–25.

Mockaitis, Caia. Public Policy Information Manager, Focus on the Family. Interview by author. Colorado Springs, 23 February 1996.

Moen, Matthew C. *The Christian Right and Congress*. Tuscaloosa: University of Alabama Press, 1989.

——. "From Revolution to Evolution: The Changing Nature of the Christian Right." In *The Rapture of Politics*, ed. Steve Bruce, Peter Kivisto, and William H. Swatos Jr., 123–35. New Brunswick, N.J.: Transaction, 1995.

Moody, Dwight L. *The Best of D. L. Moody*. Ed. Wilbur Smith. Chicago: Moody Bible Institute, 1971.

——. *Moody: His Words, Work, and Workers*. Ed. Rev. Charles H. Fowler. New York: Nelson and Phillips, 1878.

Murphy, Caryle. "They're Finding God on the Radio." *Washington Post*, 27 May 1997, A1, A8.

National Center for Health Statistics. *Health, United States, 1993*. Hyattsville, Md.: Public Health Service, 1994.

The New English Bible, with the Apocrypha. Gen. ed. Samuel Sandmel. New York: Oxford University Press, 1976.

Niebuhr, Gustav. "Advice for Parents and for Politicians: Religious Group Speaks to Family Issues and to the Right." *New York Times*, 30 May 1995, A12.

O'Connor, James. *The Fiscal Crisis of the State*. New York: St. Martin's, 1973.

Offe, Claus. *Contradictions of the Welfare State*. Ed. John Keane. Cambridge: MIT Press, 1984.

Orfield, Gary, Susan E. Eaton, and the Harvard Project on School Desegregation. *Dismantling Desegregation: The Quiet Reversal of "Brown v. Board of Education."* New York: New Press, 1996.

Parekh, Sunita. *The Politics of Preference: Democratic Institutions and Affirmative Action in the United States and India*. Ann Arbor: University of Michigan Press, 1997.

Parker, Glenn. *Congress and the Rent-Seeking Society*. Ann Arbor: University of Michigan Press, 1996.

Patterson, Orlando. "Affirmative Action: Opening Up Workplace Networks to Afro-Americans." *Brookings Review* 16, no. 2 (spring 1998): 17–23.

Piore, Michael J., and Charles F. Sabel. *The Second Industrial Divide: Possibilities for Prosperity.* New York: Basic, 1984.

Piven, Frances Fox. "Welfare and the Transformation of Electoral Politics." *Dissent* 43, no. 4 (fall 1996): 61–67.

Piven, Francis Fox, and Richard A. Cloward. *Regulating the Poor: The Functions of Public Welfare.* 2d ed. New York: Vintage, 1993.

Pollock, Friedrich. "State Capitalism: Its Possibilities and Limitations." 1941. In *The Essential Frankfurt School Reader*, ed. Andrew Arato and Eike Gebhardt, 71–94. New York: Continuum, 1982.

Putnam, Robert D. "Bowling Alone: America's Declining Social Capital." *Journal of Democracy* 6, no. 1 (January 1995): 65–78.

Rice, Mitchell F. "Health Care Reform, Managed Competition, and the Urban Medically Underserved." *Journal of Health and Social Policy* 8, no. 4 (1997): 31–52.

Rosenbaum, Sara, Kay Johnson, Colleen Sonosky, Anne Markus, and Christ DeGraw. "The Children's Hour: The State Children's Health Insurance Program." *Health Affairs* 17, no. 1 (January–February 1998): 75–89.

Ross, Andrew. *No Respect: Intellectuals and Popular Culture.* New York: Routledge, 1989.

Rozell, Mark J., and Clyde Wilcox. "Conclusion: The Christian Right in Campaign '96." In *God at the Grass Roots, 1996: The Christian Right in the American Elections*, ed. Mark J. Rozell and Clyde Wilcox, 255–69. Lanham, Md.: Rowman and Littlefield, 1997.

———. "Virginia: When the Music Stops, Choose Your Faction." In *God at the Grass Roots, 1996: The Christian Right in the American Elections*, ed. Mark J. Rozell and Clyde Wilcox, 99–114. Lanham, Md.: Rowman and Littlefield, 1997.

———, eds. *God at the Grass Roots, 1996: The Christian Right in the American Elections.* Lanham, Md.: Rowman and Littlefield, 1997.

———, eds. *God at the Grass Roots, 1994: The Christian Right in the 1994 Elections.* Lanham, Md.: Rowman and Littlefield, 1995.

Shils, Edward. "Daydreams and Nightmares: Reflections on the Criticisms of Mass Culture." *Sewanee Review* 65 (autumn 1957): 587–608.

Silverstein, Mark. "Watergate and the American Political System." In *The Politics of Scandal: Power and Process in Liberal Democracies*, ed. Andrei S. Markovits and Mark Silverstein, 15–37. New York: Holmes and Meier, 1988.

Skerry, Peter. "E Pluribus Hispanic?" In *Pursuing Power: Latinos and the Political System*, 16–30. Notre Dame, Ind.: University of Notre Dame Press, 1997.

Smidt, Corwin E., and James M. Penning. "Michigan: Veering to the Left?" In *God at the Grass Roots, 1996: The Christian Right in the American Elections*, ed. Mark J. Rozell and Clyde Wilcox, 115–34. Lanham, Md.: Rowman and Littlefield, 1997.

Sorensen, Elaine. *Comparable Worth: Is It a Worthy Policy?* Princeton, N.J.: Princeton University Press, 1994.

Starr, Paul. *The Social Transformation of American Medicine.* New York: Basic, 1982.

State of Washington, Office of the Secretary of State. *1998 Online Voters Guide for the General Election—November 3, 1998.* 18 November 1998.

Stepp, Carl Sessions. "Access in a Post-social Responsibility Age." In *Democracy and the Mass Media: A Collection of Essays*, ed. Judith Lichtenberg, 186–201. New York: Cambridge University Press, 1990.

Stepp, Laura Sessions. "The Empire Built on Family and Faith." *Washington Post*, 8 August 1990, C1 ff.

Stoesz, David, and Howard Jacob Karger. *Reconstructing the American Welfare State.* Lanham, Md.: Rowman and Littlefield, 1992.

Stone, Deborah A. "The Doctor as Businessman: The Changing Politics of a Cultural Icon." *Journal of Health Politics, Policy and Law* 22, no. 2 (April 1997): 546–52.

Thompson, Dennis F. *Ethics in Congress: From Individual to Institutional Corruption.* Washington, D.C.: Brookings Institution, 1995.

Thorpe, Kenneth E. "The Health System in Transition: Care, Cost, and Coverage." *Journal of Health Politics, Policy and Law* 22, no. 2 (April 1997): 339–61.

Toy, Vivian S. "Tough Welfare Rules Used as Way to Cut Welfare Rolls." *New York Times*, 15 April 1998, A10, A24.

Unitarian Universalist Association of Congregations. *Challenging the Radical Right.* Boston: Unitarian Universalist Association of Congregations, June 1995.

U.S. Department of Commerce, Bureau of the Census. *1990 Census School District Special Tabulations.* Washington, D.C.: U.S. Department of Commerce.

——. *Current Population Surveys: October 1996.* Washington, D.C.: U.S. Department of Commerce.

U.S. Department of Education, National Committee for Educational Statistics. *Common Core of Data: School District Fiscal Data, 1993–1994.* Washington, D.C.: U.S. Department of Education.

——. *Dropout Rates in the United States: 1996.* Washington, D.C.: U.S. Department of Education.

——. *NAEP 1996: Trends in Academic Progress: Achievements of US Students in Science, Math, Reading, and Writing.* Washington, D.C.: U.S. Department of Education.

U.S. National Center for Health Statistics. *Health, United States, 1993.* Hyattsville, Md.: Public Health Service.

Valentine, Herbert D. Letter to membership. Washington, D.C.: Interfaith Alliance, 1995.

Ward, Mike. "Focus on the Family Group Plans to Move." *Los Angeles Times*, 15 June 1990, B3.

Weinick, Robin M., Margaret E. Weigers, and Joel W. Cohen. "Children's Health Insurance, Access to Care, and Health Status: New Findings." *Health Affairs* 17, no. 2 (March–April 1998): 127–36.

Weissman, Joel S., and Arnold M. Epstein. *Falling through the Safety Net: Insurance Status and Access to Health Care.* Baltimore, Md.: Johns Hopkins University Press, 1994.

Welch, Susan, and John Gruhl. *Affirmative Action and Minority Enrollments in Medical and Law Schools.* Ann Arbor: University of Michigan Press, 1998.

Wiggershaus, Rolf. *The Frankfurt School: Its History, Theories, and Political Significance.* Trans. Michael Robertson. Cambridge: MIT Press, 1994.

Wilcox, Clyde. "Premillennialists at the Millennium." In *The Rapture of Politics*, ed. Steve Bruce, Peter Kivisto and William H. Swatos Jr., 21–39. New Brunswick, N.J.: Transaction, 1995.

Zechetmayr, Monika. "Native Americans: A Neglected Health Care Crisis and a Solution." *Journal of Health and Social Policy* 9, no. 2 (1997): 29–47.

Zettersten, Rolf. *Dr. Dobson: Turning Hearts toward Home.* Dallas: Word, 1989.

Index

Christian radio (*cont.*)

grassroots mobilization, 26, 114, 158, 188; negative-utopian moments in, 210–11. *See also* Adorno, Theodor W.; *Focus on the Family* (radio program)

Christian right and the New Deal, 81–84

Christian right as a social movement, 2, 4–7, 17–18, 26–30, 114, 158, 188, 234 n.10; and Christian radio, 26, 114, 158, 188; in Colorado Springs, 230–31; communicative engagement with, 230–31; liberal opposition to, 20, 216–18. *See also* Lowenthal, Leo, and Norbert Guterman

Civil rights movement, 164, 190; backlash against, 192–205

Class. *See* Social class

Clinton, Bill: emotional style of, 92; impeachment of, 132, 168; 1992 campaign of, 166–68; on welfare reform, 251 n.88

Clinton, Hillary Rodham, 124–26; on traditional family values, 251–52 n.91

Clinton administration: affirmative action policy, 194–95; electronic town meetings, 167; health care reform policies, 115, 117–18, 120; social policy rhetoric, 124–26; welfare policy, 90, 191–92

Coburn, U.S. Rep. Tom, 155

Colson, Charles, 142–52, 169–71

Commodity. *See* Adorno, Theodor W.; Christian radio

Communicative ethics, 230–31

Communitarianism. See *Focus on the Family* (radio program); Post-Fordism

Congress. *See* Democratic accountability

Conspiracy theory, 130–33

Critical theory, 211–12. *See also* Adorno, Theodor W.; Habermas, Jürgen; Honneth, Axel; Ideology; Lowenthal, Leo, and Norbert Guterman; Pollock, Friedrich

Cultural studies, 8–12, 46–47

Culture industry. *See* Adorno, Theodor W.

Culture, theories of politics and: in Adorno, 12–13; Foucauldian and postmodernist, 9, 12, 17–19, 158–59; Gramscian, 8–9, 12–13, 17–18; in Marx, 6–7; in Marxism, 239 n.5

Dare to Discipline, 22–23

Democratic accountability: campaign fi-

nance and, 161; and ethics scandals, 160–61, 165–66; legislative politics and, 161–63; and the media, 165; and post-Fordism, 163–68

Democratic party. *See* Post-Fordism

Desegregation. *See* School desegregation

Dialectics, 11–12, 66, 69–71, 75–76, 115. *See also* Adorno, Theodor W.

Diamond, Sara, 5–6, 29

Dobson, James: advising of presidents, 26–27; on child discipline, 22–23, 236 n.44; early career, 22–24; elections and, 1–3, 233 n.3; evangelism and, 226–27; on feminism, 95–96; image and self-presentation, 25, 91–101; television spots, 237 n.56. *See also* Focus on the Family; *Focus on the Family* (radio program); *Focus on the Family* (video series)

Enemy figures, 64–65, 85, 114. See also *Focus on the Family* (radio program)

Ethics: autonomous individuality and, 20, 96–101, 106, 127–28, 217–18; in Congress, 160–61, 165–66; physician autonomy and, 121–22, 250–51 n.80, 251 n.83; technical rationality and, 177–81, 186–88

Evangelicalism, 137–38, 215; progressive, 215

Family: in Clintonite communitarianism, 124–25; significance for Christian right, 9–10; traditional roles and *Focus on the Family*, 95–101, 107, 178–79, 187

Family Research Council, 7, 27

Fascism. *See* Adorno, Theodor W.; Lowenthal, Leo, and Norbert Guterman

Feminism: backlash against, 199–202, 204–5; comparable worth movement, 195–96; Dobson on, 95–96; in *Focus on the Family*, 176

Focus on the Family: college academic program, 229; community impact seminars, 28–29, 238 n.72; constituent characteristics, 25–26, 237 n.55; history, 22–24; international operations, 24; public policy operations, 27–29. *See also* Dobson, James; *Focus on the Family* (radio program); *Focus on the Family* (video series)

Focus on the Family (radio program): on abortion, 181–88; Adorno's theory and,

90–93, 114–15, 128–29, 133, 142, 159, 171, 174, 188–89, 207; authoritarianism in, 139–42, 147–52, 155–58; broadcast studio, 254; on capital punishment, 175, 188; on child intelligence, 93–101, 247 n.14; on the Church, 111, 148–52; and citizenship, 158–59; communitarian spirit in, 101–4, 110, 185–86; compassion in, 91–96, 102–4, 107–10; demonization of outsiders, 96–101, 104–6, 111–14, 248 n.49; dialectical relation to post-Fordism, 19, 127–29, 169–71, 205–7; egalitarianism in, 134–39, 142–47, 153–55; ethics and technical rationality in, 177–81, 186–88; on false memory syndrome, 101–7; on family trauma, 134–36; on forgiveness, 174–88; fundamentalism in, 101, 106–7, 113, 142, 152, 157; on the health care system, 127; history of, 23; on homosexuality, 107–14, 248 n.49; on Iran-Contra, 133–42; listening audience, 22, 24; narrative structures in, 221–26, 235 n.30; negative-utopian moment in, 21, 93, 128–29, 171, 207; on parenting, 94–101, 105, 109–10; on racial discrimination, 179–81; Republicans on, 153–58; salvation narratives in, 16–17, 94–96, 100–101, 104, 107–11, 133–38, 141–47, 152–55, 172–81, 184–88; on satanism, 105–6; scientific professionalism in, 95–96, 102–4, 108–10; on Watergate, 143–44, 150–52; and the welfare state, 90–93; on women and violence, 174–79

Focus on the Family (video series), 23–24, 236 n.47

Fordism, 54, 86–88; and democratic accountability, 164; and health care, 119–20; and labor, 54, 86–87. *See also* Post-Fordism

Foucault, Michel, 8, 11–12, 17–19, 158–59, 203

Frankfurt School. *See* Adorno, Theodor W.; Habermas, Jürgen; Honneth, Axel; Lowenthal, Leo, and Norbert Guterman; Pollock, Friedrich

Fundamentalism, 79, 215. *See also Focus on the Family* (radio program)

Gatewood, David, 102–6

Gender: and Christian right women, 11; and citizenship, 9; and homosexuality on

Focus on the Family, 108–13; and traditional roles on *Focus on the Family*, 95–101, 107, 178–79, 187

Gingrich, Newt, 160, 252 n.98

Gramsci, Antonio, 8–9, 12–13, 17–18

Grossberg, Lawrence, 92, 159

Guterman, Norbert. *See* Lowenthal, Leo, and Norbert Guterman

Habermas, Jürgen, 231, 241 n.47

Hall, Stuart, 8–9

Harvey, David, 200–201

Health care system, 115–23; for-profit health enterprises, 120–23; health expenditures, 116; health safety net, 117–18, 249 n.67; and managed care, 116–19; and mental health, 118–19, 250 n.73; and physician autonomy, 121–22, 250–51 n.80, 251 n.83; and public programs, 119–20; and uninsured persons, 117. *See also* Post-Fordism

Hegel, G. W. F., 34–35, 66

Hilfiker, David, 214–15, 218

Homosexuality: and antigay ballot initiatives, 5, 29. See also *Focus on the Family* (radio program)

Honneth, Axel, 38, 49–50, 241 n.47

Huffman, Heidi, 182–89, 205–6

Huffman, Tina, 182–85

Idealism, 35, 66

Ideology, 3–4, 6–7, 33, 43; critique of, 34–37, 62, 66

Immanent criticism, 66, 75–77, 115. *See also* Adorno, Theodor W.

Individualism. *See* Ethics

Institute for Social Research, 13, 38, 61–62. *See also* Adorno, Theodor W.; Lowenthal, Leo, and Norbert Guterman; Pollock, Friedrich

Instrumental reason, 13, 45–46, 57, 76

Interfaith Alliance, The, 217–18

Iran-Contra affair. See *Focus on the Family* (radio program)

Irrationalism, 63–64, 66, 70–71, 73–74, 84–85

Jay, Martin, 71, 244 n.41

Jessen, Gianna, 182–89, 205–6

Jesus Christ: as model on *Focus on the Family*, 94–96, 175–77; and the stations of the cross, 208–9

Kintz, Linda, 9–10
Kozol, Jonathan, 198–99

Labor: culture and the division of, 33; and the culture industry, 41; mobilization in the 1930s, 84. *See also* Fordism; Post-Fordism; Social class
Late capitalism, 41, 44–45, 49, 73. *See also* Market economy; State capitalism
Leonard, Stephen T., 211–12
Liberalism. *See* Christian right as a social movement
Liberation theology, 212, 215–16
Lowenthal, Leo, and Norbert Guterman: *Prophets of Deceit: A Study of the Techniques of the American Agitator*, 62–67, 71–73, 84–85, 130
Lowi, Theodore J., 162, 254 n.62
Lukács, Georg, 239 n.5

Market economy: and the culture industry, 40–43; and liberal capitalism, 49–50; and liberal-productivist ideology, 124; and state capitalism, 38–40, 49
Marx, Karl: critique of religion, 6–7; on theory and practice, 210–12
Marxism. *See* Adorno, Theodor W.; Culture, theories of politics and
Mass culture. *See* Adorno, Theodor W.
Mayfield, Margy, 174–79, 181, 186–89, 205–7
Media: Christian right, 92–93, 158; and democratic accountability, 165; and electronic populism, 166–68; industry consolidation, 165; and progressive Christianity, 216; reporting on Focus on the Family, 1–3
Meier, Paul, 102–7
Moody, Dwight L., 173

Nazism. *See* Adorno, Theodor W.
Negative dialectics. *See* Adorno, Theodor W.
New Deal: and Christian right radio, 81–84; rhetoric and social policy, 83–84
Nicolosi, Joseph, 107–14, 186
Nonidentity, 13, 50–51
North, Betsy, 134–35, 159
North, Oliver L., 134–42, 169–71

Orfield, Gary, 202

Piven, Frances Fox, 84–85
Pollock, Friedrich, 38, 49
Popular culture. *See* Adorno, Theodor W.; Cultural studies
Populism. *See* Post-Fordism
Post-Fordism, 87–89; and autonomy of culture, 87–89; and communitarian rhetoric, 124–26; and democratic accountability, 163–68; dialectical relation to *Focus on the Family*, 127–29, 169–71; and electronic populism, 166–68; and Focus on the Family's constituents, 25–26; and the health care system, 119–23, 250 n.75; and labor, 86–88, 200–201; and opposition to the Christian right, 217–18; and party coalitions, 163–64; and racist backlash, 199–205, 257 nn. 63, 65; and sexist backlash, 199–205, 257 nn. 63, 65; and social work, 122–23. *See also* Fordism
Postmodernism, 17–18
Power, theories of, 3–4, 6
Promise Keepers, 10

Race and racism. *See* Affirmative action; *Focus on the Family* (radio program); Post-Fordism; School desegregation
Radio. *See* Adorno, Theodor W.; Christian radio; *Focus on the Family* (radio program)
Reagan administration: affirmative action policies, 193–94; Dobson's involvement in, 26; liberal-productivist ideology, 124; school desegregation policies, 197
Redemption. *See* Salvation
Reification. *See* Adorno, Theodor W.
Religion and social transformation, 6–8, 18–21, 213–19, 222
Republican party: congressional leaders' policies, 2; 1995–1996 presidential primary campaign, 1–2. *See also* Christian right as a social movement; Post-Fordism
Robertson, Pat, 173

Salvation, 16–17, 93, 96–97, 100–101, 104, 110–11, 137–38, 141–44, 152–55, 159, 172–81, 184–85, 208–9, 214–16
Schlafly, Phyllis, 127
Schoenberg, Arnold, 44–46
School desegregation, 196–99, 202–3

Paul Apostolidis is Assistant Professor in the
Department of Politics at Whitman College.

Library of Congress Cataloging-in-Publication Data
Apostolidis, Paul, 1965–
Stations of the Cross : Adorno and Christian right radio /
Paul Apostolidis.
Includes bibliographical references and index.
ISBN 0-8223-2504-7 (hardcover : alk. paper)
ISBN 0-8223-2541-1 (pbk : alk. paper)
1. Radio in religion—United States—Case studies.
2. Conservatism—Religious aspects—Christianity—Case
studies.   3. Focus on the Family (Radio program)—History.
4. Christianity and politics—United States—History—20th
century.   5. United States—Church history—20th century.
I. Title.
BV656 .A66 2000   261'.06'073—DC21   99-087368